TERRORIST EVENTS WORLDWIDE 2022

EDWARD MICKOLUS, PHD

WANDERING
WOODS
PUBLISHERS

Terrorist Events Worldwide 2022

By Edward Mickolus, PhD

ISBN: 978-1-949173-19-2

Published in the United States by
Wandering Woods Publishers
EdwardMickolus.com

Book Design, Cover and Typesetting by
Cynthia J. Kwitchoff (CJKCREATIVE.COM)

DISCLAIMER

ABOUT THE AUTHOR

Edward Mickolus, PhD, is the President of Vinyard Software, Inc. He served a 33-year career with the Central Intelligence Agency, has written 50 books, and has taught intelligence tradecraft courses at numerous federal agencies. Vinyard Software's International Terrorism Data Center provides universities, research institutions, governments, the media, and others interested in international terrorism the best publicly-available data on terrorists and events around the world. His books include:

Terrorism Events Worldwide 2021

Terrorism Events Worldwide 2019-2020

Terrorism Worldwide, 2018

Terrorism Worldwide, 2017

Terrorism Worldwide, 2016

Terrorism 2013-2015: A Worldwide Chronology

Terrorism 2008-2012: A Worldwide Chronology

Terrorism, 2005-2007

with Susan L. Simmons Terrorism, 2002-2004: A Chronology, 3 volumes

with Susan L. Simmons Terrorism, 1996-2001: A Chronology of Events and a Selectively Annotated Bibliography, 2 volumes

with Susan L. Simmons Terrorism, 1992-1995: A Chronology of Events and a Selectively Annotated Bibliography

Terrorism, 1988-1991: A Chronology of Events and a Selectively Annotated Bibliography

with Todd Sandler and Jean Murdock International Terrorism in the 1980s: A Chronology, Volume 2: 1984-1987

with Todd Sandler and Jean Murdock International Terrorism in the 1980s: A Chronology, Volume 1: 1980-1983

with Peter Flemming Terrorism, 1980-1987: A Selectively Annotated Bibliography

International Terrorism: Attributes of Terrorist Events, 1968-1977, ITERATE 2 Data Codebook

with Susan L. Simmons The 50 Worst Terrorist Attacks

with Susan L. Simmons The Terrorist List: North America

with Susan L. Simmons The Terrorist List: South America

with Susan L. Simmons The Terrorist List: Eastern Europe

with Susan L. Simmons The Terrorist List: Western Europe

with Susan L. Simmons The Terrorist List: Asia, Pacific, and Sub-Saharan Africa

The Terrorist List: The Middle East, 2 volumes

The Literature of Terrorism: A Selectively Annotated Bibliography

Transnational Terrorism: A Chronology of Events, 1968-1979

Combatting International Terrorism: A Quantitative Analysis

Stories from Langley: A Glimpse Inside the CIA

More Stories From Langley: Another Glimpse Inside the CIA

Briefing for the Boardroom and the Situation Room

The Counterintelligence Chronology: Spying by and Against the United States from the 1700s through 2014

Spycraft for Thriller Writers: How to Write Spy Novels, TV Shows and Movies Accurately and Not Be Laughed at by Real-Life Spies

TABLE OF CONTENTS

Introduction	1
Activities of Key Terrorist Groups	2
Regional Developments	5
Trends in Terrorist and Counterterrorist Techniques	8

2022 CHRONOLOGY

Africa	11
Asia	43
Australia/New Zealand	58
Europe	59
Latin America	81
Middle East	94
North America	130
Updates of pre-2022 incidents	159
Bibliography	199

Find the Author at:

Books: EdwardMickolus.com

Terrorism Data: VinyardSoftware.com

INTRODUCTION

This book uses the same **definition** of terrorism as found in its predecessors, allowing comparability across decades. Terrorism is the use or threat of use of violence by any individual or group for political purposes. The perpetrators may be functioning for or in opposition to established governmental authority.

A key component of international terrorism is that its ramifications transcend national boundaries, and, in so doing, create an extended atmosphere of fear and anxiety. The effects of terrorism reach national and worldwide cultures as well as the lives of the people directly hurt by the terrorist acts. Violence becomes terrorism when the intention is to influence the attitudes and behavior of a target group beyond the immediate victims. Violence becomes terrorism when its location, the victims, or the mechanics of its resolution result in consequences and implications beyond the act or threat itself.

The book is divided into **three sections:** a **region-by-region** (and within each, a country-by-country) look at terrorist **incidents**, a separate section updating events that occurred prior to 2022, and a **bibliography**. The Incidents section is based solely on publicly available sources. This section is not intended to be analytical, but rather comprehensive in scope. As such, the section also includes descriptions of non-international attacks that provide the security and political context in which international attacks take place. In some cases, the international terrorists mimic the tactics of their stay-at-home cohorts. Often, these are the same terrorists working on

their home soil against domestic, rather than foreign, targets. Domestic attacks often serve as proving grounds for techniques later adopted for international use. I have therefore included material on major technological, philosophical, or security advances, such as: the use of letter bombs; food tampering; major assassinations; attempts to develop, acquire, smuggle, or use precursors for an actual chemical, biological, radiological, or nuclear weapon; key domestic and international legislation and new security procedures; key arrests and trials of major figures; and incidents involving mass casualties. Non-international entries do not receive an eight-digit code.

The section also provides follow-up material to incidents first reported prior to January 1, 2022. For example, updates include information about the outcome of trials for terrorist acts occurring prior to 2022 and "where are they now" information about terrorists and their victims. The update is identified by the original incident date, and I have included enough prefatory material to give some context and to identify the original incident in the earlier volumes.

The international terrorist incidents and airline hijackings are identified by an eight-digit code. The first six digits identify the date on which the incident became known as a terrorist attack to someone other than the terrorists themselves (e.g., the date the letter bomb finally arrived at the recipient's office, even though terrorists had mailed it weeks earlier; or the date on which investigators determined that an anomalous situation was terrorist in nature). The final two digits ratchet the number of attacks that took place on that date. In instances in which either the day of the month or the month itself is unknown, "99" is used in that field.

The information cutoff date for this volume is December 31, 2022.

The Bibliography section includes references drawn from the same public sources that provide the incidents, literature searches, and contributions sent by readers of previous volumes. It does not purport to be comprehensive. The citations are grouped into topic areas that were chosen to make the bibliography more accessible and includes print and web-based material. The Bibliography gives citations on key events and may be referenced for more detail on specific attacks described in the Incidents section.

Activities of Key Terrorist Groups

The Russian invasion and war atrocities in Ukraine turned the world's attention to that area, possibly drawing reporting away from terrorist attacks in other countries. Public reports of terrorist attacks were down across the board.

Although international terrorism is not only the work of the **Islamic State** (IS), a noteworthy amount of attacks in 2022 can be attributed to IS, its affiliates, and those inspired by its call to violence. Because of its international spread and radically decentralized method of operations-by-inspiration, few days go by without an attack by someone declaring fealty to, if not membership in, some form of IS.

Key developments for IS included:

The death on February 2 of Abu Ibrahim al-Hashimi al-Qurayshi, the group's emir. While he did not have the following and name recognition of his predecessor, Abu Bakr al-Baghdadi, the death once again established that ISIS leaders were vulnerable and had to spend time playing defense rather than planning grand attacks around the globe. His successor, Abu al-Hasan al-Hashmi al-Qurayshi, did not fare much better,

with ISIS announcing his passing on November 30. ISIS has always been quick to resort to a "next man up" succession plan, soon announcing yet another emir with the honorific al-Qurayshi.

A United Nations investigating committee declared that ISIS was responsible for war crimes and crimes against humanity in an earlier attack on Badush Prison in Iraq. The UN also determined that the group had worked on developing chemical and biological weapons; 3,000 people were affected by the use of mustard gas in ISIS rocket artillery projectiles. A German court found an individual guilty of such charges in his treatment of a Yazidi woman he had enslaved.

ISIS's difficulties might be exploited by remnants of the original **al-Qaeda**, from which ISIS was spawned. However, AQ will have to do so without the services of its emir, Ayman al-Zawahiri. After searching for him for two decades, counterterrorist forces used a drone strike to kill al-Zawahiri in Afghanistan in early August. This might not be a negative, however, as the decapitation removes an increasingly irrelevant figurehead who more served as a boat anchor to operations than an inspiration.

The decentralization of AQ continued throughout al-Zawahiri's tenure at the helm and is likely to continue to do so without anyone of sufficient status to replace him, much less Osama bin Laden. Perhaps tacitly admitting these difficulties, by the end of the year, AQ had yet to formally name a successor. Nonetheless, al-Qaeda tried to keep the image of him alive by releasing just before Christmas a video it claimed he had narrated. It was unclear when the video was made. Some al-Qaeda affiliates, especially in Africa, conducted numerous attacks and were far more active than the AQ central group, which as of the end of the year had not announced a succession plan.

ISIS posed a downstream problem for numerous governments around the world, as women experiencing buyer's remorse attempted to return to their home countries, with children of their ISIS husbands in tow, after a few years in the clutches of the caliphate. Western governments were unsure of the wisdom of welcoming the expats with open arms, concerned by the possibility of the returnees backtracking to their terrorist ways. While the prodigals might not be front-liners conducting attacks themselves, many ISIS sympathizers have served in support roles, particularly in obtaining money for ISIS fighters.

FATES OF KEY TERRORISTS

The death of al-Qaeda leader Ayman al-Zawahiri in Afghanistan in early August led the headlines, which were by-and-large good news stories of the ends of the reigns of notable terrorists.

In some cases, the long arm of the law captured, tried, and sentenced terrorists. Long trials for attacks from years ago included cases against 10 men accused of involvement in the two March 22, 2016 ISIS suicide bombings in Brussels that killed 32 people and injured 340; and of eight people found guilty of aiding Mohamed Lahouaiej Bouhlel, who rammed a truck into crowds in Nice's Promenade des Anglais, killing 86 people and injuring 450 during July 14, 2016 Bastille Day celebrations.

Libya extradited to the U.S. Libyan citizen and intelligence operative Abu Agila Mohammad Mas'ud Kheir al-Marimi, 71, the alleged builder of the Pan Am 103 bomb that killed 270 people in Lockerbie, Scotland in 1988. His trial is pending on charges of destruction of an aircraft resulting in death. He faced life in prison.

Some prominent terrorists found freedom, sometimes to the surprise of their victims and victims' families.

A major figure from the past, Japanese Red Army co-founder Fusako Shigenobu, 76, was released from jail in late May after serving a 20-year sentence and professing penitence.

In November, the last six co-conspirators jailed for the May 21, 1991 assassination of former Indian Prime Minister Rajiv Gandhi were released from prison, a day after India's Supreme Court ordered their release.

In December, Bali bombmaker Hisyam bin Alizein, alias Umar Patek, was released on parole after serving half of his sentence for killing 202 people in an attack in Bali in 2002.

South Africa's Constitutional Court unanimously ordered the release of Polish citizen Janusz Walus, 69, who was jailed for killing anti-apartheid leader Chris Hani, leader of the South African Communist Party and chief of staff of Umkhonto we Sizwe, the armed wing of the African National Congress, on April 10, 1993. Walus was stabbed in prison, allegedly by a fellow inmate, ahead of his release on parole.

Several Guantánamo Bay detainees were approved for release by a Periodic Review Board, but finding a final landing place proved problematic. The most prominent was Mohammed al-Qahtani, often called the would-be 20th 9/11 hijacker, who was repatriated to Saudi Arabia. Saifullah Paracha, aged 74 or 75, the oldest Gitmo inmate, was sent to his native Pakistan after nearly 20 years of detention without trial. Former detainee Mohamedou Ould Slahi, 51, sued Canada for 35 million Canadian dollars (US$28 million) over its alleged role in his imprisonment. Freed Yemeni Mansoor Adayfi remained in touch via *WhatsApp* with more than 100 fellow Gitmo alumni.

Terrorists also used mass prison breaks to replenish their numbers. Mohammed Usman, alias Khalid al-Barnawi, leader of Nigeria's Ansaru (Jama'atu Ansarul Muslimina Fi Biladis Sudan; Vanguards for the Protection of Muslims in Black Africa), was one of hundreds of prisoners who escaped in a Boko Haram prison break in July. The Islamic State in West Africa Province claimed credit. Some 64 Boko Haram convicts escaped. ISIS conducted a mass prison break in Syria's Ghwaryan prison in the Kurdish-controlled area of Hasakah Province.

In the 2013-2015 prequel to this volume, I suggested that terrorism-hunters concentrate on several key terrorists, including

- Ibrahim Hassan al-Asiri, AQAP's chief bomb maker, no longer with us
- Samantha Louise Lewthwaite, believed to be an al-Shabaab strategist not seen in years
- Abubakar Shekau, Boko Haram leader, no longer with us.

- Ayman Mohammed Rabie al-Zawahiri. The al-Qaeda leader continued to be sidelined, reduced to issuing videos with limited production values of minimal interest to the next generation of jihadis. Despite wishful thinking that he had passed away, he released a video in April referring to events in February. But President Biden announced on August 1 that a weekend (July 30-31) drone strike killed him in his hideout in Kabul, Afghanistan.

- Returning jihadis from ISIS territory. Hundreds of terrorism tourists proved a difficult task for surveillance teams.

- Lone wolves. Many popped up throughout the rest of the world. Security forces stopped many, but not all, before they could attack.

Terrorists generally do not retire peacefully, usually either dying on the battlefield or in prison. The following did not get past the year:

Senior Terrorists Killed in 2022

This list includes those killed by coalition and Russian forces, including by airstrikes, and by rival terrorist groups, plus those who died of natural causes.

Al-Qaeda

- Ayman al-Zawahiri, the group's emir and successor to Osama bin Laden

ISIS

- Maher al-Agal, leader of ISIS in Syria
- Abu Mu'ad al Qahtani, an ISIS leader responsible for prisoner affairs
- Abu al-Hasan al-Hashmi al-Qurayshi, the group's emir
- Abu Ibrahim al-Hashimi al-Qurayshi, the group's emir
- Abu-Hashum al-Umawi, alias Abu 'Ala, the No. 2 ISIS leader in Syria and one of the group's top five leaders as the group's governor in Syria

Al-Shabaab (of Somalia)

- Abdullahi Nadir, alias Abdulahi Yare, a co-founder and chief prosecutor of al-Shabaab

Hurras al-Din

- Abu Hamzah al-Yemeni, a senior leader in Syria's Idlib Province

Lion's Den Resistance Brigades

- Wadi al-Houh, variant Wadee, founder and commander
- Tamer al-Kilani, a founding member and former PFLP member

Revolutionary Armed Forces of Colombia (FARC) dissidents

- Jorge Eliecer Jimenez, alias Arturo, FARC dissident commander in Arauca
- Antonio González Contreras, alias Roque, leader of the 33rd Front of the Residual Armed Group (GAO) splinter of Revolutionary Armed Forces of Colombia (FARC) dissidents

Paraguayan People's Army (EPP)

- Osvaldo Villalba, the group's leader
- Luciano "Luchi" Argüello

Jaish e-Mohammed (JeM), a Kashmiri separatist group operating in India

- Zahid Wani, a senior commander

Other Terrorists Killed in 2022

Abu Sayyaf

- Idang Susukan

Dawlah Islamiyah of the Philippines

- Arnel Cabintoy
- Feliciano Sulayao Jr.

Al-Shabaab

- Abdullahi Ali Araaye

- Ubeda Nur Issu, commander for the Bokol area and the Ethiopian border
- Fuad Mohamed Jalaf, propaganda chief responsible for the group's financing
- Abdulaziz Abu Musa, spokesman
- Hassan Nur, a prominent leader in Middle Shabelle
- Musab Abdalla Saney

ISIS

- Anas, an ISIS Syria Province official
- Hani Ahmed al-Kurdi, a senior bombmaker known as the Wali of Raqqa
- Rakkan Wahid al Shamman, an ISIS smuggler of weapons, money, and fighters

Pakistani Taliban

- Hafiz Dawlat Khan
- Omar Khalid Khorasani, a top leader
- Mufti Hassan Swati

Palestinian Islamic Jihad

- Tayseer Jabari, a senior PIJ leader in Gaza
- Khaled Mansour, head of PIJ operations in the south of Gaza

Key Terrorists Captured/ Surrendered in 2022

ISIS

- Hani Ahmed al-Kurdi, a senior ISIS leader of Raqqa, Syria, who was an experienced bomb maker, planner, and facilitator

ISIS-K in Afghanistan

- Abdul Malik, alias Maliki, chief of financial affairs for Islamic State–Khorasan Province

Islamic State in the Greater Sahara (IS-GS)

- Oumeya Ould Albakaye, an explosives expert and regional chief of IS-GS in Gourma in Mali and Oudalan in Burkina Faso

Libyan Terrorists

- Abu Agila Mohammad Mas'ud Kheir al-Marimi, Pan Am 103 bombmaker

Regional Developments

Western governments increasingly came to the conclusion that the major terrorist threat to global stability came not from the headline-grabbing jihadi lone wolf or ISIS-affiliated operative—although they certainly remained a threat and authorities arrested and tried numerous suspected ISIS cell members—but from right-wing attacks on democracy itself. Refusals to accept electoral results in North and South America and in Europe led to numerous attacks on institutions of democracy, with rump attacks on symbols of government activity, including COVID-19 restrictions, immigration assistance, the LGBTQ community, and the like. Muddying the waters were attacks by mentally-disturbed individuals with jihadi or radical political leanings who conducted attacks that initially were treated as terrorist events.

In the **United States**, this trend was met with a barrage of successful prosecutions, including on charges of seditious conspiracy, against the rioters who would have overturned the results of the 2020 Presidential election with the attack on the U.S. Capitol on January 6, 2021. Nearly 800 individuals faced indictments, or prison time from plea bargains and jury verdicts. Successful prosecutions also took place against right-wing militia members who planned to kidnap/murder Michigan Governor Gretchen Whitmer in October 2020, and against neo-Nazi Atomwaffen Division terrorists who conducted a campaign against Jews. Neo-Nazis, white supremacists, conspiracy theorists, and other once-fringers came to prominence on Internet social media and attacked various groups, including Blacks, Asians, Jews, Muslims, leftists, LGBTQ individuals, and others, including House Speaker Nancy Pelosi's husband Paul, 82. Still others made threats against at least 57 Historically Black Colleges and Universities. Would-be anti-democratic mimics in Brazil used similar antics in attempting to keep Jair Bolsonaro in the Presidential chair, with one individual arrested for planning a bombing attack.

The U.S. also successfully prosecuted ISIS members, terrorism tourists, financiers, and wannabes. Other ISIS adherents were not so lucky, dying at their own hands or in confrontations with police.

Distinctions often blurred between politically motivated extremist lone wolves and mentally disturbed individuals in several mass casualty environments. Thoughts and prayers, but few solutions, were offered to the problem of gun violence.

Anti-indigenous attacks were also common, particularly in Latin America, although the most deadly spree occurred in Canada, when ten people were stabbed to death and 19 injured across 13 crime scenes in an Indigenous community and the surrounding area in Saskatchewan.

The anti-democratic trend was also seen in **Europe**, fueled by white supremacists, anti-foreign immigration, antisemitism, and ire over COVID-19 restrictions. In Germany, some 25 Reich Citizens Movement affiliates plotted to raid the Bundestag and install a monarchist-inspired regime while others planned to cause a nationwide blackout and kidnap prominent figures. The rightwing extremists appeared to be particularly well-organized, although occasional lone wolves inspired by their propaganda also popped up. Police in France raided homes of neo-Nazis planning a "Jew hunt". A member of the neo-Nazi Nordic Resistance Movement stabbed to death a woman at a political festival in Sweden; the leader of a centrist party was believed to be the original target.

In **Sub-Saharan Africa**, jihadis expanded the number and geographic locations of attacks, with IS naming "provinces" in West Africa, Mozambique, and Central Africa—the Greater Sahara province stepped up operations—and al-Qaeda affiliates conducting numerous attacks. IS got a toehold in South Africa. Complicating matters, many of the groups also retained their tribal and economic affiliations, drawing support from like-minded herders or farmers. Thousands of civilians were internally displaced or became international refugees.

- Al-Shabaab continued attacks in Somalia, but sometimes also aimed their guns at governments supporting anti-Shabaab efforts, principally Kenya and Ethiopia. Government officials, hotels, the military, African Union peacekeepers, and police were favorite targets, but civilians had the largest casualty toll.

- The similarly-named but separate al-Shabaab jihadis continued to plague Mozambicans.

- West Africans, including in Benin, Burkina Faso, Chad, Mali, Niger, Nigeria, and Togo, experienced ongoing violence by Boko Haram and ISIS affiliates while France drew down its anti-terrorist Operation Barkhane presence.

- Cameroon faced an ongoing Anglophone Ambazonian separatist insurgency conducted by several disparate bands. Eritrea, Ethiopia, Gambia, Senegal, and South Sudan also experienced attacks by ethnic insurgents, with tribal clashes continuing in Sudan.

- The Congo battled jihadi and separatist groups, including the March 23 Movement (M23), Cooperative for Development of the Congo (better-known as CODECO), Mai-Mai militia, and Allied Democratic Forces (ADF), allegedly aided by hostile neighbors, on numerous fronts.

- Nigeria, already plagued by get-rich-quick bandits and jihadi groups, saw activities by a new generation of Biafran separatists. Mass kidnappings and mass casualty attacks continued to be a favorite tactic of anti-government entities.

Often outmanned and out-gunned, African governments turned toward partnerships with neighboring regimes, the African Union, militias, and vigilantes to help combat homegrown and traveling terrorists. The Russian mercenary Wagner Group saw opportunities for cashing in, but also were often ambushed by armed groups. Other favorite foreign terrorist targets were UN peacekeepers, the Red Cross, Doctors Without

Borders, and other non-governmental aid organizations, Christian clergy, Chinese workers, and businesses.

The *Global Terrorism Index 2022*, produced by the Institute for Economics and Peace, reported that 48% of the 3,461 terrorism-related deaths in 2021 occurred in Burkina Faso, Democratic Republic of Congo, Mali, and Niger.

Asia saw no letup in terrorist attacks, with India and Pakistan plagued by numerous separatist and jihadi groups. Each accused the other of sponsoring the groups, which on occasion conducted cross-border operations, sometimes via Afghanistan. Violence in disputed Kashmir continued unabated, as did violence between Hindus and Muslims in India. Tehrik-e-Taliban Pakistan and Baloch separatists were especially active in Pakistan, with police, the armed forces, Chinese investors and workers, and polio vaccination programs high on terrorists' list of targets. The Afghanistan-based ISIS-K also snuck across the border to conduct mass-casualty attacks in Pakistan; one attack on a mosque in Peshawar killed 62.

- The Taliban discovered the difficulties of playing defense against a determined jihadi band unafraid of taking a page from its history when ISIS-Khorasan Province conducted suicide bombings, attacked civilians including children and co-religionists, and used increasingly unsavory methods, even by Taliban standards. Targets included mosques and other religious installations, bazaars, sports venues, educational institutions, military facilities, and civilian convoys.

- Iran, longtime patron of terrorist groups and home to many al-Qaeda semi-retirees, experienced its own difficulties with terrorism, principally by separatists and Sunni extremists. Tehran attempted to conflate these attacks with ongoing human rights demonstrations.

- The Philippines continued to battle jihadi, separatist, and communist insurgents willing to impose mass casualties on civilian populations, while violence marred campaign rallies and polling places during local

elections. Thailand experienced similar diversity among its terrorist opponents.

- **Latin America** saw the expansion of Colombian peace talks, helped by newly-inaugurated Gustavo Petro, himself a former M-19 leftist guerrilla and target of right-wing terrorists. FARC dissident splinter groups and the National Liberation Army (ELN) did not get the memo, and continued to be active in conducting attacks on government targets, civilians, and each other, and benefiting from narcotics trafficking. Rightwingers attacked Indigenous leaders and human rights workers.

- Gang violence in Haiti continued unabated.

- Latin American anti-democratic forces looked to Jair Bolsonaro for cues, despite his loss in the Brazilian presidential election.

The **Middle East** continued to be the focus of much of the anti-Israeli sentiments of the region, with constant exchanges of sorties by the Israeli Defense Force and terrorists holed up in the Gaza Strip and West Bank. Attacks in Israel and occupied territories tended to be simple methods as had been seen in previous years—shootings, car rammings, stabbings, the occasional bomb, and barrages of rockets. For a brief time, the Lions' Den Resistance Brigades was the most active militant guerrilla unit in the West Bank.

The ongoing war in Syria involving ISIS was made more complex with Türkiye attacking groups battling ISIS, claiming that Kurdish forces are not allies but anti-Turkish PKK terrorists. Turkish operations for a time shut down Syrian Democratic Forces cooperation with coalition forces against ISIS. U.S. Air Force authorities charged a Tech Sergeant in connection with a bombing in the Green Village base that injured two American personnel. Coalition forces chipped away at the ISIS leadership, taking out two emirs and numerous lieutenants during the year.

Iran-backed groups and ISIS conducted attacks in Iraq, also the site of several clashes between Turkish and Kurdish forces.

Houthis continued to fight the Yemeni regime, but also lobbed projectiles—mostly missiles and drones—over the border into Saudi Arabia, targeting airports and energy facilities, and on occasion into the UAE. Riyadh was having none of it in March, executing 81 men, including 73 Saudis, seven Yemenis, and one Syrian, for terrorism and other offences including holding "deviant beliefs", murder, and membership in militant groups such as ISIS, al-Qaeda, and Houthi rebels. Yemen also saw continued attacks by al-Qaeda in the Arabian Peninsula.

The as-of-this-writing ongoing **conventional war** pitting **Russian** invaders against **Ukrainian** defenders of their homeland diverted much of the world's attention from other forms of political violence. Surprisingly, there were few instances of international terrorist attacks against either of the combatants. The occasional phoned threat, cyberattack, firebomb or bomb, none of them definitively attributable to a government or established terrorist group, pockmarked the news. In November and December, the single terrorist campaign issuing from the conflict came in the form of *Godfather*-like sending of bloody packages containing animal eyeballs to Ukrainian diplomatic/consular facilities and installations supporting Kyiv. The blizzard of eyeballs was accompanied by only one actual bombing of a Ukrainian overseas facility (although the jury remains out on the motive behind the explosion of a gift obtained by a Polish police chief during an official visit to Ukraine).

Trends in Terrorist and Counterterrorist Techniques

Decapitation was not just used against terrorist leaders, with assassination attempts, often in broad daylight in front of crowds, being conducted in several continents. Examples included former Prime Minister Shinzo Abe in Japan, former Prime Minister Imran Khan in Pakistan, and Vice President Cristina Fernández de Kirchner in Argentina. Less-publicized attacks included apparent assassination attempts against Libyan Prime Minister Abdulhamid al-Dbeibah, Guatemalan President Alejandro Giammattei, and Haitian Prime Minister Ariel Henry and planned assassination attempts against Ukrainian President Volodymyr Zelensky, former U.S. President George W. Bush, and Canadian Prime Minister Justin Trudeau. Several other individuals planned to attack heads of state/government, but did not get close enough to their targets. Other targets and/or victims of assassinations around the world included clerics, military officials, journalists, and politicians.

Terrorists generally targeted "soft" targets with little security, including hospitals, schools, churches, mosques, and other places of worship.

The U.S. administration imposed economic sanctions against terrorists, terrorist financiers, and other individuals supporting terrorism. Washington also instituted numerous criminal cases against perpetrators and conducted targeted attacks against terrorist leaders and adherents. These techniques were used by other like-minded regimes and regional and global intergovernmental organizations throughout the world. While new leaders popped up, the counterterrorism operations chipped away at radicals' capabilities and terrorist successors tended to keep their heads down rather than run flashy attacks. Interfactional strife led to attacks by splinter factions against more well-known groups, particularly in Nigeria and Colombia.

Courts, particularly in the West and Africa, successfully prosecuted defendants for attacks that occurred years, sometimes decades, earlier. They included:

- The October 15, 1987 assassination of former Burkina Faso President Thomas Sankara and his colleagues. Former president Blaise Campaore was sentenced to life in prison.

- The October 12, 2002 Bali bombings that killed 202 people from 21 nations. The presiding judge at East Jakarta District Court sentenced Aris Sumarsono, alias Zulkarnaen, to 15 years in jail.

- The murder of prominent Bangladeshi writer and academic Humayun Azad, 56, on

February 27, 2004. A court sentenced four members of Jama'atul Mujahideen Bangladesh (JMB) to hang.

- The February 14, 2005 assassination in Beirut of former Lebanese premier Rafik Hariri in a truck bombing that killed Hariri and 21 others and injured 226. Presiding judge Ivana Hrdlickova handed down the maximum sentence of life in prison to Hassan Habib Merhi and Hussein Hassan Oneissi.

- Twenty Harkat-ul-Jihad-al-Islami (Indian Mujahideen) bombings on July 26, 2008 in Ahmedabad in Gujarat State that killed 57 people and injured 200. A judge sentenced 38 Muslim men to hang and ordered life in prison for 11 others.

- The murder-by-machete of Bangladeshi blogger and science writer Ananta Bijoy Das near his home in Sylhet on May 12, 2015. A court sentenced four people to death.

- The November 13, 2015 ISIS attacks that killed 130 in Paris. A court found Salah Abdeslam guilty on all five counts and sentenced him to life without the possibility of parole. Another 19 were convicted on other charges.

- The March 13, 2016 AQIM attack on a beach resort in Grand Bassam, Ivory Coast that killed 19 people and wounded 33. Eleven defendants received life sentences.

- The March 12, 2017 kidnap/murder of UN experts Swedish-Chilean Zaida Catalan and American Michael Sharp and their interpreter, Betu Tshintela, in the Kasai region of the Congo. Congolese officials blamed the Kamuina Nsapu militia. Several defendants were sentenced to death.

- The October 16, 2017 car bomb that killed prominent Maltese journalist Daphne Caruana. George Degiorgio, 59, and Alfred Degiorgio, 57, pleaded guilty and were sentenced to 40 years in prison.

- The April 23, 2018 murder of ten and attempted murder of 16 when an incel drove a rented van into dozens of people on a busy Toronto street. The Supreme Court sentenced Alek Minassian, 29, to life in prison.

- The mid-May 2019 massacre in northwest Central African Republic in which 46 civilians were killed. The Special Criminal Court sentenced three members of the Return, Reclamation and Rehabilitation militias (3R movement), identified as Issa Sallet Adoum, Ousman Yaouba, and Tahir Mahamat, to terms ranging from 20 years to life imprisonment for "crimes against humanity".

- The stabbing murder of UK lawmaker David Amess, 69, in a church in Leigh-on-Sea on October 15, 2021. London's Central Criminal Court sentenced Ali Harbi Ali to whole life in prison, meaning Ali will never be eligible for parole.

Other proceedings begun earlier continued into 2023, including:

- In the U.S. of Libyan citizen and intelligence operative Abu Agila Mohammad Mas'ud Kheir al-Marimi, for allegedly making the bomb which destroyed Pan Am flight 103 over Lockerbie, Scotland, in 1988, killing 270 people.

- At Guantánamo Bay of numerous individuals charged with the 9/11 attacks, inter alia.

- In Belgium for the three coordinated suicide bombings in Brussels on March 22, 2016 that killed 32 and wounded 340.

- In France for the July 14, 2016 attack on the Promenade des Anglais in Nice where ISIS sympathizer Mohamed Lahouaiej-Bouhlel, a 31-year-old Tunisian, killed 86 people and injuring 450 by driving a truck into thousands of locals and tourists celebrating France's national day.

- In France for the ISIS murder of Catholic priest Father Jacques Hamel, 85, by two 19-year-old attackers as he celebrated Mass inside a Saint-Etienne-du-Rouvray, Normandy church on July 26, 2016.

- In the U.S. for the assassination in Haiti of Haitian President Jovenel Moïse, outside his Port-au-Prince home on July 7, 2021.

ADDITIONAL
RESEARCH SOURCES

For those who prefer to run textual searches for specific groups, individuals, or incidents, a computer version of the 1960-2022 ITERATE (International Terrorism: Attributes of Terrorist Events) textual chronology is available from Vinyard Software, Inc., 502 Wandering Woods Way, Ponte Vedra, Florida 32081-0621, or e-mail via vinyardsoftware@hotmail.com

The data set comes in a WordPerfect and Word textual version and looks remarkably like the volumes in this series of hardcopy chronologies. A numeric version offers circa 150 numeric variables describing the international attacks from 1968-2022. The data sets can be purchased by specific year of interest. See www.vinyardsoftware.com for further details.

Vinyard also offers the Data on Terrorist Suspects (DOTS) project, where you will find a detailed biographical index of every terrorist suspect named in the previous volumes of this chronology.

Comments about this volume's utility and suggestions for improvements for its likely successors are welcome and can be sent to me via vinyardsoftware@hotmail.com. Please send your terrorism publication citations to me at Vinyard to ensure inclusion in the next edition of the bibliography.

Once again, there are many individuals who have contributed to this research effort. Of particular note are my family.

2022 CHRONOLOGY

WORLDWIDE

August 18, 2022: The *Washington Post* reported that a study of patterns of terrorism in the 18 countries that had fielded armed drones between 2001 and 2019 and the 11 countries that used them against any target established that obtaining armed drones reduces the amount of terrorism a country experiences and are an effective counterterrorism tool. This worked out to six fewer terrorist attacks and 31 fewer deaths from terrorism annually—a 35 percent reduction in attacks and a 75 percent decrease in fatalities. This article was based on a study by Joshua A. Schwartz, Matthew Fuhrmann and Michael C. Horowitz scheduled to be published in *International Studies Quarterly.*

AFRICA

BENIN

January 6, 2022: *Reuters* and *Radio France Internationale (RFI)* reported that a Benin army vehicle hit a mine in Pendjari National Park near a hotel that has been closed since 2019 near the border with Burkina Faso, killing two soldiers.

February 8, 2022: *Al-Jazeera* reported that in the afternoon, gunmen ambushed rangers in the West National Park, where it intersects with Burkina Faso and Niger, killing five rangers and a soldier and injuring 10 other people. No one claimed credit. 22020801

April 11, 2022: *Al-Jazeera* and *Reuters* reported that terrorists possibly linked to ISIS or al-Qaeda placed a roadside bomb that killed five soldiers in the Pendjari National Park when their vehicle rolled over it. Several other soldiers were hospitalized.

June 26, 2022: *Al-Jazeera, 24 Heures,* and *Reuters* reported that at 2 a.m., gunmen fired on the Dassari police station, killing two police officers and wounding an officer. Two terrorists died and several others were wounded. The gunmen torched impounded motorcycles. No group claimed credit.

BURKINA FASO

January 16-23, 2022: *AFP* reported on January 30 that local forces and French troops killed nearly 60 terrorists during four operations during the week. Air strikes by the French Barkhane force "guided by Burkinabe units" destroyed 20 motorcycles and several pickup trucks with weapons.

January 19, 2022: *Reuters, Le Monde, Le Figaro,* and *AFP* reported that a bomb hit a vehicle, injuring four French soldiers from the Operation Barkhane task force. The injured soldiers were evacuated toward Gao, Mali. One of the soldiers was seriously wounded. 22011901

March 12, 2022: *Al-Jazeera* reported that gunmen killed nine people at an informal gold mine in Oudalan Province.

March 13, 2022: *Al-Jazeera* reported that gunmen killed 15 people, including 13 military police officers, in Namentenga Province.

March 14, 2022: *Al-Jazeera* and *Reuters* reported that in the morning, gunmen killed eight people who were collecting water in in Arbinda, in Soum Province.

March 19, 2022: Gunmen kidnapped 15 youth in Nagre.

March 20, 2022: *France24* and *AFP* reported that jihadis were suspected of killing 13 soldiers in an attack on a patrol near Natiaboani. The government said 35 terrorists were "neutralized".

AFP reported on March 23 that the armed forces said a "complex attack" involving an improvised explosive killed 11 soldiers near Napade.

April 1, 2022: *AFP* reported that Lieutenant-Colonel Paul-Henri Sandaogo Damiba, 41, who seized power in a coup against President Roch Marc Kabore on January 24, announced the creation of local committees to meet with armed jihadist groups and help restore peace.

April 4, 2022: *Knewz, CBS News, al-Jazeera,* and *Reuters* reported that Theophile Nare, Bishop of Kaya, announced that during the night, gunmen kidnapped American nun Sister Suellen Tennyson, 83, of the Congregation of the Marianite Sisters of the Holy Cross, from the Yalgo Parish religious community in Kaya Diocese in North Central Region. The attackers vandalized the halls and sabotaged the community vehicle they failed to hijack. She had been serving at Yalgo since 2014. *NBC News* reported on August 31, 2022 that Sister Suellen Tennyson, from Louisiana, was found alive on August 29 and was in U.S. care in Niamey, Niger. *CNN* added on September 1, 2022 that Cmdr. Timothy Pietrack, U.S. Africa Command spokesperson, said that U.S. Africa Command personnel "facilitated the safe turnover". 22040401

April 8, 2022: *Al-Jazeera* reported that jihadis were suspected of attacking the Namissiguima

military base in Sanmatenga Province. During the clash, 12 soldiers and four paramilitary fighters were killed and more than 20 soldiers were wounded.

April 24, 2022: *Al-Jazeera* reported that in the morning, gunmen attacked military detachments in Gaskinde and Pobe-Mengao, killing nine soldiers and six civilians, including two members of an armed self-defense group.

May 5, 2022: *Al-Jazeera* reported that terrorists ambushed soldiers near Solle, killing two soldiers and four civilian volunteers. In a separate raid in Ouanobe, terrorists killed five paramilitary troops. Troops found the bodies of 20 attackers, and seized or destroyed weapons, ammunition, and communication devices.

May 14, 2022: *AFP* reported that several jihadi attacks killed 40 people, many of them civilian volunteers with the army.

Two attacks in the Sahel region killed 25 people, including 13 members of the Volunteers for the Defence of the Fatherland (VDP). Attackers killed 15 civilians who were in a convoy under VDP escort in Kompienga, near Burkina Faso's southeastern border with Togo and Benin. Three VDP volunteers were killed. Nearly a dozen people were wounded.

In a nighttime raid, gunmen attacked police and gendarmes' posts in Faramana, near the frontier with Mali, wounding two.

In an attack in Guessel, 20 people, including eight VDP, were killed. In Markoye, attackers killed five volunteers and a civilian.

May 25, 2022: *Reuters* and the *Jerusalem Post* reported that gunmen killed 50 people in the Madjoari rural commune in an eastern area plagued by jihadi violence. Two other attacks on the commune in May killed 17 civilians and 11 soldiers.

June 9, 2022: *Al-Jazeera* reported that gunmen attacked a security post in Seytenga in Seno Province during the evening, killing 11 military policemen. *AFP* reported that police said 40 terrorists died.

Two people were killed in an attack at a gold mine in the north.

Gunmen killed four military police in an attack in western Kossi Province.

June 11, 2022: *AFP* reported that jihadis were suspected of conducting several attacks that killed six people and injured four. The group hit the gold-mining site of Alga village in Bam Province and the nearby Boulounga village. The group torched houses and looted property. Another deadly attack occurred that night in Seytenga, which was hit two days earlier, near the Niger border. On June 13, *al-Jazeera* put the death toll at Seytenga at 50. On June 17, the *Washington Post* logged 79 deaths.

June 30, 2022: *AFP* reported that during the night, gunmen blew up the Nare Bridge on a main road connecting Kaya and Dori.

July 3-4, 2022: *Reuters* reported that during the evening of July 3 and the following morning, gunmen killed 22 civilians and wounded others in a rural commune in Kossi Province, 55 kilometers from the Mali border.

August 10, 2022: *Al-Jazeera* reported that a transport vehicle drove over a mine during an escort mission of a troop convoy on a rural road near Namsiguia district in Bam Province in Central-North region, killing several soldiers. A second remotely-detonated bomb killed first responders. Some 15 soldiers died. No group claimed credit.

August 27, 2022: *Reuters* reported that gunmen attacked a convoy from the Boungou gold mine in the east, killing six and wounding two.

September 5, 2022: A supply convoy escorted by the army hit a suspected jihadi roadside bomb while driving between Bourzanga and Djibo in Soum Province, killing at least 35 people and injuring dozens more. One of the vehicles was carrying civilians.

September 12, 2022: *News 360* and the Burkinabe news portal *Infowakat* reported that gunmen attacked an army detachment in Oudalan, killing two Burkinabe soldiers and wounding twelve soldiers, four seriously. Another dozen were missing. No group claimed credit. Jihadis were suspected.

September 26, 2022: *News 360*, the Burkinabe state news agency *AIB*, and *Radio France International (RFI)* reported that gunmen attacked a supply convoy being escorted by the army on a road near Gaskindé, some 20 kilometers from Djibo in Soum Province, killing 11 soldiers and wounding 28 people, including 20 soldiers, a "volunteer" from a self-defense group, and seven civilians. Another 50 civilians were reported missing. Gunmen on foot and on motorcycles attacked the front and rear of the convoy, destroying several trucks carrying food.

October 15, 2022: *News 360* and the *Infowakat* portal reported that gunmen ambushed a patrol of the armed forces and members of the Volunteers for the Defense of the Homeland in Silmagué, killing 14 members of the security forces, including soldiers and volunteers. The number of wounded and missing was not disclosed.

October 24, 2022: *News 360* reported that suspected jihadis attacked a military base. In the clash, 18 terrorists and ten members of the 14th Combined Arms Regiment of Djibo of the Burkinabe Armed Forces were killed and 50 wounded.

October 29, 2022: *News 360* reported that gunmen clad in the same leopard attire as Burkinabe soldiers attacked troops who had left Fada N'Gourma and were en route to Natiaboani in search of relief, killing 13 military personnel. *Radio France International (RFI)* reported that civilians and Patriotic Defense and Vigilance Brigade military auxiliaries were also in the convoy, which was attacked in Kikideni, halfway along the route the soldiers planned to travel.

CAMEROON

January 12, 2022: *AFP* reported that the bullet-riddled body of opposition senator Henry Kemende was found in Bamenda in the northwest, site of an Anglophone separatist insurgency. The lawyer was a lawmaker for the Social Democratic Front (SDF), a main opposition party. His vehicle was missing. No one claimed credit. Ambazonian separatists were suspected.

February 24, 2022: *AFP* reported that gunmen entered the building in Fotokol in the Far North area used by the French charity Doctors Without Borders and kidnapped five people, including three aid workers with Chadian, Senegalese, and French-Ivorian nationalities, and two Cameroonian security guards. Fotokol is near the Nigerian border. *AFP* reported on March 31, 2022 that the five hostages had been released in Nigeria. 22022401

April 30, 2022: Senator Elizabeth Regine Mundi, 79, and her driver were abducted in Bamenda in the Northwest Region. Shortly afterward, she appeared in a video on social media, in front of separatist flags. Two wings of the self-described Ambazonian Defence Forces (ADF) claimed credit; one demanded a ransom, the other, the release of prisoners. *AFP* reported on May 31, 2022 that the army said it had freed Mundi, who is a member of the politburo of President Paul Biya's ruling Cameroon People's Democratic Movement (RDPC) party from a "terrorist refuge" in Ashong in the late evening. Army spokesman Cyrille Atonfack Guemo said "several hostages were freed, including the senator". Guemo said 12 terrorists were killed, several other wounded and fled, and three were captured.

May 29, 2022: *AFP* reported that Mayor Ekwalle Martin said that separatist gunmen atacked the village of Obonyi II in the Anglophone Southwest Region near the border with Nigeria, killing 24 civilians and wounding 62. He said "The separatists wanted the inhabitants to pay them money each month, they refused, and that's why they (the gunmen) attacked."

June 7, 2022: *AFP* reported that during the night rebels attacked a gendarmerie post in Njitapon in the West Region, killing five gendarmes and injuring three.

June 25, 2022: *Reuters* and the *Jerusalem Post* reported that 26 villagers died in an attack on Ballin village in the Akwaya district of South-West region, near the border with Nigeria.

June 28, 2022: Separatist rebels were suspected of attacking rural villages in the Akwaya district, killing 30 people, including five Nigerians doing business in Cameroon. Several people were hospitalized with severe head and chest injuries from gunshots and machete cuts. Separatists blamed armed groups operating across the border in Cameroon and Nigeria. 22062801

November 28, 2022: *Reuters* reported that the U.S. Department of Justice arrested and charged three U.S. citizens of Cameroonian origin—Claude Chi, 40, of Lee's Summit, Missouri; Francis Chenyi, 49, of St. Paul, Minnesota; and Lah Nestor Langmi, 46, of Buffalo, New York—with raising funds for Anglophone Ambazonian separatist fighters in Cameroon. The charge sheet said the trio allegedly solicited and raised funds for supplies, weapons and explosive materials to be used in attacks against Cameroonian government personnel and security forces. DOJ also said, "In addition to more than $350,000 the defendants raised through voluntary donations, the indictment alleges Chi, Chenyi and Langmi conspired with others to kidnap civilians in Cameroon and hold them for ransom… In some instances, U.S. citizens were extorted for ransom payments to secure the release of their kidnapped relatives living in Cameroon." The trio held senior positions in a support group known as the Ambazonian Restoration Forces and other separatist fighters in Cameroon's Northwest region. They had raised funds for them since 2018.

CENTRAL AFRICAN REPUBLIC

March 15, 2022: *Al-Jazeera* reported that Chadian authorities handed over Maxime Jeoffroy Eli Mokom Gawaka, a former Central African Republic militia leader accused of war crimes and crimes against humanity, to the International Criminal Court in The Hague. Mokom led an "Anti-balaka" group. In 2019, he served as minister for disarmament and demobilization. The ICC said it has "found reasonable grounds" to suspect that in his capacity as a "National Coordinator of Operations of the Anti-balaka", he was responsible for crimes against humanity, including murder, torture, persecution, and "enforced disappearance".

October 3, 2022: *News 360* reported that the spokesman for the UN Secretary General,

Stéphane Dujarric, announced that a vehicle carrying Bangladeshi peacekeepers from the United Nations Multidimensional Integrated Stabilization Mission in the Central African Republic (MINUSCA) hit a mine during the night, killing three and seriously injuring a fourth. The explosion occurred during a MINUSCA patrol on the Koui-Bohong route, five kilometers from the mission's temporary base in Uham-Pendé prefecture. 22100301

November 25, 2022: *News 360* reported that the United Nations Mission in the Central African Republic (MINUSCA) announced that in the morning, gunmen killed a Moroccan military member of its peacekeeping contingent at Obo airfield. 22112502

November 28, 2022: *Business Insider* and *AP* reported that an unknown aircraft dropped bombs at 5 a.m. near a Russian mercenary Wagner Group base in Bossangoa, 200 miles north of Bangui. *AFP* reported that material damage was reported at the base and surrounding homes.

December 16, 2022: *AP* and *Tass* reported that Yevgeny Prigozhin, the millionaire owner of the Wagner Group mercenary contractor and Russian officials said that Dmitry Sytiy, a Wagner representative who headed the Russian House in Bangui, was severely injured when a package exploded in his hands. Prigozhin added that Sytiy said the explosive package contained a note saying "This is for you from all the French. The Russians will get out of Africa." Prigozhin accused France of orchestrating the attack and asked the Russian Foreign Ministry to declare the country a "sponsor of terrorism". 22121601

Prigozhin claimed that in November, Sytiy received a letter with a picture of his son, who lives in France, saying that next time he will get his son's head "if the Russians don't get out of the African continent and open the doors to the French." 22119901

Europa Press, Tass, Ria Novosti, Moscow Times, and *News 360* reported on December 19 that Sytiy was evacuated and rushed to Russia.

CHAD

February 21, 2022: *AFP* reported that President Mahamat Idriss Deby Itno said that Boko Haram jihadis killed five Chadian soldiers at Kaiga Kindjiria in the Lake Chad region. 22022102

October 28, 2022: *Reuters* reported that gunmen kidnapped a man with dual French and Australian citizenship, who manages an oryx park on behalf of a conservation group. The gunmen grabbed him in Wadi Fira Province. Interim President Mahamat Idriss Deby tweeted his release on October 30. 22102801

November 22, 2022: *AFP* and *al-Jazeera* reported that suspected Boko Haram jihadis attacked an army position near Ngouboua in the Lake Chad area, killing ten soldiers and wounding others. French state media *Radio France Internationale (RFI)* said four civilians and 20 to 40 Chadian soldiers were killed and others were missing. Some 150 soldiers had been setting up an advance position on Bouka-Toullorom island. An army officer said 30 troops were killed.

CONGO

January 24, 2022: *Al-Jazeera* reported on January 27 that an overnight attack by the March 23 Movement (M23) killed more than 20 Congolese soldiers at an army position in Nyesisi, North Kivu Province near the Virunga National Park. Clashes continued into January 26. Gentil Karabukala, civil society head of Kisigari near Nyesisi, claimed that 29 soldiers were killed in the attack. Lieutenant Colonel Muhindo Lwanzo, chief of staff to Rutshuru territory's administrator, added that a colonel died, as did some rebels. The Kivu Security Tracker tweeted that the M23 Tutsis killed 26 soldiers, including Colonel Ndume.

February 2022: *AFP* reported a group of eight hostage negotiators—including former warlords Thomas Lubanga, Germain Katanga, and Floribert Ndjabu —were instead taken prisoner by CODECO in Ituri Province. *AFP* reported on April 12, 2022 that the last four hostages were free. One hostage was released on March 21, 2022; three others, including the team's driver, on April 4, 2022. Reports differed as to whether the final four were freed or escaped. The last were Lubanga and Ndjabu, and two army colonels, Justin and Desire Lobho. Lubanga and Katanga served 14- and 12-year prison sentences, respectively, imposed by the International Criminal Court (ICC) for crimes committed in Ituri in the early 2000s. Ndjabu was jailed for 15 years for killing of nine U.N. peacekeepers.

February 1, 2022: *Reuters* reported that the Allied Democratic Forces (ADF) Islamist militia was believed responsible for freeing 20 prisoners in an attack in Nobil in North Kivu Province near the Ugandan border. Three people, including a child and a pregnant woman, were killed by gunshot and an ensuing stampede. *Reuters* reported on February 4 that the Islamic State Central Africa Province (ISCAP) claimed credit, saying, "The soldiers of the Caliphate attacked a post of the Crusader Congolese army in the town of Nobili, near the Ugandan border, two days ago, causing its personnel to flee... they were able to free nearly 20 Muslims detained in the prison there."

February 2, 2022: *Reuters* and *AP* reported that Cooperative for the Development of the Congo (CODECO) gunmen wielding machetes attacked the Savo camp for displaced persons in Plaine Savo in Djugu territory near Bule in Ituri Province, killing 60 people and seriously injuring others. Ituri army spokesman Lieutenant Jules Ngongo said 21 died. *AFP* said 40 died. Charite Banza Bavi, president of the humanitarian group for the Bahema-North area, said 63 were killed. The Norwegian Refugee Council (NRC) said, "59 civilians were killed and a further 40 injured". Two students at a school supported by the NRC were among the dead. *AFP* reported on February 4 that the death toll stood at 62, including 17 children, with another 46 wounded.

February 5, 2022: *U.S. News and World Report* and *Reuters* reported that a bomb exploded at a market in Beni, injuring four people. Days earlier, the U.S. Embassy warned of a possible attack.

February 15, 2022: *AFP* and *Reuters* reported that in the early morning, CODECO Lendu militiamen attacked a village in the Banyali Kilo administrative area in Ituri Province, killing 18. Jean-Robert Basiloko, who represents civil society groups in Banyali Kilo, said that the terrorists used "machetes, arrows, firearms. Seven children and six women were among the victims."

February 16, 2022: *AFP* reported that CODECO kidnapped eight people, including a general, who had been sent by President Felix Tshisekedi to try to negotiate a peace deal.

February 27, 2022: *Al-Jazeera* and *Reuters* reported that at 9 p.m., terrorists carrying machetes burned homes and killed 20 civilians in Kikura. Local authorities blamed the ADF.

March 2022: *Al-Jazeera* and *AFP* reported on October 14, 2022 that the Ituri Military court convicted and sentenced six people, including two army colonels and three other military personnel, to death for the murder of two Chinese mine workers in March 2022. Four other military personnel were sentenced to 10 years in prison. The two colonels were accused of planning an attack on a convoy with the aim of stealing four gold bars and $6,000 in cash being transported by the victims, who were returning from a gold mine. The defense planned to appeal.

March 8, 2022: *AFP* reported that at 5:30 a.m., CODECO attacked a unit of the Congolese army, then moved on to a church building in Kilo in Djugu territory in Ituri Province, in which displaced people had taken shelter, killing 18 people. They next killed another six people.

March 16, 2022: *Reuters, TDPELMedia.com,* and *CGTN* reported that ADF jihadis were suspected of killing 62 people during the previous five days in attacks on eastern villages. Two ADF gunmen died in clashes with the military.

March 19, 2022: *Al-Jazeera* and *AFP* reported that terrorists attacked a camp for displaced persons in Ituri Province with machetes, killing 14 people, including five women aged between 25 and 32, and seven children, including a two-year-old girl, and wounding five people. Jean D'Zba Banju, a community leader in Ituri's Djugu area, claimed "CODECO militiamen entered Drakpa and started to cut people with machetes. They did not fire shots in order to operate calmly...

The victims are displaced people who had fled Ngotshi village to set up in Drakpa."

March 20, 2022: *Al-Jazeera* reported that Sabiti Njiamoja, an official from the office of the governor of North Kivu Province, said that the ADF ambushed and killed four young people 1.8 miles from Eringeti in the Beni region.

March 27, 2022: *Reuters* reported that during the night, the M23 attacked army positions at Runyoni and Tshanzu near Goma and the border with Uganda and Rwanda. M23 had held the villages during an attack in November 2021.

March 29, 2022: *Reuters, BBC,* and *AFP* reported that eight U.N. peacekeepers were killed in the crash of a U.N. helicopter on a reconnaissance mission amid fighting between the Congolese army and M23 rebels in the area of Tshanzu in the Rutshuru region of North Kivu Province. The dead U.N. Stabilization Mission in the Democratic Republic of Congo (MONUS-CO) members included six crew members from the Pakistani military and two military personnel – one from Russia and one from Serbia. M23 (Congolese Revolutionary Army) denied the army's claim that the group had downed the Puma helicopter.

Uganda's army claimed it killed 14 M23 fighters near the border with Congo.

April 1, 2022: *Reuters* reported that M23 rebel spokesman Willy Ngoma announced a unilateral ceasefire after several days of clashes with the army in the east.

April 3, 2022: The Allied Democratic Forces were suspected of a nighttime attack on Masambo, 31 miles from Beni, with machetes and guns, killing 12-15 civilians.

April 6, 2022: *AFP* reported that Damien Seburazane, a representative of civil society groups, said that "The army attacked all the M23 positions in Musongati, Tchanzu and Runyoni" that the rebels took the previous week. Colonel Muhindo Lwanzo, chief aide to the territory's military administrator, said M23 had retreated from the strategic hill of Bugusa in North Kivu Province.

April 7, 2022: *Reuters* and *UPI* reported that a nighttime explosion in a bar at the Katindo military camp in Goma killed eight and wounded 15. The cause of the explosion was not clear. No one immediately claimed credit. *Africa News* quoted General Constant Ndima Kongba, governor of North Kivu, as saying "In view of the impact of the explosions, I believe that it must be an improvised explosive device… Only scientists will be able to determine what the device was." Among the dead were officers with the 34th Military Region, including a lieutenant colonel, his wife, a captain, the bar's owner, and a child, 12.

May 8, 2022: *Reuters* reported that CODECO attacked an artisanal gold mining site near Mongwalu in Ituri Province, killing 35 civilians. *Al-Jazeera* reported that many more were missing. Civil society leaders put the death toll between 30 and 50 people.

May 9, 2022: *AFP* and *al-Jazeera* reported that 14 civilians, including children, died in a machete attack on a displaced persons camp in Fataki in the Djugu area of Ituri Province. CODECO was suspected of the overnight attack.

May 26, 2022: Following days of fighting the army, the M23 advanced on the Rumangabo base in the Rutshuru area of North Kivu Province 25 miles from the provincial capital, Goma. M23 attacked other army positions in the Nyragongo and Rutshuru areas. On May 24, rebels fired some 20 shells near the Congolese Institute for the Conservation of Nature and the surrounding area.

May 27, 2022: *Al-Jazeera* reported that soldiers in Ituri Province found 17 decapitated bodies, believed to be victims of the ADF.

May 28, 2022: *Al-Jazeera* and *AFP* reported that Rwanda claimed that two of its Rwanda Defence Force (RDF) soldiers were kidnapped on patrol and were being held captive by Democratic Forces for the Liberation of Rwanda (FDLR) rebels in the Democratic Republic of Congo (DRC). The DRC accused Rwanda of supporting the M23 rebels in the east. RDF said the soldiers were Corporal Nkundabagenzi Elysee and Private Ntwari Gad.

May 28, 2022: *Al-Jazeera* and *AFP* reported that the Kivu Security Tracker said that at dawn, Allied Democratic Forces (ADF) terrorists armed with guns and machetes killed 27 civilians in Beu Manyama village in Beni region in North Kivu Province. The army claimed it killed seven ADF gunmen.

May 29, 2022: *Reuters* reported that ADF jihadis were suspected of killing 15 civilians, pillaging homes, and torching six vehicles in a 9 p.m. attack on Bulongo in North Kivu Province. *Reuters* and *VOA* reported that on May 31, the Islamic State claimed credit via *Telegram* for killing nearly 20 Christians.

June 5, 2022: *USNWR, al-Jazeera,* and *Reuters* reported that the ADF was suspected of killing 20 people in an 8 p.m. raid on Otomabere village (variant Bwanasura) in Irumu territory in Ituri Province. David Beiza, head of the Red Cross in Irumu, said volunteers counted 36 bodies at the site.

June 6, 2022: *Reuters* reported that M23 rebels firing shells killed two Congolese soldiers and wounded five in Bugusa in North Kivu Province.

June 7, 2022: *Reuters* reported that CODECO was believed responsible for a nighttime raid in the Bahema-Nord chiefdom in Ituri Province that killed 12 people and injured two near the shore of Lake Albert.

June 12, 2022: *AFP* reported that M23 seized Bunagana in North Kivu Province, forcing some 100 government forces to retreat into Uganda. Two soldiers and several rebels were killed. UNHCR reported that 368 people crossed into Uganda.

July 7, 2022: *Al-Jazeera* reported that gunmen believed to be from the ADF attacked a church clinic in Lume in North Kivu at 10 p.m., killing nine patients, including three children. Kule Mwenge Salomon, a nurse at Lume health center, said, "In the hospital ward there were four patients who all burned to death, in the pediatric unit all the mattresses are burned and in the side wards we just collected nine bodies." Kakule Vikere Lem said his father was burned to death. The army killed three fighters and captured one.

July 25, 2022: *Reuters* reported that hundreds of protesters attacked a United Nations MONUSCO peacekeeping force's warehouse and looted offices in Goma, calling for MONUSCO to leave for failing to protect the population. Protesters set fire to a gate of the mission's compound and looted equipment. The protest was called by a faction of the youth wing of President Felix Tshisekedi's UDPS ruling party.

Human Rights Watch reported that M23 rebels had summarily killed at least 29 civilians since mid-June in areas under their control.

August 9, 2022: *USNWR* and *Reuters* reported the Mai-Mai militia attacked a prison in Butembo during the night, freeing hundreds of inmates and killing two police officers. Part of the prison was damaged by fire.

August 25-29, 2022: *USNWR* and *Reuters* reported that the ADF was suspected of killing 40 civilians in a string of attacks on five villages in the east. Gunmen hit a group of villagers from North Kivu Province who had crossed into Ituri Province in a search for arable land on August 25.

October 1, 2022: *News 360* reported the ADF was suspected in an attack in Ituri Province that killed 14 civilians, including two women. Lingasa Benago, president of the civil society in Banyali-Tchabi, told Congolese news portal *7sur7* that, "After executing people, they set fire to 36 houses and looted the population's property."

October 19, 2022: *AFP* reported that ADF rebels killed seven people and kidnapped a nurse during a midnight attack on two health centers in Maboya, in the Beni territory of North Kivu Province. The terrorists torched the Maboya health center, killing three people, then killed three more people in the center of town. They moved on to the Protestant-owned Tinge hospital a mile away, killing a sentry and kidnapping a nurse.

October 23, 2022: *AFP* reported that army officials and local residents said that M23 fighters had captured the village of Ntamugenga. Four civilians were killed and eight wounded.

October 29, 2022: *Reuters* reported that M23 seized Kiwandja in eastern Congo, cutting North Kivu's capital Goma off from the northern half of the province.

Al-Jazeera reported that the Democratic Republic of the Congo's government ordered Rwandan Ambassador Vincent Karega to leave the country within 48 hours after accusing Kigali of supporting M23 rebels who seized control of Kiwanja and Rutshuru in North Kivu Province.

November 2, 2022: *News 360, AFP,* and Kenyan *NTV* reported that the Kenya Defense Forces (KDF) deployed between 6,500 and 12,000 troops in Bunangana in eastern Democratic Republic of Congo (DRC) near the border with Uganda as part of a regional operation against the M23 in North Kivu, South Kivu, and Ituri Provinces. Burundi had sent a contingent on August 15.

November 25, 2022: *News 360* reported that the M23 agreed in principle to cessation of hostilities in North Kivu Province against the Kenyan and Ugandan Army and forces of the East African Community (EAC), but reserved the right to respond to any attack.

November 28-30, 2022: *Al-Jazeera, Reuters,* and *AFP* reported on December 1 that the armed forces accused M23 and its allies of killing 50 civilians in Kishishe in North Kivu Province on November 28. The *Washington Post, Reuters, al-Jazeera, Deutsche Welle,* and *AFP* reported on December 6 that government officials, including Industry Minister Julien Paluku, said that 272 civilians were killed when M23 rebels attacked villagers in Kishishe in North Kivu Province. An earlier estimated death toll was 50. M23 said only eight civilians had been killed, and those by stray bullets. Government spokesman Patrick Muyaya said "children were killed in an Adventist church and a hospital."

Djibouti

October 7, 2022: *News 360, al-Jazeera,* and Djibouti state television reported that Djibouti's Ministry of Defense blamed the rebel armed wing of the Front for Unity and Restoration for Democracy (FRUD) for an attack in Garbtisan that killed seven Djiboutian military personnel, wounded four, and left six missing. FRUD consists largely of Afars, and began its rebellion against the Issa ethnic group in 1991.

Ethiopia

February 3, 2022: *Reuters* reported on February 18 that gunmen attacked the Barahle refugee camp in Afar region, killing five Eritreans, kidnapping several women, looting property, and occupying homes. Thousands fled. 22020301

March 2, 2022: The *Jerusalem Post*, citing the Ethiopian Human Rights Commission, reported on March 14 that gunmen ambushed a civilian convoy in Metekel, in the Benishangul-Gumuz region, killing 53 people, including 20 soldiers and three civilians. Thirty attackers died in the day-long gun battle. Another 11 people died the next day; one was burned alive. The Commission claimed that government soldiers stopped a bus, pulled out eight ethnic Tigrayan civilians who had just been released from prison, and accused them of orchestrating the attack.

March 29, 2022: *Reuters* reported that suspected Amhara gunmen in seven vehicles ambushed a vehicle carrying 100 militia members as it passed through Korke in neighboring Oromiya, killing 26 people, including two federal policemen and a driver, and injuring 15. The gunmen called Oromo militia members with a phone of one of the deceased to say they were members of the Fano volunteer Amhara militia.

April 26, 2022: *AFP, al-Jazeera,* and *EBC* reported that the Islamic Affairs Council of Amhara charged that around 7 p.m., "extremist Christians" fired heavy machine guns and threw grenades, killing more than 20 people and wounding 15 in an attack on Muslims during the funeral of a Muslim elder in a cemetery in Gondar in the Amhara region.

June 18, 2022: Witnesses and the regional government blamed Oromo Liberation Army (OLA) rebels for an attack that killed 230 people, mostly Amhara, in the Oromia region's

Gimbi County. OLA spokesman Odaa Tarbii denied involvement, blaming the military and local militia.

June 18, 2022: The *Jerusalem Post* reported on June 30 that the Ethiopian Prime Minister's spokeswoman announced that some 340 people were killed in an attack in the Gimbi district of Western Wollega Zone in the western part of Oromiya region on June 18. She blamed a militia formerly allied to an opposition party.

July 4, 2022: Prime Minister Abiy Ahmed announced that Shene rebels massacred Amhara villagers in Oromia region's Qellen Wellega area. The Amhara Association of America suggested that between 150 to 160 people were killed.

July 25, 2022: *Reuters, Shabelle Media,* and the *Islam Times* reported that the military claimed that Ethiopia forces killed 85 al-Shabaab fighters near Somalia. *ETV* said soldiers also wounded and captured more terrorists in the Ferfer district. Al-Shabaab had attacked two villages the previous week.

July 30, 2022: *News 360* and the state-owned *Ethiopian Broadcasting Corporation (EBC)* reported that the Ethiopian Embassy in Djibouti identified three senior al-Shabaab members among the more than 200 killed during recent fighting in recent days in the Somali region, near the border with Somalia. They were:

- Fuad Mohamed Jalaf, propaganda chief responsible for the group's financing
- Abdulaziz Abu Musa, spokesman
- Ubeda Nur Issu, commander for the Bokol area and the Ethiopian border.

August 29-30, 2022: *Al-Jazeera, Reuters,* and *AP* reported that residents of Wollega region's Horo Guduru area's Amuru district said an armed group from the ethnic Amhara community, known as Fano, killed 42 Oromo civilians. Some witnesses said there were up to 200 rifle-toting attackers who spoke Amharic and wore a variety of uniforms.

October 14, 2022: *News 360* reported that three people, including an International Rescue Committee (IRC) aid worker who was a member of the health and nutrition team transporting vital humanitarian aid for women and children, were killed during an attack in Shire in Tigray region. Four other civilians, including another IRC worker, were injured. IRC was founded in 1933 in the United States. 22101401

October 29, 2022: *News 360* reported that the Ethiopian Red Cross Society (ERCS) "unreservedly condemned" the killing by gunmen in the Amhara region of ambulance driver Mengist Minyil, 40, of the North Gonder division, who provided humanitarian services in West Dembiya for the Adi Remets hospital. He was transporting injured patients from Ada in Tigray Province. The ERCS did not specify the date of the incident or how many patients were killed. Mengist left behind two daughters in his home town of Belessa.

November 25, 29, 2022: *News 360* and the *Addis Standard* reported that residents of Oromia region said that hundreds of people have been killed and thousands forced to flee their homes by several Fano militia attacks on November 25 and 29 in Kiramu in eastern Welega territory.

GAMBIA

January 24, 2022: *Reuters* reported that Movement of Democratic Forces for Casamance (MFDC) gunmen killed two Senegalese soldiers and were believed to have taken nine hostage during fighting. Senegalese forces killed one rebel and captured three. The soldiers were monitoring timber trafficking. 22012403

KENYA

January 3, 2022: *Reuters* reported that al-Shabaab was suspected when gunmen killed six men in a Kenyan coastal village in Lamu County near the border with Somalia, stabbing and beheading one of the victims, torching his house, and burning four of the bodies, their hands tied behind them. Another victim had gunshot wounds to the head. 22010301

November 1, 2022: *Al-Jazeera* reported that al-Shabaab was believed responsible for kidnapping two paramedics, a driver, and a patient from an ambulance belonging to the regional county government of Mandera County near Kenya's border with Somalia. The ambulance was en route to Elwak Hospital. 22110201

December 25, 2022: During the night, al-Shabaab terrorists shot to death two people in Taa village in the Pandaguo area of Lamu County that abuts Boni forest. The gunmen then torched several homes. 22122501

A week earlier, al-Shabaab was suspected in an attack on a police vehicle in northern Kenya that killed two police officers and a civilian. 22129901

LIBERIA

January 19, 2022: The *Washington Post* and *al-Jazeera* reported that gunmen attacked a nighttime religious gathering on a fenced-in soccer field outside a school in New Kru Town outside Monrovia, sparking a stampede that killed 29 people, including 11 children and a pregnant woman. The prayer events are locally called "crusades". Doctors at Redemption Hospital said 15 people were wounded, two critically. A knife-wielding individual was arrested.

MALI

January 22, 2022: *Reuters, Stars and Stripes,* and *AP* reported that a mortar attack on a military base of France's anti-insurgent force Operation Barkhane in Gao killed French artilleryman Alexandre Martin, 24, and slightly injured nine other soldiers. *Stars and Stripes* reported on January 27 that a U.S. soldier was injured. 22012201

January 23, 2022: *Military Times* reported on April 14, 2022 that intelligence specialist Master Sgt. Steven Corley, assigned to 2nd Battalion, 20th Special Forces Group, received the Purple Heart on April 8, 2022 in a ceremony in Stuttgart, Germany, for wounds sustained during a mortar attack in Gao on January 23, 2022. The mortar attack killed a French soldier. Cor-

ley was leading a six-person team helping with intelligence exploitation. Despite his wounds, he helped partner forces locate the point from which his element was attacked.

February 3, 2022: *Reuters* reported on February 8 that the French Army Ministry said that in joint operations conducted on February 1-6 by the French-led Takuba task force and Malian soldiers that began on February 3, thirty jihadis were killed and dozens of vehicles and weapons destroyed. On that date, a drone spotted a column of fighters on motorbikes. A Mirage 2000 patrol fighter jet "led to the putting out of action of about twenty terrorists" and the destruction of a vehicle with dozens of kilograms of explosives, weapons, and motorbikes.

February 19, 2022: *BBC* reported that rebels attacked the army in Archam region, killing eight soldiers. Another five were missing. The Malian air force killed 57 militants. *AFP* reported that 40 civilians were killed in Archam the previous week.

March 2022: *Reuters* reported on April 2, 2022 that the military claimed it had killed more than 200 jihadis in a clash in Moura village in central Mali in late March. Some observers said that the Russian mercenary Wagner Group was involved.

March 4, 2022: *Al-Jazeera* reported that rebels using car bombs attacked an army base in Mondoro near the Burkina Faso border, killing 27 soldiers and wounding 33. Another seven soldiers were missing. The military said it killed 70 "terrorists".

March 7, 2022: *AFP* reported a roadside bomb killed two UN MINUSMA peacekeepers and wounded four others north of Mopti. The peacekeepers were believed to be Egyptians. 22030701

March 11, 2022: *AFP* reported that jihadis were suspected in a string of attacks on Tamalat and Insinane in the Menaka region during the week that killed more than 100 civilians and combatants from the Movement for the Salvation of Azawad (MSA), a Tuareg rebel group that signed a peace deal with the government in 2015. The MSA accused the Islamic State in the Greater

Sahara (IS-GS), an ISIS affiliate, of the attacks. MSA official Moussa Acharatoumane claimed that about 20 of the group's combatants and 40 civilians had died.

March 21, 2022: *AFP* reported on March 23 that two attacks against the military killed 16 soldiers and wounded 18. The military said it killed 37 "terrorists" and seized weapons and munitions. The Islamic State claimed credit for one of the attacks on a military outpost in the northeast.

April 2022: *AP* reported on April 25, 2022 that the JNIM claimed it had captured Russian Wagner Group mercenaries in the mountainous Segou region earlier in April. 22049901

April 19, 2022: *Al-Jazeera* and *AFP* reported that a Russian, believed to be a member of the Wagner mercenary group, operating alongside Malian soldiers was killed by a roadside bomb near Hombori in Sahel State. He was in his 30s. 22041901

April 24, 2022: *Al-Jazeera* and *Voice of America* reported that vehicle bombs were driven into three military camps at Sévaré, Niono, and Bapho near Ségou in central Mali before dawn. Six soldiers were killed and 20 wounded at the Sevare camp. Five were wounded at two other locations. Another 30 soldiers were wounded and a helicopter was damaged. The armed forces claimed it killed 11 attackers during the raid on the Sévaré military camp in Mopti Region and confiscated two AK-47 assault rifles, mobile phones, and other military equipment.

Katiba Macina, a group linked to the firebrand preacher Amadou Koufa, claimed credit for the three attacks. Katiba Macina is part of the Group for the Support of Islam and Muslims, an al-Qaeda-linked alliance operating in the Sahel. The group sent an audio to *AFP* which said, "On Sunday morning, the mujahideen of the Katiba Macina struck three camps of the (Malian armed forces)… We hit these camps at the same time within five minutes of each other. [Apart from the] deaths, we caused material damage to them."

May 9, 2022: Defense counsel Melinda Taylor told the International Criminal Court in The Hague, Netherlands that her client, Al Hassan Ag Abdoul Aziz Ag Mohamed Ag Mahmoud, a Malian rebel accused of policing a brutal Ansar Dine Islamic regime in the Malian city of Timbuktu, was only a police officer carrying out court orders who could have been killed for disobeying. Al Hassan was charged with involvement in crimes including rape, torture, persecution, forced marriages, and sexual slavery committed from April 2012 through January 2013.

June 1, 2022: *AP* and *AFP* reported that gunmen fired small arms and rocket launchers at a U.N. Multidimensional Integrated Stabilization Mission in Mali peacekeeping convoy in the Kidal region, killing a Jordanian peacekeeper and wounding three other Jordanians. Jihadis were suspected. 22060101

Al-Jazeera reported that at 6 p.m., gunmen on motorcycles fired on a vehicle transporting a Red Cross team near Kayes, killing a worker for the Dutch Red Cross and the car's driver. Two employees survived. The vehicle was marked with the Red Cross emblem. The Dutch Red Cross worker was not a Dutch citizen. Katiba Macina was suspected. 22060102

June 3, 2022: *AP, Reuters,* and *al-Jazeera* reported that a bomb exploded under an armored personnel carrier in an escort of a dozen UN Multidimensional Integrated Stabilization Mission in Mali vehicles accompanying a convoy of civilian trucks carrying fuel near Douentza on the road to Timbuktu in the Mopti region, killing two Egyptian UN peacekeepers and injuring two others. 22060301

June 11-12, 2022: *AFP* and *Reuters* reported that the French Armed Forces ministry announced that during the night, Operation Barkhane soldiers had captured Oumeya Ould Albakaye, an explosives expert and regional chief of the Islamic State in the Greater Sahara (IS-GS) in Gourma in Mali and Oudalan in Burkina Faso, close to the border with Niger.

June 15, 2022: *AFP* reported that an armed group reported the death of 22 people in the Menaka region, near Niger's western border.

June 17, 2022: *AP* reported that local officials blamed jihadis on motorbikes for attacks in Dialassogou, Segue, and Lesago in the Bankass circle that killed 40 civilians. *AFP* the next day noted that the government increased the death toll to 132 civilians, blaming Fulani religious leader Amadou Koufa's armed group, the al-Qaeda-affiliated Macina Katiba. A local official tallied more than 200 dead and missing. A police official said more bodies were found on June 21.

June 18, 2022: Suspected jihadi gunmen killed 20 civilians in the northern region of Gao.

June 19, 2022: A U.N. peacekeeper died from an improvised explosive device. 22061901

June 24, 2022: *AFP* reported Mali's army said it had killed 50 jihadis in the Diallassougou area, "two terrorist watchmen" in the Mondoro area, and arrested eight terrorist suspects in the south of the country.

July 2022: The *Washington Post* reported on July 22 that mid-month, gunmen attacked an army checkpoint 37 miles outside Bamako, killing six people and wounding several others. No one claimed credit, but the al-Qaeda affiliate Jama'at Nusrat al-Islam wal-Muslimin (JNIM) was suspected.

July 5, 2022: The *Jerusalem Post* and *AFP* reported that in the morning, a United Nations Multidimensional Integrated Stabilization Mission in Mali (MINUSMA) peacekeeping logistics convoy hit a mine, killing two Egyptian United Nations peacekeepers and severely wounding five on the road between Tessalit and Gao. 22070501

July 21, 2022: The *Washington Post* reported that gunmen attacked a police base in Kolokani, killing two Malian soldiers.

On July 23, *Reuters* reported that JNIM claimed responsibility for attacks in five central and southern Mali towns, which the Malian military said had killed one soldier and injured 15.

July 22, 2022: The *Washington Post* and *Reuters* reported that jihadis were suspected in a 5 a.m. attack on the Kati barracks of the main military base outside Bamako where Mali's interim president Lt. Col. Assimi Goita lives. The attackers set off two car bombs. Seven terrorists and one soldier died when the armed forces repelled the attackers. The military said six people were wounded. Eight terrorists were arrested. The government blamed Katiba Macina.

Reuters reported on July 23 that al-Qaeda's JNIM affiliate Katiba Macina branch claimed credit, saying it was responding to governmental collaboration with Wagner Group Russian mercenaries. JNIM said a Malian set off a car bomb at the base's gate and a fighter from Burkina Faso detonated another inside the base. 22072201

July 27, 2022: *Deutsche Welle, AFP,* and *Reuters* reported that in coordinated attacks, jihadis killed 15 soldiers and three civilians in attacks on three military bases. Nine soldiers and three civilians were killed in an early morning attack on a camp in Kalumba. Gunmen killed six soldiers and wounded 25 others, five seriously, in a raid on a military camp in Sonkolo. The army said 48 terrorists were killed. No one was injured in an attack on a military base in Mopti.

August 7, 2022: *Al-Jazeera, ORTM,* and *AFP* reported that jihadis were suspected when gunmen killed 17 Malian soldiers and four civilians, including two elected officials near Tessit in the Gao region. Nine soldiers were reported missing. Vehicles and equipment were destroyed. The Islamic State in the Greater Sahara was suspected. The Army said it had killed seven terrorists. *Al-Jazeera* added on August 11 that the government revised the tally to 42 soldiers killed, 22 soldiers wounded, and 37 terrorists killed.

August 13, 2022: *Deutsche Welle* and *AFP* reported that JNIM claimed it killed four Russian Wagner Group mercenaries in an ambush around Bandiagara in the Mopti region.

September 11, 2022: *News 360* reported that a roadside bomb exploded under a MINUSMA patrol between Ber and Timbuktu, injuring three "blue helmet" peacekeepers. 22091101

September 28, 2022: The *Bangkok Post* reported on October 25, 2022 that gunmen kidnapped Thai physician Dr. Nopparat Rattanawaraha, 49, also known as Mor Song and host of the Mor Song Tong Loke *YouTube* channel, on September

28, 2022 while driving from Burkina Faso into Mali with a driver and guide. He was released after a US$50,000 (5.5 million baht) ransom was paid. *AFP* and *Channel 3 Television* added that the plastic surgeon drank pond water to survive and that the ransom was $150,000. He said he was sleeping in the car and was rudely awakened by five or six gunmen. In his third week, he was permitted to phone his mother and girlfriend, who listened to the kidnappers' demands. 22092802

October 13, 2022: *AP, al-Jazeera,* and *AFP* reported that a bus hit an explosive device in the village of Songo on the road between Bandiagara and Goundaka in the Mopti area in the early afternoon, killing 11 and injuring 53. Jihadis were suspected.

October 14, 2022: *Reuters* reported that jihadis in the east in recent days had seized territory, killed hundreds of civilians, and forced thousands to flee. Fighting between Tuareg separatists and the Islamic State in the Greater Sahara (ISGS) was reported in Menaka region. In October, jihadis took over the rural Ansongo district, near the border with Niger.

October 17, 2022: *USNWR* and *Reuters* reported that three U.N. peacekeepers were killed and three others seriously injured when their vehicle hit an improvised explosive device in Kidal region. A fourth died of his injuries soon after. 22101701

October 23, 2022: *News 360* reported that the Malian Army General Staff reported that during the last two weeks, it had "neutralized" 30 jihadis in Operation Kélètigui and the Maliko plan against terrorism in the country. *Malijet* reported that 11 jihadis were killed on October 12 in Haroun in Gao region. Ten terrorists were neutralized in the N'dila Toridagago commune on October 20. The Army killed another four jihadis who tried to attack a detachment in Mourdiah, in the Koulikoro region on October 21.

November 18, 2022: *News 360* reported that on November 28 authorities, as part of a special forces operation carried out in Missabougou, arrested four "criminals", including two French

nationals, a French-Malian, and a French-Senegalese, allegedly behind the November 18 kidnapping of ten hostages, including six children, all of the same family, who were freed. The gunmen demanded a ransom of 900 million Central African francs (about €1.4 million) or "information on the location of cocaine recently intercepted by Malian Customs".

November 20, 2022: *AP* and *Reuters* reported that jihadis were suspected of kidnapping of German priest Rev. Hans-Joachim Lohre of the Missionaries of Africa (White Fathers institute) as he was preparing to celebrate Mass in Bamako the next morning. Investigators found Lohre's cross necklace, which had been cut off, next to his car. No one claimed credit. He had served in Mali for more than 30 years and taught at the Institute of Islamic-Christian Training. 22112001

November 21, 2022: *News 360* and *Studio Tamani Radio* reported on November 24 that at 7 p.m., gunmen attacked a camp for internally displaced persons in Kadji, in Gounzoureye commune, seven kilometers southeast of Gao in east-central Mali, killing 11 people. The terrorists killed all the men, torched IDP homes and food supplies, and stole all their livestock.

Mozambique

September 2022: *AP* reported on September 12, 2022 that the Islamic State Mozambique Province group claimed responsibility for setting fire to two churches and more than 120 homes of Christians during the first week of September in Nampula Province. During an attack on the Catholic Chipene Mission, the jihadis shot and killed Italian nun Sister Maria de Coppi, 83, and set fire to the church, health center, and residential quarters. Pope Francis said she had "served with love for nearly 60 years" as a Comboni missionary in Mozambique. 22099901

September 15, 2022: *News 360* and *Carta de Mozambique* reported that gunmen killed 16 Mozambican military personnel at a security forces checkpoint in Knoe in Macomia district, in Cabo Delgado Province (north). Army spokesman Omar Saranga said the clashes killed four prominent terrorists, including Dady and Marisco, whom he accused of participating in various attacks in Cabo Delgado.

September 30, 2022: *News 360* reported that suspected jihadis beheaded three people in the districts of Meluco and Macomia, in Cabo Delgado Province. *News 360* and *O Pais* reported that Chief of the Mozambican Police Bernardino Rafael encouraged residents of Cabo Delgado Province to "resist" jihadist attacks with knives or machetes.

The *Carta de Mozambique* news portal reported that the terrorists attacked Ntapuala, near Macomia, and beheaded a man who was working in his field. They then beheaded two people between the villages of Koko and Nangololo, between Macomia and Meluco.

NIGER

February 20, 2022: *Al-Jazeera* reported that Interior Minister Alkassoum Indatou blamed "armed bandits, aboard several motorcycles, who have not yet been identified" for an attack in the Tillaberi region near the Malian border which killed 18 civilians whose vehicle came under fire. Indatou said 13 victims were from Foney Ganda and five from Tizegorou.

March 2022: *AFP* reported on March 16, 2022 that five soldiers were killed by a mine in the Torodi region. Jihadis were suspected.

March 7, 2022: *AFP* reported that Boko Haram was suspected when gunmen on foot during the evening attacked the villages of Fiego, Ngarwa-Lawandi, and Ngarwa-Koura near the town of Diffa, shooting to death ten male villagers. The terrorists then attacked the nearby Lada village. Maman Kaka Touda, a representative for the Nigerien NGO Alternative Citizen Space (AEC), tweeted that "20 people have been killed", including "10 at Lada". 22030701

March 16, 2022: *AFP* reported that jihadis on motorcycles and a vehicle were suspected of attacking a Nigerien Modern Transport Company bus returning from Ouagadougou and truck near the Petelkole border post in the Tillaberi

region, killing 21 people, including 17 bus passengers and two police officers on the bus, and two people on the truck. The latter died when the fruit-and-vegetables truck was torched. Five people including a policeman, were wounded in the attack on the bus, which was also set alight. Four women and three men escaped from the bus. The bus company suspended departures to Burkina Faso.

June 16, 2022: *Al-Jazeera* reported that French Operation Barkhane drone strikes killed nearly 40 fighters travelling on motorcycles near Niger's border with Burkina Faso.

October 26, 2022: *News 360* reported that terrorists attacked a police station in a town near the border with Burkina Faso, killing two Niger police officers and stealing military equipment.

November 2, 2022: *News 360* reported that during the night gunmen attacked an IDP camp in the southeast, killing four people and burning down numerous homes. Nigerien news portal *Actu Niger* have indicated that the attack occurred in Ngagala Peulh, located near N'Guigmi in Diffa Province. No one claimed credit, although attacks occur often by Boko Haram and the Islamic State in West Africa (ISWA).

NIGERIA

January 2022: Gunmen kidnapped three Chinese workers and killed two local staff at the 700-megawatt Zungeru hydropower project in Niger State. *Reuters* reported on March 3, 2022 that Chinese contractors working for Sino-Hydro had stopped working, fearing for their safety. The China Export and Import Bank had provided $1.3 billion of funding. As of March 3, the hostages' fate was unknown. 22019901

January 3, 2022: *CNN* reported that local police announced on January 4 that 97 hostages were rescued in separate rescue operations in northwest Nigeria. The Commissioner of Police in northwestern Zamfara State, Ayuba Elkana, said in Gusau that on January 3, joint military operations in Zamfara's Shinkafi and Tsafe districts rescued the hostages including more than a dozen babies, 16 children between the ages of two and seven years, nursing women, and seven pregnant women. The hostages had been in captivity for more than two months. Officials said no ransom was paid.

January 4, 2022: Gunmen killed more than 100 people during a three-day attack in the Anka and Bukkuyum local government areas of Zamfara State. The group also burned down homes. No group claimed responsibility. Witnesses told *CNN* the death toll was 200.

January 14-16, 2022: *Reuters* and *U.S. News and World Report* said that dozens of gunmen on motorcycles killed 50 people, including two soldiers, dozens of villagers, and a police officer, during a raid on Dankade village in Kebbi State during the night and early morning, exchanging gunfire with soldiers and policemen, burning shops and grain silos, and stealing cattle. A witness said the terrorists also kidnapped the community leader of Dankade and many villagers, mostly women and children. Didzi Umar Bunu, son of the kidnapped community leader, added that the gunmen returned on January 16 to torch more houses.

January 20, 2022: *AFP* and *AP* reported that in an afternoon raid, Islamic State West Africa Province (ISWAP) jihadists wearing military uniforms killed two men and kidnapped 13 girls and seven boys aged between 12 and 15 in Piyemi, variant Pemi, a village near Chibok town in Borno State. The terrorists attacked a church and torched homes. Local resident Silas John said the gunmen came from the Sambisa forest and moved the "20 kidnapped children into a truck they seized from the village and drove them into the forest". One witness said eight of the girls came from one household.

January 21, 2022: *AP* reported that the Islamic State West Africa Province claimed responsibility for killing "many Christians" and setting fire to two churches and several houses during an attack on the Borno town of Bimi.

January 23, 2022: *Reuters* reported that gunmen in Kwalam in Jigawa State killed two policemen responding to an early morning distress call over

an abduction of a 60-year old. A patrol vehicle was set ablaze in the ensuing firefight. The gunmen fled.

January 29-30, 2022: *AFP* reported that gunmen killed dozens of people, including 11 security personnel, in separate attacks in northwest and central Nigeria. Niger State Governor Sani Bello said that in an attack on the remote Galadiman Kogo community in Shiroro district, motorcycle-riding "terrorists, numbering over 100 are said to have invaded the community in broad daylight, killing about 11 Joint Security Taskforce members, several villagers and leaving many injured." Security forces killed scores of the attackers.

February 22, 2022: The Islamic State West African Province claimed that it had attacked soldiers on patrol at several checkpoints in Borno State, killing and wounding more than 30. The Nigerian military said it had killed "several" terrorists and seized a "large cache of weapons" and vehicles on February 21 in a different location in Borno State.

March 1-3, 2022: *Reuters* reported that Niger State Commissioner for Security Emmanuel Umar announced that some 200 gunmen had been killed in the past three days during a security operation. Authorities seized 60 motorbikes, weapons, and cattle.

March 6-7, 2022: *AFP, Reuters,* and *AP* reported that gunmen killed 67 members of a local Yan Sa Kai self-defence vigilante group in clashes with heavily armed bandits in the Zuru district of Kebbi State. Yan Sa Kai leader and retired soldier Usman Sani said his group planned to attack bandits in the Sakaba area the night of March 6, but the gunmen were tipped off and "lay in ambush, hid their motorcycles in the shrubs, circled us, and opened fire from different directions".

March 8, 2022: *AFP* reported that in a nighttime attack, gunmen raided Kanya village in the Danko-Wasagu district in Kebbi State, killing 19 security personnel, including 13 soldiers, five policemen, and a vigilante, and hospitalizing eight other security personnel, including four soldiers, in a three-hour firefight. Local resident Musa

Arzika said the attackers came on "around 200 motorcycles riding three on each".

March 19, 2022: *Al-Jazeera* reported that two police constables were killed in an attack on Umuguma police station outside Owerri in the southeast.

Gunmen attacked the residence of Professor George Obiozor, leader of the Igbo cultural union Ohanaeze, set off explosives, and destroyed part of the building. He was not at home.

March 20, 2022: *Al-Jazeera* and *AFP* reported that gunmen set off dynamite at a police station at Oru in Imo State. Four terrorists died. State police spokesman Michael Abattam said that five bombs were recovered. The outlawed Indigenous People of Biafra (IPOB) denied responsibility.

March 23, 2022: *Al-Jazeera* and the *News Agency of Nigeria* reported that Major General Christopher Musa announced that 7,000 members of the Islamic State West Africa Province (ISWAP) and Boko Haram had surrendered in Borno State during the previous week.

March 25, 2022: *Al-Jazeera* reported that U.S. Under-Secretary of the Treasury Brian Nelson announced the imposition of sanctions on six Nigerians connected with Boko Haram. The six were found guilty of setting up a Boko Haram cell in the United Arab Emirates to raise funds for fighters in Nigeria. The UAE convicted Abdurrahman Ado Musa, Salihu Yusuf Adamu, Bashir Ali Yusuf, Muhammed Ibrahim Isa, Ibrahim Ali Alhassan, and Surajo Abubakar Muhammad of attempting to send $782,000 from Dubai to Nigeria. Adamu and Muhammad were sentenced to life in prison for violating UAE anti-terrorism laws. Musa, Yusuf, Isa, and Alhassan were sentenced to 10 years in prison followed by deportation. Treasury added, "All property and interests in property of the individuals named above, and of any entities that are owned, directly or indirectly, 50 percent or more by them, individually, or with other blocked persons, that are in the United States or in the possession or control of US persons, must be blocked and reported to OFAC."

March 28, 2022: *Al-Jazeera* and *AP* reported that during the night, suspected bandits attacked a passenger train headed to Kaduna from Abuja. Passenger Anas Iro Danmusa posted on *Facebook* that bandits had set off two bombs to halt the train and forced their way on board, engaging in a shootout with security guards on the train. After the guards were subdued, the gunmen killed several of the 970 passengers; passenger Abdulwadud Ahmad said nine died. *CNN* reported on April 1 that 26 were injured. The Kaduna state government said that the military secured the train, which was in Katari, 16 miles from Kaduna, in Kaduna State. Fidet Okhiria, CEO of the state-owned Nigerian Railway Corporation, and Nigerian state media outlet *NAN* said many people were feared to have been kidnapped. Others escaped into the nearby forests.

CNN reported on April 1 that among the dead was dental surgeon Chinelo Megafu, who had run into another section of the train from where she had been seated. She had graduated from the University of Port Harcourt's Faculty of Dentistry in Nigeria's southern region in 2016. She planned to travel to Canada on the weekend to begin her Master's program.

BBC and *Reuters* reported on April 4, 2022 that 168 people were still missing. No one had claimed credit. The governor of Kaduna State suspected Boko Haram and a kidnapping gang had joined forces. There were 18 policemen on the train.

Al-Jazeera and *AFP* reported on April 7 that the gunmen released a video of Alwan Ali-Hassan, director of Nigeria's Bank of Agriculture, who was among the passengers taken hostage, flanked by four armed masked men in military uniforms. They called on authorities to meet the demands of his captors to secure the release of other hostages who "are in a dire situation". Family members said the gunmen released him on April 6; the gunmen said he was freed out of compassion as a "Ramadan gesture" and his "advanced age". The family said they paid a ransom. The video was shot in a forest with an armored vehicle in the background. The men did not claim a group affiliation, but the video was similar to earlier propaganda videos sent by jihadis. It included an opening prayer in Arabic that was the same used in earlier propaganda videos by Boko Haram and ISWAP (and something that simple criminal bandits do not include in their videos). Bulama Bukarti, a senior analyst with the Extremism Policy Unit at the Tony Blair Institute for Global Change said the men also spoke Kanuri, principal language of Borno State, the birthplace of Boko Haram. Two speakers did not have Fulani accents, which most bandits do.

Al-Jazeera reported on April 8 that as of that date, the families were still awaiting updates on the case from the Nigerian government. Family members said that they had been contacted by the kidnappers and the hostages, but government officials remained aloof.

BBC reported on May 15, 2022 that gunmen who abducted 62 train passengers in March released a pregnant hostage. The kidnappers had earlier freed a bank executive due to his old age, although a ransom was reported paid. The government blamed Boko Haram.

USNWR and *Reuters* reported on June 11, 2022 that Minister of State for Transportation Gbemisola Saraki said that gunmen freed 11 passengers who were abducted during an attack on the night train on the Abuja-Kaduna route in late March. Dozens remained hostages.

AP and *AFP* reported on October 5, 2022 that the government announced that a committee led by Nigeria's chief of defense staff "secured the release and took custody of all the 23 remaining passengers held hostage". No arrests or ransoms were announced.

AFP reported that at 10 a.m. on December 5, 2022, Nigeria resumed a Nigerian Railway Corporation train service linking Abuja and Kaduna, eight months after it was suspended following a March 28 attack. The hostages were released seriatim following negotiations with their captors who apparently obtained large ransoms from their families.

April 5, 2022: *Al-Jazeera,* Lagos-based *Channels Television,* and *The Guardian* reported that gunmen on motorcycles and carrying heavy weapons, including a rocket-propelled grenade, attacked a military base in Birnin Gwari in Kaduna State for two hours during the night, killing 10 soldiers and wounding an undisclosed number.

April 7, 2022: *Reuters* and *al-Jazeera* reported that a federal court judge ruled that all terrorism trials were to be held in camera. Catherine Christopher, spokeswoman for an Abuja court, said in a statement dated April 5 that coverage of any part of such proceedings would require permission from Justice John Terhemba Tsoho. Anyone contravening the instructions would be deemed an offender of Section 34(5) of the amended Terrorism (Prevention) Act, 2011.

April 8, 2022: *Reuters* reported that a High Court judge ruled that Nnamdi Kanu, a British citizen who leads the banned Indigenous People of Biafra (IPOB), should stand trial and answer to charges that include terrorism and broadcasting falsehoods between 2018 and 2021. The court ruled that Kanu will stand trial on seven counts of terrorism out of 15, and struck down eight other charges. Defense lawyer Mike Ozekhome argued that Kanu could not be tried on those charges because he was not extradited from Kenya for those charges. Kanu disappeared from Nigeria after skipping bail in 2017. He had founded the secessionist IPOB in 2014. Kanu was born in 1967, when Igbos tried to secede as the Republic of Biafra and started a three-year civil war that killed more than one million people.

April 10, 2022: *AFP* and *al-Jazeera* reported that gunmen raided Kyaram, Gyambau, Dungur, Kukawa, Shuwaka villages in Garga District in Plateau State, destroying scores of homes. Two days later, President Muhammadu Buhari vowed there would be no mercy for those behind the killings of 100+ people. Local community leader Malam Usman Abdul said that 54 dead bodies were found at Kukawa village, 16 local vigilantes died at Shuwaka village, 30 villagers were recovered at Gyambahu, and four more were found around other villages. Bala Yahaya, operational commander of local vigilantes, said they had recovered 107 bodies, including 16 members of his group. *Al-Jazeera* reported that Jonathan Ishaku, spokesman for the Plateau Elders' Forum, claimed that 70 people, including women and children, were kidnapped from nine villages. *Al-Jazeera* added on April 14 that the death toll had reached 154 and 4,800 people, mostly women and children, fled their homes. Information Minister Lai Mohammed blamed armed criminal gangs and Boko Haram.

April 14, 2022: *Al-Jazeera* reported the Nigerian air force and aircraft from Niger killed or severely injured more than 70 ISWAP fighters at Tumbun Rego and a nearby training camp at the border with Niger.

April 14-15, 2022: *Reuters* reported that the Independent Electoral Commission of Nigeria suspended voter registration at 54 centers and in three local government areas in Imo State after an election official was shot dead by unknown gunmen on April 14. The government suspected the banned separatist Indigenous People of Biafra (IPOB), which denied the charges.

April 19, 2022: *Free Press Journal, Xinhua,* and *Reuters* reported that a bomb went off at a restaurant in a market area in Irawe in Taraba State, killing three and injuring 19. *Al-Jazeera* reported on April 21 that ISWAP claimed credit, saying it killed or injured 30 people at a market where alcohol was sold. ISWAP said on *Telegram* that the bombers were "soldiers of the caliphate in central Nigeria" who had attacked "a gathering of infidel Christians".

April 20, 2022: Dungus Abdulkareem of the Yobe State Police Command said Boko Haram was suspected when gunmen on foot killed nine people, including two women and a retired inspector of police, in Geidam in Yobe State. A local witness said the gunmen burned down a school, shot some persons in a bar, bound others from behind and slit their throats.

April 22, 2022: *Reuters* and the *Jerusalem Post* reported that ISWAP claimed credit for a nighttime bombing in Jalingo, capital of Taraba State, injuring 11 people, including children.

May 4, 2022: *Al-Jazeera* and *AP* reported that in the evening, gunmen attacked Kautukari village in the Chibok area of Borno State, killing seven people.

May 6, 2022: *Al-Jazeera* and *AFP* reported that dozens of gunmen on motorcycles attacked Damri, Kalahe, and Sabon Garin villages in Zamfara State, killing 48 people trying to flee. The terrorists shot to death 32 people, including patients at a hospital, in Damri. They burned a police patrol vehicle and killed two security personnel.

May 10, 2022: *Al-Jazeera* and *Reuters* reported that during the night, gunmen ambushed an army 93 Battalion patrol, killing seven soldiers in Tati village in the Takum local government area of Taraba State. A brigadier general and his aide were missing. No one claimed credit.

May 15, 2022: *CNN* reported that during the night of May 21, police found the severed head of state legislator Okechukwu Okoye, who, along with his aide, went missing on May 15 in Anambra State. His head was found along Nnobi Road in a park in the Nnewi south local government area. The Anambra state governor offered a 10 million naira ($24,000) reward for information on the killers.

Earlier in May, gunmen killed and beheaded two soldiers in neighboring Imo State. The government accused the banned Indigenous People of Biafra (IPOB) separatist group, which denied the charge.

May 17, 2022: *CNN* reported on May 27 that eyewitnesses were saying that a suicide bomber was responsible for an explosion in Kano that killed nine people and injured several others. Kano Police Commissioner, Sama'ila Shu'aibu Dikko initially blamed a gas cylinder that went off near a school in the Sabon Gari area of Kano.

May 22, 2022: *Reuters* and *Insidene.com* reported that gunmen on motorcycles and armed with guns and machetes killed 50 people working on their farms in Rann in Borno State, near the Cameroon border. Local residents blamed Boko Haram.

May 29, 2022: Police spokesperson Geoffrey Ogbonna said gunmen kidnapped His Eminence Samuel Kanu Uche, prelate of the Methodist Church Nigeria, and two other senior clerics along a highway in the Umunneochi area of Abia State.

May 30, 2022: *AFP* reported that the Multinational Joint Task Force (MNJTF) said Operation Lake Integrity ground and air attacks the previous week in the Tumbun Rago area in Borno State in the Lake Chad basin had "neutralised more than 25 terrorists". Five more terrorists were killed in a separate operation in in Kirta Wulgo in Borno state. Seven soldiers from Chad and Niger were slightly wounded. Lake Integrity began on March 21. 22053001

June 5, 2022: *BBC, Punch, Reuters, CNN, AP, UPI, al-Jazeera,* and *ABC News* reported that gunmen who had arrived on motorcycles walked into the St. Francis Xavier Catholic Church in Owo in Ondo State during a Pentecost Sunday service, killing 50 worshippers and passersby, including several children, and injuring scores more. Gunmen fired from inside and outside the church, and set off at least one bomb. The gunmen fled. No one claimed credit. Authorities blamed ISWAP. One witness claimed the terrorists had intended to kidnap a bishop. The Catholic Diocese of Ondo clarified that no one was kidnapped. *Reuters* reported that police found explosives nearby and reported that the terrorists disguised themselves as congregants. *ABC News* reported on June 9 that more than 80 were feared dead.

June 9, 2022: *USNWR* and *Reuters* reported that jihadis on motorbikes were suspected of killing 25 people, including children, and wounding others searching for scrap metal in a forest in Boboshe Mukdala village in the Dikwa local government area of Borno State.

June 13, 2022: *BBC* reported that gunmen set up roadblocks near Bismaa village and kidnapped 29 wedding guests traveling home from the ceremony in Zamfara State. The victims work as phone dealers in Gusau. Groom Jamilu Umar and his wife, Basira Abubakar Atiku, escaped the attack because their vehicles had driven by earlier. The kidnappers demanded a ransom.

June 19, 2022: *AP* and *AFP* reported that gunmen on motorcycles attacked morning church services at the Maranatha Baptist Church and at St. Moses Catholic Church in the Rubu community of Kaduna State, killing three people, kidnapping 36—most of them Baptists—looting shops, and destroying homes. They released two hostages, including a community chief.

June 30, 2022: *Al-Jazeera* reported that gunmen arriving on motorbikes and in a truck attacked a mining site at Ajata Aboki village in Niger State's Shiroro area in central Nigeria, killing eight civilians and seven policemen and abducting some workers, including four Chinese nationals. *Reuters* added on July 2 that gunmen killed 30 Nigerian soldiers deployed in three trucks to search for the hostages. 22063001

July 2022: *Al-Jazeera* reported that gunmen kidnapped two priests at a function in Kaduna State nearly two weeks after another priest was taken from his parish in Kaduna.

July 5, 2022: *Al-Jazeera* reported that suspected bandits ambushed the security convoy of Nigerian President Muhammadu Buhari in Katsina State. Two people in the convoy suffered minor injuries. The convoy was en route to Daura, Buhari's home town, to prepare for a visit by the President, who was not in the convoy.

At 11:30 a.m., some 300 gunmen on motorcycles fired AK-47 rifles and machine guns at ACP Aminu Umar, Area Commander, Dutsinma and his team that was on a clearance operation in the Zakka forest, Safana LGA of Katsina State, killing a police area commander and another officer elsewhere in Katsina State.

AP, Reuters, and *Daily Maverick* (Zambia) reported that at 10 p.m., 600 inmates escaped from the Kuje maximum security prison in Abuja. The *Washington Examiner* said the figure was 900 escapees. More than 300 were recaptured or surrendered at police stations. The government blamed Boko Haram. Shuaib Belgore, Permanent Secretary of the Ministry of Interior, said the rebels used "very high-grade explosives", killing a guard and wounding three. Minister of Defense Maj Gen Bashir Salihi Magashi said the prison held 994 inmates, including 64 Boko Haram suspects, all of whom escaped. *The Daily Beast* reported that the gunmen had freed dozens of jihadists including Mohammed Usman, alias Khalid al-Barnawi, 51—leader of the terrorist group Ansaru—and six of his close lieutenants.

Reuters and *UPI* reported that ISWAP claimed credit. *Reuters* reported on July 7 that prison authorities claimed to have captured 27 escapees.

Nigerian security agencies arrested al-Barnawi in 2016 and charged him in connection to the death of Italian engineer Franco Lamolinara and his British colleague, Chris McManus. Ansaru (Jama'atu Ansarul Muslimina Fi Biladis Sudan; Vanguards for the Protection of Muslims in Black Africa) kidnappers killed the duo in Sokoto in March 2012 after a British-Nigerian rescue operation was launched. Al-Barnawi was believed behind the abduction of Francis Collomp, a Frenchman who escaped from his captors in November 2013, and Edgar Raupach, a German who was killed during a military raid in Kano State in May 2012. In 2013, al-Barnawi and his Ansaru colleagues kidnapped two Lebanese, two Syrians, an Italian, a Greek, and a Briton, from a construction site in Bauchi, moved them to the Sambisa Forest, killed them, and buried them in a shallow grave. Ansaru announced in January 2012 that it had broken from Boko Haram because the latter was "inhuman" for killing innocent Muslims and targeting defectors.

Justice John Tshoho of Federal High Court in Abuja ordered al-Barnawi to Kuje prison on March 14, 2017 after he was charged with conspiracy, hostage taking, supporting a terrorist group, membership of a terrorist group, illegal possession of firearms, and concealing information on terrorism. His second wife Halima Aliya was charged with concealing information about Ansaru. Five of his lieutenants—Mohammed Bashir Saleh; Umar Bello, alias Abu Azzan; Mohammed Salisu, alias Datti; Yakubu Nuhu, alias Bello Maishayi; and Usman Abubakar, alias Mugiratu—faced the same charges as al-Barnawi and were jailed in Kuje. The judge later remanded him to the Department of State Service security service.

August 21, 2022: *Al-Jazeera, CNN,* and *Reuters* reported that gunmen kidnapped four Sisters of Jesus Catholic nuns on a highway near Okigwe while travelling to a thanksgiving Mass from Rivers State to Imo State. *Al-Jazeera* and *AFP* reported that the gunmen had released the nuns unharmed on August 23.

September 6, 2022: *Reuters* reported that police in Rivers State rescued 15 children, ranging from four years to 15 years old, who were abducted by traffickers. Police arrested Maureen Wechinwu, 44, who claimed to be a nun in the Delta region. One boy, 9, was taken from a market in October 2020 in neighboring Bayelsa State and had been sold to a woman in Lagos. He was returned to Wechinwu.

September 11, 2022: *Reuters* reported that in the evening, gunmen attacked the convoy of Senator Ifeanyi Ubah in Enugwu-Ukwu, a community in the Njikoka local government area of Anambra, killing five aides, including security personnel. Spokesman Kameh Ogbonna, who was riding with Ubah in his bullet-proof vehicle, said they escaped injury.

September 23, 2022: *News 360* reported that the Nigerian Army claimed it had killed 36 suspected terrorists in bombings over the past two weeks in Borno State where Boko Haram and the Islamic State in West Africa operate. Among those "neutralized" were BH and ISWAP commanders Abu Asiya and Abu Ubaida. During the fortnight, the army rescued 130 civilians and arrested 46 suspects.

Reuters reported that around 2 p.m., gunmen on motorbikes killed 15 people and injured many others during Friday prayers at the Jumu'at central mosque in Ruwan Jema in the Bukkuyum local government area in Zamfara State.

September 28, 2022: *News 360, AFP,* and the *Premium Times* reported that gunmen fired on a patrol in Umunze in Anambra State, killing five soldiers and a civilian. No one claimed credit.

October 5, 2022: *News 360,* the *Premium Times,* and the Nigerian *Daily Post* reported that suspected jihadis attacked the village of Birnin Waje in Zamfara State while residents were preparing for evening prayers. Some 30 people, most of them women and children, were killed when their two overloaded canoes sank while they were trying to flee toward Zauma across a river.

October 8-9, 2022: *News 360, Premium Times,* and news portal *PR Nigeria* reported that the Nigerian Armed Forces killed prominent terrorist

Ali Dogo and dozens of his supporters in a series of attacks carried out over the weekend in Yadi in Kaduna State. Dogo had fled to Kaduna from Niger State. The Air Force also killed several suspected terrorists in Mando, 30 kilometers away.

October 16, 2022: Motorcycle-riding terrorists attacked the Celestial Church in the Lokoja area of Kogi State during Sunday Mass, killing a woman and her young daughter. The gunmen used petrol to set the altar on fire.

October 18, 2022: *News 360, Reuters,* and the Nigerian newspaper *Leadership* reported that gunmen attacked the Abdulsalam Abubakar General Hospital in Lapai in Niger State in the afternoon, killing two patients and abducting 20 people, including one of the hospital's doctors and patient relatives. Niger State governor Sani Bello referred to the facility as Gulu General Hospital.

Reuters reported that clashes between herdsmen and farmers in Benue State killed 23 people.

October 23, 2022: *News 360* and Nigeria's *Premium Times* reported that police in Zamfara State announced the release of 37 people kidnapped a week earlier in Kawa, Gwashi, Tungar Rogo and Anka, in the municipalities of Anka and Bukkuyum by "bandits". Ten were given treatment for psychological trauma.

News 360 and the *Daily Post* reported that six people were killed in clashes between Boko Haram and ISWAP in Gajibo, Maiduguri region. ISWAP quietly infiltrated a Boko Haram camp, attacked its members, and stole five AK-47 rifles.

Two people were killed and three kidnapped in an attack in Katsina State.

October 28, 2022: *CNN* reported that the U.S. Department of State ordered non-emergency U.S. embassy employees and their family members in Abuja to leave the country "due to the heightened risk of terrorist attacks there". The Level 3 travel advisory for all of Nigeria urged that Americans "Reconsider travel to Nigeria due to crime, terrorism, civil unrest, kidnapping, and maritime crime." An October 23 advisory authorized the departure of non-emergency U.S. government employees and family members,

warning that potential terrorist "Targets may include, but are not limited to, government buildings, places of worship, schools, markets, shopping malls, hotels, bars, restaurants, athletic gatherings, transport terminals, law enforcement facilities, and international organizations".

November 3, 2022: *News 360* reported that gunmen kidnapped 40 children from a farm in Katsina State's Mai Ruwa community. The *Premium Times* reported that the kidnappers demanded a 30 million naira (about €70,120) ransom and asked for a dialogue with the farm's owner regarding their demands. *Al-Jazeera* reported that 21 hostages were aged 15-18, working on the farm in the Faskari council area. The farm's owner apparently refused to pay the kidnappers coerced contributions they had demanded from other farms. *Reuters* reported that on November 5 the 21 children, aged between 8 and 14, were freed and reunited with their families. Three parents said they paid a ransom of 1.5 million naira ($3,400). Police spokesman Gambo Isa denied a ransom had been paid. Parents said 30+ children were kidnapped on October 30 while harvesting crops at a farm located between Kamfanin Mailafiya and Kurmin Doka villages in Katsina. Some escaped.

November 12, 2022: *News 360* reported that Nigerian authorities announced that a military ambush in a forest in the area of Gengere-Kaso in Kaduna State killed bandit leader Dogo Maikasuwa, alias Dogo Millionaire, who led attacks and kidnappings along the Kaduna-Kachia road and in the communities of Chikun and Kajuru. Authorities seized an AK-47 assault rifle, a magazine, five rounds of ammunition, two motorcycles, and a camouflage military uniform. *Premium Times* reported that other bandits escaped, but were wounded.

November 15, 2022: *News 360, Channels TV,* and the *Daily Post* reported that Fulani herdsmen were suspected of an 11 p.m. attack on a Maikatako community in a district of the Bokkos Local Government Area of Plateau State, killing 11 and injuring six.

November 17, 2022: *AP* and *al-Jazeera* reported ed that a Nigerian soldier opened fire at the

Damboa base in Borno Province, killing an aid worker with Medecins du Monde (Doctors of the World) and a fellow soldier and injuring a helicopter co-pilot for the U.N. Humanitarian Aid Service. Soldiers returned fire, killing the attacker. 22111702

November 19, 2022: *Reuters* reported that ISWAP gunmen attacked Malam Fatori in the afternoon, killing eight soldiers and two policemen and injuring 25 soldiers and residents. The Borno State government requested for 300 Civilian Joint Task Force (CJTF) militia to help the military clear out jihadi insurgents. ISWAP said it had killed 20 soldiers and seized weapons and ammunition.

November 20, 2022: *Reuters* reported that gunmen raided four villages in Zamfara State, kidnapping more than 100 people, including women and children. More than 40 people were abducted from Kanwa village in the Zurmi local government area of Zamfara; 37, mostly women and children were taken in Kwabre community. Another 38 people working on their farms were kidnapped in the Yankaba and Gidan Goga communities of the Maradun local government area.

November 22, 2022: *Reuters* reported that gunmen attacked Ryuji community in Zamfara State's Zurmi local government area, which is adjacent to Kaura Namoda, killing 19 people.

November 23, 2022: *Reuters* reported that gunmen on motorbikes kidnapped 60 people in the remote Magami Tandu community of the Kaura Namoda local government area in Zamfara State during the evening. The hostages were mostly women observing Mawlid—Prophet Muhammad's birthday. Abdulkarim Haruna's wife was kidnapped.

December 3, 2022: *Reuters* reported that gunmen on motorbikes killed 12 worshippers, including the chief imam, and kidnapped several others from Maigamji mosque in Funtua in Katsina State during night prayers. Katsina State police spokesman Gambo Isah said state-backed vigilantes and some residents rescued some worshippers.

SENEGAL

June 10, 2022: *AFP* reported authorities arrested Movement of Democratic Forces of Casamance (MFDC) rebels seeking independence for the Casamance region.

SOMALIA

January 12, 2022: *Al-Jazeera, AFP, Somali National News Agency,* and *Reuters* reported that al-Shabaab claimed credit when a bomb hit a convoy, which included bulletproof cars, on Avisione Street in Mogadishu's Hamarweyne district on the route to the airport, killing eight people and damaging four cars and two tuk tuk motor rickshaws. At least one person was injured. The terrorists said they were targeting "foreign officers". *AFP* quoted witnesses who said the convoy was escorting foreigners. 22011201

January 16, 2022: *Reuters, al-Jazeera,* and the *Somali National News Agency* reported that a suicide bomber injured Somalia's government spokesman as he was passing in his vehicle at a road junction in Mogadishu outside the house of Mohamed Ibrahim Moalimuu, who was rushed to a hospital. A photographer saw body parts lying on the ground. Al-Shabaab claimed credit.

January 18, 2022: *Al-Jazeera, AFP,* and the state-run *SONNA* news agency reported that police officer Abdirahman Adan said an al-Shabaab suicide bomber set off his explosive vest at a Mogadishu tea shop near the Nacnac military base, killing four people and injuring ten. The base is near a Turkish military garrison that trains Somali troops.

February 16, 2022: *AP, AFP,* and *Reuters* reported that al-Shabaab attacked at least five police stations and security checkpoints in the morning in the Mogadishu area, killing five people, including two girls, and wounding 19, including 16 civilians and three security forces. Gunmen seized a police vehicle at the station in Kaxda district. The multiple injuries came during an attack in suburban Darussalam suburb. Al-Shabaab claimed it hit six locations.

February 19, 2022: An al-Shabaab suicide bomber set off his vest at a restaurant at lunch hour in Beledweyne, capital of Hiran region, killing 15 people, mostly civilians, and wounding 20.

February 22, 2022: *Military Times* reported that al-Shabaab attacked coalition forces near Duduble. U.S. Africa Command and Somali forces conducted an airstrike against al-Shabaab within the week, killing three terrorists.

March 23, 2022: *Reuters, AFP,* and *Somali National Television* reported that security forces shot to death two gunmen who tried to enter the army's Halane base near Adan Abdulle International Airport in Mogadishu. A witness said the gunmen had gotten past the gates and started shooting. They also fired mortars. Al-Shabaab claimed credit on *Radio Andalus*. The camp hosts African Union (AMISOM) peacekeeping troops; a witness said some of them were wounded. *Al-Jazeera* and *Reuters* added the next day that a Somali policeman and two security guards, possibly Kenyans, died, and four people were wounded. 22032301

Reuters and al-Jazeera reported that in the evening, an al-Shabaab suicide bomber killed 15 people, including a prominent Somali female legislator and government critic Amina Mohamed Abdi, as she approached a building housing Hirshabelle State leaders in Beledweyne. *AP* reported that others were wounded. Abdi was campaigning to retain her seat in the National Assembly. Eyewitness Dhaqane Hassan added, "I was at a walking distance to the polling station when a suicide bomber rushed towards the member of parliament Amina and embraced her and blew himself up… Shots were fired in the air by the soldiers who seemed shocked, but unfortunately she instantly died at the scene." Abdi had been pressing for an investigation of the killing of female intelligence officer Ikram Tahlil.

April 5, 2022: *Reuters* reported that the National Intelligence and Security Agency tweeted that al-Shabaab senior leader Mohamed Mahir planned to attack Somali President Mohamed Abdullahi Mohamed and Prime Minister Mohamed Hussein Roble.

April 14, 2022: *Al-Jazeera* and *Irish Times* reported that during the swearing-in ceremony for more than 200 new Somali MPs, al-Shabaab fired mortar shells near the Halane Camp venue, where African Union peacekeeping forces, many diplomats, and international organizations are based.

April 22, 2022: *BBC, AP,* and *Reuters* reported that a bomb went off at a seaside restaurant in Mogadishu's Lido Beach, killing six people and injuring seven who had gathered for an evening Iftar meal to break the Ramadan fast. Several high profile individuals, such as the Somali police commissioner, were at the venue. Al-Shabaab claimed credit.

May 3, 2022: *WIONews* of India, *Reuters, AP, CNN,* and *AFP* reported that before dawn, a car bomber knocked down the main gate, allowing al-Shabaab gunmen inside the compound of an African Union (AU) Transition Mission in Somalia (ATMIS) base housing Burundian peacekeepers near Ceel Baraf in the Shabelle region, sparking a gun battle that killed several people. *Al-Jazeera* reported that witnesses saw two helicopters overflying the scene and that three civilians had died and five others were wounded. *Reuters* reported that a local resident said three people had died. *AFP* said ten Burundian peacekeepers, among them a battalion commander colonel, and 20 al-Shabaab terrorists died, 25 soldiers were injured, and five were missing. *Reuters* later reported that the Burundian military said ten soldiers died, while a security source said "dozens" of Burundian soldiers were killed. Al-Shabaab claimed it controlled the camp, had killed 173 AU soldiers, and injured dozens more. A senior Burundian military officer said 400 jihadis stormed the base. ATMIS—made up of troops from Burundi, Djibouti, Ethiopia, Kenya, and Uganda—succeeded the AMISOM peacekeeping force when its mandate expired in late March. 22050301

May 11, 2022: An al-Shabaab suicide bomber hit a checkpoint near Mogadishu's airport, killing four people, including two government soldiers, wounding several people, and destroying several small businesses along the street. Presidential candidates were heading into the airport area to address lawmakers.

May 17, 2022: *AFP* reported that newly-elected president Hassan Sheikh Mohamud thanked U.S. President Joe Biden for redeploying around 500 U.S. troops to Somalia to combat al-Shabaab.

July 17, 2022: *USNWR, al-Jazeera, Bloomberg,* and *Reuters* reported that U.S. Africa Command announced that an air strike killed two al-Shabaab fighters near Libikus in the Lower Juba region.

Al-Shabaab claimed credit for a car bomb that went off outside a popular hotel in Jowhar, killing five and wounding 14.

August 2, 2022: The government of President Hassan Sheikh Mohamud announced the appointment as Religious Affairs Minister of Mukhtar Robow, former deputy chief of al-Shabaab. He defected from al-Shabaab in 2017, when the U.S. was offering $5 million for his arrest. The U.S. named him a "specially designated global terrorist" and imposed sanctions on him in 2008. He studied shariah in Sudan and is believed to have participated in the anti-Soviet fighting in Afghanistan. He once praised Osama bin Laden and tried to impose a caliphate in Somalia.

August 9, 2022: The *Washington Examiner* and *Military Times* reported that U.S. Africa Command announced its three airstrikes killed four al-Shabaab terrorists in response to an attack on Somali troops near Beledweyne.

August 14, 2022: *Bloomberg* and state-owned national television reported that a U.S. air strike killed 13 al-Shabaab terrorists in the Hiiran region of central Somalia.

August 19, 2022: *Reuters, AFP, Jerusalem Post, al-Jazeera,* the *Somali National News Agency,* and the *Washington Post* reported that after two car bombs exploded during the night, al-Shabaab gunmen took control of the upscale four-storey Hotel Hayat in Mogadishu. One car hit a barrier near the hotel and the other hit the hotel's gate, injuring first responders. The Somali Police Special Unit rescued several people, including

children. The *Los Angeles Times* reported that 20 people were killed and 40 injured, five critically, in hours-long clashes between security forces and the terrorists. *CNN* said 50 were injured. Al-Shabaab claimed it was holding several politicians hostage. *CNN* reported that two security officials, including Mogadishu intelligence chief Muhidin Mohamed, were wounded. Al-Shabaab spokesman Abdiaziz Abu-Musab said on *Andalus* radio that its forces were still in control of the hotel and had "inflicted heavy casualties". *BBC* reported on August 21 that 106 people were rescued by the end of the 30-hour siege at midnight. *UPI, News360, Voice of America,* and *BBC* reported that Somali Minister of Health Ali Haji Adan said that 21 people were killed and 117 injured, 15 critically; police said 30 died.

August 20, 2022: *AFP* reported that district commissioner Mucawiye Muddey said that mortar shells hit the seafront neighborhood of Hamar Jajab, injuring 20, including a newlywed bride and her groom and a family of three children, a mother, and their father. No one claimed credit.

September 2, 2022: *Al-Jazeera, AFP,* and *SONNA* reported that al-Shabaab killed 19 civilians and destroyed trucks laden with food aid en route from Baladweyne to Mahas in a nighttime attack in the Hiran area in the semi-autonomous state of Hirshabelle.

September 12, 2022: *News 360* and Somali news portal *Goobjoog News* reported that the military killed more than 100 suspected al-Shabaab members in the states of Galmudug, Hirshabelle, and Southwest and seized control of more than 20 locations from the terrorists.

September 16, 2022: *News 360* reported that the Somali National Army killed 35 suspected al-Shabaab terrorists at 2 a.m. near Aborey in the Hiran, variant Hiiraan, region, north of Mogadishu.

The government announced the arrest of ten al-Shabaab members in Waydow, Yaaqshid, and Heliwaa who were allegedly involved in assassinations and bombings in Mogadishu. Authorities seized weapons and other materials.

News 360 and *SONNA* reported on September 19, 2022 that by September 17, the Somali Army claimed it had killed 75 al-Shabaab members and arrested multiple terrorists in the region.

September 18, 2022: *Al-Jazeera, News 360,* and *Reuters* reported on September 21 that U.S. Africa Command (AFRICOM) said a September 18 air strike killed 27 al-Shabaab fighters who were attacking Somali military forces near Buulobarde in the Hiran region.

September 25, 2022: *News 360* and *Garowe Online* reported that an al-Shabaab suicide bomber killed 15 people and wounded 20 at an army training facility in Mogadishu.

September 26, 2022: *News 360* reported the Somali government confirmed it was using Turkish-made Bayraktar TB2 drones in recent operations against al-Shabaab in the center of the country.

September 30, 2022: *Al-Jazeera* reported that two al-Shabaab raids killed 16 people.

October 1, 2022: *Al-Jazeera* reported that the Information Minister announced that the government, in an operation with unnamed international partners, had killed Abdullahi Nadir, alias Abdulahi Yare, a co-founder and chief prosecutor of al-Shabaab. He was in line to replace the group's leader, Ahmed Diriye, who is ill. The *Washington Examiner* added that U.S. Africa Command, in coordination with the Somali government, conducted the airstrike near Jilib, 230 miles southwest of Mogadishu. *Military Times* reported that the U.S. had offered a $3 million bounty for Nadir's capture.

October 3, 2022: *Al-Jazeera, SONNA,* and *Reuters* reported that al-Shabaab claimed credit for setting off two car bombs in Beledweyne, variant Beledueine, capital of the Hiiraan region, killing five people and injuring more than a dozen others. *News 360* indicated that 12 had died and 20 were injured. *Radio Dalsan* added that the dead included regional health minister Zakaria Mohamed Ahmed and the deputy governor of Hiiraan, Abukar Madey. Al-Shabaab claimed the target was "a security square" in Beledueine.

October 7, 2022: *News 360* and *SNTV* reported that the Somali Army repelled an al-Shabaab attack on a military base near Balad in the Middle Shabelle region, killing 19 suspected terrorists.

October 9, 2022: *News 360* reported that the Ministry of Information, Culture and Tourism shut down 40 digital social networking pages that it considers to be propaganda tools of al-Shabaab.

October 15, 2022: *News 360* reported that the Somali Army killed more than 30 al-Shabaab terrorists in Xawaadley region. Some were killed while attempting to attack the army, others while escaping in stolen civilian vehicles.

News 360 and the *Goobjoog* portal reported that the Somali government announced that it would revoke the operating licenses of any company that transfers money or makes payments to al-Shabaab. The Somali Ministry of Industry and Trade added that it would confiscate the property of companies in which members of the organization are found to be involved.

October 17, 2022: The U.S. Department of the Treasury's Office of Foreign Assets Control pursuant to Executive Order (E.O.) 13224, as amended, imposed sanctions on more than a dozen senior members of al-Shabaab who liaise with local Somali companies and use funds to buy weapons and finance recruitment. One was accused of using digital currency to launder money for the group.

Simultaneously, the Department of State designated five al-Shabaab leaders for diplomatic penalties, naming Mohamed Mire, Yasir Jiis, Yusuf Ahmed Hajji Nurow, Mustaf 'Ato, and Mohamoud Abdi Aden.

Treasury announced that the sanctioned individuals had engaged in the following actions:

- **Abdullahi Jeeri**, as of late 2021, smuggled weapons for al-Shabaab. He served as al-Shabaab's head of weapons procurement and acquired weapons for al-Shabaab from both local markets and foreign suppliers, primarily in Yemen. Jeeri is one of the serving members on the terrorist group's Shura Council leadership body, and commanded a unit of al-Shabaab fighters. He oversaw the consolidation of weapons and vehicles from various groups for al-Shabaab.

- **Khalif Adale**, as of early 2022, has served as al-Shabaab's finance leader for collecting money from non-governmental organizations (NGOs) and has reported directly to al-Shabaab's emir Ahmed Diriye, who was designated as a Specially Designated Global Terrorist (SDGT) pursuant to E.O.13224 in 2015. He was part of al-Shabaab leader Mahad Karate's team within the al-Shabaab organizational structure and maintained communication with Karate. The U.S. Department of State designated Karate as an SDGT on April 10, 2015. As of 2018, Adale had served as an al-Shabaab finance officer who brokered business deals between al-Shabaab and legitimate businesses, handled higher-level payments imposed on businesses, acted as a clan liaison to settle disputes between clans, and recruited for al-Shabaab. In late 2017, al-Shabaab senior leaders, including Adale, arranged for approximately 600 fighters to be trained by al-Shabaab and paid for by members of a local clan. Al-Shabaab ultimately recruited up to 600 children between the ages of 10 to 15 from local villages for training to support future al-Shabaab operations.

- **Hassan Afgooye.** State's Rewards for Justice program offered a reward of up to $5 million for information on the key leader of al-Shabaab. He oversees a complex financial network, whose activities range from involvement in sham charities and fundraising to racketeering and kidnapping in support of al-Shabaab. Afgooye is considered critical to al-Shabaab's continuing operations. As of early 2021, he was a senior official in al-Shabaab's Finance Department under Mahad Karate. Afgooye previously served as al-Shabaab's Chief of Finance. He continued to serve in an influential leadership position in al-Shabaab's Finance Department and was involved with al-Shabaab's overseas financial transactions. Afgooye also managed al-Shabaab's financial relationships with local companies, personally conducting negotiations on behalf of al-Shabaab.

- **Abdikarim Hussein Gagaale** served as a deputy within al-Shabaab's Finance Department under Mahad Karate.

- **Abdi Samad** is an al-Shabaab militant who has been in close contact with the al-Shabaab Senior Leadership Council. In 2010, al-Shabaab provided funding for his university degree, including travel and tuition expenses. In 2018, Samad performed surveillance and conducted research on behalf of al-Shabaab.

- **Abdirahman Nurey** is an interlocutor between al-Shabaab and the local private sector. Nurey has securely stored, transferred, and laundered fiat and digital currency for al-Shabaab. Nurey has gathered financial transfers from al-Shabaab local finance officials to al-Shabaab finance leaders. Nurey has facilitated al-Shabaab's use of meeting space and has assisted in fundraising for al-Shabaab.

The Department of the Treasury also singled out the following members of an al-Shabaab weapons trafficking network, alleging that these individuals were involved in the following actions:

- **Mohamed Hussein Salad**, **Ahmed Hasan Ali Sulaiman Mataan**, and **Mohamed Ali Badaas** are part of an al-Shabaab smuggling and weapons trafficking network in Yemen. The network members have served as representatives for terrorists, criminals, and weapons dealers from Somalia, some of whom were middlemen.

As of early 2018, Salad received payment for a shipment of weapons for al-Shabaab that included 15 PK machine guns, about 80 AK-47s, and nearly a dozen boxes of grenades, ammunition, and military uniforms used by the Somali security forces. Al-Shabaab intended to use the uniforms to confuse people and facilitate entry into guarded installations. Mataan was the owner of the vessel used for the shipment.

Between 2017 and 2020, Mataan owned dhows (sailboats used for regional trade and capable of carrying heavy loads) that took supplies for al-Shabaab militants to Somalia. In 2017,

Mataan and al-Shabaab reached an agreement to transport weapons, improvised explosive device (IED) equipment, ammunition, and small arms to Somalia. Mataan's dhows were involved in transporting IED components to al-Shabaab that were used to make explosive devices used in the Soobe bomb attacks on October 14, 2017, that killed circa 400 and wounded hundreds. Mataan was a Somali businessman who primarily profited from trafficking weapons and facilitating criminal groups. Mataan operated a fleet of more than half a dozen boats and a single shipment paid approximately $15,000.

As of late 2021, al-Shabaab placed an order with Mataan for weapons and IED materials from Yemen. Mataan procured the weapons from a Yemeni weapons dealer and, in preparation for the shipment, a boat owned by Mataan arrived in Somalia to carry illegal seafood, including fish and lobster, to Yemen.

As of early 2022, a dhow owned by Mataan departed Yemen with a shipment of weapons intended for al-Shabaab members in central Somalia. Salad was involved with facilitating the weapons shipment to Somalia.

Mataan and Salad were business partners who jointly owned a boat used in a shipment for al-Shabaab. The shipment carried weapons, including AK-47s and shoulder-fired missiles, ammunition, and food and military uniforms typically worn by the Somali military.

Salad has also been in contact with at least two companies that engage in illegal, unreported, and unregulated (IUU) fishing. These companies were part of a forced labor fishing operation, and the contact with a prominent arms trafficker may provide a preliminary nexus between IUU fishing and arms trafficking networks.

Over the course of five years, Salad received more than $700,000 in remittances from Puntland-based arms importers. He is a key intermediary in facilitating the transport of arms consignments from Yemeni suppliers to Puntland purchasers.

As of late 2018, Salad owned a boat transporting a shipment of weapons, including AK-47s, hand grenades, pistols, ammunition, and materials for making IEDs, for the Islamic State of Iraq and the Levant branch in Soma-

lia (ISIS-Somalia). The supplies for this shipment were purchased through Badaas. In mid-2019, Mataan also sold a weapons shipment to ISIS-Somalia.

Badaas is an al-Qa'ida in the Arabian Peninsula (AQAP) member and is part of an al-Shabaab smuggling and weapons trafficking network in Yemen. Badaas has facilitated a shipment of ammunition from Yemen for al-Shabaab militants.

In 2018, Badaas purchased a weapons consignment for al-Shabaab that included more than 30 anti-vehicle land mines, a dozen rocket-propelled grenades (RPG)-9s, RPG-7s, nearly 50 AK-47s, several PK machine guns, sniper rifles, Makarov pistols, rifle silencers, and rifle scopes.

As of 2017, Badaas was one of the most important AQAP commanders in the Shabwah region of Yemen. Badaas was responsible for monitoring personnel movements, smuggling operations, and managing AQAP members. Since at least 2015, Badaas has been a road guide for AQAP and facilitated travel for AQAP leaders throughout Shabwah, Yemen.

October 20, 2022: *News 360* reported that al-Shabaab claimed responsibility for two attacks that killed 21 people in two towns in Hirshabelle State. A terrorist set off a car bomb at a checkpoint near local government buildings and a military base in Jalalaqsi where the African Union's Djibouti peacekeepers are deployed when he ignored orders to stop and soldiers fired on his vehicle. The bomb killed 15 people, including the town's mayor and district chief, Mohamed Omar Dabashe, and injured several others, including soldiers and civilians.

A motorcycle crashed into the main bridge in Bulobarde. A bomb it was carrying went off, killing six, including four civilians. One of the two men on the motorcycle jumped off the motorcycle before it crashed, while the other blew himself up with it. *VOA* reported that security forces shot dead the surviving terrorist.

October 23, 2022: *AP, al-Jazeera, Reuters, Somali National Television, Somali Times,* and *News 360* reported that al-Shabaab took credit when a suicide car bomb exploded at the gates of Kismayo's

Tawakal Hotel and three gunmen stormed in. Several small businesses were destroyed. Members of the Jubaland regional administration usually work inside the hotel. *News 360* and *Garowe Online* added that the security minister of the Somali state of Jubaland, Yusuf Hussein Osman, announced that nine civilians, including students, died and 47 others were injured.

CNN reported that U.S. Africa Command conducted an airstrike against an al-Shabaab contingent that was attacking Somali National Army forces near Buulobarde, killing two terrorists.

October 24, 2022: *News 360* and *Garowe Online* reported that the Executive of Hassan Shaykh Mohamud opened a hotline for Somali citizens to report extortion by al-Shabaab.

News 360 reported that Deputy Information Minister Abderraman al-Adallah announced that nearly 100 al-Shabaab members, including several of its leaders, were killed in joint operations with the National Intelligence and Security Agency (NISA) and international forces in Shabeellaha Dhexe in the south of the country since October 22. The dead leaders included Abdullahi Ali Araaye and Musab Abdalla Saney.

October 29, 2022: *Al-Jazeera, UPI, AP, Somalia National News Agency, Somali Times, News 360,* and *Reuters* reported that at 2 p.m., two car bombs exploded at the Ministry of Education headquarters on Sobe Road in Mogadishu's K5 intersection, causing scores of casualties, including civilians traveling on public transport. One vehicle crashed into the ministry compound, followed by gunfire. Another explosion was heard minutes later in front of a crowded restaurant, injuring an Aamin Ambulance Service driver and a first aid worker as their ambulance came to transport casualties from the first blast. Somali president Hamza Abdi-Barre blamed al-Shabaab. *News 360, Voice of America, DPA,* and *SONNA* reported that at least 12 people, including a journalist and a police officer, were killed. *NPR,* the *Washington Post, al-Jazeera,* and *Reuters* reported on October 30 that the death toll had reached 100, with 300 injured.

Among the dead was Fardawsa Mohamed, mother of six, who was killed by the second blast

when she ran to the scene to help. Her husband was Mohamed Moalim. Abdullahi Aden added that his friend, Ilyas Mohamed Warsame, was killed while travelling in his three-wheeled tuk tuk taxi to see relatives before returning to his UK home. The *Somali Guardian* and *SONNA* tweeted that journalist Mohamed Eise Koona, variant Mohamed Isse Kona, died.

On October 31, 2022, *AP* reported that the death toll had risen to 120 with 320 injured and more than 150 still hospitalized. Some people remained missing.

October 30, 2022: The *Washington Post,* the *SONNA* government news agency, and *News 360* reported that the Somali Army killed circa 100 al-Shabaab terrorists while soldiers captured territory in Masajid Ali Gadud in the Middle Shabelle region.

November 1, 2022: *Reuters* reported that the U.S. Department of the Treasury issued sanctions against the Islamic State in Somalia, designating members of the group and others it accused of being involved in a "terrorist weapons trafficking network" in Eastern Africa. Several of the designees have sold weapons to or were active al-Shabaab members. Among the designees were

- Abdirahman Mohamed Omar, whom the Treasury accused of being an ISIS-Somalia member and, as of 2020, considered the most active illicit arms importer in Puntland state in Somalia.

- Isse Mohamoud Yusuf, who Treasury said is an ISIS-Somalia weapons and logistics facilitator in Bari in Puntland and an arms smuggler

- Abdirahman Fahiye Isse Mohamud, an ISIS-Somalia emir

- Mohamed Ahmed Qahiye, who Treasury said heads Amniyat, ISIS-Somalia's intelligence wing.

November 3, 2022: *News 360* reported that three people, including two children, were killed in a bomb attack on Sadiq Aden Ali Dudishe, deputy mayor of Mogadishu. He was not in his vehicle at the time of the attack.

U.S. Africa Command announced that an airstrike in support of the Somali government's operations killed some al-Shabaab members near Cadale in the Middle Shabelle region.

November 4, 2022: *News 360* reported that Somali authorities announced the deaths of more than 100 suspected al-Shabaab members in clashes in Garas Magan and El Hariri in the Hiran region.

November 7, 2022: *Al-Jazeera* reported that al-Shabaab was suspected when gunmen set off two suicide car bombs at 5 a.m., then fired on a Somali military base in Qayib in Galgaduud region.

November 9, 2022: *Reuters* reported that the army and clan militias killed 20 al-Shabaab terrorists in central Somalia. Six soldiers were wounded.

November 21, 2022: *AP* and *al-Jazeera* reported that a gunman entered the Sarira Forward Operating Base in the Lower Jubba region of southern Somalia, shot to death three Kenyan peacekeepers, and injured five soldiers before he was shot to death. Al-Shabaab claimed credit. 22112103

November 22, 2022: *Reuters* reported that the government announced that a military operation had killed 49 al-Shabaab fighters in Bulo-Madino village in Lower Shabelle region.

November 26, 2022: *News 360, Hiran on Line,* and *Goobjoog* reported that the Somali Army announced that the 5th Battalion of the National Army and special commandos of Danab had regained control of El Dhere Burale, between the regions of Hiraan and Middle Shabelle, killing 100 al-Shabaab terrorists, including ten senior AS officials, among them a prominent leader in Middle Shabelle, Hassan Nur.

November 26, 2022: *News 360, AFP,* and *Hiran on Line* reported that Somali authorities intercepted 20 suspected Pakistani and Iranian sailors and fishermen who claimed they had been held hostage for years by al-Shabaab in the Galmudug region on the central coast. The 14 Iranians and six Pakistanis were traveling in two boats between Hobyo and Haradhere. Police said "Some of these people were kidnapped by al-Shabaab

in 2014, while others were abducted on the Harardhere coast, near Qosol-tire, in southern Somalia in mid-2019… Four of them have physical injuries." 14999901, 19999901

November 27, 2022: *Al-Jazeera, News 360, BBC, AP, CBS News, AFP, Garowe Online, UPI,* and *Reuters* reported that at 8 p.m., al-Shabaab attacked the Villa Rose Hotel in Bondhere district with guns and explosives, killing four and injuring dozens, including government officials. Government officials frequent the facility, which is near the Villa Somalia presidential palace in Mogadishu. State Minister for the Environment Adam Aw Hirsi, tweeted that he was safe after a "terrorist explosion targeted at my residence" at the hotel. Some government officials escaped through a window. Fisheries Minister Abdilahi Bidhan Warsame and Senator Dunia Mohamed escaped. *News 360* and *DPA* put the death list at ten, including two people with dual Somali and British nationality. Civilians and officials were evacuated. *News 360* and *Radio Shabelle* reported the Somali Parliament postponed a joint session scheduled to discuss the 2023 Budget. After 18 hours, the terrorists were holed up in a top-floor room of the hotel, battling Gaashaan and Haramcad special forces units who stormed the hotel, killed all five terrorists, and rescued the remaining 60 hostages. Another terrorist blew himself up at the start of the siege. The terrorists had killed eight civilians and one member of the security forces.

The United Nations announced earlier in November that 613 civilians had been killed and 948 injured in violence in 2022 in Somalia, mostly caused by improvised explosive devices (IEDs) attributed to al-Shabaab, the most since 2017 and more than 30 percent higher than 2021.

Mogadishu resident Mohamed Suleyman told *AP* that two of his relatives, both civilians, died. Mogadishu resident Ali Moalim said he saw "two bodies of the security forces carried by their fellow soldiers".

December 3, 2022: *News 360* and *Garowe On Line* reported that al-Shabaab recaptured several strategic towns, including Deynunay and Gofgadud Buurey, in central Somalia after days of heavy fighting. Meanwhile, *Goobjoog* reported that al-Shabaab abandoned Adan Jabal in the northern region of Middle Shabelle.

Garowe on Line noted that since January 2022, al-Shabaab killed 613 people and wounded more than 900, mostly civilians.

December 4, 2022: *News 360* and *Hiiraan On Line* reported Somali government forces and local militias recaptured eastern Hiiraan region from al-Shabaab, plus several localities in the Middle Shabelle region in the south. The freed towns included Gulane, Darusalam, Harga-Dhere, and Mabah, the last town recovered in Hiiraan. The army said it killed 16 al-Shabaab jihadis, including four in Middle Shabelle and ten in Hiiraan.

December 5, 2022: *News 360* and *Garowe Online* reported that the Islamic State branch in Somalia pledged allegiance to the new ISIS leader, Abu al-Hussein al-Husseini al-Quraishi. The local affiliate was led by Abdulkadir Mumin.

SOUTH AFRICA

January 2, 2022: *Al-Jazeera, AFP, SABC,* and *AP* reported on January 11 that homeless South African man Zandile Christmas Mafe, 49, was charged in Cape Town Magistrates' Court with "terrorism" after being arrested on January 5 on suspicion of starting a fire that gutted South Africa's 138-year-old parliament in Cape Town on January 2. He first was charged with breaking into parliament, arson, and intention to steal property, including laptops, crockery, and documents. *Newsweek* added that the charges included housebreaking with intent to steal, theft, arson, and possession of an explosive device. *AP* noted that prosecutors said that Mafe had intended to "deliver, place, discharge or detonate" an explosive device at the Parliament complex. He was represented by defense attorney Dali Mpofu, who said Mafe was "taken for mental observation on January 3" and diagnosed with "paranoid schizophrenia". No casualties were reported in the fire, which took four days for 300 firefighters to extinguish. The main chamber of the National Assembly building was destroyed, and other buildings were heavily damaged.

March 1, 2022: The U.S. Department of the Treasury imposed financial sanctions against four men in South Africa it accused of being recruiters and fundraisers for ISIS. Three provided money for the extremist group in Iraq and Syria; the fourth helped move money and buy weapons for an IS branch in Mozambique. Treasury said the four raised money via kidnap for ransom, extortion, and training members to conduct robberies. Two of them are South Africans, one an Ethiopian, and one a Tanzanian.

Treasury claimed that Farhad Hoomer formed and led an IS cell in Durban, South Africa. He and associates were arrested in 2018 and charged with plotting to plant bombs at various sites in the city and for an attack at a mosque where worshippers had their throats cut. The case was eventually dropped in 2020 because of delays by the prosecution in submitting evidence.

Treasury reported that Abdella Hussein Abadigga had strong links to an IS leader in Somalia.

June 6, 2022: A court convicted pastor Harry Johannes Knoesen, 61, a leader of the National Christian Resistance Movement, of high treason, incitement to carry out violent attacks, and recruiting people to commit attacks by plotting to overthrow the government and to kill thousands of Black people by using a biological weapon, including poisoning of water reservoirs supplying Black communities. The Middelburg High Court in Mpumalanga Province found him guilty of unlawful possession of firearms. He was arrested in November 2019. The sentencing proceeding was to begin on June 10, 2022.

November 26, 2022: *Face2FaceAfrica* and *BBC* reported that gunmen stormed the Johannesburg Central SDA church and robbed worshippers of their valuables during a sermon.

SOUTH SUDAN

July 22, 2022: *News 360* reported that the South Sudan People's Movement Army (SSPM/A) attacked an administrative building in Mayom, killing 12 people, including the county commissioner.

July 26, 2022: *News 360* reported that Mayom authorities spokesman Wour Weah announced that SSPM/A rebels led by Stephen Buay Rolnyang ambushed a three-vehicle South Sudanese Army convoy between Thiebder and Kotong towns in Unity state, killing 15 South Sudanese soldiers. *Radio Tamazuj* reported that both military and civilians were traveling in the vehicles. SSPM/A spokesman Luk Gattiek said seven soldiers died while "carrying arms and ammunition to launch a military operation".

Sudan

March 14, 2022: *Al-Jazeera* reported on March 18 that Janjaweed militia riding ten pickup trucks plus horses and motorbikes and carrying artillery and anti-aircraft weapons killed 17 people, including three workers with Darfur-based Human Rights Monitors, in the gold-rich Jabal Moon mountain area.

June 7, 2022: *AFP* reported that fighting over a land dispute near Kolbus in West Darfur killed 16, while an argument between rival Arab groups of Hawazma and Kenana near Abu Jebeiha in South Kordofan State expanded into clashes that killed 11 an wounded 35.

July 13-16, 2022: *NPR* and *Reuters* reported that several days of tribal clashes killed 31 people in Damazin and Roseires in southeastern Blue Nile State, close to the border with Ethiopia. Another 39 were wounded and 16 shops were destroyed.

November 3, 2022: *AP* reported that the U.N. Office for the Coordination of Humanitarian Affairs announced that four months of tribal clashes killed 359 people, injured 469, and displaced 97,000 people in Sudan's south Blue Nile state.

November 19-25, 2022: *News 360* reported that the United Nations Office for the Coordination of Humanitarian Affairs (OCHA) announced that fighting between factions of the Sudan Liberation Army-Abdel Wahid (SLA-AW) in western Central Darfur State broke out on November 19 in Shamal Yamal Marra and spread to nearby areas, killing 13 people, injuring four, and displacing 5,600. Another 12 were missing and six were kidnapped.

Togo

May 11, 2022: *Reuters* and *al-Jazeera* reported that suspected jihadis killed eight soldiers and wounded 13 in a pre-dawn attack on an army post in the Kpendjal prefecture in the north near the border with Burkina Faso, possibly the first deadly Islamist attack in the country. No one claimed credit. The government blamed "terrorists". Security analysts suspected an al-Qaeda affiliate based in Mali and operating in Burkina Faso.

July 11, 2022: *Al-Jazeera* and *Reuters* reported that a nighttime explosion killed seven children, aged between 14 and 18, and injured two others in Margba village in Tone Prefecture, in Savanna region. Authorities suspected that jihadis had crossed the border from Burkina Faso. The teens were returning home from Eid al-Adha celebrations.

July 14, 2022: *Reuters* reported that gunmen killed 12 civilians in overnight raids on villages in northern Togo's Kpendjal district. A local rights activist said jihadis killed ten civilians in Sougtangou and ten in Blamonga.

ASIA

AZERBAIJAN

November 1, 2022: *Intellinews* reported that the State Security Service announced that it had rounded up a network of 19 armed Shi'a jihadis backed by Iran. The Service said the group was founded and funded by Huseyniyyun (the Azerbaijani version of Hizballah), headed by Tohid Ibrahimli, who had been wanted by Azerbaijan since 2018 and is currently in exile in Iran. The Service charged that "Over the past period, citizens of the Republic of Azerbaijan, selected by an illegal armed formation, mainly from among persons previously convicted of various crimes, as well as persons who consider themselves members of an organization they call the 'Muslim Unity Movement', were transported through the territory of third countries to the city of Tehran in Iran where their mobile phones and passports were confiscated, they were instructed on the secrecy of communications and secrecy requirements, they were given religious nicknames and they were taken to the city of Damascus in Syria by military cargo planes with forged documents. On the territory of Syria, they were involved in military exercises, where they learned the rules for the use of various firearms and combat tactics, they took part in the exercises." Among the detainees was Mammadov Fagan.

CHINA

July 4, 2022: A man was arrested after going on a stabbing spree in Shanghai's downtown Jingan district.

July 9, 2022: *Reuters* reported that a man with a knife stabbed four people at Shanghai's 100-year-old Ruijin Hospital in the morning. He held a crowd hostage on the seventh floor of the outpatient department. When the man threatened to hurt the hostages, the police opened fire.

August 3, 2022: *Beijing Daily, Metro, CBS News,* and *Weibo* reported that Liu Xiaohui, 48, a "lone wolf gangster" wearing a cap and mask, conducted a knife attack at a private kindergarten in Anfu County in Jiangxi Province at 10 a.m., killing three people and injuring six. He escaped but was later killed when hit by a car while on the run from police.

REPUBLIC OF CHINA

August 2, 2022: *Newsweek* reported that the Aviation Police Bureau were investigating a bomb threat made against Taoyuan international airport after an unsigned e-mail said it sought to "stop the U.S. House speaker's visit". U.S. Speaker of the House Nancy Pelosi (D-Calif.) was to visit the island, despite loud Chinese protests, six hours later. No suspicious items were discovered. The *Central News Agency* reported that the email to Taoyuan International Airport Corporation claimed that three explosive devices would be placed on the grounds of the airport. 22080201

INDIA

January 14, 2022: *AFP* and the *NDTV* news channel reported that a bomb was found hidden in an abandoned bag at the busy Ghazipur wholesale flower market in New Delhi. Police carried out a controlled explosion.

January 29, 2022: *Al-Jazeera* reported that Indian forces killed five suspected rebels, including senior Jaish-e-Muhammad (JeM) commander Zahid Wani and a Pakistani national, Kafeel, in two separate operations in Pulwama and Budgam districts in Indian-administered Kashmir. The operations began the evening of January 29 and lasted into the morning of January 30. The family of Inayat Ahmad Mir, one of the four people killed in Pulwama, said he was just an innocent teenager who "had nothing to do with militancy". Police said he was a "hybrid militant" who was killed along with the other rebels hiding inside his house in Pulwama's Naira village. Police chief Vijay Kumar said Mir had "joined the terror fold recently" and that police will book Mir's father under anti-terror laws for "providing shelter" to the rebels. Police also detained Mir's elder brother Naveed. Kumar said Indian forces launched their operation after the suspected rebels killed a police officer on January 29 outside his home in the south of Srinagar.

March 6, 2022: A terrorist threw a grenade at a bus market in Srinagar in Kashmir, killing one person and injuring more than 20. Local media suggested that the target was security personnel in the area.

April 12, 2022: *Free Press Journal* reported that the Anantnag Police recovered a short barrel AK-56, two AK magazines, two pistols, three pistol magazines, six hand grenades, 44 rounds of AK-47 ammunition, 58 rounds of 9 mm ammunition, and one sling from a vehicle near Mehmoodabad bridge Dooru.

April 14, 2022: The *Free Press Journal* reported that the Ministry of Home Affairs (MHA) declared al-Umar-Mujahideen founder Mushtaq Ahmed Zargar, 52, alias Latram, to be a terrorist under the Unlawful Activities (Prevention) Act, 1967. He was one of the terrorists freed in the 1999 Indian Airlines Flight IC-814 hijacking. MHA called Zargar a "threat to peace, not only to India but across the world, with his contacts and proximity to radical terrorist groups like the al-Qaeda and Jaish-Mohammed". MHA charged that Zargar had been affiliated with the Jammu-Kashmir Liberation Front terrorist group and had gone to Pakistan for obtaining illegal arms and ammunition training. Zargar resides in Gani Mohalla in Jammu and Kashmir's Srinagar. MHA said Zargar was "involved in various terror crimes including murder, attempt to murder, kidnapping, planning and execution of terrorist attacks and terror funding" and constituted "a threat to peace".

April 16, 2022: The *Free Press Journal* reported that security forces in Rajouri recovered and destroyed a bomb found on Rajouri Gurdan road. Jammu and Kashmir police had received a tipoff regarding suspicious movements in Gurdan Chawa village on Rajouri Gurdan road. Rajouri Police added "Jammu and Kashmir police teams from Army, Special Operation Group of Police, and teams of the Army launched a joint Cordon and Search Operation in the area in the early morning hours."

Jammu and Kashmir Police and the army arrested a terrorist associate in Handwara and recovered a Chinese pistol, two pistol magazines, 13 live rounds of 9 mm ammunition, and a mobile phone.

April 18, 2022: *Free Press Journal* reported that police and the army seized ten pistols, 17 pistol magazines, 54 pistol rounds, and five hand grenades during a search operation in Tad village in Karnah Tehsil near the Line of Control (LoC) in Kupwara district of Jammu and Kashmir.

April 22, 2022: *Al-Jazeera* reported that six alleged rebels and an Indian paramilitary officer died in two clashes in Indian-controlled Kashmir, days before Prime Minister Narendra Modi's scheduled visit.

In the morning, a gun battle began in the suburbs of Jammu after police and soldiers noticed gunmen in the garrison town of Sunjwan. Two gunmen and a paramilitary officer were killed, and two soldiers and two police officers were wounded. Dilbag Singh, director-general of police, said the "suicide squad from Pakistan… were planning a major attack" as a likely part of a "conspiracy to sabotage" Modi's visit.

A gun battle with rebels in Malwah, a village northwest of Srinagar, went into its second day, leaving four rebels dead. Police and soldiers on April 21 raided a cluster of civilian homes in Malwah. Four soldiers and a policeman were wounded. Police said the dead rebels included Yousuf Kantroo, the longest surviving rebel commander in Kashmir.

May 25, 2022: *BBC* reported on June 1, 2022 that Amreena Bhat, 30, a television actor and singer who had 19,000 *Youtube* subscribers and 25,000 followers on *Instagram*, was shot to death in Indian-administered Kashmir's Budgam district during the evening. Her brother said he was praying in a mosque when he heard the shots. Nephew Farhan, 11, who was with her, said two men approached her on the pretext of booking her for a program. They shot her, then followed her inside and shot her again. A bullet hit Farhan's arm. Local militants were suspected. On May 27, Kashmir police said had killed the terrorists, whom they said had recently joined Lashkar-e-Taiba.

Days earlier, a government employee from the minority Hindu community was shot dead inside his office by militants in Budgam district.

Earlier in the week, a female government school teacher was killed in what a former chief minister called a "despicable targeted attack".

May 25, 2022: The *Washington Post* reported that an Indian court sentenced Kashmiri separatist leader Mohammed Yasin Malik, 56, head of the banned Jammu and Kashmir Liberation Front, to life in prison after declaring him guilty of terrorism and sedition. Protesters and police clashed, leading to a partial shutdown of businesses in the Indian-controlled portion of Kashmir. He was arrested in 2019 and convicted in mid-May 2022 for committing terrorist acts, illegally raising funds, belonging to a terrorist organization, and criminal conspiracy and sedition. He lived in Srinagar. The judge rejected the prosecution's request for a death sentence. Malik had earlier been arrested in 1990 and released in 1994. He moved his organization toward non-violent resistance. He married Pakistani artist Mushaal Hussein, with whom he has a daughter, 10.

May 31, 2022: *USNWR* and *Reuters* reported that gunmen shot to death Hindu school teacher Rajni Bala, 36, outside a government school in Kulgam, south of Srinagar, Kathmir. More than 100 Hindu families fled Kashmir.

June 2, 2022: *Reuters* reported that gunmen shot to death Hindu bank manager Vijay Kumar, originally from western Rajasthan State, inside a branch of the Ellaquai Dehati Bank in southern Kashmir's Kulgam, where a schoolteacher was shot dead on May 31. The little-known Kashmir Freedom Fighters claimed credit on social media, telling non-locals not to settle in the Kashmir valley. "Anyone involved in the demographic change of Kashmir will meet the same fate."

Gunmen shot at two non-Kashmiri laborers working in a brick kiln in Chadoora area of Budgam district in Kashmir, killing one.

June 28, 2022: *AP*, the *Los Angeles Times,* and *Press Trust of India* reported that two cleaver-wielding Muslim men posted a video of themselves slitting the throat of Hindu tailor Kanhaiya Lal Teli, 48, in his shop in Udaipur in Rajasthan State. Lal

had reportedly shared a posting that supported spokespeople from Prime Minister Narendra Modi's Hindu nationalist Bharatiya Janata Party who made remarks in May that were seen as insulting Islam's Prophet Muhammad and his wife, Aisha. A few hours later, police arrested Udaipur residents Gos Mohammad and Riyaz Akhtari. Their second video accused Lal of blasphemy and threatened to kill Modi in the same way.

India's *Latest News and Updates* reported on July 1 that Prafulla Kumar, a senior police officer based in Udaipur, announced "We have now arrested two masterminds and earlier we arrested two who committed the heinous crime."

August 10, 2022: *Al-Jazeera* reported that government counterinsurgency forces killed three rebels in Budgam district.

August 11, 2022: *Al-Jazeera* reported that two Kashmir rebels armed with guns and grenades stormed an India army camp in the remote Darhal area of southern Rajouri district in Indian-administered Kashmir, killing three soldiers and injuring two more before they died in the morning attack that lasted three hours.

August 16, 2022: *Times Now* reported that a bomb exploded under the car of Sub Inspector Dilbagh Singh in Amritsar, Punjab. CCTV caught two individuals arriving on a motorcycle and planting the bomb.

A terrorist shot to death a Kashmiri pandit in the Chotipora area of Shopian in South Kashmir. Several terrorists fired in an apple orchard, killing one and injuring one; both were minorities. The next day, *Times Now* reported that police arrested relatives of "terrorist Adil Wani".

August 18, 2022: *Times Now* reported that authorities seized a boat smuggling AK-47s into Raigad district.

September 28, 2022: *AFP* reported that India banned the Islamist Popular Front of India (PFI) and its affiliates for five years for alleged terrorism links to, inter alia, ISIS and Jamaat-ul-Mujahideen Bangladesh (JMB). The government arrested more than 300 PFI members in raids across the country since September 23. The government said PFI was responsible for at least 10 murders in the south since 2016 and accused the group of "pursuing a secret agenda" to radicalize society and undermine democracy. Thirteen PFI members were jailed in 2015 for hacking off the hand of a university lecturer accused of insulting the Prophet Mohammed. The government claimed that some PFI activists had joined ISIS and participated in terrorist activities in Syria, Iraq, and Afghanistan. *NDTV* reported that investigators found bomb-making manuals and ISIS videos.

Several JMB bombings in Bangladesh in 2005 killed 28 people.

October 3, 2022: The *Hindustan Times* and *Reuters* reported that Mahan Air tweeted that its Airbus A340 flight W581 landed safely and on time in Guangzhou, China after a hoax bomb scare. Punjab and Jodhpur air bases scrambled Indian Air Force Su-30MKI fighter jets to escort the plane. Lahore's Air Traffic Control (ATC) at 9 a.m. had informed the pilot about a possible bomb threat.

October 15, 2022: *News 360* and the *Hindustan Times* reported that terrorists killed Puran Krishan Bhat, a member of the Kashmiri Pandit minority who did not convert to Islam during the Middle Ages, on his way to an orchard in Choudhary Gund in Shopian district in Indian-controlled Kashmir.

October 18, 2022: *Reuters* reported that terrorists threw a grenade into the rented home of two migrant laborers from Uttar Pradesh State, killing them, in Indian Kashmir's Shopian district.

INDONESIA

February 3, 2022: *UPI* reported that the U.S. Department of the Treasury announced economic and financial sanctions on World Human Care, charging that the NGO was founded by the U.S.-designated Indonesia-based Majelis Mujahidin Indonesia terrorist group to support its extremist activities in Syria under the guise of humanitarian work. Treasury froze all of its property and interests in property and barred U.S. citizens from doing business with the entity. Treasury said WHC hosts events near Ja-

karta to raise funds to be transferred to al-Qaeda-linked terrorists. Treasury added that in early 2016, WHC sent money to Syria for weapons and fighters, including to an unnamed Southeast Asian foreign terrorist. The U.S. Department of State on June 12, 2017, designated MMI as a terrorist group.

July 16, 2022: *Reuters* and *Antara* reported that in the morning, separatist gunmen were suspected in the killing of nine people and wounding of another in the remote highland area of Nduga in Papua region.

December 7, 2022: *AFP*, the *New York Post*, *Reuters*, *Metro TV*, and *Kompas TV* reported that a suspected jihadi suicide bomber crashed his motorcycle into the entrance of the Astana Anyar police station in Bandung in West Java Province during morning muster, killing a police officer and wounding 10 other people, including at least six police officers and a civilian. *AFP* reported that the bomber had served four years in a maximum security prison for his involvement in a 2017 bombing.

JAPAN

May 28, 2022: The *Washington Post*, *AFP*, *AP*, and *al-Jazeera* reported that Fusako Shigenobu, 76, co-founder of the Japanese Red Army terrorist group, left jail in Akishima, Tokyo after completing a 20-year sentence. She apologized for her actions, saying, "I apologise for the inconvenience my arrest has caused to so many people… It's half a century ago … but we caused damage to innocent people who were strangers to us by prioritising our battle, such as by hostage-taking… Although those were different times, I would like to take this opportunity to apologize deeply… I feel strongly that I have finally come out alive." She was convicted of masterminding a siege at the French embassy in The Hague, the Netherlands, in 1974. She was at-large for 30 years, but was arrested in Osaka in 2000. Several JRA members remain fugitives in the Middle East. She founded the JRA in 1971 while in Lebanon. She was believed behind a 1972 machinegun and grenade attack on Tel Aviv's Lod Airport, which killed 26 people and wounded 80 others.

She was born into poverty in Tokyo after WWII. He father was a WWII major who became a grocer. She had earlier worked for a soy-sauce firm. She passed by a sit-in at age 20, and soon became caught up in the left-wing movement. She left Japan at age 25. Her daughter, May, was born in 1973 to a father from the Popular Front for the Liberation of Palestine (PFLP). She announced the disbanding of the JRA in April 2001 while in prison. In 2008 she was diagnosed with colon and intestinal cancer and underwent several operations. She wrote to the *Japan Times* in 2017 that "Our hopes were not fulfilled and it came to an ugly end."

July 8, 2022: *CNN* reported that at 11:30 a.m., an unemployed man fired two shots from a homemade double-barreled gun from ten feet away, killing former Prime Minister Shinzo Abe, 67, as Abe was delivering a campaign speech for a fellow politician from the ruling Liberal Democratic Party (LDP) in the street near Yamato-Saidaiji train station in Nara in western Japan. Abe was hit in the right side of his neck and in his chest. Police immediately wrestled to the ground and arrested Tetsuya Yamagami, 41, who told police he was "dissatisfied" with Abe. *NHK* added that he clarified that the attack was "not a grudge against the former Prime Minister's political beliefs". The grudge was over his mother's bankruptcy, after having sent large donations to the Japan branch of South Korea's Unification Church. He told Nara-nishi police that he hated a certain group, which he believed Abe had links to (he was not a member of the Unification Church, also known as the Family Federation for World Peace and Unification, founded by the late Sun Myung Moon). The attacker was dressed in a grey t-shirt and cargo pants. *Asahi Shimbun* said police held him on suspicion of attempted murder and seized the weapon.

One of the bullets reached Abe's heart and a team of 20 doctors could not stop the bleeding. Abe died at 5:03 p.m.

Business Insider and *NHK* reported that Yamagami had worked for Japan's Maritime Self-Defense Force for three years until 2005. He had been a contract forklift driver at a Kyoto warehouse. The Defense Ministry said he had live-firearms training. *Kyodo* reported that police found explosives and several handmade pistol-like items at his condominium apartment in Nara. The *New York Times* reported on July 24, 2022 that Yamagami was born into wealth, but his dad killed himself when Yamagami was four years old.

The gun appeared to be two metal barrels taped to a wooden board.

BBC reported that Abe's speech was confirmed only late the previous night.

Abe had stepped down from the Prime Ministership in 2020 due to ulcerative colitis. He had served in 2006 to 2007 and from 2012 to 2020, becoming the country's longest-serving PM and also its youngest. He was the first world leader to meet with then-president-elect Donald Trump in New York, two weeks after his election, and the first Japanese PM to visit Pearl Harbor. Abe, born on September 21, 1954, was a member of a prominent political family which included his grandfather and great uncle serving as prime minister, and his father as an LDP secretary general. His younger brother Nobuo Kishi was Defense Minister. He was known for, inter alia, Abenomics, a mixture of fiscal stimulus, monetary easing, and structural reforms.

In 2018, Japan reported nine deaths from firearms; the U.S. had 39,740.

CNN reported on July 11 that Japan's ruling coalition (led by Abe's Liberal Democratic Party) won the upper house election.

AP, Kyodo, and *UPI* reported on August 25, 2022 that Itaru Nakamura, general commissioner of the National Police Agency, announced his resignation, taking responsibility for failing to prevent Abe's assassination.

The *Daily Beast* reported on September 16, 2022 that the September cover of the weekly Japanese magazine *SPA!* was devoted to the cult of hero worship for Tetsuya Yamagami, 42, Abe's killer. Online fans are Yamagami Girls. An online petition calling for a reduced sentence received more than 8,000 signatures.

AFP, CNN, NHK, and *TV Asahi* reported on September 21, 2022 that a man believed to be in his 70s doused himself in oil and set himself on fire near the Japanese Prime Minister's office in opposition to holding a state funeral for Abe scheduled for September 27. Police found the burned man at 7 a.m. A police officer who tried to extinguish the fire was injured. The ceremony at Tokyo's Budokan venue was projected to cost $12 million.

On December 24, 2022, *UPI, NHK,* and *Kyodo News* reported that prosecutors decided to indict Tetsuya Yamagami, 42, claiming that had been determined mentally fit to stand trial after a psychiatric evaluation. His detention for mental evaluation was due to expire on January 10, 2023. Prosecutors were expected to indict him by January 13, when his detention was to end.

KAZAKHSTAN

December 2, 2022: *Newsweek* reported that the Ukrainian Foreign Ministry announced that "the embassy in Kazakhstan received a message of a mine {bomb} that was later unconfirmed." 22120212

MYANMAR

May 31, 2022: At 3:20 p.m., a bomb exploded in central Yangon, killing a man, 30, who sustained wounds in his chest and abomen, and wounding nine others. The state-run *Global New Light of Myanmar* newspaper blamed the People's Defense Forces, the opposition movement's armed wing, who used a "handmade bomb planted by PDF terrorists at a bus stop" one block from the Sule Pagoda.

State media also blamed the PDF for another fatal bombing at an education office in Naung Cho township in Shan State in eastern Myanmar. The *Global New Light of Myanmar* said a headmistress died and six educational personnel and a civil servant were injured.

June 8, 2022: *Reuters* reported that the United Nations condemned the fatal shooting of Myo Min Htut, a World Health Organization driver for five years, while riding his motorcycle in Mawlamyine in Mon State, close to Thailand. The junta people's defence force in Mawlamyine, which has pledged its support for the shadow National Unity Government (NUG), claimed responsibility and accused the victim of being a junta informant and of harassing people who

joined strikes and protests against the 2021 coup. "We let him retire from this human world." The militia called him an "informer" and a "dog". The junta earlier outlawed the NUG as a "terrorist" organization.

August 23, 2022: *UPI* and *Myanmar Now* reported that Tiger Force Mandalay, a resistance group, apologized for the shooting death of married couple Ko Sithu Ko Ko and his wife Ma Hnin Wai Hlaing, blaming a case of mistaken identity. The couple had dropped their daughter off at school. The terrorist scout team erred in identifing its target, Police Major Soe Ko Ko of the Mandalay Criminal Investigation Department, and instead fired on the couple.

On August 21, another resistance group had killed a family in Saw Township in the Magwe Region.

September 25, 2022: *The Diplomat* and *AP* reported that the Inya Urban Force claimed credit for assassinating retired Army general and former ambassador Ohn Thwin, 72, in his home in Yangon's Hlaing Township at 3 p.m. His son-in-law, retired captain Ye Tay Za, also died. Thwin had been ambassador to the Maldives, Sri Lanka, Bangladesh, and South Africa.

October 19, 2022: *UPI, Myanmar Now, Irawaddy News, Deutsche Welle,* and *AFP* reported that parcel-packaged bombs exploded at 9:40 a.m. in the postal room of Yangon's Insein Prison, which holds about 10,000 inmates, including many political prisoners, killing three staffers and five visitors, including a girl, 10, and wounding 18. Another bomb found in a plastic bag did not detonate. One of the civilian victims was the mother of student activist "James" Lin Htet Naing, who was delivering a care package to her son. No group claimed credit for the attack on people leaving parcels for inmates. The junta blamed "terrorists". Detainees held in the prison include the former UK ambassador to Myanmar, Vicky Bowman, and Japanese journalist Toru Kubota.

December 5, 2022: *News 360* and *The Irrawaddy* reported that 100 soldiers of the 108th Infantry Battalion launched an offensive to recapture localities on the road linking Demoso to Nanmekhon seized in late November by Karenni

Nationalities Defense Force (KNDF) rebels. The insurgents killed 20 soldiers and captured four others in Demoso in Kayah State in central-eastern Myanmar. The rebels also seized weapons and ammunition.

NEPAL

December 25, 2022: *USNWR* and *Reuters* reported that former Maoist guerrilla Pushpa Kamal Dahal, 68, who uses his guerrilla name Prachanda ("terrible" or "fierce"), was scheduled to take over the prime ministership for the first half of the five-year term with the support of the opposition Communist Unified Marxist-Leninist (UML) party and some other smaller groups. He will step down in 2025.

PAKISTAN

January 17, 2022: Mohammad Khurasani, spokesman for the outlawed Tehrik-e-Taliban Pakistan (TTP, Pakistani Taliban), tweeted to claim credit for an overnight gun attack on police in Islamabad that killed an officer and two terrorists. He added that the TTP had targeted police in two separate attacks on police in Khyber Pakhtunkhwa Province. *AFP* said two other police officers were injured. The gunmen were riding a motorcycle when they fired on a police checkpoint.

January 20, 2022: *Reuters, al-Jazeera, dawn.com, U.S. News and World Report,* and the *Jerusalem Post* reported that a timebomb attached to a motorcycle exploded outside a shop in a crowded market in Balochistan Province, killing three people, including a boy, 9, and wounding more than 20. A newly-formed Balochistan-based separatist group claimed credit, saying a bank was its target.

January 25, 2022: *Reuters* and *al-Jazeera* reported that Baloch Liberation Front (BLF) separatists claimed credit for a nighttime attack on a Pakistani army post in Kech district in Baluchistan Province, north of Gwadar port, in which China is investing. The army said 10 soldiers and an attacker were killed and three gunmen were

arrested. BLF claimed that 17 soldiers and one of its members were killed.

February 2, 2022: *Al-Jazeera, AFP,* and the *Jerusalem Post* reported that Interior Minister Sheikh Rasheed Ahmad said that the army fought off the Baluch Liberation Army (BLA) in two attacks on bases in Baluchistan Province within hours of each other. The clashes killed four soldiers, a civilian, and 15 terrorists. The gunmen hit paramilitary posts in Panjgur and Noshki, 205 miles away. Ahmad said four or five terrorists were still being hunted in Panjgur and that six attackers were killed. Another four soldiers and nine attackers died in Noshki. Local police official Khalid Badini said that a civilian died in the crossfire. BLA spokesman Jeayand Baluch said on *Telegram* that the raids were carried out by attackers who were prepared to "self-sacrifice" and that it had killed 100 Pakistani troops. *AFP* said seven Pakistani soldiers died. *AFP* reported that the gun battle lasted into February 4 in an attempt to derail Prime Minister Imran Khan's visit to China. By then, 13 rebels had died. *Reuters* reported on February 5 that the clashes had killed 20 gunmen and nine soldiers.

February 6, 2022: *Reuters* reported that Tehrik-e-Taliban Pakistan claimed credit when gunmen firing from Afghanistan killed five Pakistani soldiers at a border post in northwestern Kurram district. 22020601

March 2, 2022: Gunmen shot to death female polio worker Iqra Iqbal as she was returning home from work in the Peshawar suburbs. No one claimed credit.

March 4, 2022: *AP, Dawn, CNN,* and *Reuters* reported that a suicide bomber hit the Shi'ite Kucha Risaldar Mosque in Peshawar during Friday prayers, after which gunmen hopped off their motorcycle, ran inside, and fired on worshipers in the main hall, killing 62 and wounding 196, many critically. Several had limbs amputated. The dead included police officers and prayer leader Allama Irshad Hussein Khalil. Retired army officer Sher Ali was injured by shrapnel.

Pakistani police tweeted that two terrorists shot police officers who had stopped the motorcyclists for a security check, killing one and critically wounding another. The suicide bomber then ran inside the mosque, setting off his 12 pounds of explosives hidden beneath his large black shawl. The device was packed with ball bearings. *UPI* reported that ISIS-K later claimed credit. The *New York Times* and *AFP* reported that ISIS-K claimed that a single Afghan bomber was responsible. *AFP* said the bomber, in his 30s, had moved to Pakistan with his family decades earlier, but had trained for the attack in Afghanistan. 22030401

March 8, 2022: *Reuters* reported that an ISIS-K suicide bomber killed six paramilitary soldiers and injured 22 people. Nasroor Alam Kolachi, a senior police officer of the Sibi District in South-West Balochistan Province, said, "The bomber first hurled a grenade which failed, after which he blew himself up close to paramilitary men, killing six." The guards were at the end of their shift of security duties after an annual cultural festival attended by President Arif Alivi, who had left the venue.

March 29, 2022: *AFP* reported that a woman colleague and two students killed Safoora Bibi, a teacher at the all-girls Jamia Islamia Falahul Binaat religious school in Dera Ismail Khan in Khyber Pakhtunkhwa Province, after they accused her of blasphemy. The trio ambushed her at the main gate of the school, attacking her with a knife and stick. Police official Saghir Ahmed said that "She died after her throat was slit." Police believed that the main suspect, Umra Aman, planned the crime with two nieces studying at the school. The girls told police a relative had dreamt Bibi "had committed blasphemy".

April 14, 2022: *Al-Jazeera* reported that gunmen ambushed a military convoy near the Afghan border in the Isham area of North Waziristan District in Khyber Pakhtunkhwa Province, killing seven Pakistani soldiers. Four gunmen also died. The area had been a stronghold of the Pakistan Taliban. No one claimed credit. The military said that since January, it had killed 128 gunmen in the region, while nearly 100 soldiers had died.

April 23, 2022: *Al-Jazeera* reported that gunmen in Afghanistan fired heavy weapons across the border into a Pakistani military outpost in the North Waziristan region, killing three troops.

April 26, 2022: *Reuters, CNN, Dawn,* and *BBC* reported that a Baloch Liberation Army (BLA) female suicide bomber hit a passenger van during the evening, killing three Chinese tutors and a Pakistani driver near Karachi University's Confucius Institute. Another Chinese teacher was injured. The BLA released a photo of a woman in fatigues raising two figures in a salute, saying she was Shariah Baloch, 30, alias Bramsh. BLA said the bomber was a married mother of a girl, 8, and boy, 4, and was a science teacher studying for a master's degree at the university. 22042601

Al-Jazeera said that the next day, the BLA warned of more violent attacks on Chinese targets. BLA spokesman Jeeyand Baloch said "Hundreds of highly trained male and female members of the Baloch Liberation Army's Majeed Brigade are ready to carry out deadly attacks in any part of Balochistan and Pakistan," and that attacks would be "even harsher" unless China halts "exploitation projects" and "occupying of the Pakistani state". 22042701

Al-Jazeera reported on July 6, 2022 that Pakistan on July 4 arrested Dad Bakash, variant Dad Bukhsh, 26, a man who allegedly provided technical support for the bombing, in Karachi's district west. Sindh Province information minister Sharjeel Memon blamed the Balochistan Liberation Front (BLF) and the Balochistan Liberation Army (BLA). Memon claimed Bakash admitted being a commander of a BLF sleeper cell and that "He confessed to carrying out surveillance of Chinese nationals at Karachi University and important installations on the task given by Balochistan Liberation Army (BLA) and met and provided assistance to the female suicide bomber and her husband." Bukhsh was wanted for suspected involvement in previous attacks on Chinese targets. Officials said he had travelled from Karachi to Kandahar, Afghanistan in December 2020. There he was trained in bomb making and armed combat and met several leaders of the Baloch insurgency. Bukhsh returned to Karachi in July, 2021, and began to surveil the KANUPP nuclear plant, which is being expanded with Chinese assistance.

Reuters reported on October 31, 2022 that the BLA continued to make threats against Chinese workers. *Reuters* noted that the bomber was schoolteacher Shari Hayat Baloch, 30, who was filmed thanking fellow Baloch separatist fighters for giving her the "opportunity" to become the BLA's first female suicide bomber. The science teacher had a master's degree in Zoology and was planning to enroll in a second master's degree, but instead set off explosives in her rucksack as a minivan carrying the three Chinese teachers drove by. She began her radicalization at the university in Quetta through the Baloch Students Organization (BSO). Hayat was active in the BSO Azad as a zoology student from 2011 to 2014. The man she later married, dentist Habitan Baloch, was a leading figure in BSO Azad.

Also influential in Hayat's life was Karima Baloch, a leading Baloch activist featured in the *BBC*'s list of 100 inspirational and influential women in 2016. Baloch moved to Canada in 2016 after receiving threats in Pakistan. Her body was found in the waters off Toronto in late 2020. Toronto police deemed the death a non-criminal matter.

Chinese investigators traveled to Pakistan in July-August to assist in the case via CCTV footage enhancement and data retrieval from cell phones. Seven Baloch students were detained but later released.

May 18, 2022: *Al-Jazeera* and *AP* reported that Pakistani Taliban spokesman Mohammad Khurasani announced that the group had extended its ceasefire with the government, begun on May 10, until May 30 during talks in Kabul brokered by Afghanistan's Taliban.

June 27, 2022: *AP* and *al-Jazeera* reported that Pakistan sentenced Sajid Majeed Mir, 43, one of the men linked to the 2008 Mumbai attacks that killed 166 people, to 15 years in prison for terror financing unrelated to the 2008 assaults. He was arrested in 2020 and sentenced by a court in Gujranwala on May 16, 2022 to 15 years; his detention and sentencing had not been disclosed by Pakistan. The U.S. Rewards for Justice Program offered up to $5 million for information on his involvement in the Mumbai attacks by Lashkar-e-Taiba. The U.S. designated him a terrorist and indicted him on 2011. He was placed on the FBI's Ten Most Wanted Fugitives list. *Dawn* had reported on June 25-26 that he had

been quietly arrested in Gujranwala in Punjab Province. Mir was a member of a charity set up by Hafiz Saeed, also designated a terrorist by the U.S. Department of Justice.

June 28, 2022: Gunmen on motorcycles shot at Pakistani police escorting a team of polio workers during a door-to-door inoculation campaign, killing two policemen and a polio worker and injuring a passerby in North Waziristan district in Khyber Pakhtunkhwa Province. The campaign began the previous day after North Waziristan registered 11 new polio cases; Pakistan had only one case in 2021. The attackers escaped.

July 7, 2022: Terrorists threw a hand grenade at a roadside police post in Mardan district in Khyber Pakhtunkhwa Province near the Afghanistan border, killing an officer and wounding four people. The attackers fled. No one claimed credit.

July 12, 2022: *Arab News (Pakistan)* and *Reuters* reported that around 8 p.m., Lieutenant Colonel Laeeq Mirza Baig was kidnapped in the Ziarat district of Balochistan Province. Gunmen intercepted Baig's car in the Warchoom area. Two days leader, Baig and his friend were found shot dead in the Mangi Dam area between the Ziarat and Harnai districts. The Baloch Liberation Army claimed credit for the kidnap/murder. The military and local authorities confirmed that up to 15 insurgents disguised as police killed him. *AP* reported on July 15 that Pakistani forces backed by helicopters killed nine separatists near the area of Harnai and Manga dam. The colonel's civilian cousin—Umar Javed, who was traveling with him—was also abducted and remained a hostage.

August 9, 2022: *News 360* reported that a suicide bomber set off explosives while passing a military convoy in the Mir Ali district in the North Waziristan region, killing four soldiers.

August 13, 2022: *News 360* and *Geo TV* reported that a bomb planted on a motorcycle on the side of a road exploded in the Mir Ali district in the North Waziristan region, killing three motorcyclists and injuring five others. No group claimed credit.

August 16, 2022: Gunmen on motorcycles shot at police escorting four polio workers in Gomal in Khyber Pakhtunkhwa Province bordering Afghanistan, killing two policemen. No polio workers were harmed. The four polio workers and their police escort were all traveling on motorcycles. No one claimed credit.

September 5, 2022: *AP* and *AFP* reported that Pakistani security forces raided a suspected Pakistani Taliban hideout in Boyya in the North Waziristan district of Khyber Pakhtunkhwa Province, near the border with Afghanistan. The ensuing gun battle killed five soldiers and four insurgents.

September 13, 2022: *AFP* and *News 360* reported that the Pakistani Taliban claimed credit for killing three soldiers identified as Naik Muhamad Rehman, Naik Mauiz Jan, and Irfan Ula in Kurram district on the Afghan border. The shots came from across the border, according to the Pakistani Armed Forces. 22091301

AFP, AP, and *News 360* reported that during the night, a remotely-detonated roadside bomb exploded under a pickup truck in Bara Bandai Kotkay in Kabal in the Swat Valley of Jiber Pakhtunkhwa Province, killing Idrees Khan, variant Idris Jan, the former head of a pro-government militia, local policemen Rambail Jan and Tauhid Jan, two private guards, a child, and two bystanders believed to be day laborers. Idris was driving his car. The Pakistani Taliban claimed credit, saying that he was involved in killing its members since 2007.

News 360 and *Dawn* added that Tehrik-e-Taliban Pakistan attacks killed around ten, with seven workers of a telephone company abducted.

News 360 and *The News* reported that the TTP had recently set up a check point at Balasur in Matta in Swat district. The Pakistani Taliban kidnapped a man and demanded a ransom of 10 million rupees through a cell phone located in Afghanistan. 22091302

September 28, 2022: *Reuters* reported that a gunman in his early 30s posing as a dental patient killed a Chinese-Pakistani dual national and injured two others at a clinic in Karachi. Senior Superintendent of Police Asad Raza said

the dental clinic was run by one of the victims, identified by police as Dr. Richard Hu, Mrs. Margrate Hu and Ronald, all Chinese-Pakistani dual nationals. No one claimed credit. Baloch separatists had targeted Chinese in recent years. 22092801

September 30, 2022: *News 360* reported that one person was killed and more than 20 injured, ten critically, in an attack at a market in Kohlu in Balochistan Province.

Later, a suicide bomber blew himself up in Mardan in Jiber Pakhtunkhwa, without causing any other casualties.

September 30, 2022: *News 360* reported that gunmen fired from Afghan soil and killed Pakistani soldier Yamshed Iqbal, 27, in Kurram.

October 23, 2022: *News 360* and *Dawn* reported that a Pakistani Armed Forces soldier Lance Daffadar Waqar Ali, 32, died in Hassan Jel, North Waziristan Province, in a firefight between troops guarding the border with Afghanistan and gunmen firing from the Afghan side.

November 3, 2022: *CNN, Reuters,* and *al-Jazeera* reported that a would-be assassin fired on the campaign bus of former Prime Minister Imran Khan, hitting him in the leg (or foot; reports differed) and injuring several others attending a rally for Khan's Pakistan Tehreek-e-Insaf (PTI) party outside Gujranwallah. *NPR* reported that the attacker was detained. Khan was demanding snap elections.

November 13, 2022: *News 360* and *GEO TV* reported that gunmen in Afghanistan fired across the border, killing a Pakistan Frontier Corps soldier and injuring two others in Chaman district, Balochistan Province. Kabul claimed that the attackers were disguised as Taliban. 22111302

November 16, 2022: In the morning, Pakistani Taliban gunmen ambushed a police vehicle in the Dadewala area of Lakki Marwat district in Khyber Pakhtunkhwa Province during a routine patrol in a suburban area, killing all six people in the vehicle. The terrorists fled on motorcycles. Tehreek-e-Taliban Pakistan spokesman Mohammad Khurasani said that the patrol was ambushed on the way to a raid and the attackers acquired five police weapons from the confrontation.

November 28, 2022: *AFP* reported that TTP called off a fragile ceasefire agreed with the government in June and ordered fighters to stage attacks across the country.

November 29, 2022: The military claimed it had killed ten "terrorists" in a raid in the Hoshab district of Baluchistan Province.

November 30, 2022: *News 360, AP, Deutsche Welle,* and *GeoTV* reported that a suicide bomber hit a police truck in Quetta, killing three—a policeman, a civilian, and a minor—and wounding 24, including 20 officers and four civilians. Two policemen were in critical condition. Deputy inspector general of police in Quetta, Ghulam Azfar Mahesar, said, "The explosion took place near a police truck, the vehicle overturned and fell into a ditch due to the impact (of the explosion)." He said 25 kilograms of explosives were used. Remains of an attacker were found near the scene. The officers were en route to protect polio workers. The bomb damaged a nearby car carrying members of a family. TTP said the attack in Baluchistan targeted police to avenge their former spokesperson, Abdul Wali, alias Omar Khalid Khurasani, who was killed in a bombing in Afghanistan's Paktika Province in August.

December 1, 2022: The *Independent* and *al-Jazeera* reported that the United States Department of State announced the naming as "Specially Designated Global Terrorists" Tehrik-e-Taliban Pakistan (TTP, the Pakistani Taliban) and al-Qaeda in the Indian Subcontinent, triggering sanctions. The groups operate from Afghanistan and maintain hideouts in Pakistan's former tribal regions in the northwest. State announced that "As a result of these actions… all property and interests in property of those designated (Thursday) that are subject to U.S. jurisdiction are blocked, and all U.S. persons are generally prohibited from engaging in any transactions with them."

State named four members of TTP and AQIS: Osama Mehmood, AQIS emir; Atif Yahya Ghouri, the deputy chief of AQIS; Muhammad Maruf, who is responsible for AQIS recruitment; and TTP's leader, Qari Amjad, who oversees attacks in northwest Pakistan's Khyber Pakhtunkhwa Province.

December 3, 2022: *Reuters* reported that the Pakistani Taliban claimed credit for ambushing a police patrol in Nowshera, a district of northern Khyber Pakhtunkhwa Province which borders Afghanistan, during the night, killing three police officers.

December 18, 2022: Gunmen attacked a police station in the Lakki Marwat district during the night with grenades and automatic weapons, killing four Pakistani police officers and critically injuring another four before fleeing.

The *Globe and Mail* reported that Pakistani army forces killed all 20 Pakistani Taliban gunmen who had taken over a counter-terrorism center on December 20, two days after they had held six security officers and detainees hostages at the facility. One militant used a brick to overpower an interrogator and seize his weapon. Other prisoners then broke into a storeroom where they obtained other weapons. Two soldiers died and several were wounded. The gunmen demanded safe passage to Afghanistan; the government refused. The TTP later said Pakistan's former tribal regions were also acceptable for the militants. *Reuters* reported that security forces killed 25 of 35 Taliban gunmen who took over the center in Bannu. One hostage—a security official—and two commandos died. Seven gunmen surrendered; the other three were arrested while trying to escape. Ten soldiers, including three officers, were wounded.

December 25, 2022: Gunmen conducted nine attacks in Baluchistan Province, killing six troops and wounding 17 civilians.

Five soldiers, including Army Captain Mohammad Fahad Khan, died when a roadside bomb exploded near a security forces' vehicle during a clearance operation in Kahan. No one claimed credit.

A sixth soldier died in a shootout with the Pakistani Taliban in the Sambaza area of Zhob district. A gunman also died.

Twelve people were wounded when assailants threw a hand grenade in a bazaar near a residential area in Quetta. Another five people were wounded in attacks in Kalat, Khuzdar, and Hub.

PHILIPPINES

January 11, 2022: *Al-Jazeera* reported that a bomb exploded on a public bus travelling along a highway near Cotabato City on Mindanao island, killing a boy, 5, and wounding six others, including a five-month-old baby and a three-year-old child. A victim saw a male passenger leave "baggage" on the bus when he disembarked which later exploded. No group claimed credit.

January 15, 2022: *Yahoo News* reported that human rights organization Karapatan Sorsogon said that two gunmen on a motorcycle shot to death husband and wife farmers Silvestre Fortades Jr. and Rose Marie Galias in Barcelona, Sorsogon, then fled. The duo were members of Sorsogon's chapter of Anakpawis (Toiling Masses) Party-list. The two were selling agricultural goods in Brgy, San Vicente. Anakpawis Party-list and Kilusang Magbubukid ng Pilipinas (Peasant Movement of the Philippines; KMP) said there were 347 politically-motivated farmer killings.

January 28, 2022: *Reuters* reported that Department of Justice (DOJ) Secretary Menardo Guevarra announced that police and the National Bureau of Investigation (NBI) would investigate a *TikTok* posting that threatened to assassinate presidential candidate Ferdinand Marcos, Jr., also known as Bongbong and BBM. Charito Zamora, head of the DOJ' s cybercrime unit, said a citizen alerted her office to a *TikTok* post that read "We are meeting everyday to prepare to have BBM assassinated. Get ready."

February 12, 2022: *UPI,* the state-run *Philippine News Agency,* and *Rappler* reported that an 8 a.m. ambush in Maguindanao Province killed nine people and injured three. Police and military officials attributed the attack to a feud between the families of two commanders of the Bangsamoro Islamic Armed Forces-Moro Islamic Liberation Front (BIAF-MILF). Police believed the main target was BIAF-MILF commander Peges Lentagi Mamasainged, alias Black Magic, who died along with eight others, including his sons Johari, Sadam, and Sadr. Maguindanao Police Captain Fayeed Cana said the group was led by Jordan Malalintang and his son Morsid. Malalintang is Mamasainged's cousin. The victims were traveling on a narrow road in a remote area en route to a banquet in Barangay Kitapok village. Authorities found nine bodies on the ground and inside a Mitsubishi Montero and a Ford Ranger. Empty shells at the scene came from M14 and M16 rifles.

February 15, 2022: The *Jerusalem Post* reported that Philippine National Police thwarted a Hamas plan to target visiting Israelis. Intelligence Group director Police Brig.-Gen. Neil Alinsangan said, "Our Filipino source identified the Hamas operative as 'Bashir,' who was reportedly attempting to establish a foothold in the Philippines with pledges of financial support to some local threat groups, including militant extremists with links to the international terrorist organizations." Bashir's true name was Fares al-Shikli, who Filipino police claimed is a member of Hamas's foreign relations department. He added that Shikli has an "Interpol Red Notice and is charged with an Offense of Terrorism Logistic Support".

March 13, 2022: *Yahoo News* and *Davao Today* reported that at 6 a.m., a gunman shot Larry Villegas, 64, Bayan Muna Progressive Party-list coordinator for General Santos, in Villegas's house in Barangay Buayan, General Santos City. The gunman used a short firearm, wounding Villegas in his legs. He had earlier been threatened by soldiers. Villegas chairs the local transport group TIRES-PISTON, both of which have been repeatedly red-tagged by the National Task Force to End Local Communist Armed Conflict (NTF-ELCAC).

May 8, 2022: *Al-Jazeera* reported that five grenades exploded outside a polling station in Datu Unsay in Maguindanao Province, injuring nine.

May 9, 2022: *Al-Jazeera* reported that gunmen killed three members of local peacekeeping forces near a school being used as a polling station in Buluan municipality on Mindanao island in the southern Philippines during national elections. Maguindanao provincial police spokesman Major Roldan Kuntong said a fourth guard was wounded.

Gunmen attacked a polling station in Lanao del Sur Province in Mindanao, killing one voter and wounding two others.

July 24, 2022: *ABC News, Reuters,* and *AP* reported that a gunman armed with two pistols killed three people waiting to attend a graduation ceremony at Ateneo de Manila University's law school in Quezon City, including Rosita Furigay, a former mayor of Lamitan town in Basilan Province, her aide, and a university guard. Furigay's daughter was hospitalized with injuries. Witnesses blocked the gunman who tried to escape in a carjacked vehicle before police arrested him outside the university gates. Commencement speaker Supreme Court Chief Justice Alexander Gesmundo was advised to turn back en route to the event. Quezon City Police Chief Brig. Gen. Remus Medina said the killer, apparently a medical doctor, feuded with Furigay.

August 7, 12 and 26, 2022: *News 360* and Human Rights Watch reported on November 20, 2022 that the New People's Army (NPA) executed three alleged "counterrevolutionaries" in Negros Occidental Province on August 26, 2022 after a judicial process without any guarantees. The trio were accused in a "people's court" of spying for the army and rape.

NPA spokeswoman Roselyn Jean Pelle confirmed the execution in his house on August 26 of Benjamin Javoc, 54, chairman of the village of Lalong in Calatrava, Negros Occidental. She said he was "notorious for protecting drug trafficking in the area" and conducted "crimes against the people and the revolutionary movement for working for the military by giving them information". Renato Estrebillo, 43, a Calatrava worker, was executed while leaving his house on August 12 for "tipping off" the 79th Infantry Battalion that prompted a military intervention on July 6 during which two children were wounded and the military detained a civilian. She added that Estrebillo was "a known thief of animals and agricultural products". Rodel Nobleza of Calatrava was executed while he was driving a motorcycle with two minors on August 7 for giving information to the Army, which sparked an April 2019 raid during which two guerrillas and a civilian were killed. She alleged that Nobleza was a drug trafficker.

October 3, 2022: *NPR* reported that during the night, two gunmen on a motorcycle fired two shots into the head of longtime Manila radio commentator Percival Mabasa, 63, in suburban Las Pinas City, while he was driving his vehicle. The attackers escaped. He used the broadcast name Percy Lapid.

Al-Jazeera added on October 17, 2022 that Interior secretary Benjamin Abalos announced that Quezon City resident Joel Estorial, 38, surrendered to police and handed over a gun which he said was the murder weapon. The official *Philippine News Agency (PNA)* reported that Estorial surrendered due to "fear for his personal safety" after his photo was released and a 110,000 reward for his capture "placed on his head". Estorial said that he and three others took part in the ambush on orders from an unnamed person at the country's national prison, and that after the killing they shared a 550,000-peso ($9,340) payment. His co-conspirators remained at large.

October 9, 2022: *AP, ABS-CBN,* and *News 360* reported that Philippine National Police killed three detained militants, including senior Abu Sayyaf leader Idang Susukan, linked to ISIS after they staged a foiled escape attempt at dawn from the maximum-security facility in the PNP Custodial Compound in Camp Crame police headquarters in Manila. A police officer delivering breakfast in an open outdoor exercise area was stabbed. The prisoners briefly held hostage former opposition Senator Leila de Lima, who was unhurt but taken to a hospital for a checkup. A police officer in a sentry tower killed two prisoners when they refused to yield. Police commandos killed a third inmate who had raided de Lima's cell, blindfolded her, and held a blunt instrument to her chest. Another prisoner was injured in the rampage. The hostage-taker demanded a helicopter for him to escape and later asked for water. A police officer delivering the water shot him.

Susukan was blamed for dozens of killings and beheadings of hostages, including foreign tourists, and other terrorist attacks. He was arrested two years earlier in Davao city.

The other two dead inmates, Arnel Cabintoy and Feliciano Sulayao, Jr., were suspected members of the Dawlah Islamiyah, linked to bombings and other deadly attacks in the country's south. They were arrested in 2019 in suburban Quezon city and faced non-bailable charges like Susukan.

De Lima, 63, was detained in 2017 on drug charges she claimed were fabricated by former President Rodrigo Duterte.

October 27, 2022: *News 360* and the *Inquirer* reported that the New People's Army (NPA) attacked members of the Army carrying out rescue operations in Licuan-Baay after the 6.4 earthquake earlier in the week. Two soldiers died and a third was missing.

SINGAPORE

September 28, 2022: Public state broadcaster *Channel News Asia*, *Reuters*, and *Newsweek* reported that a man, 37, on Singapore Airlines flight SQ33 that left from San Francisco at 1:05 p.m. Singapore time claimed there was a bomb in his hand luggage. Two Republic of Singapore Air Force (RSAF) F16C/D fighter jets escorted the plane to Singapore's Changi International Airport. No bomb was found. The man was arrested. The crew said he had assaulted the cabin staff. He was held under anti-terrorism laws and for suspected drug consumption. The Singapore Police Force was alerted of the threat at 2:40 a.m. All passengers and crew disembarked safely at 9:20 a.m.

SRI LANKA

February 14, 2022: *AFP* reported that before dawn, gunmen attacked the home of high-profile Sri Lankan television journalist Chamuditha Samarawickrama, who had criticized the ruling Rajapaksa family and their allies in recent broadcasts, including on *YouTube*. He was not hurt. He

said the trio traveled in a white van. A police official said they intimidated the guard and gained access to the housing compound. Samarawickrama said, "I heard shots fired. They smashed my windows and threw feces at the house."

TAJIKISTAN

May 18, 2022: The *Jerusalem Post* reported that 200 gunmen killed an officer and wounded 13 troops in an ambush on a convoy in Gorno-Badakhshan Province, which borders Afghanistan and China. Security forces returned fire, killing eight anti-government terrorists and detaining more than 70 people.

THAILAND

April 15, 2022: *Reuters* reported that two bombs were set off by G5, a militant group of the Patani United Liberation Organization (PULO), killing a civilian and injuring three policemen. PULO president Kasturi Mahkota claimed that peace "talks are not inclusive enough and it is going too fast".

August 17, 2022: *Deutsche Welle*, *Reuters*, and *AFP* reported that after midnight, 17 locations, including convenience stores and a gas station, were attacked by bombs and arson in Pattani, Narathiwat, and Yala Provinces, injuring seven people. No one claimed credit. Military spokesperson Pramote Promin said the attackers "dressed up as women, using motorcycles and in many cases using petrol bombs, throwing them into the target sites… It is clear that the insurgents remain committed to using violence on people, damaging confidence in the economy, creating uncertainty and undermining the government system." Police Captain Sarayuth Kotchawong said that at a convenience store of a gas station in Yala's Yaha district, a suspect left a black bag inside and told employees to leave if they "do not want die". The bag exploded 10 minutes later. Kasturi Makhota, leader of the Patani United Liberation Organisation (PULO), denied involvement.

September 14, 2022: *AFP* reported that a gunman shot to death one person and wounded two others at the Army Training Command Department, part of a large complex of military buildings in the north of Bangkok. Deputy national police spokesman Kissana Phathanacharoen said a suspect had been detained. *News 360* added that he was a Thai Army sergeant, and had killed two soldiers inside a military academy. The Thai Army later said on *Facebook* that Colonel Yongyuth Mungkornki was arrested soon after fleeing. Thai Army deputy spokeswoman Sirichan Ngathong said Yongyuth entered his office and fired on several colleagues. The *Bangkok Post* identified the dead as Nopparat Inthornsunthorn and Prakarn Sinsong.

September 20, 2022: *Al-Jazeera* reported that a roadside bomb detonated in the night as a police motorcycle and patrol truck passed near a hospital in Mai Kaen in Pattani Province, killing a Thai policeman and injuring four others. Police believed that the remotely detonated bomb was hidden in a trash can in front of the hospital. The exterior of the Mai Kaen hospital was damaged and a shrapnel hole was seen at the Mai Kaen Kittiwit School, which was ordered closed for the day.

October 6, 2022: *NPR, CNN,* the *New York Times, Khaosod Online, Insider, al-Jazeera, Thairath TV,* the *Washington Post,* and *BBC* reported that at 12:30 lunchtime, former police sergeant Panya Kamrab, 34, killed 38 people, including 23 children, two teachers, and a police officer, at the Child Development Center in Utthai Sawan Na Klang district, Nong Bua Lamphu Province, in north-east Thailand. Armed with a shotgun, 9 mm pistol, and knife, he broke into a locked room and killed 23 of 24 napping children, some age two. *Reuters* reported that he first shot four or five officials before attacking the children. One of the dead was a teacher, wife of Seksan Sriraj, 28; she was eight months pregnant. A dozen people were injured, six critically, and taken to Nong Bua Lamphu district hospital. *The Nation* reported that people rushed to the hospital to give blood. Kamrab fled in a white four-door Toyota pick-up truck with Bangkok registration plates. He crashed into bystanders, killing nine and injuring several others, during his escape. The killer went home, barricaded it, then killed his wife and stepson, 2, before killing himself. He had been suspended in January and fired in June for using and selling methamphetamine. A surviving teacher said that the attacker used to drop off his child at the nursery and had seemed polite. Regional police spokesman Paisal Lauesomboon told the *Thai Public Broadcasting Service* that the attacker had appeared in court in Nong Bua Lamphu Province that morning on charges related to the use and possible sale of methamphetamine. The verdict was scheduled to be delivered on October 7. He went to the daycare center looking for his son, and began his attack when he did not find him. Police said the gun had been legally obtained.

The dead included Tawatchai Sriphu, 4, grandson of Oy Yodkhao, 51; the niece of Pensiri Thana; and the 3-year-old niece of Som-Mai Pitfai.

November 22, 2022: *Al-Jazeera* reported that a car bomb killed a police officer and injured 30 civilians and officers when an individual left his car in a police compound in Narathiwat Province. No one claimed credit.

Australia/Oceania

Australia

August 14, 2022: *USNWR, BBC, the Sydney Morning Herald,* and *Reuters* reported that police evacuated Canberra's airport and arrested a man after five gunshots were heard in the main terminal's check-in area in the afternoon. No injuries were reported. Police recovered a firearm.

October 29, 2022: *News 360* and *Sydney Morning Herald* reported that Australian authorities began repatriating 60 women married to ISIS fighters, as well as their children, who were held in the Roj camp in northeastern Syria. Four women and their 13 children arrived in Sydney in the first phase.

November 27, 2022: *News 360* reported that Australia's national intelligence agency (ASIO) downgraded the terror threat level from "probable" to "possible" for the first time since 2014. Australian Director General of Security Mike Burgess observed, "Since 2014, there have been eleven terrorist attacks on Australian soil, while 21 significant plots have been detected and disrupted. Fortunately, there have been no major attacks this year."

New Zealand

June 20, 2022: The *Washington Post* and *UPI* reported that on June 20, New Zealand police, under the authority of Police Commissioner Andrew Coster, designated two U.S. far-right groups, the Proud Boys and the Base, as terrorist organizations. The government published the declaration in the official *New Zealand Gazette* on June 27. The UK earlier labeled the Base an extremist organization; Canada designated the Proud Boys a terrorist group in February 2021. New Zealand residents may not fund or support either group, which join ISIS and al-Shabaab on the list, under the Terrorism Suppression Act. The Base had tried to expand into Australia. Coster added, "The designations of The Base and the Proud Boys will expire on 20 June 2025 unless earlier revoked or extended."

July 27-28, 2022: *Al-Jazeera* and *Radio New Zealand (RNZ)* reported that hoax bomb threats were phoned to four schools in Gisborne, Thames and Waikato, on the country's North Island. Bomb threats were made on July 28 at a dozen schools amid suggestions of a possible cyberattack from overseas. Schools were either locked down or evacuated in Ashburton, Dunstan, Geraldine, Greymouth, Kaikoura, Levin, Masterton, Queenstown, Rolleston, Takaka, Palmerston Northwere, and Whanganui. An overseas cyberbot was suspected. No explosive devices were found. In 2016, more than 30 schools received telephoned bomb threats.

October 27, 2022: *News 360* and *New Zealand Herald* reported a woman, 57, was arrested after breaking the office door of Prime Minister Jacinda Ardern in Morningside, Auckland with a sword around 8:20 a.m. She also threw a smoke bomb inside the office. No injuries were reported. She told the *Herald* that she had a dispute with the PM's office and other government offices regarding health issues.

EUROPE

May 30, 2022: *UPI* reported that the European Council, which oversees the 27-member European Union's political direction, imposed terrorism-related sanctions against Syria-based al-Qaeda affiliate Hurras al-Din, its leader, Faruq al-Suri, and its religious leader, Sami al-Aridi, announcing asset freezes and travel bans. Hurras al-Din was formed in late February 2018 by seven Syrian rebel factions; 10 more joined in the following months. The United States deemed Hurras al-Din and al-Suri as Specially Designated Terrorists in September 2019. The U.S. Department of State's Rewards for Justice program offers a $5 million reward for information on al-Suri.

June 20, 2022: *UPI* reported that the European Union imposed economic and financial sanctions on two senior commanders with Jama'at Nusrat al-Islam Wal-Muslimin and its Burkinabe branch, Ansarul Islam, on accusations of being behind terrorist attacks in West Africa.

August 4, 2022: *AP* reported that Spanish police were looking into 50 reports of women being jabbed with medical needles during parties or at night clubs. Some 23 attacks were in the Catalonia region. Spanish police found ecstasy in a 13-year-old girl's system in Gijon.

    Similar jabs at musical events were reported in France, the UK, Belgium, and the Netherlands. French police counted 400 reports in recent months. It was not clear if any substances were injected.

October 14, 2022: *CNN* reported that 99 out of 100 members of the Parliamentary Assembly of the Council of Europe (PACE), an assembly of representatives drawn from 46 national parliaments across Europe, voted for a resolution calling on European countries to "declare the current Russian regime as a terrorist one." A Turkish MP from the Republican People's Party abstained.

November 23, 2022: *Le Monde, Reuters,* and *AFP* reported that the 27-nation European Parliament in Strasbourg declared Russia a state sponsor of terrorism, with 494 MEPs backing the resolution, 58 opposed, and 44 not voting. The resolution noted, "The deliberate attacks and atrocities carried out by the Russian Federation against the civilian population of Ukraine, the destruction of civilian infrastructure and other serious violations of human rights and international humanitarian law amount to acts of terror... recognizes Russia as a state sponsor of terrorism and as a state which uses means of terrorism." *Deseret News* reported that hours later, the European Union Parliament website was hit with a cyberattack by a pro-Kremlin group.

December 1, 2022: *Reuters,* the *Daily Beast, Interfax Ukraine,* and the *Jerusalem Post* reported that three Ukrainian diplomatic missions, including two outside Spain, received threatening letters. Ukrainian Foreign Minister Dmytro Kuleba said that "If they have already started attacking embassies... it means that they are afraid of us, they are trying to stop us... Inside these letters was a symbolic threat to Ukraine... all the envelopes were soaked in red liquid at the time they were received... We certainly have a guess but we need to trace the entire network of agents and people involved in this campaign." 22120101-03

December 2, 2022: *Newsweek, Kyiv Independent, AP,* and *CNN* noted that Ukraine's Foreign Minister Dmytro Kuleba charged that "a well-planned campaign of terror and intimidation" was behind the sending of exploding letters and blood-soaked packages containing animal eyes, mostly those of cows and pigs, covered in a liquid to Ukrainian embassies in Hungary, the Netherlands, Poland, Croatia, Italy, and Austria, Consulates General in Naples, Italy and Krakow, Poland, and the consulate in Brno in the Czech Republic.

    CNN reported on December 4 that a senior top Russian government official and the leader of the Moscow-aligned Wagner mercenary group denied involvement with the packages. Russian Foreign Ministry spokesperson Maria Zakharova sent *CNN* a single word comment to the allegation: "psycho." Yevgeny Prigozhin, Russian oligarch and head of the Wagner group, said the Wagner Group would "never engage in boorish stupid antics". 22120202-10

ALBANIA

July 22, 2022: *The Independent* reported that Iranian Mujahedeen-e-Khalq dissidents said they had canceled the Free Iran World Summit scheduled for July 23-24 following warnings from local authorities of a possible terrorist threat. Some 3,000 MEK members live at Ashraf 3 camp in Manez, 19 miles west of Tirana. U.S. senators and members of the House of Representatives and other former personalities from Western countries were scheduled to participate.

BELARUS

May 18, 2022: *UPI* reported that Belarusian President Alexander Lukashenko signed a law making people who attempt an act of terrorism eligible for the death penalty. The *Kyiv Post* reported that the new law will go into effect May 29. Observers believed that Belarus would use the law to oppress people supporting Ukraine in Russia's invasion.

BELGIUM

May 17, 2022: *U.S. News and World Report* and *Reuters* reported that Spanish rapper Josep Miguel Arenas Beltran, alias Valtonyc, won his fight to avoid extradition to Spain. In 2017, a Spanish court sentenced him to 3½ years in prison for praising the violence of Basque separatist group ETA and a now-defunct left-wing group in song lyrics, insulting the Spanish monarchy, and other charges. Spain requested extradition when he arrived in Belgium in 2018 after losing an appeal. A lower court ruled in December 2021 that the offences were not crimes in Belgium, thus preventing his extradition. Prosecutors in Ghent appealed to the court of appeal. They can still appeal to the Supreme Court. He was represented by Belgian lawyer Simon Bekaert.

September 28, 2022: *Reuters* reported that police raided ten addresses, most of them in Antwerp and the Flemish region of Belgium, in an investigation of far-right sympathizers suspected of planning an attack and illegally possessing arms. Police killed one man, Yannick V., 36, in a shootout. Police seized more than 100 weapons and other military and assault equipment, plus ammunition. *News 360* added on September 29 that Belgian authorities filed terrorism charges against two of the six individuals who were detained. *Nieuwsblad* reported that the other four were released.

November 11, 2022: *Dailymotion, CNN, De Standaard, UPI,* and *VRT News* reported that a terrorist stabbed to death a Belgian police officer in his 20s and injured a second around 7:15 p.m. on Rue Aerschot in the Brussels municipality of Schaerbeek. Reinforcements shot the suspect in the leg.

November 28, 2022: *News 360, Sudinfo, La Libre,* and *DPA* reported that during the night, three stabbing attacks in several municipalities in southwestern Brussels killed two people and injured two. At 6 p.m., an assailant stabbed a cyclist and a pedestrian in the Anderlecht district. The victims, aged 28 and 62, did not know each other. One was in critical condition. At 6:20 p.m., a 20-year-old was stabbed in the neck and died in the Saint-Gilles neighborhood. At 6:30 p.m., a person died of a knife attack in the Molenbeek district. Local police arrested the attacker. It was not clear if he was responsible for all three incidents.

DENMARK

February 4, 2022: *BBC* and *AP* reported that the Roskilde District Court found three male members of an Iranian opposition group guilty of "promoting terrorism" by supporting its armed wing in Iran and for spying for Saudi Arabia. Police detained the trio in February 2020. The men, aged between 41 and 50, belonged to the Saudi-backed Arab Struggle Movement for the Liberation of Ahvaz (ASMLA), which seeks a separate state for ethnic Arabs in Iran's Khuzestan Province. One is a Danish citizen. Police had arrested them in February 2020 in Ringsted. The court also found the men guilty of supporting Jaish al-Adl, which operates in Iran and the U.S. lists as a terrorist organization. Sentencing was scheduled for March 2022; the defendants faced up to 12 years in prison and deportation.

Prosecutors said the three received 15m kroner (£1.27m) from Saudi intelligence operatives. Prosecutors said the money helped finance the activities of ASMLA's armed wing in Iran, the Mohiuddin Nasser Martyrs Brigade.

In 2018, one of the trio was the target of an assassination attempt believed to have been sponsored by Tehran. A Norwegian-Iranian was jailed for seven years for his role in the plot.

July 3, 2022: *CNN, UPI, AP, BBC, DR, TV2, NPR,* and the *Washington Examiner* reported that at 5:37 p.m., a gunman fired for 15 minutes in several locations inside the Field's shopping center in Orestad, Copenhagen, killing three people and injuring 30, four seriously. Police arrested an ethnic Danish man, 22, near the mall 13 minutes after receiving the first call. Police chief Soeren Thomassen said that he could not rule out an "act of terrorism". Witness Mahdi al-Wazni said that the shooter had carried a "hunting rifle". The shooter was also carrying a knife, according to the *BBC*. *Berlingske* reported that the gunman was charged with manslaughter and attempted manslaughter.

Newsweek and *Ekstra Bladet* reported that the suspect had posted five videos, including a claim that the anti-psychotic medication Quetiapine "does not work". He also had posted videos of himself pressing the muzzle of a handgun and rifle against his head and into his mouth. He uploaded several playlists to *YouTube*, with the titles "Killer Music" and "Last Thing to Listen To". Video showed him walking around the mall with a rifle.

Police announced on July 4 that he had killed two Danish 17-year-olds, a girl and boy, and a Russian man, 47. He injured two Danish women, aged 19 and 40, a Swedish girl, 16, and a Swedish man, 50. Police were now saying that the attack was not terrorism and that he chose his targets at random. Police said he did not have a gun permit.

October 7, 2022: *News 360, Mehr,* and *Berlingske* reported that police arrested an Iranian man, 32, after he tried to enter the Iranian Embassy in Copenhagen armed with a knife. He was charged with two counts of vandalism under the Criminal Code for attacking a diplomatic institution.

November 18, 2022: *Reuters* reported that a court sentenced a Danish woman, 35, evacuated from a Syrian detention camp in 2021, to three years in prison for aiding ISIS and illegally travelling to and residing in conflict zones. She and her husband traveled to Syria in 2013. The duo were captured by Kurdish forces in 2018 while attempting to escape the caliphate. She was sent to the al-Roj detention camp in northeastern Syria due to their association with ISIS. His fate is unknown. Danish authorities evacuated her, her five children, and two other women and their nine children in 2021. In that evacuation, Germany took in eight other mothers and 23 children from Syrian camps. The Danish woman pleaded guilty to aiding ISIS by working as a housewife and to illegally travelling to and residing in a conflict area.

FRANCE

February 7, 2022: *AFP* reported that French prosecutors in Nanterre outside Paris opened an investigation after death threats were issued against journalist Ophelie Meunier after the *M6* channel broadcast her "Off Limits" report on radical Islam, mainly in Roubaix near Lille. She was given police protection, as was Roubaix resident Amine Elbahi, who denounced the rise of radical Islam in the area.

February 14, 2022: *Reuters, Le Parisien, BFMTV, BBC,* and *RMC* radio reported that Minister of Transport Jean-Baptiste Djebbari said that Paris police killed a man who attacked two police with a 12-inch knife at the Gare du Nord station at 7 a.m. The man's knife included an anti-police inscription. Djebbari said the attacker was known to the police "as someone who wandered around in the station".

March 2, 2022: *Reuters* reported that French prosecutors began a terrorism investigation after a prisoner strangled Corsican nationalist and shepherd Yvan Colonna in the prison gym in Arles in southern France. The attacker was serving a nine-year sentence for planning terrorist attacks. Colonna was serving a life sentence for the 1998 murder of Claude Erignac, prefect of Corsica. On March 21, *Reuters* and *Le Parisien* reported that Yvan Colonna died of his injuries while still in a coma.

March 12, 2022: *Reuters, U.S. News and World Report*, and *ABC News* reported that a French man with a knife injured three police officers in the Old Port of Marseille on the Mediterranean in the morning. Police shot him to death after he ignored warning shots. The motive was unclear. Police said he had no criminal record, and were considering opening a terrorism investigation. The attack occurred near a site that is collecting aid for victims of the war in Ukraine.

April 24, 2022: *Reuters, BFM TV, France Info* radio, and *Le Figaro* newspaper reported that during the night, police fired on a car driving the wrong way near the Pont Neuf in central Paris, killing two people and injuring another. *AFP* reported on April 28 that a French policeman, 24, was charged with involuntary manslaughter after using his assault rifle to shoot dead a driver who sought to evade police. He said he acted in self-defense, as the car was aiming at his colleagues on the Pont Neuf bridge. A police report indicated that a dozen rounds were fired, and five or six hit the occupants. He was also charged with "willful violence by a person in authority" for the death of the front-seat passenger, and the injury of a person in the back seat. The two dead occupants had extensive criminal records, including for drug charges.

April 24, 2022: *Fox News* and *BFM TV* reported that French priest Father Christophe was stabbed multiple times and Sister Marie-Claude, who intervened, was also injured in the forearm in a knife attack at Église Saint-Pierre-d'Arène de Nice, a Catholic church along the French Riviera. French national and municipal police arrested a suspect, 31. Nice Mayor Christian Estrosi said the suspect was a mentally unstable French national who was born in Fréjus, a port town on the Côte d'Azur. Bernard Gonzalez, the prefect of the Alpes-Maritimes department of southeast France added that the suspect had no criminal record and was unknown to the police, but was the subject of psychiatric monitoring with several stays in the Sainte-Marie psychiatric hospital in Nice. He purchased the knife several days ago.

Meanwhile, French voters reelected President Emmanuel Macron.

May 23, 2022: *AP, Reuters,* and *Le Parisien* reported that around 6:30 a.m., a security guard at the Qatari Embassy in Paris's posh 8th district was killed and a suspect, 38, arrested. The guard was apparently beaten and strangled to death. French media suggested that the suspect was mentally unstable. The special prosecutor for terrorism cases was not involved in the case, suggesting the authorities were ruling out a terrorist motive. *Al-Jazeera* said the suspect and the guard were fighting in front of the embassy. *Le Parisien* added that "Originally from Sevran, he is known for acts of violence against the police, outrages and rebellion. He was also on cocaine at the time. He is undergoing a medical examination."

May 31, 2022: *BBC, AFP,* and the *Washington Examiner* reported that French police discovered a cache of weapons, including machine guns, 18 legal guns, 23 illegal guns, 167 magazines, 30 kilograms of gun powder, the equivalent of at least 120,000 bullet cartridges, plus extremist, anti-Semitic literature that denies the Holocaust after raiding houses belonging to men suspected of being part of a neo-Nazi gang in the eastern Alsace region of France. Police also found equipment to produce bullets and $26,800 worth of euros in cash. Intelligence services believe the men were engaged in a "Jew hunt" of Jewish people to attack during a soccer game in Strasbourg. Authorities arrested four men, aged 45 to 53, in Mulhouse and charged them with arms trafficking. They faced up to 10 years in prison.

June 28, 2022: *AFP* reported that a French appeals court was to determine whether to extradite to Italy eight men and two women, aged 61 to 78, believed to be former Italian Red Brigades members. Among them was Sergio Tornaghi, 64, wanted for assassinations conducted during the Years of Lead in the late 1960s to mid-1980s. He had been sentenced in absentia for being behind the murder of his factory's manager in the Milan underground in 1980. *Reuters* reported on June 29, 2022 that the Paris Court of Appeal denied extradition, citing the right to respect for private and family life and the right to a fair trial as laid out by articles 8 and 6 of the European Convention on Human Rights. In April 2021, France arrested seven of the at-large Italian leftists. They included Giorgio Pietrostefani, a co-founder of the Lotta Continua (Continuous Struggle) group, sentenced to 22 years in prison for his role in the 1972 murder of Milan police commissioner Luigi Calabresi. The other six were members of the Red Brigades, including Marina Petrella, Roberta Cappelli, and Sergio Tornaghi, all sentenced to life in prison for murders and kidnappings.

July 5, 2022: *Al-Jazeera* reported France repatriated 35 French children and 16 mothers from Kurdish-run camps in northeastern Syria that hold family members of suspected ISIS fighters. The minors were handed over to child protection services while the mothers faced judicial proceedings.

The *Washington Post* added that Iraq had also accepted several camp residents, including Hadeer Khalid, 34, and her children.

September 2, 2022: *BFM TV* and *AP* reported that national anti-terrorism prosecutor Jean-Francois Ricard warned of an elevated threat of attacks on French soil by Islamic extremists coming from Iraq and Syria.

September 16, 2022: *CoinDesk* and *Le Figaro* reported that a Paris criminal court sentenced Franco-Algerian Sami Allem to three years in prison and one year of probation and Franco-Moroccan Abderrahman Cheikh to two years in jail and two years of probation on charges of funding terrorism in Syria via cryptocurrencies and participation in a terrorist criminal association. France's anti-terrorism prosecution Parquet national antiterroriste (Pnat) arrested the duo in September 2020. They were among 29 people arrested on suspicion of funding Islamist extremists in Syria with crypto. The duo were believed to have financed jihadists in Syria using crypto worth €280,000 ($280,268) between 2018-2020.

October 18, 2022: *UPI* and *CNN* reported that Paris-based Lafarge, S.A., a French global building manufacturing company, pleaded guilty in a Brooklyn federal court to a federal count of conspiring to provide material support to ISIS and another terrorist organization as part of a deal with the Department of Justice and agreed to pay a $777.78 million fine for paying ISIS $5.92 million for permission to operate in Syria. The U.S. Department of Justice said that the firm operated Lafarge Cement Syria in Damascus, paying ISIS and al-Nusrah Front "fixed monthly donations" from 2013 to 2014, allowing the company to operate there and make about $70.3 million in revenue. *CNN* added that DOJ said it was an unprecedented corporate prosecution under the material support of terrorism law. DOJ said that when Lafarge evacuated the cement plant in 2014, ISIS sold the cement it had produced for circa $3.2 million.

On December 26, 2022, *ABC News* reported that families of three U.S. servicemen killed by ISIS sued Lafarge. Lee Wolosky, Partner at Jenner & Block LLP, lawyer for the plaintiffs, said, "Defendants' payments to and business partnership with ISIS provided ISIS the seed capital it needed to transform from a fledgling militia in the early 2010s into a brutal terroristic behemoth with the capability and intent to kill Americans… Defendants aided and abetted ISIS's and ANF's acts of international terrorism by knowingly providing substantial assistance, including by making cash and covert payments through foreign shell companies and intermediaries to, purchasing raw material from, and making anti-competitive agreements with, the foreign terrorist organizations, and by failing to safely shut down and evacuate the Cement Plant, thereby placing tons of valuable cement and raw materials in the hands of ISIS and ANF… Defendants knew that this material support was paid to foreign terrorist organizations and would be used to commit acts of international terrorism… Lafarge has already pled guilty to federal crimes and admitted to paying millions of dollars to ISIS. This lawsuit is intended to hold it accountable to the military families devastated by its heinous and unlawful conduct. We expect more families to join the lawsuit and we look forward to bringing the case to trial before a jury of New Yorkers."

The victims were:

- Navy Chief Petty Officer Jason Finan of California, killed by an ISIS-planted bomb in Iraq on October 20, 2016.

- Navy Senior Petty Officer Scott Cooper Dayton of Virginia, killed by an ISIS-planted bomb in Ayn Issa, Syria, on November 24, 2016.

- Former Marine David Berry, a 12-year combat veteran from Virginia working for a private contractor, killed by an ISIS attack on the Corinthia Hotel in Libya on January 27, 2015.

December 23, 2022: *CNN, BBC, UPI, Sky News, Fox News, France24,* and *Reuters* reported that at midday, a gunman attacked the Ahmet-Kaya Kurdish Cultural Center, a nearby restaurant, and a hair salon on Rue d'Enghien in Paris's 10th arrondissement near the Gare de l'Est train station, killing three, including a woman, and wounding four, one critically, before he was arrested. *AP* reported that police said the shooter had earlier been charged with attacking migrants at a refugee tent encampment and conducted another attack.

The *Washington Post* added that French Interior Minister Gérald Darmanin said the assailant "clearly wanted to attack foreigners" and probably acted alone. A witness told *AFP*, "We saw an old white man enter, then start shooting." The suspect was treated for face injuries. The retired French train driver, William Malet, 69, was earlier charged with racially motivated violence in a saber attack on a tent encampment housing migrants in eastern Paris, injuring two of them. He was released from prison on December 12 under judicial supervision, ordered to get psychiatric care, and banned from carrying weapons. Police opened an investigation against him for "assassination," "attempted assassination", and "intentional violence with weapons". Darmanin added that the suspect was not known to have been an active member of right-wing extremist groups, and practiced at shooting ranges. He owned several registered weapons. Police said the Caucasian man was known for two previous attempted murders in 2016 and December 2021.

AFP reported that Kurdish demonstrators railed against the Turkish government and blamed French officials for not protecting them. Protesters threw projectiles at police, who responded with tear gas.

A construction worker saw the assailant wound three people before two passersby in the salon intervened and stopped him.

Forbes reported that police were investigating whether the shooting was a hate crime.

BBC added that the accused man told investigators he had a "pathological" hatred of migrants and had planned to kill "non-European foreigners". He told police he had become "depressed" and "suicidal" after his home was burgled in 2016. He first went to Saint-Denis, a high-immigration suburb in northern Paris, in order to kill "non-Europeans", but after finding few people there, went to the Ahmet-Kaya Kurdish Center.

Malet was formally charged on December 26.

Al-Jazeera and *AFP* added on January 3, 2023 that thousands of Kurds from across Europe attended the victims' funeral in Villiers-le-Bel, north of Paris. The three coffins were wrapped in the flags of the Kurdistan Workers' Party (PKK) and the Kurdish-controlled Rojava territory in northern Syria. The victims were Abdurrahman Kizil; singer and political refugee Mir Perwer; and Emine Kara, a leader in the Movement of Kurdish Women in France.

GERMANY

January 24, 2022: *Reuters, AP, CNN, DPA, KFOR, France24,* and *AFP* reported that a gunman, 18, killed a German woman, 23, and seriously injured two German women, aged 19 and 20, and a German-Italian man, 20, in an attack with a long gun in a lecture hall at the Neuenheimer Feld campus of Heidelberg University on the northern bank of the Neckar River. The gunman fled, but died after turning his weapon on himself. German media reported that he appeared to have no religious or political motive. Police found indications that he had been a member of a far-right party, which he left in 2019, while still a minor. *AP* reported that he had earlier suffered a mental illness. *DPA* and *AP* said that the gunman, who lived in Mannheim, was a biology student at the university. Heidelberg, founded in 1386, is Germany's oldest university. Its Neuenheimer Feld campus hosts natural sciences departments, part of the university clinic and a botanical garden. *AP* reported on January 26 that police said that the gunmen purchased three weapons a week earlier in Austria. Police seized two of the weapons, bought from a weapons dealer, and 150 rounds of ammunition, at the scene. Austrian police found a rifle, purchased from a private individual, in a room the gunman had rented during his stay in Austria. He had no valid German weapons license. *Deutsche Welle* reported on January 26 that police were investigating possible ties to neo-Nazis.

March 29, 2022: *DW* and *DPA* reported on March 31 that Foreign Minister Annalena Baerbock confirmed that nearly all German women who moved to ISIS territory but wanted to return to Germany had done so. Many, aged between 23 and 36, were arrested upon arrival on terrorism-related charges. Ten women and 27 children arrived in Frankfurt the evening of March 29 following an "extremely difficult operation" to extract them from the Roj detention camp in northeast Syria.

April 12, 2022: German federal prosecutors charged Jalda A., a German woman who allegedly abused a Yazidi slave while in ISIS territory, with membership in a foreign terrorist organization, crimes against humanity, war crimes, and being an accessory to genocide. Jalda A. was arrested upon her arrival back in Germany on October 7, 2021. Kurdish forces had detained her in 2017. She traveled to Syria via Türkiye on April 2014 and soon married an ISIS fighter, giving birth to a son the next year. Her first husband died; she married two other men in succession. She lived with yet another man in the area of Mayadin from September to October 2017; he kept a Yazidi woman as a slave and regularly raped her with A.'s knowledge. Prosecutors said A. physically abused the woman "almost every day" by punching and kicking the woman, pulling her hair, slamming her head against the wall, and on one occasion hitting the woman in the head with a flashlight.

April 13, 2022: *AP, ARD,* the *Washington Post, Reuters, U.S. News and World Report,* and *DPA* reported that prosecutors in Koblenz and Rhine-land-Palatinate's state criminal police office said that raids at 21 properties led to four arrests of German citizens and seizure of weapons in an investigation begun in October 2021 into suspected anti-government United Patriots (Vereinte Patrioten) extremists who allegedly planned via *Telegram* to cause a long nationwide blackout and kidnap well-known figures including Health Minister Karl Lauterbach. The detainees were associated with the protest movement against COVID-19 restrictions and with the Reich Citizens (Reichsbürger) movement, which disputes the legitimacy of the post-World War II German constitution. Police confiscated 22 firearms, including 14 rifles, seven handguns, hundreds of rounds of ammunition, thousands of euros (worth $20,000) in cash, and numerous gold bars and silver coins. The detainees were accused of preparing a serious act of violence and of violating weapons laws. They had hoped to spark a "civil war" that would lead to the collapse of the country's democracy. Three people were held for "preparation of a serious crime endangering the state"; a fourth with financing terrorism. A fifth suspect was at large.

May 6, 2022: *Reuters* reported that Berlin authorities found and destroyed a device thrown at a window of a residential building housing Russian state-run *RIA* news agency staff in the city's Steglitz district. The Russian news agency said it had journalists living in the block. 22050601

May 11, 2022: *AP, DPA,* and *ZDF* reported that state interior minister Herbert Reul announced that during the night police detained a student, 16, for allegedly plotting an attack on the Don-Bosco-Gymnasium secondary school, which he attends, in Essen. Police confiscated weapons, bomb-making materials, spears, other sharp weapons, and large amounts of right-wing extremist, anti-Semitic, and anti-Muslim writings from his apartment. Another potential target was his previous school, the Realschule am Schloss Borbeck. Reul added that the suspect "had massive mental problems and suicidal thoughts", including recordings that could be seen as "an urgent call for help from a desperate young man". No bombs were found at the schools.

May 13, 2022: The *Florida Times-Union, DPA,* and *AP* reported that an Iraq-born man, 31, wounded five people with a knife on a regional train traveling near Aachen before he was overpowered by three passengers, including a police officer.

June 1, 2022: *DW* reported that the German federal prosecutor's office arrested German national Matthias B. in Röderaue in Saxony State, for belonging to a far-right criminal organization that sought to spread anti-Semitic and Nazi propaganda by selling books. His right-wing extremist criminal organization allegedly had store rooms stocked with thousands of texts. Authorities raided his home and that of three others. The group ran Der Schelm publishing house (translations include *the rogue, the knave, the imp*).

June 1, 2022: The state court in Celle convicted Romiena S., a German woman who took her daughter, 4, to Syria in 2014 against the wishes of the child's father, joined ISIS, successively married several ISIS members, and allegedly took advantage of an enslaved Yazidi woman, of membership in a terrorist organization, being an accessory to a crime against humanity, abducting a minor, and breaching her duties of welfare and education, sentencing her to three years and three months in prison. She raised her daughter and two Syria-born sons in line with ISIS ideology, taking the girl to the stoning of a woman when she was 6 and showing her execution videos. She exploited an enslaved Yazidi woman at the home of a slave trader for a few days and guarded her as she went into town. She tweeted support of terrorist attacks in Nice, France, and Wuerzburg, Germany, in 2016. In October 2021, authorities arrested her at Frankfurt airport when she arrived with other women and children repatriated from a camp in northeastern Syria where suspected ISIS members were held.

June 8, 2022: *ABC News, N-TV, ARD, ZDF,* the *Washington Post, Reuters, CNN, UPI, Der Spiegel, RBB24,* and *Insider* reported that at 10:30 a.m., a silver Renault Clio drove into pedestrians on the sidewalk of the popular Kurfürstendamm shopping district on Tauentzienstrasse in Berlin, killing a female teacher and injuring 30 others, eight seriously, before crashing into a storefront window of the Douglas drugstore. The *Washington Post* reported that Police Chief Anja Dierschke said that the injured belonged to a Bad Arolsen, Hesse State high school group traveling together. *Bild* quoted an investigator observing "by no means an accident–someone on the rampage, an ice-cold killer". Bystanders detained a German-Armenian dual national, 29, living in Berlin. Police soon arrested him; he was given medical treatment for his injuries. The incident took place near Breitscheidplatz in Berlin's Charlottenburg district, where 12 people were killed and nearly 50 injured when Tunisian ISIS jihadi Anis Amri drove a black truck into a Christmas market in 2016. *BBC* reported that authorities said the suspect is "severely mentally impaired" and gave "confused statements". Interior Minister Iris Spranger said posters were found in the man's car "in which he expressed views about Türkiye" but denied a *Bild* report that a letter of confession had been found in the car. *Reuters* and *Bild* reported that the driver lived with his mother and sister, and the car belonged to the latter. He became a naturalized German citizen in 2015. Spranger said he was earlier connected to incidents of bodily harm and trespassing.

June 10, 2022: *CNN* reported that students overpowered a man, 34, suspected of stabbing several people, injuring three women and one man, at Hamm-Lippstadt University of Applied Sciences in Hamm.

June 13, 2022: In a joint operation with Swiss authorities, police in Roemerberg, southwest of Heidelberg, detained Aleem N., a man suspected of having prepared a serious act of violence endangering the state and of membership in ISIS. The federal prosecutor's office said he had "long been a follower of jihadist and radical Islamic ideas". In mid-September 2020, he went to Türkiye en route to Syria, where he planned to join ISIS, receive military training, and participate in combat operations or terrorist attacks. However, he returned to Germany in late October 2020. Since April 2021, N. had conducted extensive ISIS propaganda activities, translating official ISIS Arabic texts, videos, or audio messages into German and to distribute them on *Telegram* in German-speaking countries.

June 15, 2022: *Der Spiegel, al-Jazeera, BR,* and *Reuters* reported that the trial in Munich began of Valid D., a Russian citizen charged with agreeing in 2020 to carry out the contract killing of Chechen dissident Mokhmad Abdurakhmanov, 27, on behalf of people linked to Ramzan Kadyrov, strongman ruler of Russia's autonomous Chechnya region. Federal Prosecutor Frank Stuppi said the planned murder was to intimidate into silence the victim's elder brother, Tumso, a Chechen independence activist living in exile in Stockholm. Tumso was the target of an assassination attempt in February 2020. Prosecutors said Valid D. obtained a gun with ammunition and a silencer and surveilled the area where the target lived. Police were tipped off and arrested Valid D. on January 1, 2021. The trial was expected to run into December 2022, with 39 hearing dates. Authorities said Valid D. selected a hitman, with whom he conducted shooting exercises.

June 16, 2022: *DW* and *DPA* reported that 550 police officers raided properties of suspected drug dealers and a neo-Nazi network in Thuringia, Schleswig-Holstein, and Berlin, arresting six people. One was arrested while on vacation in Greece. Fourteen individuals were suspected of money laundering. Police confiscated property worth €1.4 million ($1.48 million), cash, drugs, several cell phones, three functioning handguns, gas-powered and disabled weapons and objects with Nazi symbols. Four suspects were believed to be members of far-right factions of the Brotherhood Thuringia, which wear leather cuts similar to those of biker gangs.

July 15, 2022: The *Washington Post, AP, AFP,* and *DPA* reported that the Regional Court in Frankfurt am Main convicted German Bundeswehr First Lieutenant Franco Albrecht, 33, who registered in Bavaria as a Syrian asylum seeker named Benjamin David, of preparing a "serious act of violence endangering the state" against senior politicians and sentenced him to 5½ years in jail. He was arrested in 2017 after trying to retrieve a loaded Nazi-era pistol from a restroom in Vienna, Austria's airport. A cleaning lady had found the gun, and police staked out the site awaiting someone to come collect it. Prosecutors

said he planned to make terrorist attacks seem to be attributable to "radical Islamist acts of terrorism". The court added that he harbored "nationalist, right-wing extremist sentiments". He had hoarded a semiautomatic rifle, two semiautomatic pistols, more than 1,000 rounds of ammunition, more than 50 explosive devices, and five machetes (hidden under his mattress). Prosecutors added that some of the materiel had been stolen from German military stocks. Defense lawyers said the weapons were for defense of his three children in case of collapse of the state.

He was arrested in February 2022 en route from Strasbourg, France, with a box of Nazi memorabilia and notes that described the threats to the German nation from migration and intermarriage. He had listed cabinet ministers, MPs, and a prominent Jewish human rights activist as potential targets.

He was also convicted of weapons law violations and fraud.

His lawyers planned to appeal.

August 2, 2022: *Deutsche Welle* and *ZDF* reported that the trial in Frankfurt began of Marvin E., 20, aspiring carpenter and local politician, who was arrested in a police raid on his house in September 2021, for trying to launch a local branch of the neo-Nazi Atomwaffen Division terrorist group. He had stood as a candidate for Germany's mainstream conservative party. Police confiscated several handmade "unconventional" explosive devices, a racist manifesto, and material intended for a recruitment campaign. Authorities said he wanted to spark a "race war... to preserve the white population" by 2024. He was chairman of the Christian Democratic Union (CDU) in Spangenberg in Hesse State.

September 7, 2022: *Reuters* reported that a Duesseldorf court sentenced an unnamed ISIS member to ten years in prison for war crimes and murder committed in Syria, including the beating of a prisoner who later died in custody. He traveled from Germany to Syria to join ISIS in March 2014, later becoming a prison guard. He and three other men were ordered to punish a prisoner. He beat the handcuffed man, who was suspended from the ceiling by his hands tied behind his back. The victim died two days later.

October 8, 2022: *Der Spiegel, Swissinfo,* and *Reuters* reported that the state-owned rail operator Deutsche Bahn (DB) said that sabotage on cables was behind a nearly three-hour halt in all rail traffic through the states of Lower Saxony and Schleswig-Holstein and the city states of Bremen and Hamburg in northern Germany that morning. Cables for DB's communication network had been cut in two places. International rail journeys to Denmark and the Netherlands were also affected.

October 19, 2022: *Deutsche Welle* reported that officials believed arson was responsible for extensive damage to a shelter for Ukrainian refugees near Wismar in Mecklenburg-Western Pomerania State. No injuries were reported in the nighttime blaze. During the previous week, swastikas had been found on the shelter's entry sign. 22101901

October 28, 2022: At 5 a.m., a fire broke out in a former hotel outside Bautzen scheduled to be used to house refugee families from Syria, Afghanistan, and Russia, starting November 3. Anti-foreigner arson was suspected. Windows were broken. Four employees of the owner who were staying in the building were unharmed. The building had housed refugees between 2015-2017. *DPA* reported that in 2016, three young men threw Molotov cocktails over a fence toward the building.

November 18, 2022: The *Jerusalem Post* reported on November 27 that the Attorney General's Office in Düsseldorf announced that a German-Iranian man, 35, was arrested on suspicion of committing arson at a synagogue in Bochum on November 18. Bullet holes were found in at the door of a synagogue in Essen. A witness testified that he tried to convince him to attack a Dortmund synagogue on the same night of the attack in Bochum. The suspect was seen on security camera footage. In a search of his apartment and car, police confiscated his electronic devices.

December 5, 2022: *Reuters* reported that Duesseldorf closed Christmas markets in the city center after police received a threat against one of them. *Bild* reported that a caller had threatened to crash a truck into the market at the city hall.

A week earlier, Berlin police closed roads and stepped up security around the Alexanderplatz Christmas market due to a phoned-in threat. *Berliner Zeitung* reported that someone called police saying he planned to crash his car into the crowds of revelers.

December 7, 2022: The *Washington Post, BBC, DPA, AP, CNN, Reuters,* and *UPI* reported that authorities arrested 25 right-wing extremists suspected of plotting to use armed force to storm the Bundestag to violently overthrow the state. The public prosecutor said 22 were accused of membership in a "terrorist organization"; the other three, including a Russian national, were detained on suspicion of being supporters. Police searched the properties of another 27 individuals investigated on an "initial suspicion" of being a member or having supported the organization. More than 3,000 police officers were involved in the raids in 11 of Germany's 16 states. *The Week* and *New York Times* reported that 150 sites were raided and that suspects were also detained in Perugia, Italy and Kitzbuehel, Austria; Germany requested the extradition of the duo. Authorities seized guns, ammunition, tasers, night-vision goggles, crossbows, knives, combat helmets, swords, 100,000 euros, gold, silver, and an enemies list of 18 names, including Chancellor Olaf Scholz and Foreign Minister Annalena Baerbock. Police were investigating another 54 people.

The accused supported such conspiracy theories as QAnon and the Reichsbürger movement, which denies the existence of the modern German state, which they believe is governed by a "deep state". The group's central "council" was headed by Heinrich XIII P.R., whom German news media identified as Prince Heinrich XIII, 71, a descendant of the House of Reuss, a royal dynasty from the German state of Thuringia. Prosecutors said another leader was Ruediger v. P., 69, a former paratrooper. The prosecutor said "Since November 2021, the members of the 'Council' have regularly met in secret to plan the intended takeover of power in Germany and the establishment of their own state structures." Such "liberation" would be aided by intervention of the

"Alliance" secret society of military and governments, including those of Russia and the United States. The group's military arm included former members of Germany's armed forces. The group attempted to recruit members of the military and police.

The *New York Times* reported that the Reichsbürger movement apparently was founded by Wolfgang Ebel, a West Berlin railroad worker who was fired for joining a strike in the 1980s.

Der Spiegel reported that authorities raided the barracks of a unit of Germany's Special Forces Command (KSK) in Calw in the southwest.

Die Zeit reported that one defendant posted on *Telegram* that public prosecutors, judges and health authorities would "soon find themselves in the dock at Nuremberg 2.0".

Reich Citizen activists and members had joined protests against COVID-19 restrictions.

BBC and the *Daily Mail* reported that the group planned to establish a state "modelled on the Germany of 1871–an empire called the Second Reich".

The *New York Times* reported on December 9, 2022 that the detainees included a judge, a doctor, a cook, a pilot, a classical tenor, and three police officers. Fifteen had links to the military, including former or current soldiers and two reservists with access to weapons. Judge and former AfD parliamentarian Birgit Malsack-Winkemann was among those arrested.

December 11, 2022: *Reuters* and *Der Spiegel* reported that unknown attackers cut cables belonging to the Deutsche Bahn public railway near Essen.

December 12, 2022: Stephan Balliet, 30, a right-winger earlier convicted of murder and sentenced to life in prison after shooting two people to death at a synagogue in Halle on Yom Kippur in 2019, took two Burg Prison guards hostage during an attempted jailbreak. Other guards overwhelmed him. He was injured during the incident; the hostages were not. The prison is in Saxony-Anhalt near Magdeburg.

DPA reported that during his trial in 2020, Balliet tried to escape from another prison by climbing over an 11-foot-tall fence during a yard exercise.

GREECE

February 1, 2022: *Al-Jazeera, Skai Television, Kathimerini.gr,* and the state-run *AMNA* news agency reported that in the morning, two bombs exploded outside the residences of Greek journalist Dimitris Kambourakis and the head of the country's police union, Vasilis Doumas.

A security camera showed a hooded and masked figure placing an explosive device made of small cooking gas canisters outside the apartment building of Kambourakis in the southern suburb of Argyroupoli at about 2:30 a.m. The bomb set a door on fire. One of the canisters did not explode.

Simultaneously, a similar bomb went off in the central Athens district of Kypseli, outside the home of Doumas.

July 13, 2022: *Deutsche Welle* and *al-Jazeera* reported that a morning arson attack was suspected at the offices of the center-left *Real News* and *Real FM* in the *Real FM* building in Athens. *AFP* reported that firebombs were used. Some 18 firefighters needed two hours to extinguish the fire. Some people were hospitalized with respiratory problems. Investigators found three gas canisters taped together on an outside staircase between the basement and first floor of the building. Pundits suggested a connection with the ongoing hunger strike by the imprisoned anarchist Yannis Michailidis.

The broadcaster's transmission equipment was seriously damaged the previous day.

September 25, 2022: *News 360* and *Ethnos* reported that at 1 a.m., two masked individuals on a motorcycle threw Molotov cocktails at the Iranian embassy in the Psichiko neighborhood of Athens. The façade was not damaged. 22092501

December 2, 2022: *Reuters* reported that arsonists torched cars in the parking lot of the Italian deputy ambassador's home in Athens. One car was destroyed and a second sustained limited damage in the early morning attack. Italian Prime Minister Giorgia Meloni suggested that attack was "probably anarchist in origin". 22120201

December 12, 2022: *Ukrinform.net* and *NPR* reported that a blood-soaked package arrived in the morning at Ukraine's Embassy in Athens. The Ukraine foreign ministry said "The address of the sender is the same as on the rest of the envelopes that were previously sent to Ukrainian embassies and consulates: the Tesla car dealership in the German town of Sindelfingen." 22121202

Holy See

December 2, 2022: *Newsweek* reported that the entrance to the residence of the Ukrainian Ambassador to the Vatican was vandalized. 22120211

Iceland

September 23, 2022: *Reuters, Euronews, UPI,* and public broadcaster *RUV* reported that National Police and special forces conducted nine raids in Reykjavik and the suburban towns of Kopavogur and Mosfellsbaer, arrested four Icelandic men in their 20s (*UPI* said they were in their 30s) suspected of planning an attack using high-powered weapons against public buildings, including the Icelandic parliament and police, and seized semi-automatic firearms, ammunition, computers, cellphones, and other digital items. They were also suspected of trying to make guns using 3D-printers. Two men were released after questioning; two others were remanded in custody. State police superintendent Karl Steinar Valsson said investigators could not rule out links with foreign radical organizations.

Ireland

May 30, 2022: *AFP* reported that Judge Tony Hunt announced that three judges at the Special Criminal Court in Dublin found former soldier Lisa Smith, 40, guilty of membership in ISIS in Syria between October 28, 2015 and December 1, 2019. The trial of the Muslim convert from Dundalk had lasted nine weeks. She was acquitted of financing terrorism by sending €800 ($900) to aid medical treatment for a Syrian man in Türkiye. The court said that there was reason-

able doubt that she intended the money to be used for humanitarian purposes rather than to fund terrorism. A sentencing hearing was scheduled for July 11. Smith was a member of the Irish Defence Forces from 2001 to 2011. In 2012, she went on a hajj to Mecca, and expressed a desire on an Islamic *Facebook* page to live under Sharia law and to die a martyr. She bought a one-way ticket from Dublin to Türkiye, crossed into Syria, and lived in Raqqa. Her husband refused to join her, so she divorced him in 2016 and married a Briton involved in ISIS armed patrols. With ISIS territory collapsing, she fled to Baghouz. She had been held in the al-Hawl and Ain Issa refugee camps in northern Syria, then returned to Ireland, where she was arrested on arrival at Dublin airport on December 1, 2019 with her young daughter.

On July 22, 2022, *AFP* reported that Dublin's Special Criminal Court sentenced Lisa Smith to 15 months in jail. Judge Tony Hunt said that although she had shown no remorse, Smith was a low risk for reoffending. Three judges acquitted Smith on a separate charge of financing terrorism by sending €800 ($810) to aid medical treatment for a Syrian man in Türkiye. She was represented by attorney Michael O'Higgins.

October 30, 2022: *BBC* reported that at 9:30 a.m., a priest in his 30s was hospitalized after he was injured in an assault in Ardkeen in County Waterford. Irish broadcaster *RTÉ* reported that he was stabbed. Gardaí (Irish police) announced that a man in his 20s was arrested and was being held at Waterford Garda station.

Italy

January 7, 2022: *Business Insider* and *BBC* reported that immunologist Antonella Viola, one of Italy's top COVID-19 experts, said she and her family were threatened with a letter and a bullet in the mail after publicly calling for children to get vaccinated.

April 6, 2022: *The Daily Beast, Yahoo!, AGI, La Regione,* and *Newsweek* reported that at dawn, an arsonist attacked a lavish villa owned by Vladimir Putin's top propagandist and Russian state TV presenter Vladimir Solovyov, 58. The villa in Loveno Sopra Maneggio was undergoing full renovation thanks to COVID-19 bonus payouts for construction projects. It sits on the flanks of Lake Como. Italian officials had confiscated it as part of a campaign of economic sanctions. Firefighters said someone had thrown burning tires over the villa wall. Two of Solovyov's three properties—worth €8 million—are sequestered by Italy's financial police. 22040601

Yahoo! reported that soon after, police announced that a second villa he owns on the lake had been vandalized, with red paint spelling out "war" and "killer". Water in the pool was dyed red to look like blood.

October 27, 2022: The *Washington Post* and *UPI* reported that at 5:30 p.m., a man with a knife fatally stabbed a male supermarket employee and injured four others, including Arsenal central defender and Spanish citizen Pablo Mari, 29, who has been playing this season for Serie A side Monza, at a Carrefour grocery store in Assago, near Milan. The attacker, 46, was arrested. Three people were hospitalized in serious condition. Another was treated at the scene. The 6'4" Mari was walking with his wife and pushing his son in a shopping cart when he was stabbed in the back.

December 7, 2022: *Reuters* reported that police arrested in a hotel in Perugia a former German army officer, 64, connected to the far-right group suspected of preparing a violent overthrow of the state in Germany. Police found "material related to the subversive activity". Authorities initiated extradition procedures.

Kosovo

April 15, 2022: *USNWR* and *Reuters* reported that gunmen armed with a hand grenade and an AK-47 assault rifle attacked two police patrol cars in the morning near the Serbian border. No injuries were reported in the fourth attack in three days. Interior Minister Xhelal Svecla deemed it a terrorist attack aimed at intimidating police and Kosovo citizens.

September 19, 2022: *Reuters* and Tirana-based television *A2* reported that the government announced that Kosovo's intelligence agency had foiled a plot by an Albanian citizen to assassinate Prime Minister Albin Kurti in 2021 based on data published online by Iranian hackers.

Lithuania

January 10, 2022: *The Guardian* and *UPI* reported that Lithuania paid €100,000 ($113,500) to Guantánamo detainee Abu Zubaydah in compensation for having allowed the CIA to hold him at the secret Violet site outside Vilnius in 2005 and 2006. Three years earlier, the European Court of Human Rights ordered the Lithuanian government to pay compensation for violating European laws banning the use of torture. His legal team included Mark Denbeaux.

May 10, 2022: *The Hill* and the *Washington Examiner* reported that the Seimas (parliament) announced the unanimous adoption of a resolution in which it called Russia "a state supporting and carrying out terrorism", recognized Russia's actions in Ukraine as a genocide, urged that a special international criminal tribunal be established to look into Russia's actions in Ukraine, and called on international governments and organizations "to recognize and prosecute the genocide, war crimes and crimes against humanity committed by" Russia. The declaration said the war crimes with the intent to destroy the country included Russia's attacks against civilians in Bucha, Irpin, Mariupol, Borodyanka, and Hostomel.

May 18, 2022: *BBC* reported that Ireland extradited to Lithuania Liam Campbell, 59, from Upper Faughart, Dundalk to face charges related to weapons smuggling for the Real IRA. In 2009, Campbell was held liable for the 1998 Omagh bombing that killed 29 people. In earlier May 2022, the Irish Supreme Court dismissed an appeal, paving the way for his extradition. He was detained in Dundalk, County Louth, in December 2016 on a second European Arrest Warrant issued by Lithuania regarding preparation of a crime, illegal possession of firearms, and terrorism. The latter carries a 20-year sentence.

MOLDOVA

July 5, 2022: *Al-Jazeera* reported on July 29, 2022 that on July 5, Moldovan authorities received an e-mail indicating that bombs had been planted at more than 50 state institutions. Since then, more than 100 hoax bomb threats were sent to landmarks, including the Chișinău International Airport, parliament and government buildings, the Supreme Court, commercial centers, hospitals, and churches around the country. On July 18, prosecutors identified several bomb threat suspects within the country and abroad. Days later, the Organization of the Himmler-Kult Nationalist-Socialists Fighters called for military action in Transnistria and a stop to Moldova joining the EU and NATO.

August 19, 2022: Since early July, the country logged nearly 60 emailed bomb threats, including 15 in the previous week. Threats were made against Chișinău's city hall, the airport, the supreme court, shopping malls, and hospitals. The emails were traced to computer addresses in Russia, Ukraine, and Belarus. An August 15 bomb threat against a plane flying to the capital led air traffic controllers to send the plane back to Türkiye.

MONTENEGRO

August 12, 2022: *UPI, AP, BBC,* and *TV Vijesti* reported that Vuk Borilović, 34, used a hunting rifle to shoot to death 11 people, including a mother and her two children, aged 8 and 11. A civilian passerby shot him to death after Borilović shot at police officers. He first attacked a family of tenants living in his home, then shot at random people walking through the Medovina neighborhood in Cetinje, 22 miles west of the capital Podgorica. Zoran Brđanin, Director of Montenegro's police administration, told state media *RTCG* that six people, including a police officer, were injured.

NORTHERN IRELAND

March 25, 2022: *Reuters* reported that two gunmen hijacked and placed a suspect device—later deemed a hoax—in a van whose driver was ordered to drive to an event where Irish Foreign Minister Simon Coveney was speaking. Assistant Chief Constable Mark McEwan said pro-British loyalist militant groups were believed to have aimed at causing maximum disruption, adding, "The victim believed he was driving a van with a live bomb and that his family were being threatened. ... At this early stage of the investigation our assessment is that these crimes were carried out by loyalist paramilitary groups."

November 17, 2022: A homemade bomb damaged a police vehicle in Strabane; two officers inside were unharmed. The Police Service of Northern Ireland (PSNI) was treating the attack as attempted murder, possibly by the New IRA.

NORWAY

June 25, 2022: *CNN, UPI, ABC News, Business Insider,* and the *New York Times* reported that a 1:14 a.m. shooting at Oslo's London Pub gay bar, a second bar, and a fast-food restaurant killed two men in their 50s and 60s and injured 21, ten seriously. *Reuters* said that the arrested male suspect, a Norwegian citizen originally from Iran, was a radicalized jihadi with mental health issues. Norwegian news media reported that the suspect and his family left Iran for Norway in the 1990s when he was 12. Prosecutor Christian Hatlo said that the suspect was "known to the police" for "minor convictions". Police charged the suspect, 42, with "murder, attempted murder, and terrorist acts", basing the latter on the number of injured and dead people, the number of crime scenes, and an "overall assessment" that the accused intended to "create serious fear in the population".

The suspect was armed with two weapons. The *Washington Post* added that authorities raised the terrorist threat to its highest level. Roger Berg, head of the domestic intelligence and security service, said the attack was an act of "extreme Islamist terror".

Authorities canceled Oslo's annual Pride parade, which had been scheduled for hours later. The *New York Times* reported that hundreds of people participated in a march and rally near the club.

The London Pub calls itself Oslo's gay headquarters since 1979.

AP reported that the suspect had a prior narcotics offense and a weapons offense for carrying a knife. The Norwegian Police Security Service had been aware of him since 2015. Police seized a handgun and a "not modern" automatic weapon.

On June 27, *USNWR* and *Reuters* reported that a Norwegian court identified the suspect as Zaniar Matapour, who had been part of a network of Islamist extremists in Norway. He was represented by defense attorney John Christian Elden. *VG* reported that the suspect lived in Oslo, became a father, and for several years was on welfare.

POLAND

November 14, 2022: *Deutsche Welle* reported that a bomb threat was made against a Hungarian Airbus A321 carrying more than 200 passengers from Poland to the United Kingdom. The pilot made an unscheduled landing in Paderborn, Germany.

November 17, 2022: *News 360* reported that a Molotov cocktail was thrown at the Russian Embassy in Warsaw. 22111701

November 29, 2022: *Reuters* reported that a man who fired an automatic weapon at police died after being shot during a raid on his home in Straszyn, near Gdansk. Police spokeswoman Iwona Jurkiewicz said a police officer was injured. *PAP* reported that the shooter was suspected of having weapons and ammunition in his home.

December 4, 2022: *CNN* reported the low-cost British EasyJet flight EZY6276 bound for Bristol from Krakow, Poland was diverted to the Czech Republic following a report of a "possible bomb" on board. Prague Airport officials tweeted that the plane landed safely at 10:50 p.m. local time. No bomb was found.

December 14, 2022: *CNN* reported that at 7:50 a.m., Polish police chief Jaroslaw Szymczyk was hospitalized with minor injuries after a gift that he had received during a visit in Ukraine exploded in a room adjacent to his office. He visited Ukraine on December 11-12, meeting with the heads of the Ukrainian Police and Emergency Situations Service. The Polish government alleged the gift came from one of the heads of Ukrainian services. A member of the staff from the Police Headquarters suffered minor injuries. 22121402

ROMANIA

April 6, 2022: *Al-Jazeera, Newsweek, Reuters, AP,* and the *Washington Examiner* reported that at 6 a.m., a driver crashed his sedan into the gate of the Russian embassy in Bucharest. The car burst into flames, killing him. *AP* reported that the car carried containers of flammable materials. Romania had taken in 624,000 refugees since Russia's invasion of Ukraine on February 24. Hours earlier, Ukrainian President Volodymyr Zelenskyy had addressed the Romanian Parliament over video. Romania had expelled ten Russia diplomats. The Russian embassy said that no employees were harmed. *Tass* reported that Russian Ambassador Valery Kuzmin claimed that the embassy has "repeatedly" received e-mailed threats.

Newsweek and *Digi24* said Bogdan Drăghici, leader of TATA (Anti-Discrimination Alliance of All Dads), allegedly shouted at the security guards and set himself and the sedan on fire. TATA advocates for equal rights for mothers and fathers. *Digi24* reported that the previous day, Drăghici was sentenced to 15 years and four months in jail for sexually assaulting and raping his daughter, a minor.

December 6, 2022: *News 360* reported that the Ukrainian Embassy in Bucharest said it received several envelopes with suspicious contents. 22120601

RUSSIA

April 26, 2022: *Reuters* and *Interfax* reported that a gunman killed two children and a teacher and wounded another teacher before committing suicide in a kindergarten in Ulyanovsk region.

May 2, 2022: *Newsweek, Baza* (a *Telegram* news channel with links to Russian security services), *MediaZona*, and the Latvia-based Russian-language news outlet *Meduza* reported that during the evening, a man threw a Molotov cocktail at a riot police vehicle near the Karl Marx monument on Revolution Square in central Moscow. Two Russian security officials detained a Moscow man, 45, on a grassy area near the vehicle. The state-backed Russian news website *Life.ru* said he had previously disobeyed police officers and "held rallies".

August 20, 2022: *UPI, CNN,* the *Washington Post,* and *The Guardian* reported that a car bomb exploded at 9 p.m. in the Odintsovo district near the village of Bolshie Vyazyomy, on the outskirts of Moscow, killing Darya Dugina, 29, daughter of ultra-nationalist philosopher and Putin supporter Alexander Dugin. She was driving her father's Toyota Land Cruiser from a festival they both attended. They left in different cars. Russia's Investigative Committee said the bomb was planted under the bottom of the car on the driver's side. Ukraine denied responsibility, blaming "various political factions" in Russia.

Dugin helped shape Putin's expansionist foreign policy. The United States and UK sanctioned Dugin and Dugina for working to destabilize Ukraine. The U.S. sanctioned Dugin, on occasion called Putin's Rasputin and Putin's Brain, in 2015. The *Washington Post* cited U.S. officials who indicated that Dugin, as a leader of the Eurasian Youth Union, recruited individuals with combat experience to fight on behalf of the self-proclaimed Donetsk People's Republic. Dugin also controls *Geopolitica*, another propaganda website.

Dugina was chief editor of *United World International*, a Russian disinformation website. The UK Office of Financial Sanctions Implementation called her a "frequent and high-profile contributor of disinformation in relation to Ukraine and the Russian invasion of Ukraine on various online platforms". The U.S. Department of the Treasury's Office of Foreign Assets Control sanctioned her in March 2022; the UK, in July 2022. She was born in 1992 and studied Philosophy at Moscow State University.

Dugin's friend Andrey Krasnov, head of the Russky Gorizont (Russian Horizon) social movement, told *Tass* that he believed Dugin, who has no official position, was the target.

Metro reported on August 24 that the anti-Putin National Republican Army claimed credit. The FSB blamed Natalia Vovk, whom it claimed was a female Ukrainian spy.

September 14, 2022: The *Daily Mail, Newsweek,* and the *Mirror* reported an unconfirmed claim indicated that President Vladimir Putin's limousine was hit by a "loud bang" on its "left front wheel followed by heavy smoke". Putin was unharmed and the car drove away safely. His security service made several arrests. The *Mail* claimed that several other bodyguards vanished. The General SVR *Telegram* channel reported rumors that information about Putin's movements had been compromised.

September 26, 2022: *Reuters,* the *Washington Post, Tass, Business Outsider,* and *UPI* reported that Russian conscript Ruslan Zinin, 25, fired at least three shots inside a military draft office full of other potential draftees in Ust-Ilimsk in Siberia's Irkutsk region. Two military officials, one of whom had just delivered a pep talk to conscripts, were on stage. *The Guardian* reported that Zinin yelled "Nobody is going to go anywhere", "no one will go to fight", and "we will all go home now", then pulled his gun and shot office chief Alexander Vladimirovich Eliseev, a military commandant who also runs the local draft board in the Irkutsk region. Irkutsk regional governor Igor Kobzev wrote on *Telegram* that the draft office head was hospitalized in critical condition. Zinin was held on felony charges of endangering the life of a police officer and illegal weapons possession. The *Washington Post* reported that the gunman's mother, Marina Zinina, told *ASTRA* that he was distraught that his close friend had been called up despite having no military experience. President Vladimir Putin said in the upcoming partial mobilization, only experienced veterans would be tapped.

YA62.ru and the *Washington Post* reported that a man tried to self-immolate at a bus station in Ryazan, 115 miles southeast of Moscow, shouting that he did not want to fight in Ukraine.

He was not severely injured, and was led away by police and ambulance workers.

Arson was reported at a military enlistment office in Uryupinsk.

September 26, 2022: *NPR, NBC News, AP, ABC News, Tass, CNN, Reuters, UPI,* and the *Washington Post* reported that Artem Kazantsev, 34, born in 1988, wearing Nazi symbols, including a red swastika on his black t-shirt, shot to death 17 people, including 11 children, a school security guard, and two teachers, at School No. 88 in Izhevsk, which he had earlier attended. *AP* reported that he injured 24, including 22 children. The gunman, armed with two unregistered non-lethal handguns adapted to fire real bullets, then killed himself. Izhevski is the capital of the Udmurt Republic west of the Ural mountains. Regional government leader Alexander Brechalov said that Kazantsev was registered with a psycho-neurological clinic. He first shot the security guard, then walked into the school and fired at the children, some age 7. *Moskovsky Komomolets* reported that a seventh-grade boy jumped from a third floor window to escape, but broke his leg.

Police found ammunition clips with the word "hatred" in red paint. Two pistols near Kazantsev's body had braided cords with the words Columbine, Dylan, and Eric, referring to the 1999 Columbine school massacre in which 13 people were killed by Eric Harris and Dylan Klebold.

October 7, 2022: *News 360* and *Interfax* reported that the Federal Security Service (FSB) announced that it had dismantled a suspected ISIS cell about to attack transport infrastructure in the Stavropol region. Several cell members had Russian citizenship but were acting on the orders of "foreign logistical elements". The FSB seized "subversive components and elements purchased by them for the manufacture of an improvised explosive device (IED) and means of secret communication".

October 15, 2022: *Business Insider, Tass, Newsweek, Reuters,* and *RIA* reported that the defense ministry announced that during a firearms demonstration for volunteer soldiers at a military training center in Belgorod region's Western Military District, which shares a border with Ukraine, two volunteer soldiers from a former Soviet republic fired on their colleagues, killing 11 and injuring 15. The two shooters, who used small firearms, were killed at the scene.

The *Washington Post* and *Radio Ozodi*, RFE/RL's Tajik service, reported on October 29, 2022 that Russian authorities identified the shooters as

- Ehson Aminzoda, 24, who had worked as a bricklayer, then at a local restaurant, saving his income in hope of returning to his native Tajikistan to marry. On October 10, he was seen leaving the Lyublino subway station in southeast Moscow. He was not a Russian citizen and not eligible to be mobilized into the Army.

- Mehrob Rakhmonov, 23, also a Tajik immigrant

Human rights advocates suggested that the duo were dragooned into service. 22101501

November 24, 2022: *Reuters* and *Tass* reported that a gunman fired on people in a shopping district in Krymsk in Russia's southern Krasnodar region near the Crimean peninsula as he walked down a street, killing three. The gunman also died.

December 26, 2022: *Europa Press, Tass,* and *News 360* reported that the Russian Federal Security Service (FSB) Public Relations Center claimed that the FSB dismantled an ISIS-related group active in the Urals and North Caucasus that was transporting militiamen to Syria and Ukraine to fight against the Russian Armed Forces. FSB claimed it had arrested the organizer and ten others in the republics of Dagestan, Chechnya, in the Tyumen region or the Khanty-Mansi district and confiscated communication tools, photographs, and videos.

SLOVAKIA

October 12, 2022: The *Washington Examiner* and the *Times of Israel* reported that during the night, an extremist gunman killed two people, Matus H., 23, and Juraj V., 26, one of them a university student, and wounded a woman, Radoslava T., 28, in her leg outside Teplaren, a gay bar on Bratislava's Zamocka Street. The gunman, Juraj K., 19, was found dead the next morning near the headquarters of the Ministry of Education; police suspected suicide. He had used a gun with a laser sight, registered to a relative. He reportedly tweeted a manifesto against Jews and the LGBT community. *Reuters* reported that Special Prosecutor Daniel Lipsic suggested treating the hate crime as an act of terrorism. Prime Minister Eduard Heger called the shooter a "radicalised teenager". President Zuzana Caputova posted on *Facebook* that the shooting was a crime of hatred.

News 360 added on October 19, 2022 that Chief of Police Stefan Hamran told *JOJ Television* that the gunman had originally intended to kill Prime Minister Heger. The gunman had been in the area of Heger's home the same night.

Spain

November 24-December 1, 2022: The *Washington Post* and *Reuters* reported on December 1 that at least six pyrotechnic letter bombs were sent to various officials in Spain, including to the Ukrainian embassy in Madrid, the U.S. embassy, Prime Minister Pedro Sanchez's office, the defense ministry, the European Union satellite center located at the Air Force base of Torrejon de Ardoz, and the Spanish arms manufacturer Instalaza, maker of the C90 rocket launcher that Spain has supplied to Ukraine, in Zaragoza. Four of the devices were received on November 30 and December 1. The Ukrainian embassy letter bomb caused a minor injury to an embassy security officer; the other five were rendered safe by the security services. All the letters appeared to originate from inside the country and were designed to burn rather than explode. *El Pais* reported that the packages were addressed with the same handwriting. *Reuters* reported on December 3 that Spanish police said that the six letter bombs appeared to have been posted from the northern city of Valladolid. 22113001, 22119901

November 30, 2022: *CNN* and the *New York Post* reported that a bomb exploded at the Ukrainian Embassy in Madrid, slightly injuring a security officer who handled a letter where the bomb was believed hidden. Ukrainian Ambassador Serhii Pohoreltsev told the Ukrainian news site *European Pravda* that the suspicious package was addressed to him. The guard hurt his hands and suffered a concussion. 22113001

December 5, 2022: The *Kyiv Independent* reported that Spain's Foreign Ministry's spokesman Oleh Nikolenko said that Spanish police seized three envelopes allegedly containing animal eyes, which were addressed to Ukraine's embassy in Madrid, the Consulate General in Barcelona, and the Consulate in Malaga. 22120501-03

Sweden

January 4, 2022: The *New York Daily News* and the *Jerusalem Post* reported the Swedish Prosecution Authority charged a Swedish woman, 49, with war crimes for allegedly helping to recruit her then-12-year-old son to fight as a child soldier in Syria for ISIS between April 2013 and 2016, when they lived in Syrian territory previously controlled by ISIS. Prosecutor Reena Devgun said that the child was given weapons and military equipment and "was used in combat and for propaganda purposes and for other missions that formed part of warfare". *SVT* reported that the mother was a Muslim convert who returned to Sweden in 2020. Her husband died in Syria, as did two sons, aged 14 and 18. She was represented by attorney Mikael Westerlund. She faced a minimum sentence of four years. On March 4, 2022, *al-Jazeera* reported that the Stockholm district court found Swedish woman Lina Ishaq, 49, guilty "grave violation of international law and grave war crime" for failing to prevent her son Joan, 12, from becoming an ISIS child soldier in Syria, where he was killed in the civil war in 2017. She was sentenced to six years in prison. The son was born in 2001.

July 6, 2022: *AFP* reported that around 2 p.m., a woman was stabbed to death at the Almedalen Week (also known as Politicians' Week) political festival in Visby on the Swedish island of Gotland. Expressen reported that the male detainee, 32 or 33, was believed linked to the neo-Nazi Nordic Resistance Movement (NMR). The Swedish Association of Local Authorities and Regions (SALAR) announced that the victim was Ing-Marie Wieselgren, 64, a medical doctor and psychiatrist working as a project manager and coordinator with SALAR for Sweden's municipalities and regions. She was stabbed near where Centre party leader Annie Loof was scheduled to hold a news conference.

AP and *SVT* reported on July 11, 2022 that Sweden's domestic security agency SAPO was investigating the case as an act of terrorism. Swedish media identified the suspect as Theodor Engström, who confessed to the killing. In August, Loof was appointed a plaintiff's counsel. Prosecutor Henrik Olin said that Loof was the intended victim. Loof stepped down as party leader in September.

Reuters reported on November 1, 2022 that Swedish prosecutors indicted a man, 33, suspected of murdering a woman and planning to kill a senior politician with "terrorist crime through murder", and "preparation of terrorist crime through the preparation of murder". The accused had a history of mental illness.

Reuters reported that on December 6, 2022 a Swedish court found Theodor Engström, 33, guilty of murder and of "preparation of terrorist crime" and sentenced him to psychiatric care. Prosecutors said they suspected the man had also planned to murder Centre Party leader Annie Loof. Judge Per Sundberg of the Gotland district court said the attacker had mapped Loof's agenda.

August 21, 2022: *Reuters* reported that a police bomb squad disarmed a bag containing explosives that was found in a Stockholm park during the night.

December 1, 2022: *Moscow Times, RFE/RL's Russian Service,* and *Radio Svoboda* reported on December 5 that Chechen blogger Tumso Abdurakhmanov, 36, critic of Chechnya's strongman leader Ramzan Kadyrov, was shot to death nearly a week after he went missing. The Chechen opposition 1ADAT posted that "Tumso was shot at night by a group of people." Tumso had been attacked in his apartment by a hammer in Sweden in February 2020; he claimed it had

been ordered from within Russia. A Swedish court sentenced a man in that attack to 10 years in prison and a woman to eight years. Abdurakhmanov had been living in hiding in Sweden since 2019 after being denied asylum in Poland. He had lived in exile since 2015 to escape threats to his life in Chechnya. *Yahoo! News* and *The New Voice of Ukraine* reported that his brother, Mukhammad Abdurakhmanov, was under the protection of Swedish security forces.

While living in Grozny, capital of Chechnya, Abdurakhmanov worked as Deputy Director of the Federal State Unitary Enterprise Electrosvyaz.

December 2, 2022: *News 360* and *Reuters* reported that Swedish authorities extradited to Türkiye Mahmut Tat, a member of the Union of Kurdish Communities and the Kurdistan Workers' Party (PKK), considered by Ankara to be a terrorist organization. Türkiye had refused Sweden's admission to NATO, charging that it harbors individuals wanted for PKK membership. *Anatolia* reported that he had been sentenced to six years and ten months in prison in Sweden. He had applied for asylum in Sweden in 2015 due to his sentence, but was denied. Turkish state television *TRT* said Tat was sent to an Istanbul prison upon arrival.

SWITZERLAND

June 13, 2022: In a joint operation with German authorities, police detained three people suspected of ISIS membership and searched seven locations. The trio were detained in the cantons of Zurich, St. Gallen, and Lucerne.

September 1, 2022: Swiss police in Francophone western Switzerland arrested two people suspected of supporting or participating in ISIS. Authorities searched four houses in the Geneva and Vaud cantons. The case centered on a Swiss-Macedonian dual national and a citizen of Kosovo, who lived in the two Swiss regions.

TÜRKIYE

January 18, 2022: *Anadolu* reported that a nighttime explosion shut down a BOTAS pipeline near Pazarcik in Kahramanmaras Province, causing a huge fire. Authorities shut down a highway. No one was hurt. The pipeline brings oil from the Kirkuk oil fields in Iraq to the Turkish port of Ceyhan and on to world markets. Authorities were investigating the cause of the blast. Kurdish rebels had earlier bombed pipelines in the region, including the Kirkuk-to-Ceyhan pipeline.

April 20, 21, 2022: *Reuters* reported that a bomb hit a bus in Bursa Province, killing a prison guard. Interior Minister Suleyman Soylu blamed two banned far-leftist groups, MLKP and the DKP-BOG, linked to the PKK.

April 21, 2022: *Reuters* reported that an attacker placed a bomb in Istanbul's Gaziosmanpasa district outside the offices of a non-governmental organization. Interior Minister Suleyman Soylu told *NTV* that he blamed two far-leftist groups, MLKP and the DKP-BOG, linked to the PKK.

May 28, 2022: The *Jerusalem Post* and *Sözcü* reported that the Turkish judiciary released 29 Turkish Hizballah terrorists who were jailed for their role in the murders of 114 civilians in the Kurdish-majority city of Diyarbakir in the 1990s. One reporter said that they had apparently been released before the local elections in March 2019, but the media did not cover the story.

May 31, 2022: *Al-Jazeera* reported that Turkish racist Sakir Cakir kicked in the face Syrian refugee Leyla Muhammed, 70, in Gaziantep while she sat on a bench. Police arrested him for willful injury. Cakir said he had been told that Muhammed was a kidnapper. Muhammed is mentally disabled. Former Gaziantep parliamentarian Samil Tayyar tweeted that Cakir has an extensive criminal record. *Middleeasteye.net* reported that hundreds of Syrians and others posted photos of themselves covering one side of their face with their palm, imitating an image of Muhammed after the attack.

September 1, 2022: Gunmen fired seven bullets at an Istanbul building housing the headquarters of the Turkish soccer association during a board meeting. No injuries were reported.

September 26, 2022: *AP, Reuters, Anadolu,* the *Jerusalem Post*, and *News 360* reported that Interior Minister Suleyman Soylu told reporters that at 10:40 p.m., two suspected Kurdish gunwomen got out of a vehicle and shot at police guarding a hotel for security officers in the Mezitli district in Mersin Province, killing one policeman and wounding another police officer and a civilian woman who was sitting on a balcony near the scene. The terrorists, too seriously wounded in the ensuing gun battle to be able to escape, set off suicide bombs, killing themselves. The government blamed the PKK.

September 27, 2022: *News 360* and *Hurriyet* reported that Turkish anti-terrorism police detained 24 suspected ISIS members in Istanbul and Mersin Province. Police raided 14 locations in Istanbul, detaining 16 suspects preparing operations, and arrested another eight in Mersin. *Hurriyet* reported that police had investigated the Mersin group for the last six months for their propaganda activities and fundraising.

November 13, 2022: *CNN, UPI, Firat, Anadolu, AFP, NTV, A News, News 360, al-Jazeera, Reuters,* and the *Washington Post* reported that an explosion at a store on Istiklal Street in Beyoglu Square in Istanbul at 4:20 p.m. killed six and wounded 81. Turkish Vice President Fuat Oktay labeled it a terrorist attack. Police arrested 46 people, including Ahlam Albashir, a Syrian woman who was the main suspect; she had sat on a bench for 45 minutes, leaving just before the bomb exploded. The government blamed the PKK, which denied involvement. The government claimed the woman was trained by Kurdish rebels and that instructions for the attack came from Kobane (Ayn al-Arab), a majority Kurdish city in northern Syria that borders Türkiye. No one claimed credit.

Istanbul Governor Ali Yerlikaya identified the victims, all born in Türkiye, as Arzu Ozsoy and her daughter, Yagmur Ucar; Yusuf Meydan and his daughter, Ecrin Meydan; and Adem Topkara and his wife, Mukaddes Elif Topkara. Two girls, aged nine and 15, were killed.

News 360 reported on November 15 that police detained two more people. *TRT Haber TV* reported that 37 of the 48 suspects were foreigners, mostly Syrians. Authorities seized nearly $4,000, €5,000, 10,000 lira, and jewelry from the home of the main suspect.

The Hill and *Anadolu* reported that Interior Minister Süleyman Soylu accused the U.S. of being complicit in the bombing and rejected a U.S. statement of condolence.

The *LA Times* and *Anadolu* reported on November 17 that Turkish police during the night detained a suspect, identified only by his code name Husam, in an operation in Azaz, in a Turkish-controlled area in northwestern Syria. There were now 51 suspects in custody.

The Independent, Deutsche Welle, and *Anadolu* reported on November 18 that a Turkish court ordered 17 suspects jailed pending trial in connection with the bombing, accusing them of attempts against the unity of the state, deliberate killings, and attempts to kill. The court released three other suspects from custody pending trial and ordered the deportation of 29 people.

News 360, USNWR, Reuters, and *NOVA* reported on November 19 that Bulgarian authorities arrested another five suspects in the early morning. Three had Moldovan citizenship; a man and woman were of Syrian Kurdish descent. One was believed to be an accomplice of a right-winger wanted by Interpol for terrorism.

News 360 reported on December 7, 2022 that Interior Minister Suleyman Soylu said that the bomb was made "live" with the help of social networks and that Ahlam al-Bashir, a woman of Syrian origin whom the government accuses of being linked to the Kurdistan Workers' Party (PKK), received instructions from other members on "how to produce the bomb and where to place it". 22111301

November 21, 2022: Turkish officials blamed Kurdish Syrian Democratic Forces militants for firing two rockets across the border from Syria into Karkamis in Gaziantep Province, killing two people and wounding ten. One rocket landed near a school, smashing the window of a teachers' room, killing a teacher, 22. Another rocket hit a house, killing a boy, 5. A pregnant woman was hospitalized in serious condition. 22112101

Shelling by suspected Kurdish militants injured a soldier and seven Turkish police officers overnight in nearby Kilis. 22112102

November 23, 2022: *News 360* and *Anadolu* reported that the Turkish government said its Operation Sword Claw airstrikes since November 21 had hit 471 targets and "neutralized" 254 suspected members of the Kurdistan Workers' Party (PKK) and the People's Protection Units (YPG) in northern Iraq and Syria.

Ukraine

January 27, 2022: *Al-Jazeera, BBC, Syevodnya.ua, Newsweek,* the *New York Times, Business Insider, CNN,* and *UPI* reported that at 3:40 a.m., Ukrainian National Guard soldier Artemiy Ryabchuk, 21, fired his AK-47 assault rifle on security guards at the Pivdenmash missile factory (Yuzhny Machine-Building Plant Yuzhmash) in Dnipropetrovsk region, killing four soldiers and a civilian woman and critically wounding five other people, before fleeing. He attacked during a shift change, as weapons were being issued to the guards. Ryabchuk surrendered to police in Pidgorodne, outside of Dnipro. State news agency *Ukrinform* said that the plant partners with Ukraine's State Space Agency to produce rocket and airspace technology, including missile systems and space launch vehicles.

March 4, 2022: *Business Insider, Mail Online,* the *Daily Beast,* and *Newsweek* reported that the head of Ukraine's National Security Council, Oleksiy Danilov, said that President Volodymyr Zelensky survived three assassination attempts in one week thanks to tip-offs by anti-war intelligence officers in Russia's Federal Security Services (FSB). Danilov said on *Telegram* that two groups of assassins from Chechnya were involved.

March 9, 2022: *Newsweek* and *Ukrayinska Pravda* reported that Mikhail Podolyak, head of the office for the President, said that President Volodymyr Zelensky had survived over a dozen assassination attempts since the beginning of the Russian invasion.

August 17, 2022: The *Jerusalem Post* and *Reuters* reported that Sergei Aksyonov, the top official in Russian-annexed Crimea said that the FSB security service had broken up a six-person terrorist cell of the banned Hizb ut-Tahrir Islamist group, a day after explosions rocked one of Russian occupation forces' military bases in Mayskoye in Crimea's Dzhankoi district.

United Kingdom

February 16, 2022: *UPI* reported that a court sentenced Greek-born eco-terrorist Nikolaos Karvounakis, 35, to eight years and four months in prison for planting a bomb in Edinburgh, Scotland's Princes Street Gardens, a popular tourist district, four years earlier, apparently motivated by the Mexico-based International Terrorist Mafia eco-terror group. The device failed to explode. He was radicalized online. The bomb contained an obscene message and 58 nails. He pleaded guilty and received a lesser sentence. He was to be on the UK's counter-terror list for 15 years.

April 18, 2022: Canada's *National Post* and *Reuters* reported that at 8:50 a.m., British police closed a road near 10 Downing Street and tasered and arrested a man, 29, armed with a knife who had confronted two Ministry of Defense police officers at Horse Guards Parade, a ceremonial parade ground which overlooks St. James's Park. He was held at a central London police station on suspicion of attempted murder and possession of an offensive weapon.

April 22, 2022: *Al-Jazeera* reported that Manchester Crown Court sentenced UK citizen Thomas Leech, 19, of Preston, who had pleaded guilty to inciting terrorism against Jews and Muslims, to two years in a young offenders' institution. He had posted a "call to arms", said the Holocaust was a hoax, and lauded Anders Breivik and Brenton Tarrant. Leech was given a 12-month extended license period to be applied on completion of his prison sentence, plus 10 years on the sex offenders register, a 10-year Sexual Harm Prevention Order, and a 10-year notification requirement under Part Four of the Terrorism Act 2008.

May 4, 2022: *Business Insider* reported that former pub landlord Tarek Namouz, 42, faced eight charges at the Old Bailey of funding a terrorist organization, sending thousands of pounds of taxpayer-funded COVID-19 "bounceback" loans to ISIS in Syria between November 2020 and May 2021. The *Guardian* reported that he also faced two counts of possessing terrorist information relating to videos. The *Times* reported that authorities seized suitcases of cash suspected to have come from bounceback loans that people tried to smuggle out of the country. The UK government spent £47 billion on bounceback loans.

May 17, 2022: The *Evening Standard* reported that officers from the Metropolitan Police Counter Terrorism Command detained a boy, 13, in west London on suspicion of sharing Islamist terrorist material. He was released on bail until mid-June.

August 11, 2022: The *Washington Post, UPI*, and *al-Jazeera* reported that British police at Luton Airport arrested Aine Lesley Junior Davis, 38, a member of the four-person ISIS Beatles group that grew up in west London and tortured, starved, and killed hostages in Syria, after Turkish authorities deported him. The Crown Prosecution Service charged Davis with offenses since 2014 under the Terrorism Act, soliciting funds for a terrorist purposes, and possession of a firearm for a purpose connected with terrorism. Türkiye had arrested him in 2015 and convicted him in 2017 for membership in a terrorist organization. He had been imprisoned for seven and one half years. He appeared in Westminster Magistrates' Court. U.S. investigators said the ISIS Beatles beheaded 27 hostages from the U.S., UK, Europe, New Zealand, Russia, and Japan, including American journalists James Foley and Steven Sotloff.

Two ISIS Beatles, Alexanda Kotey, 38, and El Shafee Elsheikh, 34, are imprisoned in the United States. Their leader, Mohammed Emwazi, alias Jihadi John, died in a U.S.-U.K. drone strike in Syria in 2015.

In 2014, Amal el-Wahabi, Davis's wife, became the first person in the UK to be convicted of funding ISIS after trying to send €20,000 ($25,000 at the time) to him in Syria. She was jailed for 28 months and seven days.

AFP reported on August 17, 2022 that British police released extensive information on their probe of the ISIS Beatles that began in 2012.

October 30, 2022: *Deutsche Welle, al-Jazeera, UPI, AP,* and *Reuters* reported that at 11 a.m., a white man in a striped top threw three gas-filled plastic bottles from his white SEAT SUV at a Border Force migrant processing center in Dover, the main arrival port for migrants crossing the English Channel from France in boats. He had taped fireworks to the bottles before lighting the Molotov cocktails. Two people were slightly injured and an exterior wall was damaged. One of the petrol bombs did not go off. A *Reuters* photographer said that the attacker drove to a nearby petrol station near the Viaduct in Dover, tied a noose around his neck, attached it to a metal pole, and drove off, killing himself. Police found another explosive device in his vehicle.

November 16, 2022: *BBC* reported that MI5 head Ken McCallum announced that there were 10 potential threats by Iran to kidnap or kill British or UK-based people since January 2022. In addition, since 2017, MI5 and the police had disrupted 37 late-stage terrorist attack plots, including eight in 2022, which involved jihadis and extreme right-wingers.

LATIN AMERICA

ARGENTINA

September 1, 2022: *CNN, Reuters, Washington Post, TV Publica, UPI, TN Argentina, NBC News, AFP,* and *CBS News* reported that at 9 p.m., a gunman pointed his five-shot .380 handgun and pulled the trigger inches away from the face of Argentine Vice President Cristina Fernández de Kirchner, 69, near her home in Buenos Aires's upscale Recoleta neighborhood after she had exited her car, but the gun jammed. She was President from 2007 to 2015 and faced corruption charges, accused of fraudulently awarding public works contracts to Austral Constructions in her political stronghold of Patagonia and defrauding the state out of $1 billion. The attorney had succeeded her late husband, Nestor Kirchner, as president. She became vice president in 2019. Hundreds of people had gathered in front of her home.

Police arrested a Brazilian, 35, identified by *Télam* as street vendor Fernando Andre Sabag Montiel. *CNN* reported on September 3 that he was arrested on March 17, 2021 for "improper use of a weapon" by carrying a large knife in public. He had a weapons permit. He had a tattoo with Nazi symbols. Migration office officials told *CNN* he was born in São Paulo, Brazil, on January 13, 1987, and had lived in Argentina since 1993. His girlfriend, Ambar, said in a live interview on Argentine national television that he was a "good, hard-working man". He was assigned a public defender.

UPI reported that the Argentinian Football Association suspended three matches in the AFA's First Division—Patronato vs. Union, Rosario Central vs. Talleres, and Lanus vs. Tigre.

AFP and *Télam* reported that police at a train station on September 4 arrested Brenda Uliarte, 23, under a warrant issued by the magistrate in charge of the investigation. Video footage showed the Argentinian with Sabag Montiel on the day of the attack. Fernández de Kirchner's lawyers said he "didn't act alone". Uliarte had told local television channel *Telefe* that she had been living with Sabag Montiel for more than a month but had not seen him in the two days before the incident. Fernández de Kirchner's lawyer wanted authorities to interview "Mario", who had identified himself as Sabag Montiel's friend since they were teenagers but had not seen him in 10 months.

BBC reported that on September 7, Judge María Eugenia Capuchetti charged Fernando Sabag Montiel and Brenda Uliarte with attempting to kill Vice-President Cristina Fernández de Kirchner.

Al-Jazeera reported on September 14, 2022 that on September 12, authorities arrested a third suspect, Agustina Diaz, in Buenos Aires suburb San Miguel. Information about her was found on the mobile phone of the partner of alleged gunman Fernando Sabag Montiel. Diaz was believed to be a close friend of Uliarte.

The year continued to go poorly for de Kirchner. *CNN* reported that on December 7, 2022 a court sentenced her to six years in prison and disqualified her from holding public office again after finding her guilty of "fraudulent administration" during her presidential terms from 2007 to 2011 and 2011 to 2015.

BRAZIL

June 5, 2022: *CNN* and *UPI* reported on June 9, 2022 that British journalist Dom Phillips, 57, and indigenous affairs expert Bruno Araújo Pereira, 41, were reported missing on a boat in the Itui and Itaqui rivers in the São Rafael community in the Javari Valley in the far western part of Amazonas State near the border with Colombia and Peru. They were due to return to Atalaia do Norte. Days earlier, they had received death threats. On June 7, Brazilian authorities in the São Gabriel riverine community detained a suspect found in possession of "a lot of drugs" and ammunition used for illegal hunting. *AP* reported on June 10 that the family of fisherman Amarildo da Costa de Oliveira, alias Pelado, claimed that he was innocent and police were torturing him into a false confession. His mother said that blood that police found in her son's boat was likely from a pig he had slaughtered a few days earlier. Federal Police were analyzing human matter found in the Itaquai River, near

Atalaia do Norte's port. *CNN* reported police also questioned five other suspects. The *Guardian* reported that illegal hunting and fishing gangs were suspected.

AP reported on June 12, 2022 that divers from a local firefighter corps found a backpack and laptop in a flooded area where the duo went missing. The backpack was tied to a half-submerged tree. Indigenous volunteers found a tarp that had been in the boat used by the missing men and a T-shirt that belonged to Pereira.

On June 13, 2022, *USNWR*, *G1*, and *Reuters* reported that Phillips's wife told the media that two bodies were found. *Al-Jazeera* reported that Brazilian police and an Indigenous search group dismissed the claim that the bodies were found. The Brazilian ambassador to the UK apologized to Phillips's family for the miscommunication.

BBC reported on June 14 that Brazilian police arrested a second suspect, Oseney da Costa de Oliveira, alias Dos Santos, 41, on suspicion he was involved in the case with his brother, Amarildo da Costa de Oliveira. *Reuters* and *TV Globo* reported on June 15 that police sources said that the two suspects confessed. *Band News* reported that one suspect had confessed. The *Washington Post* reported that the confessor, fisherman Amarildo da Costa de Oliveira, reportedly threatened Pereira. *CNN* added that Amarildo da Costa de Oliveira indicated where the bodies had been buried. Federal Police representative Eduardo Alexandre Fontes said police found to-be-identified human remains.

BBC noted on June 18, 2022 that Brazilian police announced that Phillips and Pereira were shot to death with hunting ammunition (Phillips by one bullet; Pereira by three) and that a third suspect, Jeferson da Silva Lima, alias Pelado da Dinha, turned himself in at a police station in Atalaia do Norte.

BBC and *O Globo* added on June 19 that eight people had become suspects. The new five allegedly helped to hide the bodies.

September 24, 2022: *News 360, O Globo,* and *O Povo* reported that a man stabbed to death Antônio Carlos Silva de Lima, 39, a supporter of former president and presidential candidate Luiz Inácio Lula da Silva after he expressed sympathy for the Workers' Party (PT) leader at a bar in Cascavel in Brazilian Paraná State. The attacker escaped. He had yelled, "Who is a Lula voter here?" When a man responded "Me!" he was stabbed. *News 360* added on September 27 that police arrested Edmilson Freira da Silva, 59, in the case. The Civil Police of the State of Ceará attributed the motive to political issues. *O Povo* said he had a criminal record for physical injuries due to gender violence. The victim left behind a son, 10.

October 23, 2022: *BBC* reported that Brazilian politician Roberto Jefferson, 69, former leader of the PTB political party and ally of far-right President Jair Bolsonaro, threw grenades at police officers who came to his house in Levy Gasparian in Rio de Janeiro State to arrest him. Two officers were wounded. He also fired several shots from a rifle, shattering the window of a police car. He surrendered and was placed into custody. Supreme Court Judge Alexandre de Moraes had ordered his detention for insulting Chief Justice Carmen Lucia. Jefferson was under house arrest for threatening her.

October 26, 2022: *News 360* reported that death threats were made against former Brazilian President Luiz Inácio Lula da Silva. A day after he won the first round of the elections, he received an e-mail warning that he would be shot at the headquarters of the Lula Institute in Sao Paulo.

October 28, 2022: *News 360* reported that a gunman shot to death Reginaldo Camilo dos Santos, 51, aka Zezinho, who had run for federal deputy in the October 2 elections as a member of the Workers' Party (PT), in Jandira municipality, Sao Paulo State. The three shots were fired from inside a vehicle very close to his home. He had received 9,000 votes, not enough to win. In 2020, he ran for mayor of Jandira, finishing third. He served as a councilman. The gunman shouted "Bolsonaro", Zezinho responded "Lula", and the shots were fired.

November 13, 2022: *News 360* and *O Globo* reported that an individual fired ten shots into the headquarters of the Brazilian newspaper *Rondoniaovivo* in Porto Velho, Rondônia State. No injuries were reported. The paper had been threatened by the extreme right for gathering information on the activities of coup and anti-democratic groups that do not accept the victory of Luiz Inácio Lula da Silva in the elections of October 30.

November 25, 2022: A former student, 16, armed with a semiautomatic pistol and a revolver and wearing a swastika pinned to his vest killed three teachers and a student and wounded 12 at a public school with elementary and middle school students and a private school in Aracruz in Espirito Santo State. Police said he had been planning the attacks for two years. He used to study at the public school. He drove his family's car to the scenes and hid the license plate with a cloth. He was wearing a bulletproof vest. He entered the teachers' lounge in the public school by breaking a lock. The semiautomatic weapon belonged to the military police; the revolver was registered to his father, a military police officer. The student had received psychiatric treatment.

December 12, 2022: The *Washington Post* reported that supporters of defeated President Jair Bolsonaro attacked federal police headquarters in Brasilia during the night. Police prevented their entry into the building. The Supreme Court accused detained Indigenous activist and Bolsonaro supporter José Acácio Serere Xavante of having "expressly summoned armed people to prevent the certification of elected" officials.

December 24, 2022: *CNN* and *Folha de Sao Paulo* reported that police at Brasilia International Airport arrested gas station manager George Washington de Oliveira Sousa, 54, on suspicion of planting and possessing explosive devices one week ahead of president-elect Luiz Inácio Lula da Silva's inauguration. He told police that he intended to "create chaos" "to prevent the establishment of communism in Brazil" and "provoke an intervention of the armed forces" so a "siege state in the country" would prevent Lula from officially succeeding incumbent President Jair Bolsonaro in office on January 1. Bolsonaro had not conceded the October 30 election.

Police seized an explosive device found by a truck driver in a tanker truck close to the airport, plus a rifle, two shotguns, revolvers, more than 1,000 pieces of ammunition and five explosive devices in the suspect's rented apartment in Brasilia. Sousa said he was inspired by far-right President Bolsonaro to spend over $30,000 to purchase the arms. Sousa arrived in Brasilia from his home state of Para on October 12 to join other Bolsonaro supporters.

Al-Jazeera added that Lula had served two terms as president from 2003 to 2010.

Sousa's initial lawyer was Wallison dos Reis Pereira, who was replaced by Jorge Chediak, who claimed Sousa's confession to police contained "contradictions".

The *Independent* added that incoming Minister of Justice Flavio Dino said that election-denying protesters camping outside army bases in Brazil have become "incubators of terrorism".

CHILE

October 20, 2022: *Reuters* and *Radio Biobio* reported that Chile's police found and defused a bomb placed in eastern Santiago in an area comprised of corporate buildings in the wealthy business district of Las Condes. Local media reported that the bomb was in a building housing offices of the Empresas Copec industrial group.

COLOMBIA

January 2, 2022: *Al-Jazeera* reported that Defence Minister Diego Molano announced that fighting between the National Liberation Army (ELN) and Revolutionary Armed Forces of Colombia (FARC) Martin Villa 10th Front dissidents killed 23 people in Arauca near the border with Venezuela.

January 7, 2022: *AFP* reported that at least 11 Colombian police officers of the Mobile Anti-Riot Squad were wounded, three seriously, in a bomb attack against their truck in Cali. No civilians were reported injured. *Reuters* added that the ELN claimed credit for injuring 13 ESMAD officers in the 9:55 p.m. attack. General Jorge Vargas, the country's seniormost police official, said Colombia offered a 1 billion peso reward for information regarding El Rolo, the leader of the ELN's urban front, and 350 million pesos for information concerning those who planned and

executed the attack, said the country's top police official. The two rewards total around $334,000.

January 14, 2022: *The Guardian* reported that gunmen shot to death indigenous Nasa activist Breiner David Cucuñame, 14, while on patrol with the Indigenous Guard, an unarmed group which seeks to protect indigenous lands from incursions by armed groups. The Association of Indigenous Councils of Northern Cauca (ACIN) said that Cucuñame was accompanying his father when he and two other Guard members were killed in an ambush. Indigenous authorities blamed FARC dissidents.

January 28, 2022: *Al-Jazeera* reported that gunmen attacked a convoy of the United Nations Office for Humanitarian Affairs (OCHA) and the Norwegian Refugee Council travelling to the rural area of Guayabero to meet with communities in southeastern Colombia, forcing people from their vehicle, burning two of the three vehicles, but causing no injuries in Puerto Nuevo, in a rural area of Guaviare Department. Senior presidential adviser Emilio Archila said that the "criminals presented themselves as dissidents" of former FARC rebels under the command of Gentil Duarte. 22012801

February 23, 2022: *Reuters* reported the ELN blew up a bridge, torched vehicles, blocked roads, and set off bombs that injured eight people during the first day of a three-day "armed strike" to protest the government's economic and social policies. The ELN destroyed a bridge in Pailitas in Cesar Province, halting traffic. In Santander Province, a bomb on a road between Socorro and San Gil injured eight people. A bombing in Cucuta, capital of Norte de Santander Province, killed a police explosives dog. ELN torched vehicles on the road connecting Popayan and Cali.

February 24, 2022: *Reuters* reported that the armed forces killed 23 FARC dissidents in a bombardment by planes and helicopters in the municipality of Puerto Rondon in Arauca Province near the Venezuelan border. Defence Minister Diego Molano said Jorge Eliecer Jimenez, alias Arturo, the FARC dissident commander in Arauca, was killed. His group had battled with the ELN for control of drug trafficking in the region

March 26, 2022: *Reuters* reported that explosives went off at a police station in a working-class neighborhood of southern Bogota during the night, killing two children—Ivanna Rangle, 5, and Daniel Stiven Duque, 12—and injuring 39 others. Colombian President Ivan Duque blamed former FARC dissidents. National police director General Jorge Luis Vargas said preliminary investigations indicated that the attack was ordered by dissident leader John Mechas. Mechas took responsibility in 2021 for ordering both an attack against Duque's helicopter and a car bombing at a military base in Cucuta.

April 19, 2022: *Al-Jazeera* and *Blu Radio* reported that around midnight, a bomb killed six Colombian soldiers and wounded five soldiers from the Fourth Brigade as their vehicle was passing by. One soldier went missing. Gulf Clan cartel drug traffickers were suspected of the attack in the Antioquia department.

May 2, 2022: *Reuters* reported that former April 19 Movement (M-19) guerilla and Bogota mayor Gustavo Petro, 62, leftist front-runner in Colombia's May 29 presidential election, canceled events scheduled for May 3-4 in the coffee region and Manizales due to an assassination plot by La Cordillera criminals.

May 10, 2022: *BBC, AFP,* and *El Tiempo* reported that two gunmen shot to death high-profile Paraguayan prosecutor Marcelo Pecci, 45, who fought against organized crime in his home country, during the sixth and final day of his honeymoon on the tourist island of Baru near Cartagena. Hours earlier, his wife, journalist Claudia Aguilera, had announced on *Instagram* that she was pregnant. She said the gunmen arrived via boat or jet ski. The couple was staying at the Decameron Hotel. Pecci specialized in cases involving organized crime, drug trafficking, money laundering, and terrorist financing.

On June 4, 2022, *Reuters* and *BBC* reported that Colombian President Ivan Duque announced that Colombian authorities in Medellin arrested five suspects in the murder. *Reuters* reported on June 17 that four people who confessed were each sentenced to 23 years and six months in prison. Colombian authorities said

that Brazilian prison gang First Capital Command (PCC), a major exporter of cocaine, was involved in coordinating the murder. Authorities also suggested that the murder could be connected to international drug trafficking and "radical terrorism". A fifth person pleaded innocent; a sixth remained at large. The full sentence of 47 years was halved as part of a plea deal. Colombian Attorney General Francisco Barbosa said that the organizers of the murder allegedly paid $500,000 for the killing.

Al-Jazeera reported on November 17, 2022 that the U.S. Department of State offered a $5 million reward for information on anyone involved in the murder of Pecci.

May 26, 2022: *BBC* reported that police in Bolivar killed Juan Castro, alias Matamba, a fugitive who had escaped from Bogota's La Picota maximum-security jail. He had walked out of his cell dressed in a prison guard uniform. He led the Cordillera Sur splinter of the Gulf Clan drug cartel and was expected to be extradited to the U.S. on charges of drug trafficking. A prison officer suspected of providing the uniform and leaving the cell door open was arrested.

June 10, 2022: *Reuters* reported federal prosecutors in Brooklyn announced that Colombia extradited to the U.S. Martin Perez, alias Richard, who led FARC's 30th Front from 2011 to 2014, to face drug trafficking charges. The group shipped thousands of kilograms of cocaine to the United States and elsewhere, earning millions of dollars. Perez was arrested in Colombia in 2014. He was arraigned before U.S. Magistrate Judge Vera M. Scanlon on six criminal counts, including international cocaine distribution.

June 13, 2022: *Al-Jazeera* reported that President Ivan Duque announced that a military operation killed FARC dissident leader Leider Johany Noscue, alias Mayimbu, in mountainous terrain close to Suarez municipality in Cauca Province. He was accused of murdering soldiers and community leaders, including the 2019 murder of a mayoral candidate in Suarez in Cauca Province, kidnapping, extortion, and cocaine trafficking in alliance with Mexican cartels. The government had offered a reward of $256,000 for information regarding his location. His group was accused of attacking local environmental activist Francia Marquez, the running mate of left-wing presidential candidate Gustavo Petro.

June 19, 2022: *CNN* reported that former M-19 guerrilla Gustavo Petro, 62, won just barely more than 50 percent of the votes in the presidential election, becoming the country's first leftist leader. Vice Presidential running mate Francia Marquez became the first Afro-Colombian to hold executive powers. Petro had lost two presidential tries in 2010 and 2018. His M-19 nom-de-guerre was Aureliano Buendia, taken from Gabriel Garcia Marquez's magical realism classic, *One Hundred Years of Solitude.*

June 21, 2022: Seven former members of FARC's last secretariat admitted to the Special Jurisdiction for Peace that FARC was responsible for war crimes, including the kidnapping of thousands of civilians for ransom and holding politicians as hostages for several years in the hopes of exchanging them for imprisoned rebels. Rodrigo Londoño, FARC's last commander, said that the kidnappings only required that hostages not be killed without the FARC leadership's approval. Londoño admitted that some hostages were tied with chains to trees, or held within barbed wire fences. Some female hostages were sexually abused. Londoño testified, "In the name of our revolutionary ideals we committed war crimes and crimes against humanity… For years we condemned hundreds of human beings to live in inhumane conditions and to suffering that had a lot of impact on their families." The hearing also included five kidnapping survivors who demanded that the former rebels discuss several high profile cases, including the 2002 kidnapping of 12 members of the Valle del Cauca state assembly, who were held for five years. In 2007, eleven of those hostages were executed in a remote jungle camp. Sigifredo Lopez was the only survivor. "The sons and daughters of my colleagues want to know who are the people who shot them… There are people who have not been able to grieve over the bodies of their brothers or their parents."

July 8, 2022: *BBC* reported on July 11 that Colombian forces attacked a rebel camp in Caquetá region run by Nestor Vera, alias Iván Mordisco, leader of the Armando Rios front, a FARC breakaway faction, killing six men and four women members of the dissident group. The Air Force bombed the camp before 300 soldiers and police of Operation Jupiter moved in. Vera assumed command of the 2,000 fighters previously led by Gentil Duarte, who was killed in Venezuela in May 2022. *AFP* reported on July 15 that Defense Minister Diego Molano announced that Colombian forces had killed Vera in an air force-led raid on July 8. A reward of $700,000 had been offered for information on Vera's whereabouts. He was the first FARC leader to reject the peace process in 2016. His group was battling for control over the drug trade with FARC splinter Segunda Marquetalia, led by former FARC chief Ivan Marquez, who was hospitalized after a recent attack in Venezuela.

July 17, 2022: *News 360* and *Radio Caracol* reported that Colombian authorities announced that special forces of the National Police and the Army supported by Judicial Police and Intelligence conducting an operation against a house in the Largo neighborhood of Tibú in the Catatumbo sub-region of Norte de Santander killed Roque Antonio González Contreras, alias Roque, leader of the 33rd Front of the Residual Armed Group (GAO) splinter of FARC dissidents. Authorities seized a pistol, ammunition, and a cell phone.

July 28, 2022: *News 360* and *El Espectador* reported that Colombian Police General Jorge Luis Vargas announced that FARC 33rd Front dissidents, led by Javier Alonso Velosa, alias John Mechas, offered a reward of up to 7 billion Colombian pesos—more than €1.56 million—for an attempt against President Iván Duque. Police said the group also offered up to 2,000 million Colombian pesos—about €446,000—for a hit on Minister of Defense Diego Molano or high-ranking members of the Armed Forces. Police said Mechas was behind the attack against Duque in Cucuta in May 2021, plus two incidents in Cucuta and Bogota, that killed two and wounded more than 70. Colombian authorities believe Mechas was sheltering in Venezuela.

July 29, 2022: *News 360* and *El Espectador* reported the death of Vladimir Herrera, a FARC signatory of the peace agreements in 2016. The Colombian Ombudsman's Office tweeted that authorities found Herrera's body next to that of Jaime León Rodríguez, who had been held in the department of Arauca by an illegal armed group two weeks earlier. The Office said, "We request the release of nine people being held, who are part of the group in which the two victims were." The hostages included several minors, former combatants, and local peasants. Herrera was the 28th FARC alumnus killed in 2022, and the 334th signatory killed since the 2016 signing of the treaty.

August 17, 2022: *News 360* reported that the ELN released five members of the Colombian Army—two non-commissioned officers and three soldiers—and a police officer who had been kidnapped between July and August 2022. The ELN told *El Tiempo*, "We welcome the willingness of the new Government, of President Gustavo Petro, to recognize the previous commitments made by the Colombian State with the ELN, to respect the agreed protocols, to recognize the legitimacy of our delegation of dialogues, to guarantee the political and legal measures that allow the resumption of the talks, in the search for peace with transformations and social justice."

The former hostages were Jovan David Rudas and José Ángel Yate, kidnapped on June 6; Milton Moreno and Mauro Muñoz, on June 25; and Sherman Santana and Gustavo Anacona, on August 13.

August 20, 2022: *News 360* reported that Colombian President Gustavo Petro announced that he would suspend arrest and extradition warrants against the chief negotiators of the ELN involved the peace talks between the government and the guerrillas. He added, "I invite those who are part of the so-called self-defense groups to initiate a similar path and jointly deliver this region to peace."

August 25, 2022: *Al-Jazeera* reported that Defence Minister Ivan Velasquez announced that the new government suspended aerial bombings against armed groups, in an effort to protect child soldiers forcibly recruited by the rebels.

September 2, 2022: *BBC,* the *New York Times,* and *Reuters* reported that police officers en route to an afternoon social welfare event in San Luis in Neiva municipality in Huila Department hit a road mine in Corozal and then were fired on. Seven police officers were killed; the youngest was 18. An eighth officer was badly injured and hid in the forest before police found him and brought him to a hospital. Colombia's *Blu Radio* blamed guerrilla groups operating in the area. FARC dissidents are active in Huila.

September 12, 2022: *News 360* reported on October 9, 2022 that 139 social leaders had been killed in 2022. Some 1,366 were killed since the 2016 signing of the Peace accords, according to Indepaz. Gunmen shot to death Nancer Barrera Herrera, president of the Junta de Acción Comunal (JAC) in the Cerro Negro village, Baraya municipality, Huila department, at his farm, also killing farmer Carlos Andrés Arias Rodríguez.

The Attorney General's Office said that ELN and FARC splinters operated in the area.

September 26, 2022: Jesús Alberto Bautista, president of the Junta de Acción Comunal de la verdad Agüita Alta, Muzo municipality, Boyacá department, was murdered.

October 9, 2022: *News 360* and Colombian radio station *RCN* reported on October 11, 2022 that Revolutionary Armed Forces of Colombia-People's Army (FARC-EP) dissidents had released three people, including the governor of the indigenous reservation of San Andrés de Pisimbalá, Weimar Pencué, who was freed thanks to the actions of the indigenous guard. During the night of October 9, gunmen forced Pencué onto a motorcycle. The indigenous guard searched between Inzá and Páez.

The International Committee of the Red Cross (ICRC) reported the release of two people who were being held by the Carlos Patiño Column of the FARC in Cauca Department.

October 19, 2022: *News 360* reported Staff Sergeant Ramiro Cruz and Lance Corporal Jairo Velasco Medellín of the Rural Special Forces

Battalion N1 died in clashes between the army and FARC dissidents in a rural area of the Araucanian municipality of Puerto.

October 23, 2022: *News 360* and *W Radio* reported that two gunmen on a motorcycle seriously wounded former FARC combatant Juan Antonio Castro, a signatory of the peace treaty with the government, at his Tibú home in Norte de Santander.

November 17, 2022: *News 360* reported that President Gustavo Petro named Otty Patiño, political scientist and former M-19 guerrilla, to serve as the Government's chief negotiator in the peace talks with the ELN.

November 19-20, 2022: *Reuters* reported that Defense Minister Ivan Velasquez announced that 18 people died in fighting between two FARC dissident factions for control of a drug trafficking area in the southern jungle in a rural area of Putumayo Province, bordering Ecuador and Peru.

Government negotiators resumed peace talks with ELN rebels.

November 22, 2022: *Al-Jazeera* reported that the Colombian government and the ELN, Colombia's largest remaining rebel group, began new peace talks in neighboring Venezuela aimed at ending nearly 60 years of conflict. Pablo Beltran led the ELN delegation. ELN leader Israel Ramírez Pineda said the group aims to make "fundamental changes."

News 360 and *Semana* reported that during the night, FARC dissidents kidnapped Army Corporal Duván Arley Prado Moreno and Private Fabián Andrés Zambrano Hurtado in Palmichal village in Briceño municipality in Antioquia region. They were freed the next day.

November 28, 2022: *News 360* reported that authorities freed 18 young people who were being held in Tolima, in the southern Pacific region, by the Iván Ríos column of the Segunda Marquetalia, one of the main dissident factions of the FARC.

December 4, 2022: *Al-Jazeera* reported that President Gustavo Petro said Colombia reached an agreement with the left-wing National Liberation Army (ELN) rebel group to allow the Indigenous Embera community to return to its lands in the departments of Choco and Risaralda in western Colombia.

News 360 reported that the Carlos Patiño Front of the Revolutionary Armed Forces of Colombia (FARC) killed a non-commissioned officer and two professional soldiers and wounded two other soldiers in a rural area of the village of El Plateado in Argelia in Cauca department. The deceased soldiers were third corporal Andrés David Aguilar, from Tierralta, Córdoba, and professional soldiers Dubán Alfonso de Oro and Hair Domínguez Narváez, from Soledad, Atlántico, and Buesaco, Nariño, respectively.

December 7, 2022: *Al-Jazeera* reported that FARC dissidents armed with grenades, bombs, and guns killed six Colombian soldiers, aged 18-20, in Cauca region.

GUANTÁNAMO BAY

January 11, 2022: The *Washington Post* reported that the Periodic Review Board approved for transfer five detainees held at the Guantánamo Bay military prison in in Cuba, including a "high-value" prisoner suspected of having been a key figure in al-Qaeda's East Africa franchise. Attorneys identified the five men as Guled Hassan Duran, Moath al-Alwi, Suhail al-Sharabi, Zakaria al-Baidany, and Abdulmalik Bajabu. None had been charged with a crime.

- Moath al-Alwi, a Yemeni, garnered international attention when the John Jay College of Criminal Justice in New York displayed an exhibition of his and other detainees' artwork in 2017.

- Zakaria al-Baidany, a Yemeni whom the government refers to as Omar Mohammed Ali al-Rammah, was represented by attorney Beth Jacob. The U.S. government said he "held a key role in al-Qaida linked plans to conduct explosives operations in Georgia and Chechnya".

- Abdulmalik Bajabu, a Kenyan, was accused of belonging to East Africa al-Qaeda. He was among the last five detainees to arrive at Guantánamo, after his 2007 arrest by Kenyan authorities.

- Guled Hassan Duran, a Somali and key member of the East Africa al-Qaeda branch, was represented by attorney Shane Kadidal. He was captured in Djibouti in 2003.

- Suhail al-Sharabi, a Yemeni, was accused of belonging to al-Qaeda and serving as a bodyguard to Osama bin Laden.

Khaled Qassem, a Yemeni, was not cleared, despite that the review board noting his "low level of training and lack of leadership in al Qaida or the Taliban. However, the Board remains concerned in light of the following factors: The detainee's susceptibility to reengage due to his inability to manage his emotions and actions, the detainee's high level of significant non-compliance in the past year, and the detainee's lack of plans for the future if transferred." Qassem's attorney Clive Stafford Smith said his client had made two suicide attempts.

February 4, 2022: The *Washington Post* and *New York Times* reported that a Periodic Review Board recommended the repatriation of detainee Mohammad al-Qahtani from Gitmo to his native Saudi Arabia for participation in an extremist rehabilitation program. His attorneys claimed he was suffering from severe mental illness when he arrived at Gitmo two decades earlier. Al-Qahtani allegedly developed schizophrenia after suffering a traumatic brain injury. He joined al-Qaeda and was believed to have been slated to become the 20th 9/11 hijacker. He tried to enter the U.S. on August 4, 2001, but was sent back to Saudi Arabia after being questioned by Customs and Border Protection officials. Psychiatrist Emily Keram evaluated him in 2016 and determined that his confinement led to post-traumatic stress disorder which could not be treated at Gitmo. He was represented by attorneys Ramzi Kassem and Shane Kadidal.

On March 8, 2022, *BBC* and *CNN* reported that the U.S. announced that Guantánamo Bay Saudi detainee Mohammed al-Qahtani, 46, was repatriated to Saudi Arabia after a review board determined that he no longer posed a "significant threat" due to his "significantly compromised mental health condition". The review board said he must participate in Saudi Arabia's Prince Mohammed Bin Nayef Centre for Counselling and Care for treatment for jihadis, where he could receive comprehensive mental health care. American authorities believed that he was meant to be on board United Airlines Flight 93, but he had been prevented from entering the U.S. in August 2001. He was captured in December 2001 on the Afghanistan-Pakistan border and brought to Gitmo in February 2002. The *New York Times* reported that a psychiatrist told a U.S. court that his treatment in detention had aggravated a childhood brain injury and schizophrenia that he developed as an adolescent. He had refused psychotropic medication and repeatedly tried to kill himself in recent years.

April 2, 2022: *UPI* and the *New York Times* reported that the United States sent Sufiyan Barhoumi, who had been held at Guantánamo Bay since his capture in Pakistan in 2002, back to his home country of Algeria. The Periodic Review Board deemed him eligible for repatriation in 2016. He was initially held because he was believed to be a jihadi bombmaker working in the Punjab area of Pakistan. A court later ruled that the Pentagon had no jurisdiction over charges of providing material support to terrorism, a civilian offense. He was represented by attorney Shayana Kadidal of the Center for Constitutional Rights.

April 22, 2022: *Al-Jazeera* reported that former Guantanamo detainee Mohamedou Ould Slahi, 51, was suing Canada for 35 million Canadian dollars (US$28 million) over its alleged role in his imprisonment. He was held for 14 years without trial. He claimed Canadian authorities gave the U.S. false information concerning when he was a permanent resident in Montreal in 1999. He complained of "physical beatings, sleep deprivation, forced standing, incessant noise, sexual assault, mock assassination, death threats, religious humiliation, and more". He was arrested in 2001 in Mauritania, then held in prisons in Jordan and Afghanistan before being jailed in 2002 in Guantánamo. He was released in 2016.

June 12, 2022: The *New York Times* on June 12, 2022 ran a collection of newly-released photos of Gitmo prisoners.

Coincidentally, the same day *BBC* ran a long report on how Gitmo alumni were doing after release, featuring Yemeni Mansoor Adayfi, now 39, who was resettled in Belgrade, Serbia in July 2016 after 14 years in Gitmo. He published a memoir, *Don't Forget Us Here*, in 2021. He was represented by attorney Beth Jacob of New York, who had represented nine Gitmo detainees pro bono. He remained in touch via *WhatsApp* with more than 100 fellow Gitmo alumni, including Yemeni Sabry al-Qurashi, who was released after 12 years to Semey, Kazakhstan in 2014. Al-Qurashi married remotely in 2015 to a woman in Yemen. Fellow detainee Asim Thahit Abdullah al-Khalaqi died of kidney failure four months after arriving in Semey, Kazakhstan. Lotfi Bin Ali, who could not get treatment in Semey for a heart condition, died in 2021 after being deported to Mauritania. Abu Bakker Qassim, 52, a Uighur resettled in a suburb of Tirana, Albania, had similar experiences. Zakir Hasam, an Uzbek detained in Guantánamo from 2002 to 2006, also went to Albania. Qassim and Hasam both married and have children (Hasam's two children are autistic.). Qassim's friend and fellow former detainee, Ala Abd al-Maqsut Mazruh, released in 2005, died from COVID-19 in early 2022 in Albania, which cut off financial assistance to his wife Hatiche and their three young children.

June 13, 2022: Abd al-Hadi al-Iraqi, 60-ish, an Iraqi man who has been held at Gitmo for more than 15 years, pleaded guilty before a military commission to war crimes for his role in al-Qaeda attacks against U.S. and allied forces along with civilians in Afghanistan in 2003-2004 as a commander for al-Qaeda and the Taliban; sentencing was postponed until 2024. A deteriorating spinal condition left him partially paralyzed. He claimed his true name is Nashwan al-Tamir. He was arraigned at Guantánamo in 2014. He pleaded guilty to four of five charges against him, including conspiracy and several violations of the international laws of war. He had faced life in prison. He was expected to be transferred to a third country via his plea agreement. Prosecutors said he was a senior figure in al-Qaeda since the mid-1990s, leading a training camp for operatives in Afghanistan. The military said he helped the Taliban with the March 2001 destruction of

the giant, sixth century sandstone Buddha statues built into a cliff in Bamiyan Province. The *New York Times* reported on November 13, 2022 that the U.S. military sent a surgical team to Gitmo to consider emergency spine surgery on al-Iraqi, who had undergone several other spinal operations.

June 24, 2022: *AFP* reported that the Taliban claimed that the U.S. had released Afghan detainee Asadullah Haroon, circa 40, after 15 years. His refugee family lives in Peshawar, fleeing the Soviet invasion in 1979. Haroon was sent to Qatar. He was arrested by American forces in 2006 while working as a honey trader. He was transferred to Gitmo in 2007, accused of being a courier for al-Qaeda and being a commander with Hezb-i-Islami.

October 29, 2022: *NPR* and *al-Jazeera* reported that the U.S. released to his native Pakistan Saifullah Paracha, aged 74 or 75, the oldest inmate of the Gitmo detention facility, after nearly 20 years of detention without trial. He was arrested in 2003 in Thailand, accused of financing al-Qaeda. The U.S. approved his release in May 2022, indicating he was "not a continuing threat" to the U.S. Paracha had studied in the U.S. and ran an import-export business supplying major U.S. retailers. He was accused of contact with Osama bin Laden and Khalid Sheikh Mohammed. In 2008, his lawyer said Paracha met bin Laden in 1999 and 2000 regarding the production of a television program.

GUATEMALA

July 30, 2022: *News 360, Prensa Libre,* and *Sonora Radio* reported that gunmen fired on the motorcade of President Alejandro Giammattei in the village of La Laguna, Jacaltenango, in Huehuetenango. He was not harmed. The Army said a vehicle approached military units and shots were fired. Authorities responded, wounding Carlos José López Velásquez, 27, a Mexican and alleged member of the armed group. The other vehicle occupants fled 30 kilometers away to Mexico, where local armed forces detained four Guatemalans. Army spokesman Ruben Tellez clarified that "The incident occurred in a distant security post, but in the direction of where the president was."

December 5, 2022: *News 360* reported that the body of human rights activist Tereso Carcamo Flores, 41, was found in a ditch and covered in a sheet in Jalapa, in the southeast. He was an activist in the indigenous and peasant movement and a member of the Committee for Peasant Development (CODECA). *Radio Victoria* reported that his father, Eusebio Carcamo, confirmed the death of his son in the hamlet of El Volcán, village of La Paz, in the Jiménez sector. Carcamo left behind a wife and five children, three of them minors.

HAITI

January 1, 2022: Haitian Prime Minister Ariel Henry fled Gonaïves where he and other government officials were attending a New Year's Day Mass to mark the country's independence from France, after a shootout killed one person during a possible assassination attempt. His office claimed that "bandits and terrorists" put soldiers behind walls to shoot at his convoy and threatened the bishop by surrounding the Cathedral of St. Charles Borromeo where the Mass was taking place. *Le Nouvelliste* reported that two people were wounded. The attack prevented Henry from giving a speech. Local media reported that gangs had warned Henry against attending the Mass.

April 29, 2022: Dominican newspaper *Listín Diario* and *BBC* reported on May 2 that Dominican Republic officials believed that the 400 Mawozo gang was responsible for the kidnapping of Carlos Guillén Tatis, the trade attaché at the Dominican embassy in Port-au-Prince, while he was travelling by road to Jimaní, a city across the border in the Dominican Republic. Dominican Ambassador Faruk Castillo said the kidnapping occurred in the Croix-des-Bouquets area, east of the capital. Local media reported that the gang demanded a $500,000 ransom. The *Washington Post* reported on May 4, 2022 that that Guillén was freed in May.

Meanwhile, the Haitian National Police announced that Germine Joly, alias Yonyon, head of the 400 Mawozo ("400 simpletons" or "400 inexperienced men" in Creole) kidnappers of Guillén and 17 American and Canadian missionaries associated with the Ohio-based Christian Aid Ministries charity in 2021, was extradited to the United States on May 2. He had been running the gang from his jail cell. After two months in captivity, the missionaries were freed—they said they had escaped—after payment of a ransom. A warrant issued by the U.S. District Court in D.C. charged Joly with conspiracy and the kidnapping for ransom of U.S. citizens. Recent clashes between the 400 Mawozo and rival Chen Mechan killed 26 people, including a family of eight.

The *Washington Post* added on May 4 that the U.S. attorney's office for the District of Columbia on May 3 charged Joly, a U.S. citizen, and two Haitians based in Florida with 28 counts, including conspiracy to violate export control laws and to defraud the United States, violating export control laws, money laundering, and smuggling. He appeared virtually before Magistrate Judge Robin M. and was remanded into custody.

The three Florida-based defendants were arrested in October and November and pleaded not guilty. Prosecutors said, "Specifically, certain of the firearms and ammunition were wrapped in garbage bags, loaded into large multi-gallon drums/barrels, and then covered with various products such as clothes, shoes and Gatorade to hide the presence" from September to November 2021. Haitian police posted on *Facebook* that a warrant issued by the U.S. District Court in D.C. charged Joly with kidnapping U.S. citizens for ransom.

The *Washington Post* reported on May 10 that a federal grand jury in Washington indicted Joly, 29, on charges of conspiracy to commit hostage-taking for his alleged role in the kidnapping of 16 American missionaries with an Ohio-based charity in 2021.

The *Florida Times-Union* and *AP* reported on May 11, 2022 that Joly was arrested in Jamaica in January 2022 with his wife and two sons. He was represented by attorney Donahue Martin.

May 9, 2022: *BBC*, the *Washington Examiner*, the Dominican Republic newspaper *El Día*, and Haiti's *Standard* newspapers reported that the 400 Mawozo gang kidnapped 17 passengers from a tourist bus in Croix-des Bouquets outside Port-au-Prince. Eight are Turkish missionaries who had crossed into Haiti from the Dominican Republic, another eight are Haitian, and the driver is from the Dominican Republic. 22050901

October 25, 2022: *Al-Jazeera* reported that popular journalist Roberson Alphonse, who works at the daily newspaper *Le Nouvelliste* and radio station *Magik9*, was shot in his car while on his way to work in Port-au-Prince. He underwent two operations.

Authorities found the body of Garry Tess, a journalist who hosted a political talk show in Les Cayes. He had been missing for several days.

October 28, 2022: *CNN* reported that during the night, gunmen shot to death Eric Jean Baptiste, leader of the Rally of Progressive National Democrats Party (RNDP), a minor political party in Haiti, outside his home in Port-au-Prince. A guard also died. Baptiste ran for president as a longshot in 2016. Baptiste sustained a bullet wound in a 2018 assassination attempt.

November 14, 2022: *CNN* and *Reuters* reported that the U.S. Department of State announced that "Armed individuals fired shots at the Haitian National Police vehicles, US Embassy vehicles, and Haitian commercial vehicles this morning." A Haitian commercial driver was slightly injured. No embassy staff were hurt. One local media report blamed the 400 Mawozo gang. 22111401

November 25, 2022: Gang violence was suspected when Harington Rigaud, director of Haiti's National Police Academy, was shot and killed inside an official police vehicle at the doors of a police training facility in a Port-au-Prince.

Martinique

March 24, 2022: *Reuters* and the *National Post* reported that French government ministers said that security staff at a hospital were attacked with acid, attributing the attack to anger over government policies and COVID-19 protocols. French Health Minister Olivier Veran and Overseas Territories Minister Sebastien Lecornu said the next day, "Yesterday morning, during a meeting between the new hospital chief Jerome Le Briere and hospital trade unions, around thirty demonstrators tried to disrupt the meeting, with six security staff getting acid thrown onto their faces."

Mexico

March 19, 2022: During the night, three masked gunmen broke into a home in Tijuana hosting a party. They robbed partiers, but when Mexican lawyer and Indigenous rights activist Patricia Rivera Reyes demanded her cell phone back, a gunman shot her in the head. A man was hospitalized with a gunshot to the head.

May 23, 2022: *UPI* reported that 15 hooded gunmen arrived in two trucks and fired more than 50 shots at the Gala Hotel and two adjoining bars in Celaya, killing 11 and injuring others during the night. They then threw homemade bombs that set the facilities on fire.

August 12, 2022: Prosecutors in the State of Mexico announced that a Cuban doctor, a nurse, and a woman who had been visiting a relative undergoing treatment were shot to death in a hospital in the Ecatepec suburb. President Andrés Manuel López Obrador's administration had announced plans to hire more than 500 specialized Cuban doctors to work when Mexican doctors are unavailable, or in dangerous or remote areas where they do not want to work, including the western states of Nayarit and Colima. The victim's sister identified the doctor in *Facebook* as Ernesto Oliva Legra. Prosecutors in the State of Mexico said two gunmen entered the hospital in the early morning and asked for a female patient at the reception desk. The gunmen then forced the receptionist to open the door to a second-floor medical area, where they opened fire. 22081201

September 1, 2022: Gunmen in two vehicles shot people gathered in the nighttime after a soccer match in Yecapixtla, killing four people, including former mayor Refugio Amaro Luna, 57, and wounding eight others.

October 5, 2022: The *Los Angeles Times* and *Milenio TV* reported that gunmen killed Mayor Conrado Mendoza and his father, himself a former mayor, and 16 other people and wounded two other people at City Hall in San Miguel Totolapan township in Tierra Caliente in Guerrero State.

Later that day, two gunmen riding a motorcycle shot to death state lawmaker Deputy Gabriela Marín, a member of the Morelos Progress party, as she exited a vehicle in front of a pharmacy in Cuernavaca in Morelos State. A person with her was wounded.

December 3, 2022: *Reuters, Reforma,* and *El Universal* reported that judge Roberto Elias was shot as he was leaving his Zacatecas home in the morning, hospitalizing him with serious injuries.

December 15, 2022: *Reuters* reported that during the night, two gunmen on a motorcycle shot at television and radio presenter Ciro Gomez Leyva as he was driving his car some 200 yards from his home. He survived because of his vehicle's armor, and broadcast his Friday morning radio show the next day.

PARAGUAY

October 23, 2022: *BBC* reported that Osvaldo Villalba, 39, leader of the violent leftist Paraguayan People's Army (EPP) rebel group, which has carried out a string of killings and kidnappings in rural Paraguay, was killed in a clash with soldiers on patrol in Amambay Province. The soldiers discovered that the rebels had killed two indigenous people and wounded another. In a shootout, they killed three rebels, including Vilalba.

Osvaldo was the younger brother of Carmen Villalba, an EPP founder currently serving a lengthy jail sentence for the attempted murder of three police officers during a foiled jailbreak in 2004. Also killed in the clash was Luciano "Luchi" Argüello, an EPP member whose two brothers Jonny and Benicio, also EPP members, were found shot dead two years ago.

The EPP still held former Vice-President Óscar Denis, who was kidnapped in September 2020; Félix Urbeita, a rancher it kidnapped in 2016; and police officer Edelio Morínigo, seized eight years earlier in Concepción Province.

PERU

November 3, 2022: The *Independent* reported on November 5 that a group of indigenous community leaders in Cuninico released 248 tourists, including U.S. and U.K. nationals, after holding them on their riverboat since 10 a.m. on November 3 in protest against the government after more than 40 oil spills in the area. The hostages included pregnant women, a one-month-old baby, and elderly people. Hostages included 228 Peruvian citizens, among them Angela Ramirez. Community leader Wadson Trujillo told national outlet *TVPeru Noticias* "Our very punctual request is that the government declares a state of emergency due to the constant oil spills in our territory, and a committee presided by the president is then commissioned."

VENEZUELA

March 28, 2022: Human Rights Watch charged that Venezuelan National Guard soldiers conducted joint operations with the Colombian National Liberation Army (ELN) against Joint Eastern Command (former FARC) rebels in Apure State earlier in 2022, kidnapping civilians from villages and battling for control of the drug trade.

May 25, 2022: *U.S. News and World Report* and *Reuters* reported that Colombia's Defense Minister Diego Molano told journalists that the leader of a FARC dissident faction, Miguel Botache Santillana, alias Gentil Duarte, was believed killed in Zulia State, Venezuela in a clash with drug trafficking and terrorist groups.

MIDDLE EAST

March 10, 2022: *Reuters* reported that ISIS announced the appointment of Abu al-Hassan al-Hashemi al-Quraishi, brother of slain former caliph Abu Bakr al-Baghdadi, as its new leader. *Al-Jazeera* added that this was the first time that ISIS had admitted that the previous ISIS emir, Abu Ibrahim al-Hashimi al-Qurayshi, blew himself up in a U.S. raid of his hideout in Atmeh, Syria, on February 3. The statement was issued by the group's new spokesman, Abu Omar al-Muhajer. The al-Qurayshis are not believed to be related. The term al-Qurayshi comes from Quraish, the name of the tribe that Islam's Prophet Muhammad belonged to. *AFP* added that ISIS adherents "pledged allegiance" to "Abu Hasan al-Hashemi al-Qurashi as an emir over believers and the caliph of Muslims".

April 6, 2022: The *Independent* and *AP* reported that al-Qaeda's *as-Sahab Media* wing released a video of Ayman al-Zawahiri praising Muskan Khan, an Indian Muslim woman who defied a ban on Islamic headscarves in Karnataka State, India. In February, large groups of people wearing saffron scarves to symbolize their fealty to the Hindutva ideology heckled Muslim students wearing hijab, yelling "hail lord ram". Al-Zawahiri hailed the "noble woman of India" and "a sister". "May Allah reward her for showing a moral lesson to sisters plagued by an inferiority complex via-a-vis the decadent Western world."

May 6, 2022: The *Independent* and *AP* reported that al-Qaeda leader Ayman al-Zawahiri issued a 27-minute video marking the 11th anniversary of the death of Osama bin Laden. He said, "Here (the U.S.) is after its defeat in Iraq and Afghanistan, after the economic disasters caused by the 9/11 invasions, after the Corona pandemic, and after it left its ally Ukraine as prey for the Russians." He was shown sitting at a desk with books and a gun.

November 30, 2022: *AP, Fox News, Reuters,* and *CNN* reported that the ISIS media affiliate *al-Furqan* ran an audio by ISIS spokesman Abu Omar al-Muhajer announcing the death in recent battle of ISIS emir Abu al-Hassan al-Hashimi al-Qurayshi, whose predecessor, Abu Ibrahim al-Hashimi al-Qurayshi, died in a February 2, 2022 U.S. raid. CENTCOM reported that he was killed in a raid in Dar'a Province in October by the Free Syrian Army. The spokesman observed "He died fighting the enemies of God killing some of them before being killed like a man on the battlefield," and was succeeded by Abu al-Hussein al-Husseini al-Qurayshi, variant Abu al-Husain al-Husaini al-Quraishi, "one of the veteran warriors and one of the loyal sons of the Islamic State".

The *Jerusalem Post* and *Reuters* reported that Abu al-Hassan al-Hashimi al-Qurayshi blew himself up with a suicide belt when cornered in Jasem in southern Deraa Province.

December 23, 2022: *Reuters* and *USNWR* reported that al-Qaeda released a 35-minute undated recording it claimed was narrated by Ayman al-Zawahiri, who was believed to have been killed in a U.S. raid in August 2022.

AFGHANISTAN

January 10, 2022: *Al-Jazeera* reported that a cart selling food hit a mortar shell in Baiganan village in Lalopar district in Nangarhar Province, killing nine children and wounding four others.

January 22, 2022: *Reuters* and the *Jerusalem Post* reported that an explosion went off at 6 p.m. under a public transport minivan in Herat, killing six people and wounding nine, three seriously. *Reuters* added on January 24 that ISIS-K took credit in a *Telegram* post.

February 7, 2022: *Newsweek* and *al-Jazeera* reported that the U.S. Department of State's Rewards for Justice Program offered a $10 million reward for information regarding the location Sanaullah Ghafari, alias Shahab al-Muhajir, who was appointed to lead ISIS-K in June 2020. The State Department labeled him a Specially Designated Global Terrorist in November 2021.

Reuters added that the reward was also offered for information that would help arrest or convict individuals responsible for the August 26, 2021, ISIS-K suicide bomb attack at the Kabul airport, which killed 13 U.S. troops and at least 170 Afghans. U.S. Central Command announced that the bomb contained ball bearings. The damage was caused by a single explosive device.

February 24, 2022: *AFP* reported that gunmen conducted four attacks against polio vaccination teams, killing eight workers. One person died in Takhar Province, the other several in Kunduz Province, including four in Kunduz city. Javid Hajir, a spokesman for the Ministry of Health, said, "Our policy is clear, we want to vaccinate and protect all the children in Afghanistan under the age of five."

April 3, 2022: *Al-Jazeera* reported that an explosion at Sarai Shahzada, Afghanistan's largest money changing market in Kabul, killed one person and injured 59 others.

April 6, 2022: *Al-Jazeera* reported that a grenade went off in the Pul-e-Khisti mosque in Kabul, wounding six people, minutes after midday prayers. Authorities arrested a suspect.

April 19, 2022: *AP, CNN, ABC News,* and *Reuters* reported that two bombs went off at 10 a.m. and 10:10 a.m. outside the main entrance of the Abdul Rahim Shahid High School in West Kabul, killing six people and wounding 17 as 11th- and 12th-graders were changing classes. The second bomb went off in an alleyway against the compound's wall. Shi'ites and Hazara reside in the Dasht-i-Barchi area. More than 16,000 students attend the school in four shifts. No one claimed credit; ISIS-K was suspected. *ABC News* reported that a suicide bomber apparently set off the first bomb.

Another bomb went off near the Mumtaz Education Center several kilometers away, causing no casualties.

April 21, 2022: *Reuters, AP,* and *UPI* reported that an ISIS-K bomb at the Sai Doken Shi'ite mosque in the 2d district of Mazar-e-Sharif during midday Ramadan prayers killed 12 people and wounded 58. *AFP* reported on April 22 that the Taliban claimed it had arrested ISIS-K member and Afghan citizen Abdul Hamid Sangaryar, who was believed to have planned the bombing.

An ISIS-K roadside bomb targeted a van of military mechanics in Kunduz, killing four and injuring 18, including school students.

The Interior Ministry said a roadside bomb in the Dasht-e-Barchi neighborhood of Kabul wounded three, including two children.

In the evening, gunmen attacked Taliban forces at a property in Mazar-e-Sharif during the evening, sparking a gun battle.

UPI reported that during the night, a bomb exploded in Khogiani in Nangarhar Province, killing several Taliban security officers.

Al-Jazeera reported that an attack on the Abdul Rahim Shaheed school in Kabul killed seven children.

April 22, 2022: *USNWR, Tolo News, CNN,* and *Reuters* reported that a bomb exploded inside the Sunni Mawlawi Sekandar mosque in the Imam Sahib district of Kunduz Province, killing 33 people and wounding 43 during Friday prayers.

April 28, 2022: *Al-Jazeera* reported that two vehicle bombs went off within minutes of each other, killing nine and wounding 13 in Mazar-i-Sharif, capital of Balkh Province. The Shi'ite Hazara victims were travelling home to break their Ramadan fast. ISIS-K claimed credit on its *Telegram* account.

April 29, 2022: *CNN,* the *Washington Post,* and *TOLO* reported that a bomb exploded at the Sahib Khalifa mosque in the Serahi Alauddin area of Kabul's Sixth District after Friday prayers, killing ten and wounding 30. Two UN staff members and their families were inside the Sufi mosque at the time of the attack near the national parliament and the American University of Afghanistan. Mosque leader Sayed Fazal, 45, said more than 50 were killed, including two of his nephews, and another 70 were injured. No one claimed credit. It was not clear whether it was a planted bomb or a suicide bombing.

April 30, 2022: *Reuters* reported that a bomb hit a passenger van in Kabul, killing one woman and injuring three others.

May 25, 2022: *U.S. News and World Report, CNN,* and *Reuters* reported that bombs hit three passenger vehicles in Mazar-i-Sharif in Balkh

Province, killing nine people and injuring 15. One bomb hit a minivan in police district 10, followed by a second nearby.

A fourth bomb hit a mosque in Kabul's police district 4 during the evening, killing five and injuring more than a dozen people, according to the Emergency Hospital.

No one claimed credit.

June 11, 2022: *Al-Jazeera* and *TOLOnews* network reported a bomb on a minibus in the eastern Bagrami district of Kabul killed four people and injured several others. The area is occupied mostly by Sunni Pashtuns. No group claimed credit.

June 17, 2022: *Al-Jazeera* reported that a bomb exploded at a mosque in Kunduz, killing one person and injuring two.

June 18, 2022: The *Washington Post, New York Times, CNN, AP, al-Jazeera, BBC, Reuters, Tolo,* and the state-run *Bakhtar* news agency reported that Kabul police chief spokesman Khalid Zadran said that at 6:30 a.m., seven terrorists set off a car bomb, threw grenades at security guards, and stormed into a Sikh Gurdwara in Kabul's Bagh-e Bala neighborhood (the *New York Times* said it was the Karte Parwan neighborhood), killing a member of the Taliban security forces and a Sikh worshiper and injuring seven people. A doctor at a nearby military hospital said the bodies of six worshippers arrived at his facility. Zadran said authorities killed all seven gunmen after an hours-long standoff. ISIS-K claimed credit via *Telegram,* saying it conducted an "act of revenge" for insults made by members of India's ruling Bharatiya Janata Party about the Prophet Mohammed. Nupur Sharma, a BJP spokesperson, had made derogatory remarks regarding the Prophet Mohammed during a panel discussion on a news channel; another party leader allegedly posted additional anti-Islam tweets. ISIS-K said suicide bomber Abu Muhammad al-Tajik threw a hand grenade at the security guard officer at the entrance, killing him. "Armed with a rifle, pistol and hand grenades, he proceeded to shoot." ISIS-K claimed its members battled with Taliban government fighters en route to reach the temple for three hours, setting off a car bomb and four other explosive devices.

June 20, 2022: *USNWR* and *Reuters* reported that an attack on a crowded bazaar in Nangarhar Province killed and wounded scores of people, including children. Quriashi Badloun, the Taliban administration's head of media and information for Nangarhar, confirmed that 10 were wounded.

July 29, 2022: *Reuters, al-Jazeera, AP,* and the *Jerusalem Post* reported that a grenade went off among spectators at an afternoon cricket match in Kabul's International Cricket Stadium, killing two people and injuring 13. Afghan Cricket Board (ACB) Chief Executive Nassib Khan said no ACB staff, players, or foreigners were hurt. No one claimed credit, although ISIS-K was suspected. The game resumed, pitting the Band-e-Amir Dragons and Pamir Zalmi in the eight-team domestic T20 Shpageza Cricket league.

Ramiz Alakbarov, UN Humanitarian Coordinator for Afghanistan and deputy at the U.N. mission in Afghanistan, was at the stadium and was to address the Afghan cricket association.

July 30, 2022: U.S. President Biden announced on August 1, 2022 that on July 30 at 6:18 a.m., a U.S. drone strike using two Hellfire missiles killed al-Qaeda leader Ayman al-Zawahiri, 71, in an upscale section of Kabul where senior Taliban officials were his neighbors. The U.S. had placed a $25 million bounty on his head after 9/11. *Sky News* and *voi.id* reported that the CIA identified his family members. *AP, al-Jazeera,* and *Politico* reported that a CIA drone carried out the strike. The takedown was in keeping with the motto of CIA's Counterterrorism Center: Anywhere, Any time, No Matter How Long It Takes. Coincidentally, the *Washington Examiner* reported that retired CIA officer Gary Schroen, 80, author of *First In: An Insider's Account of How the CIA Spearheaded the War on Terror in Afghanistan,* passed away on August 1, in time to know that al-Zawahiri died after a 20-year search.

President Biden, still quarantining with a positive COVID-19 test, addressed the country, saying:

My fellow Americans, on Saturday, at my direction, the United States successfully concluded an airstrike in Kabul, Afghanistan, that killed the emir of al Qaeda, Ayman al-Zawahiri.

You know, al-Zawahiri was bin Laden's leader. He was with him all the—the whole time. He was his number-two man, his deputy at the time of the terrorist attack of 9/11. He was deeply involved in the planning of 9/11, one of the most responsible for the attacks that murdered 2,977 people on American soil.

For decades, he was a mastermind behind attacks against Americans, including the bombing of the USS Cole in 2000, which killed 17 American sailors and wounded dozens more.

He played a key role—a key role in the bombing of U.S. embassies in Kenya and Tanzania, killing 224 and wounding over 4,500 others.

He carved a trail of murder and violence against American citizens, American service members, American diplomats, and American interests. And since the United States delivered justice to bin Laden 11 years ago, Zawahiri has been a leader of al Qaeda—the leader.

From hiding, he coordinated al Qaeda's branches and all around the world—including setting priorities, for providing operational guidance that called for and inspired attacks against U.S. targets.

He made videos, including in recent weeks, calling for his followers to attack the United States and our allies.

Now justice has been delivered, and this terrorist leader is no more.

People around the world no longer need to fear the vicious and determined killer. The United States continues to demonstrate our resolve and our capacity to defend the American people against those who seek to do us harm.

You know, we—we make it clear again tonight that no matter how long it takes, no matter where you hide, if you are a threat to our people, the United States will find you and take you out.

After relentlessly seeking Zawahiri for years under Presidents Bush, Obama, and Trump, our intelligence community located Zawahiri earlier this year. He had moved to downtown Kabul to reunite with members of his immediate family.

After carefully considering the clear and convincing evidence of his location, I authorized a precision strike that would remove him from the battlefield once and for all.

This mission was carefully planned and rigorously minimized the risk of harm to other civilians. And one week ago, after being advised that the conditions were optimal, I gave the final approval to go get him, and the mission was a success. None of his family members were hurt, and there were no civilian casualties.

I'm sharing this news with the American people now, after confirming the mission's total success through the painstaking work of our counterterrorism community and key allies and partners.

My administration has kept congressional leaders informed as well.

When I ended our military mission in Afghanistan almost a year ago, I made the decision that after 20 years of war, the United States no longer needed thousands of boots on the ground in Afghanistan to protect America from terrorists who seek to do us harm.

And I made a promise to the American people that we'd continue to conduct effective counterterrorism operations in Afghanistan and beyond.

We've done just that.

In February, our forces conducted a daring mission in Syria that eliminated the emir of ISIS.

Last month, we took out another key ISIS leader. Now we have eliminated the emir of al Qaeda. He will never again—never again allow Afghanistan to become a terrorist safe haven because he is gone, and we're going to make sure that nothing else happens. You know, it can't be a launching pad against the United States. We're going to see to it that won't happen.

This operation is a clear demonstration that we will, we can, and we'll always make good on the solemn pledge.

My administration will continue to vigilantly monitor and address threats from al Qaeda, no matter where they emanate from.

As Commander-in-Chief, it is my solemn responsibility to make America safe in a dangerous world. The United States did not seek this war against terror. It came to us, and we answered with the same principles and resolve that have shaped us for generation upon generation: to protect the innocent, defend liberty, and we keep the light of freedom burning—a beacon for the rest of the entire world.

Because this is the great and defining truth about our nation and our people: We do not break. We never give in. We never back down.

Last year, on September 11th, I once more paid my respects to Ground Zero in New York City, at that quiet field in Shanksville, at the Pentagon—and at the Pentagon.

Standing at the memorial at Ground Zero, seeing the names of those who died forever etched in bronze, is a powerful reminder of the sacred promise we made as a nation: We will never forget.

The memorial also bears a quotation from Virgil: "No day shall erase you from the memory of time." "No day shall erase you from the memory of time."

So we continue to mourn every innocent life that was stolen on 9/11 and honor their memories.

To the families who lost fathers and mothers, husbands and wives, sons and daughters, brothers and sisters, friends and co-workers on that searing September day, it is my hope that this decisive action will bring one more measure of closure. No day shall erase them from the memory of time.

Today and every day, I am so grateful to the superb patriots who serve the United States intelligence community and counterterrorism communities. They never forget. Those dedicated women and men who tirelessly worked every single day to keep our country safe and to prevent future tragedies—it is thanks to their extraordinary persistence and skill that this operation was a success. They have made us all safer.

And to those around the world who continue to seek to harm the United States, hear me now: We will always remain vigilant, and we will act. And we will always do what is necessary to ensure the safety and security of Americans at home and around the globe.

Today, we remember the lost. We commit ourselves to the safety of the living. And we pledge that we shall never waver from defending our nation and its people.

Thank you, all. And may God protect our troops and all those who serve in harm's way.

We will never—we will never give up.

Al-Zawahiri was often credited for being the operational planner of the 9/11 attacks (despite the claims of "I did it all" by Guantánamo Bay detainee Khalid Sheikh Muhammad), the USS Cole bombing, and the bombing of the U.S. embassies in Tanzania and Kenya. He could be counted on to issue long videos and audios espousing his calls to the Ummah, which had mostly passed him by.

Al-Zawahiri's having taken up residence with his wife and daughter in the exclusive Sherpour part of Kabul shortly after the U.S. withdrawal from the country in August 2021 proved troubling for relations between the Taliban and Washington. The administration and Taliban had quietly cooperated against ISIS-K, but allowing al-Qaeda's leader sanctuary was clearly in violation of the 2020 Doha Agreement between the two countries and put possible international aid and recognition in doubt. Taliban spokesman Zabihullah Mujahid's whining about a "clear violation of international principles" fell on deaf ears as praise for the strike rolled in from around the world. The Taliban also claimed that it was unaware of al-Zawahiri's presence in Kabul.

Reactions among jihadis ranged from "goodbye, dear martyr" to "good riddance". In one of his last videos, possibly recorded at the apartment safehouse, he chastised former allies, referring to them individually as an "imbecile", "idiot", "corrupt", and guilty of "moral deviation".

The commentariat speculated as to who might succeed al-Zawahiri, and if anyone would want to. Under al-Zawahiri's boring style of speaking, tendency to be prickly and pedantic, and willingness to become divisive, jihadis had either left the group entirely or established regional splinters that operationally ignored him. His decision to decentralize al-Qaeda ultimately sapped his ability to control the organization.

Calls to attack American and Western interests gave way to local battles. ISIS took up the fight against the West, but not under al-Zawahiri's tutelage.

Some observers suggested that the al-Qaeda Central members who harked back to the bin Laden days were the likeliest candidates. Some were under a form of house arrest in Iran, and it was no sure thing that Tehran would be willing to set them free.

Saif al-Adel's name appeared on most of the successor suggestion lists; he was the titular deputy of the group but his apparent residence in Shi'ite Iran was problematic. The Wanted poster for al-Adel indicated that he was wanted for conspiracy to kill U.S. nationals, to murder, to destroy buildings and property of the United States, and to destroy the national defense utilities of the United States. The *Washington Examiner* added that he was wanted for the "Black Hawk Down" attack on U.S. soldiers in Somalia in 1993 and for the U.S. embassy bombings in Africa. The former Egyptian special forces Lieutenant Colonel had a background in explosives and was wanted by the U.S. for the bombing of the U.S. Embassy in Kenya in 1998. The State Department put a $10 million bounty on his head.

AFP added another Egyptian, Abu Abd al-Karim al-Masri, part of the leadership of the Syrian jihadist group Hurras al-Din, who was believed to be in Syria.

A U.N. report suggested Abd-al-Rahman al-Maghrebi, Zawahiri's son-in-law, believed hiding in Iran. The U.S. offers a $7 million reward for al-Maghrebi.

Other candidates were less well-known, and less likely to develop a following, much less a revival, in a terrorist group that had become a shadow of its prominence under Osama bin Laden.

BBC suggested that the drone used the "switchblade" non-explosive AGM-114R9X Hellfire, which sprouts six blades which swing out from the side of the missile as it approaches the target.

BBC also quoted the Biden administration as indicating that members of the Haqqani Network spirited the family members away from the house, while the Taliban claimed that an unoccupied house had been hit. It was unclear what happened to al-Zawahiri's remains.

AP reported that a top aide to senior Taliban leader Sirajuddin Haqqani owned the safehouse. Al-Zawahiri never left the house, but sometime ventured onto a balcony, where he was standing when the strike hit. The interagency team used a model in the White House Situation Room of the safehouse for planning purposes.

The U.S. had placed a $25 million bounty on al-Zawahiri's head after 9/11.

CIA Director William Burns said, "Today, CIA mourns the passing of Gary Schroen, a legend and inspiration to every Agency officer. In Afghanistan more than two decades ago and in every other role he served at CIA, Gary embodied the very best of our organization. We will never forget his unwavering dedication, loyalty, and perseverance to protect and defend our country."

The Department of State warned Americans traveling abroad that al-Qaeda might conduct retaliatory strikes.

Task and Purpose and *The Guardian* reported on August 4 that Dan Smock, who lived in Kabul in 2012 and 2013 while he was a contractor for the U.S. Agency for International Development (USAID), said that the bombed house was the one he had lived in during that period.

August 3, 2022: The *Washington Post* reported on August 5, 2022 that the Taliban and ISIS-K engaged in a seven-hour gun battle in a Shi'ite district of West Kabul during the ten-day Muharram festival. Rumors spread that ISIS-K had taken over the residential Karte Sakhi Tower, seizing families as hostages. The Taliban announced at 6 p.m. that the battle was over, with four ISIS-K terrorists killed and one captured. Two Taliban forces, including a female officer, had died, but no civilians were harmed.

August 5, 2022: *USNWR* and *Reuters* reported that ISIS-K claimed credit for a bomb planted in a roadside vegetable cart that exploded in Sar-e-Karez, a Shi'ite area of western Kabul that killed eight people and wounded 18. ISIS-K claimed 20 were killed. The explosion killed or wounded 50, including women and children. The *Washing-*

ton Post reported that women and children had been meeting at the mosque when the bomb exploded.

August 6, 2022: *USNWR* and *Reuters* reported that a bomb exploded in a Shi'ite area of western Kabul. The *Washington Post* added that two people died and 22 were wounded. Khalid Zadran, police spokesman, tweeted that the explosives were planted in a vase. Some reports suggested that the bomb killed two participants in a meeting between Taliban security officials and Shi'ite elders. No group claimed credit.

August 7, 2022: The *Washington Post* and *AP* reported that Omar Khalid Khorasani, alias Abdul Wali, a top leader of the Pakistani Taliban, was killed in a late night bomb explosion in Paktika Province. Ehsanullah Ehsan, an aide to Khorasani, claimed that his driver and two other Pakistani Taliban leaders, Mufti Hassan Swati and Hafiz Dawlat Khan, who were traveling with Khorasani, also died. The Pakistani Taliban blamed Pakistani intelligence.

August 11, 2022: *NPR, Reuters, al-Jazeera, BBC,* and *AP* reported that a suicide bomber set off explosives hidden in his plastic artificial leg at a madrassa in Kabul, killing Sheikh Rahimullah Haqqani, a prominent cleric who graduated from Darul Uloom Haqqania in Pakistan, a Taliban-affiliated Islamic university. ISIS-K said the bomb went off in his office. Haqqani had survived two earlier assassination attempts, including an ISIS bombing in Peshawar, Pakistan in 2020 that killed seven people. Haqqani, while a Taliban supporter, had issued a fatwa that favored educating girls. He was not related to the Haqqani network.

August 17, 2022: *CNN* and *UPI* initially reported that a bomb exploded during evening prayers inside a mosque in Kabul's police district 17, killing three people and hospitalizing 27, including five minors, among them a boy, 7. The *Washington Post,* citing Khalid Zadran, a spokesman for the Kabul police, put the death toll at 21 with another 33 injured in the blast in the Khair Khana area. The *Washington Examiner* claimed that 50 people were killed in the explosion at the Abu Bakr al-Sadiq Mosque, variant Siddiquiya Mosque.

The dead included Maulvi Amir Mohammad Kabuli, a prominent religious scholar, as well as other worshippers who are thought to be from northern Afghanistan. No group claimed credit, but ISIS-K was suspected.

September 2, 2022: The *Los Angeles Times, Deutsche Welle,* and *AFP* reported that a bomb exploded in the Guzargah Mosque in Herat during Friday noon prayers, killing 18 people, including Mujib-ul Rahman Ansari, a prominent pro-Taliban cleric who advocated beheading for "the smallest act" against the government, and injuring 23. No one claimed credit. ISIS-K was suspected.

September 3, 2022: Children brought unexploded ordnance inside their religious school in Helmand Province and started playing with it. It detonated, killing four children aged between 7 and 14 and injuring three others.

September 5, 2022: *AFP, USNWR,* and *Reuters* reported that at 10:50 a.m., a suicide bomber set off his explosive device at the entrance to the consular section of the Russian Embassy in Kabul, killing six people, including two embassy employees and four Afghan civilians, and wounding ten people, including Afghan citizens. Taliban guards shot the attacker as he approached the gate, but the bomb still went off. No one claimed credit. The *Washington Post* reported that embassy second secretary Mikhail Shakh and a Russian security guard died. *RIA Novosti* reported that an embassy official had exited the building to read out names to a crowd waiting to hear about visas. 22090501

September 13, 2022: *Al-Jazeera* reported that the Taliban claimed that it had killed 40 National Resistance Front (NRF) rebels in Panjshir Province. Taliban spokesman Zabihullah Mujahid tweeted, "Due to a clearance operation against rebels in Rekha, Dara and Afshar (areas) of Panjshir Province, 40 have been killed including four commanders and 100 more have been arrested." Ali Nazary, head of NRF's foreign relations, told *AFP* that the numbers were inflated, observing, "Only a small group of our forces were captured and killed by the Taliban. Our forces fought fiercely till the last bullet." The son of rebel leader

Ahmad Shah Massoud, who was assassinated on September 9, 2001, leads the NRF.

September 21, 2022: A bomb went off in a restaurant in the Dehmazang neighborhood of Kabul, killing three and injuring 13.

September 23, 2022: *AP* reported that a car bomb went off following Friday prayers at the Wazir Akbar Khan Mosque, variant Uazir Akbar Jan Mosque, in a Kabul diplomatic neighborhood, a "green zone" in Police District 10, killing seven and wounding 41, including several children. No one claimed credit.

September 30, 2022: The *Washington Post, Khaama Press, Tolo, News 360, CNN, AFP,* and *The Hill* reported that a suicide bomber hit the Kaaj education center, where students were taking a practice university entrance exam at 7:30 a.m., in the predominantly Hazara neighborhood of Dasht-i-Barchi in Kabul's 13th district, killing 23 and injuring 36. No group claimed credit. ISIS-K was suspected. Many of the casualties were young women. *Al-Jazeera* reported the next day that the death toll had risen to 35, with 82 injured. *News 360* reported on October 3 that the United Nations Assistance Mission in Afghanistan (UNAMA) said that 53 people were killed and 110 wounded.

    AP reported that 31 students between the ages of 17 and 20 died. Among the dead were Vahida Heydari, 20; Wahida, 21, daughter of Mohammed Amir; and Nasrin, 14, who was visiting the center with her cousin, Layeqa, 19, who also died.

October 5, 2022: In the afternoon, a bomb went off at a mosque at the Interior Ministry as workers and visitors were praying.

October 5, 2022: The *Jerusalem Post* reported that a senior Afghan Special Intelligence Unit official announced that special forces arrested Abdul Malik, alias Maliki, chief of financial affairs for Islamic State–Khorasan Province (IS-KP, also known as ISIS-K), in a remote area of the country. *The Media Line* that reported that Malik was responsible for collecting funds from Germany, Ukraine, and Spain to distribute among IS-KP terrorists. A Taliban official claimed that Mali-

ki was responsible for recent terrorist attacks in the country, as well as motivating, recruiting, and training newly inducted youth. Maliki told the Taliban that he collected $15,000 from Ukraine, €5,000 from Germany, and €1,500 from Spain for the group.

October 22, 2022: *News 360* and *Tolo News* reported that the Taliban announced the deaths of eight ISIS-K suspects linked to recent attacks in western Kabul on the Wazir Akbar Jan mosque or the Kaaj educational center and other areas. Taliban spokesman and deputy information minister Zabiullah Mujahid added that the terrorists were killed in an operation in Kabul's eighth police district. The Taliban seized grenades, explosives, and a vehicle.

November 2, 2022: *News 360* and *Tolo News* reported that a roadside parcel bomb exploded in Kabul's district 5, hitting a bus carrying officials of the Taliban's Ministry of Rural Rehabilitation and Development, injuring eight people. ISIS-K was suspected.

November 4, 2022: *News 360* and *DPA/EP* reported that during the night a gunman killed three men, including two miners and a Taliban member, in a salt mine in Andkhoi in Faryab Province. No one claimed credit.

November 12, 2022: *News 360* and *Pajhwok* reported that the Taliban killed five suspected ISIS-K jihadis at a hideout in the 15th security district in the Jairjana district of Kabul.

November 23, 2022: *News 360* and *Tolo TV* reported that a gunman killed five people and wounded another inside a mosque in the Juaja Rauash area of Kabul. Officials suggested a private dispute was a possible motive. The attacker fled.

November 30, 2022: The *Washington Post, AP, AFP, Reuters,* and *Etilaat Roz* reported that a bomb exploded at the Al-Jahadi boys' madrassa in Aybak, capital of Samangan Province, during a gathering of all students for noon prayers, killing 16 people, mostly students, and injuring at least 24. ISIS-K was suspected.

December 2, 2022: *Reuters* reported that several gunmen conducted an attack near a mosque in the vicinity of the Kabul office of the Hezb-e-Islami party associated with former Afghan Prime Minister Gulbuddin Hekmatyar, injuring several guards before being killed by Taliban forces. All senior leaders, including Hekmatyar, were safe. No one claimed credit.

Shots were fired from a nearby building at the Pakistani Embassy in Kabul, wounding Israr Mohammad, the Pakistani guard of Pakistan's head of mission in Afghanistan, Ubaid-ur-Rehman Nizamani, who himself was uninjured. Kabul's police chief spokesman Khalid Zadran said police detained a suspect and recovered two light weapons from a nearby building. The embassy told *AFP* a lone gunman was involved. *Deutsche Welle* added on December 3 that ISIS-K said on *Telegram* that two of its members, using "medium and sniper weapons... attacked the apostate Pakistani ambassador and his guards". *News 360* reported on December 5 that the Taliban announced the arrest of a suspected foreign ISIS-K member for his role in the attack. 22120212

December 6, 2022: *News 360, Reuters,* and *Pajhwok* reported that nine people were injured when a bomb exploded at 1:45 p.m. at a foreign exchange market in Jalalabad's Talashi Square.

Reuters and *AFP* reported that at 7 a.m., a car bomb exploded next to a bus carrying oil employees from Hairatan in Mazar-e-Sharif in Balkh Province, killing eight and injuring ten. Azim, whose right leg was hit by shrapnel, said, "I was reading the Koran on my phone screen and there was a boom." Mohammad Hanif, who was also injured, said there were 52 people on the bus.

December 12, 2022: *AP, AFP, CBS News, Xinhua, New York Post,* and *Reuters* reported that at 2:30 p.m., gunmen attacked the ten-storey Kabul Longan Hotel in Kabul's Shaw-e Naw, variant Shahr-e-naw, neighborhood that is used predominantly by Chinese nationals. Three gunmen were killed. An Italian-run hospital received 21 patients, three of whom were DOA. Two foreign residents were injured after jumping out of windows to escape. *AFP* reported that the Chinese foreign ministry said that five of its nation-

als were wounded. The Taliban said the attack lasted for several hours. ISIS-K claimed credit. 22121201

EGYPT

January 30, 2022: *Reuters* and *MENA* reported that an Egyptian court sentenced to death 10 Muslim Brotherhood members for planning attacks on the police and forming the armed Helwan Brigades.

May 7, 2022: *Reuters* and *AFP* reported that the Islamic State claimed responsibility on its *Telegram* channel for killing an officer and 10 Egyptian soldiers in an attack against a water pumping station in the Sinai Peninsula. IS claimed on *Amaq* that it seized the weapons of soldiers it killed and torched a military post.

May 11, 2022: *Reuters* and *AFP* reported that at dawn, gunmen fired at a security post in the Sinai coast bordering the Gaza Strip, killing five members of the security forces, including an officer and four soldiers, and injuring four others, including two soldiers. Seven jihadis died.

June 28, 2022: *USNWR* and *Reuters* reported that an Egyptian court sentenced 10 people to death and more than 50 others to life in prison after they were convicted of supporting or carrying out Muslim Brotherhood attacks against security forces and sabotage of state infrastructure in Cairo between 2013 and 2015. The mass trial included more than 200 defendants.

December 30, 2022: The *Jerusalem Post* reported that ISIS claimed credit on *Amaq* for an attack on a police checkpoint in Ismailia that killed three police officers, saying "A cell of soldiers of the caliphate managed to attack an Egyptian police roadblock ... with a machine gun."

GAZA STRIP

January 1, 2022: *Reuters* reported that the IDF announced that Palestinians in Gaza fired two rockets toward the Mediterranean Sea, causing an explosion off the shore of Tel Aviv, entailing no casualties or damage. There was no immediate claim of responsibility. The Hamas-affiliated *Paltimes* news website claimed that the launch was not deliberate and was probably caused by a malfunction. Israel retaliated with airstrikes.

April 18, 2022: *Reuters* reported that the IDF's Iron Dome Air Defense System shot down a rocket launched from the Gaza Strip. *UPI* and the *Times of Israel* reported that the IDF launched an airstrike into Gaza against Hamas targets, including a military compound used by Hamas's air defense forces, the next morning. The *Jerusalem Post* reported that Defense Minister Benny Gantz charged that Hamas was responsible.

April 25, 2022: Gunmen fired a rocket that was intercepted by the IDF's Iron Dome missile defense system.

June 18, 2022: *USNWR* and *Reuters* reported that Palestinian militants fired a rocket toward Ashkelon in southern Israel. The IDF blamed Hamas, and conducted air strikes against Hamas targets in the Gaza Strip. There were no reports of casualties.

July 16, 2022: *Al-Jazeera* and *Reuters* reported that Palestinians fired rockets at Israel. One missile was intercepted; three others landed in open spaces. No one claimed credit. The IDF responded with more than two dozen missiles, hitting a rocket-manufacturing site in central Gaza run by Hamas. No one was injured.

August 5, 2022: The *Washington Post* and *CNN* reported that the IDF launched air strikes on targets inside Gaza, killing Tayseer Jabari, a leader of the Palestinian Islamic Jihad, in Operation Breaking Dawn. Palestinians had issued threats in recent days following the arrest of Bassam al-Saadi, a PIJ leader, in Jenin in the West Bank earlier in the week. The Palestinian Ministry of Health said at least seven people were killed and 40 injured in attacks in Gaza City and Khan Younis in southern Gaza.

The *Washington Post* reported on August 6 that air and rocket attacks continued from both sides, with 13 killed and 114 injured in Gaza. Gunmen fired 200+ rockets during the night at Israel. Two Israeli civilians received minor inju-

ries and two IDF soldiers sustained minor shrapnel wounds. The Iron Dome air-defense network intercepted circa 95 percent of the rockets. The IDF took 20 men into custody during raids near Hebron, Ramallah, and other West Bank locations. Among the dead was Alaa Qaddoum, a girl, 5.

NPR reported that after 44 deaths in Gaza as of August 7, the two combatants agreed to a ceasefire.

August 7, 2022: The *Washington Post* reported Palestinians fired rockets toward Jerusalem in the morning, following overnight IDF air strikes in Rafah that killed killed Khaled Mansour, the head of the Palestinian Islamic Jihad's (PIJ) operations in the south of Gaza. Israel said that Mansour had survived at least five other assassination attempts and blamed him for dozens of terrorist attacks against Israelis. The death toll in Gaza had reached 31 and the number of rockets fired surpassed 600. The Israeli army said that it had struck 139 PIJ targets.

August 17, 2022: The *Jerusalem Post* reported that Palestinian Islamic Jihad was preparing to carry out operations, including infiltrating into Israeli territory during Operation Breaking Dawn.

November 4, 2022: *Al-Jazeera*, the *Times of Israel*, and *News 360* reported that in the morning, Israeli fighter jets conducted several air attacks in the Gaza Strip, including a Hamas subway rocket production and development complex, used by Palestinian armed resistance factions in the Maghazi refugee camp, after four rockets were fired into Israel at 9 p.m. the previous evening at the towns of Kissufim, Ein HaShlosha, and Nirim. Air defense systems knocked down one rocket; the other three did not reach Israeli territory. No group claimed credit. The rockets were fired to avenge the army's killing earlier in the day of Islamic Jihad member Farouk Salameh in Jenin.

December 3, 2022: *AFP* reported that Palestinians fired a rocket from Gaza into Israel without causing any casualties. No one claimed credit. The Israeli Army fired on two observation posts operated by Hamas east of Gaza City.

Iran

April 5, 2022: *AFP* reported that an attacker stabbed to death Iranian Shi'ite hojatoleslam Mohammad Aslani and wounded two other Shi'ite clerics identified as Mohsen Pakdaman and Sadegh Daraei, in Imam Reza shrine's courtyard in Mashhad. One imam was seriously injured. *Fars* and *IRNA* reported that authorities arrested the assailant, believed to be a foreigner, and four suspected accomplices. The month of Ramadan had begun two days earlier. An official said "preliminary investigations show that the attacker committed this action under the influence of takfiri currents", a reference to Sunnis who charge others with apostasy, a capital crime in their eyes. Imam Reza is the eighth of the 12 holy Shi'ite imams. Thousands of people attended Aslani's funeral at Shohada Square near the shrine. *AFP* added on April 7 that cleric Sadegh Darai died of his wounds. *Tasnim* reported that the attacker stabbed one victim 20 times.

Tasnim reported that the main suspect was Abdolatif Moradi, 21, an ethnic Uzbek who had illegally entered the country from Pakistan a year earlier. He had "worked in transport" in a poor city district. Active on social media, he used pseudonyms including Abdolatif al-Salafi and "spread takfiri ideology and confront Shi'ites". Authorities arrested six suspected accomplices, including Moradi's two brothers.

The *Jerusalem Post* reported on June 7, 2022 that a court sentenced an Uzbek man, 21, from Afghanistan with radical Sunni views to death for killing two clerics and wounding a third in a knife attack at Iran's largest Shi'ite shrine in Mashhad in April. His lawyer appealed to the Supreme Court. 22040501

May 22, 2022: *Reuters, Tasnim,* and *Asharq al-Awsat* reported that the Revolutionary Guards announced that two gunmen on a motorcycle assassinated Colonel Sayad Khodai in Tehran, firing five shots into his unarmored Iranian-made Saipa (Kia) Pride off a secure street near Iran's Parliament (Majlis). "Anti-revolutionary" elements and "global arrogance" were blamed.

July 24, 2022: *News360* reported that the dissident Iranian National Congress claimed that

Iranian Revolutionary Guard engineer Said Thamardar Mutlak, who specialized in missile design, was killed in Shiraz a few days earlier.

September 30, 2022: *AP, Tasnim,* and *IRNA* reported that separatists attacked a police station in Zahedan in Sistan and Baluchestan Province, killing 19 people, including four members of the Islamic Revolutionary Guard, and injured 32 Guard members, including volunteer Basiji forces. The attackers hid among worshippers near a mosque. *IRNA* said the dead included Hamidreza Hashemi, a Revolutionary Guard colonel; Mohammad Amin Azarshokr, a Guard member; and basijis Mohamad Amin Arefiand Saeed Borhan Rigi. The head of the Guard's intelligence department, Seyyed Ali Mousavi, was shot and later died.

October 26, 2022: *Reuters, AFP, Fars, al-Jazeera,* and *Tasnim* reported that during the evening gunmen in a car shot at pilgrims and staff at the entrance to the Shi'ite shrine of Shah Cheragh in Shiraz, killing 15, including several women and children, and injuring 45. *Nournews* said the attackers were foreigners. Judiciary chief Kazem Mousavi said that just one attacker was involved; news agencies had cited three gunmen. *IRNA* blamed "takfiri terrorists", its term for Sunni hardliners, and said two were arrested. One remained at large. The Shah Cheragh mausoleum holds the tomb of Ahmad, brother of Imam Reza, the eighth Shi'ite imam. *CNN* reported that ISIS said on *Amaq* that one of its fighters had "targeted groups of Sunni refusal infidels inside the shrine with his machine gun, causing the death of tens of them". *AP* later reported that authorities had captured the single gunman, who used a Kalashnikov-style rifle. Iran tried to link ongoing protests to the attack. *News 360* and *IRNA* reported on October 29 that the main suspect died from wounds sustained from gunfire by security forces. 22102601

On October 31, 2022, *AFP, Tasnim, News 360,* and *IRNA* reported Iran announced the evening arrest on October 30 of a suspected accomplice and revised the death toll to 13. The Ministry of Intelligence and National Security later arrested the "second operational element" and "six supporting elements of the terrorist criminal team". A local official said gunman Hamed Badakhshan died of wounds sustained while he was being arrested. Several Iranian media services blamed the "terrorist attack" on radical Wahhabi groups, vice ISIS.

October 28, 2022: *Reuters* and the *Sepah News* agency reported that the Revolutionary Guards claimed that its intelligence unit had foiled a bomb attack in Mo'ali Abad Street in Shiraz.

November 3, 2022: *Reuters* and *IRNA* reported that Sajjad Shahraki, a cleric at a Shi'ite mosque in the mostly Sunni city of Zahedan in Sistan-Baluchistan Province, was shot to death.

November 16, 2022: *News 360, IRNA,* and *INSA* reported that a shooting at a market in Izeh in Khuzestan Province killed five, including a minor, and injured 15. The attackers arrived on motorcycles, then opened fire on the crowd gathered at the site as part of anti-government protests. *IRNA* reported that the dead included civilians and police officers.

November 28, 2022: The *Jerusalem Post, Tasnim,* and *ISNA* reported that Reza Dastani, a member of the Iranian Islamic Revolutionary Guard Corps (IRGC), was assassinated on his way to work in Isfahan. *Tasnim* reported that he served as an adviser for the IRGC Aerospace Force in Syria and was among one of the Iranian officials responsible for the seizure of two U.S. Navy command boats carrying ten U.S. personnel in the Persian Gulf in January 2016. *Intelli Times* reported that Jafari was involved in the deployment of Iranian air defense systems in Syria and Lebanon.

December 6, 2022: *News 360* reported that Iranian authorities claimed they dismantled several cells allegedly linked to the People's Mujahedin Organization of Iran (PMOI). The Intelligence Ministry added that "multiple operational sleeper cells linked to the PMOI terrorist group have been identified and dismantled by intelligence forces" in Tehran, Isfahan and the Kurdistan region. *Mehr* reported that ten suspects were arrested. The Intelligence Ministry claimed that "all terrorist activities (by these dismantled cells) were carried out under direct orders from the PMOI stronghold in Albania."

IRAQ

January 3, 2022: *Reuters, Task and Purpose,* and *Military Times* reported that authorities shot down two armed drones approaching an Iraqi military base hosting U.S. forces near Baghdad's international airport. No one was hurt. The attack came on the second anniversary of the drone assassination of Iranian General Qassem Soleimani, which was ordered by then U.S. President Donald Trump. One of the wings of a drone read "Soleimani's revenge"; another read "revenge operations for our leaders". No one claimed credit. 22010302

January 4, 2022: *Al-Jazeera* and *Task and Purpose* reported for the second time in 24 hours, in the morning, the anti-ISIS coalition foiled a drone attack by two armed drones on the Ain al-Asad airbase in Anbar Province hosting American troops. No one was hurt. No one claimed credit. 22010401

January 5, 2022: *Military Times* and *AP* reported that a Katyusha rocket hit an Iraqi military base hosting U.S. troops at Baghdad's international airport, causing no damage or casualties. Authorities found a rocket launcher with one rocket in a residential district in western Baghdad.

January 6, 2022: *Task and Purpose* reported on January 10 that on January 6, a drone was shot down near Ain al-Asad Air Base in western Iraq.

January 13, 2022: *CNN* reported that in the evening, several rockets launched from the Dora neighborhood hit Baghdad's Green Zone, including the U.S. Embassy, injuring a woman and a child. 22011301

January 14, 2022: The *Jerusalem Post* reported that a hand grenade exploded outside the headquarters of Iraqi parliament speaker Mohammed Halbousi's Taqaddum party in Baghdad in the morning, wounding two guards and damaging the building's doors and windows. No one claimed credit.

Hours later, a bomb exploded at the Baghdad headquarters of the Azm party of Sunni Muslim politician Khamis al-Khanjar, causing light damage. No one claimed credit.

January 21, 2022: The *Washington Post* reported that gunmen in Diyala Province killed 11 soldiers overnight in an apparent ISIS ambush. *Al-Jazeera* and *AP* reported added that the attack occurred in the early morning in the al-Azim district, a mountainous area 75 miles north of Baghdad. No one claimed credit. Two officials told *AP* that ISIS terrorists broke into the barracks at 3 a.m. and killed the soldiers before fleeing.

January 28, 2022: The *Jerusalem Post, al-Jazeera, UPI, Military Times,* and *AFP* reported that six rockets landed in the Baghdad International Airport compound and near an adjacent U.S. air base, known as Camp Victory, hitting runways and parking areas, causing a hole in the nose of an out of use Iraqi Airways civilian B-767, but causing no injuries. 22012802

February 13, 2022: The *Jerusalem Post* and *Shafaq News* reported that the international coalition shot down a drone after several were detected flying from the eastern border toward Erbil.

March 17, 2022: *Arabnews.com, Reuters, Military.com* and the *INA* state news agency reported that four rockets fell in open areas in Balad air base north of Baghdad, damaging a nearby home but causing no casualties. The base hosts American contractors and Iraqi fighter jets. No group claimed credit.

April 6, 2022: *Al-Jazeera* reported that three missiles fell near the KAR oil refinery in Erbil, causing no casualties.

April 26, 2022: *Al-Arabiya* and *AFP* reported that a suicide bomber killed an Iraqi major and another soldier and wounded soldiers during an army raid targeting ISIS in Tarmiya. A second terrorist died while trying to set off his bomb.

April 30, 2022: *Al-Arabiya* and *AFP* reported two rockets fell outside the Ain al-Asad base in Anbar Province, which hosts U.S.-led coalition troops, causing no casualties or damage. The previously unknown International Resistance claimed the attack on a pro-Iran *Telegram* channel. 22043001

May 1, 2022: *Al-Jazeera* reported that the Kurdistan Regional Government (KRG) counterterrorism forces said that six missiles fired from Bartella in Nineveh Province had landed around the KAR oil refinery in Erbil, causing minor damage. Security forces found a launching pad and defused four missiles in the Nineveh Plain.

May 21, 2022: The *Jerusalem Post* reported that the Ahrar Sinjar claimed credit for a drone attack on a Turkish base at Bashiqa, east of Mosul, in northern Iraq on Sunday. Reports differed as to whether four or six drones were involved in the attack on Zilkan base, located on the borders of the autonomous Kurdistan region of northern Iraq and areas of Nineveh Province that are governed by Iraqi federal forces. The group said "Our operation was carried out in response to the recent aggression on the outskirts of Kirkuk and Dohuk… These drones hit the intended targets with high accuracy, as a result of which the occupiers suffered material and human losses." *Tasnim News* reported that some sources claimed that two Turkish soldiers and a Turkish army contractor were killed. Erbil-based *Rudaw* media said a chef was killed.

May 24, 2022: During battles between Turkish forces and PKK gunmen, five Turkish soldiers were killed and two injured.

May 30, 2022: The *Jerusalem Post* reported Iran-backed groups may have targeted the al-Asad base in Iraq. *Military Times* and *AP* added that five Grad missiles hit inside the base in Anbar Province, causing minor damage but no casualties. 22053002

June 8, 2022: The *Jerusalem Post* reported that an explosive drone was shot down over Pirmam road in Erbil's suburbs at 9:35 p.m., injuring three people and damaging several cars. Two security sources said the drone was shot down. No one claimed credit. A security source claimed that the attack targeted the U.S. consulate. 22060801

June 15, 2022: The *Jerusalem Post* reported that Turkish air strikes against the Sinjar Resistance Units (YBS), a militia affiliated with the Kurdistan Workers Party (PKK), killed people, including a child, and injured seven.

June 17, 2022: The *Jerusalem Post* reported that Iraqi Kurdistan's counter-terrorism service said a 6 a.m. Turkish drone strike on a vehicle killed four PKK militants and injured one in Kalar, Sulaimaniya Province.

June 25, 2022: *USNWR* and *Reuters* reported that missiles targeted facilities owned by UAE energy firm Dana Gas in Sulaimaniya Province, causing no damage or casualties. No one claimed credit.

July 27, 2022: *AFP,* the *Jerusalem Post, Anadolu,* and *Reuters* reported that in the morning, four mortar rounds landed near the Turkish consulate in Mosul, causing damage to cars but no casualties. No one claimed credit. 22072701

July 30, 2022: *NINA* and *News 360* reported that Iraqi Air Force F-16 strikes killed three ISIS members in Mujaisa in Diyala Province.

August 26, 2022: A bomb exploded near Baghdad's Green Zone as an Australian diplomatic convoy made its way into the area, causing no injuries. 22082601

September 12, 2022: *News 360* and the Turkish *Daily Sabah* reported that the Turkish National Intelligence Organization killed three PKK members, including Vedar Aksac, alias Sahan, which it claimed was a member of a PKK assassination squad, in Halifan in Erbil Province. Türkiye claimed Aksac belonged to the PKK youth wing Revolutionary Patriotic Youth Movement (YDG-H), and fled Türkiye in 2015. He trained in assassinations and bombings in northern Iraq. 22091201

Al-Jazeera added that the Turkish Ministry of Defense announced that four Turkish soldiers carrying out a Claw-Lock cross-border operation against the PKK were killed in a nighttime clash with fighters in northern Iraq. 22091202

September 28, 2022: *News 360* and *INA* reported that three Katyusha rockets crashed inside Baghdad's Green Zone; one of them hit an area close to the headquarters of the Iraqi Parliament. *AFP* added that seven security personnel were wounded.

October 13, 2022: The *Washington Post* reported that nine rockets landed in Baghdad's Green Zone near parliament, which elected Abdul Latif Rashid, a veteran Kurdish politician and former water minister, as Iraq's new president. Several people were injured and cars were damaged in the parliament's parking lot.

November 7, 2022: The *Washington Post, CNN, AP, al-Jazeera,* and *UPI* reported that U.S. citizen Stephen Edward Troell, 45, who worked at the Global English Institute together with his wife and four children, including one son, was shot dead by two gunmen as he drove through central Baghdad near his home in the Wahda area of the Karrada district in Baghdad. His employer, Bellaire, Texas-based Millennium Relief and Development Services, said that the Tennessee native had worked in promotions and advertising at GEI; his wife, Jocelyn, was the manager at GEI's Harthiya neighborhood's facility. His teen daughters were teachers. The couple arrived in December 2012, and had done some missionary work. No one claimed credit for the attack. *Kurdistan24* claimed it was a failed kidnapping attempt. One car cut him off, gunmen in a second car opened fire. His wife and child were in the car but were not harmed. 22110701

December 6, 2022: *News 360* and *al-Sumaria TV* reported that the Iraqi Army killed eight suspected ISIS members in an aerial bombing raid in the Hamrin Mountains.

Kurdish TV channel *Rudaw* reported that two members of the Popular Mobilization Forces (PMF) were killed in Babil when a suspect set off the explosives he was carrying.

December 18, 2022: *AFP, INA, Reuters,* and *Deutsche Welle* reported that ISIS said it had bombed a federal police vehicle near Shalal al-Matar and Safra in the Kirkuk area, killing nine police officers and critically wounding two others. The group machine-gunned and threw grenades at those who survived the bombing. Authorities said they had killed one attacker.

December 19, 2022: *News 360, Rudaw, Shafiq,* and *Europa Press* reported that during the night, ISIS was suspected of firing on several vehicles in Al Jalis, northeast of Baquba, in Diyala Province, killing six and wounding eight. Terrorists then battled security forces.

ISRAEL

January 4, 2022: The *Jerusalem Post* reported the Israeli Air Force's Monitoring Command shot down a Hizballah-controlled drone that crossed the Lebanese border into Israel.

January 30, 2022: The *Jerusalem Post* reported that during the night, Palestinian youths threw Molotov cocktails towards an Israel Police station in the Palestinian neighborhood of Sur Baher.

February 3, 2022: The *Jerusalem Post* and *Walla* reported that during the night, Palestinian youths threw Molotov cocktails at an east Jerusalem police station, causing no injuries.

February 7, 2022: *AFP* reported that the Israel Prison Service said Spanish aid worker Juana Rashmawi, also known as Juana Ruiz, 63, who pled guilty to inadvertently funding the Popular Front for the Liberation of Palestine (PFLP), was released after 10 months in jail. She had been sentenced in November 2021 to 13 months in prison after a military court convicted her. She was arrested in April 2021 for unknowingly funding the PFLP via her work for a Palestinian group, the Union of Health Work Committees, which Israel said sent European donations to the PFLP.

March 6, 2022: *Al-Jazeera* and *UPI* reported Israeli forces shot dead Karim el-Kusami, 19 after he stabbed a police officer at Bab Hutta, one of the gates to the al-Aqsa Mosque compound in the Muslim Quarter of the Old City in East Jerusalem, at 4:30 a.m. A second officer was injured in the leg by friendly fire aimed at the terrorist. Local media said the youth was a resident of the al-Tur (Mount of Olives) neighborhood in East Jerusalem. *Haaretz* reported that Israeli forces raided al-Tur hours later and arrested his brother, Muhammad.

March 7, 2022: *AFP* reported that a Palestinian in his 20s stabbed with a knife and wounded two

Israeli officers at the Cotton Merchant's Gate in in Jerusalem's Old City before being shot dead by security forces. The terrorist had come from the Temple Mount. He was from the West Bank.

March 19, 2022: *Al-Jazeera* reported that Israeli forces shot a Palestinian man, 20, after a stabbing attack in West Jerusalem, seriously wounding him. An Israeli in his mid-30s was lightly wounded.

March 22, 2022: *AFP,* the *Times of Israel, Channel 13 TV, Reuters,* and *Newsweek* reported that around 4 p.m., a man stabbed several people with a knife and ran over another outside a gas station and a shopping center in Beersheba, killing four and injuring several others. Prime Minister Natfali Bennett promised to crack down on "terrorists". Israeli media outlets said the attacker was Mohammed Abu al-Kiyan, a Bedouin in his thirties who had previously been convicted in 2016 and sentenced to four years in prison for seeking ties with ISIS. The elementary school teacher from Hura was also convicted of teaching children and members of the community during sermons featuring content inspired by ISIS. He stabbed a woman at the gas station, got back into his car and crashed into a male bicyclist in his 60s at the BIG shopping center. He then stabbed at least two more people. Police spokesman Eli Levy said that a civilian shot and killed the suspect. ISIS later claimed credit

March 27, 2022: *CNN,* the *Jerusalem Post,* and *UPI* reported that at 8:30 p.m., ISIS gunmen jumped out of a vehicle, shot to death two people, and injured 12, including police and civilians, in Hadera, 31 miles north of Tel Aviv. ISIS claimed credit via *Amaq,* which referred to a "twin immersive commando attack by Islamic State Fighters". Members of the Police's YAMAS undercover unit were eating dinner 30 meters away. Within two minutes, they shot to death the two gunmen, who were from the Arab-majority Israeli city of Umm al-Fahm in the northern district of Haifa. The gunmen had fired at local police in Hadera, killing two passers-by who were members of the border police force. Police said the victims were Shirel Aboukrat, 18, a French-Israeli citizen from Netanya, and Yazan Falah, 18, from Kasra Samia

(*UPI* said they were 19). *AFP* reported that authorities arrested five suspects. Israeli police and the Shin Bet security agency conducted raids in Umm al-Fahm, arresting three suspects on suspicion of membership in a terrorist organization. The other two were detained elsewhere. Police seized weapons and ISIS books. Hamas said the attack was a "natural and legitimate response" to Israeli "crimes against our people". Islamic Jihad and Hizballah also welcomed the attack.

The *Jerusalem Post* reported that the terrorists were armed with 1,100 bullets, three sidearms, and knives, and wore flak jackets. The *Jerusalem Post* added that one of the terrorists shot a victim four times in 40 seconds, manhandled her, stole her weapon, and used it to shoot others in the area.

Haaretz reported that gunman Ibrahim Agbarieh had tried to join ISIS. The *Jerusalem Post* said an attacker had posted photos of him next to Raed Salah, leader of the Northern Branch of the Islamic Movement in Israel.

UPI added that U.S. Secretary of State Antony Blinken and the foreign ministers of Bahrain, Morocco, and the UAE were in the country for an historic summit regarding the Iran nuclear negotiations.

AFP reported that hundreds of people attended the funerals of the two police officers.

The *Jerusalem Post* added that the terrorists posted a video on *Facebook* before the attack showing them swearing allegiance to ISIS. The brother of one of the terrorists is an Israel Police officer. One of the attackers had been imprisoned for trying to join ISIS in Syria. 22032701

Police arrested another man from southern Israel on suspicion of supporting ISIS.

March 29, 2022: *Al-Jazeera, Forbes, Reuters, CNN, AFP, UPI,* and *AP* reported that at 8 p.m., Diaa Hamarsheh, 26, a gunman riding a motorcycle and carrying an M16 assault rifle, killed five people in Bnei Brak, an ultra-Orthodox suburb of Tel Aviv, before being shot dead by officers at the scene. The ZAKA rescue service said that another person suffered life-threatening injuries. The terrorist shot at passers-by in two locations. He walked through the town, shooting two Ukrainian citizens sitting at the entrance of a convenience store. He then shot to death two

Israeli men before he was shot by Amir Khoury, 32, an Israeli Arab police officer from Nof Hagalil. The gunman fired back, mortally wounding the officer. Officer Khoury had served with the Bnei Brak station's motorcycle unit in the Dan area of Tel Aviv. *Reuters* reported that the terrorist shot at apartment balconies and at people on the street and in a car. The terrorist's weapon jammed before he could shoot Menachem Englander, a medic with the national ambulance service. Two motorcycle officers arrived and shot the terrorist to death near the entrance to Ramat Gan.

UPI reported that three men in their 30s died at the scene; a man in his 40s was killed 300 feet away.

Israeli media, *Reuters,* and *AP* reported that the terrorist was a Palestinian man 27, from Yabad near Jenin in the West Bank. He had been staying in Israel illegally. The *New York Times, Forbes,* and an Israeli public broadcaster said the terrorist had earlier been jailed for arms trafficking and membership in a terrorist group.

CNN reported that Islamic Jihad praised the attack. The *New York Times* and a Hamas-run TV channel said that Hamas deemed the attack a "heroic action against the occupation in Tel Aviv" and a "quick response to the summit of shame and disgrace held in the Negev," referring to the meeting with Israeli officials of U.S. Secretary of State Antony Blinken and the foreign ministers of Israel, Bahrain, Egypt, Morocco, and the United Arab Emirates. The Al Aqsa Martyrs Brigades said it was "a clear message written in blood in response to the Negev summit".

Reuters and the Palestinian *Wafa* news service reported that Palestinian Authority President Mahmoud Abbas condemned the killing of Israeli civilians, observing that killing Israelis and Palestinians would only lead to a deterioration of the situation.

Israeli security forces raided the homes of 12 Palestinian citizens of Israel and arrested two suspected of having ties to ISIS.

Ramadan was to begin on April 1. 22032901

April 7, 2022: *AP, AFP, UPI, ABC News,* and *Reuters* reported that in a 9 p.m. attack, a Palestinian gunman from the West Bank shot and killed three men and injured 15, most of them in their chests and stomachs, at Ilka, a popular pub on Dizengoff Street in Tel Aviv. The killer fled. The victims were cared for at Ichilov, Sheba Tel Hashomer, and Wolfson hospitals. A man, 20, a woman, 28, and a man, 38, were in serious condition. Hamas praised the "heroic operation" that "led to the killing of a number of occupying soldiers and Zionist settlers", but did not claim credit. The Israeli Ministry of Foreign Affairs and Israel's Shin Bet internal security service announced that Israeli security forces tracked down and killed the terrorist in a 6 a.m. shootout on April 8 near a mosque in Jaffa, an Arab neighborhood in southern Tel Aviv. Shin Bet said the gunman was Raad Hazem, 28, a Palestinian man from Jenin, in the occupied West Bank. He did not belong to an organized militant group and had no prior record. He had entered Israel illegally without a permit. *AP* reported that the dead were Tomer Morad and Eytam Magini, both 27, childhood friends from Kfar Saba, north of Tel Aviv, and Barak Lufen, 35, a coach on Israel's national kayak team, from the central Israeli town of Givat Shmuel.

The *Jerusalem Post* reported that the terrorist's father, a former Palestinian Authority security officer, said outside his house, "You will see the victory soon… God, liberate the al-Aqsa Mosque from the occupiers." The terrorist's uncle praised the killer on *Facebook*. A reporter for the pro-Hizballah *al-Mayadeen* tweeted that the killer was "a Palestinian hero". His colleague Fatima Ftouni tweeted about the death toll with a heart emoji, and said that "the occupier is destined to leave or die."

On April 10, *Reuters* and *Today Online* reported that Israeli soldiers fired on a vehicle near Jenin carrying two brothers of Raad Hazem. The vehicle fled the scene.

The October 23, 2022 *New York Times* ran an opinion piece entitled "Is Trauma Really the Best Comedy Material" by Israeli comedian Noam Shuster Eliassi, who was at the scene two doors down. The victims included a person who had recently gotten engaged; another man left behind three young children. The writer noted that the Israelis had raided the shooter's home in Jenin in 2002, when he was eight. In early September, the Israeli Army demolished the shooter's family's home.

April 9, 2022: *Al-Jazeera* reported that the Israeli army and border police killed a Palestinian, 25, who was a member of Islamic Jihad, during heavy gun battles. Another 13 Palestinians were wounded, including a woman, 19, hit by a bullet to her stomach.

April 12, 2022: *Al-Jazeera* and *AFP* reported that in the morning, Israeli police in Ashkelon shot to death a Palestinian man in his 40s after lightly wounding a police officer by stabbing him with a kitchen knife. The attacker was from Hebron.

April 27, 2022: *Al-Jazeera* reported that the Jerusalem Magistrate's Court convicted seven Jewish men of inciting violence and terror and of several other charges for their involvement in a 2015 wedding in which participants celebrated an arson attack that killed Palestinian 18-month-old Ali Dawabsheh and his parents Riham and Saad. The court found them guilty of "glorifying with dance and song the murder of the Dawabsheh family" in Duma in the West Bank by illegal Jewish settlers in July 2015. One man was found guilty of incitement to racism, supporting a "terrorist" group, and illegal possession of a weapon. Another was convicted of a weapons charge. The male wedding singer was acquitted. They faced a five-year jail term. *Haaretz* reported that a sentencing hearing was scheduled for November. Months after the attack, Israeli television broadcast a wedding video tnat appeared to show guests brandishing rifles and dancing to music with lyrics calling for revenge, while some stabbed photos of Ali Dawabsheh. Lyrics included "the mosque will burn" and "the mosque will explode". One of those convicted, Dov Morell, tweeted, "My deeds do not represent who I am today, and I regret them… I don't think this constitutes a felony and it looks like I will appeal the conviction."

April 28, 2022: *UPI*, the *Jerusalem Post*, and *Walla* reported that Israeli Prime Minister Naftali Bennett's eldest son, Yoni, 17, received a death threat in an envelope containing a bullet. It was the second death threat of the week against the Bennett family. The Israel Security Agency (Shin Bet) and the Lahav 433 unit of the Israel Police were investigating the death threats.

April 29, 2022: The *Times of Israel* reported that two gunmen in a blue Suzuki killed Israeli security guard Vyacheslav Golev, 23, in a terrorist attack at the entrance to the West Bank settlement of Ariel, got out of the car to continue firing improvised Carlo submachine guns into the guard post, then drove into the night. A second security guard was unharmed. Hamas praised the shooting as a "heroic operation" and a "natural response to the crimes of the occupation and its settlers". The al-Aqsa Martyrs' Brigade claimed credit, saying "We claim responsibility for the heroic operation in the colony of Ariel in which a Zionist officer was killed, in response to violations committed by the occupation government in Jerusalem." Hamas did not claim its members were involved. *AFP* reported on April 30 that Israeli forces arrested two suspected killers in the Palestinian village of Qarawat Bani Hassan, northwest of Ariel.

May 5, 2022: *CNN, Reuters,* and *BBC* reported that two suspected attackers killed three people and injured four, one critically and one seriously, in a park in Elad on Israeli Independence Day. Police said one fired a rifle while the other wielded an axe, hammer, or a knife. *AP* reported a sole attacker, believed to be Palestinian, fled in a vehicle. Hamas spokesman Hazem Qassem praised the attack, saying, "The storming of al-Aqsa Mosque can't go unpunished… The heroic operation in Tel Aviv is a practical translation of what the resistance had warned against." The dead included Yonatan Habakuk, 44, and Boaz Gol, 49, both from Elad, and Oren Ben Yiftach, 35, an Israeli.

The *Jerusalem Post* reported that the two Palestinian suspects were Assad Yussef al-Rafai, variant As'ad Yousef As'ad al-Rifa'i, 19, and Tzabahi Abu Shakir, variant Subhi Imad Abu Shukair, variant Subhi Emad Sbeihat, 20, who worked in Elad. *Army Radio* reported that they had illegally entered into Israeli territory after breaching the Seam Line. *KAN* reported that Israeli authorities arrested Imad Abu Shakir, Abu Shakir's father. *AFP* and *UPI* reported on May 8 that Israeli security services arrested without incident the two Palestinian suspects after they were spotted in a forested area near a quarry outside Elad. The duo were unarmed, but police

found the axes nearby. The Israeli military said bloody banknotes, possibly dropped by the suspects, helped lead to their hideout.

May 8, 2022: *AFP* reported that a Palestinian, 19, without an entry permit for Israel stabbed a police officer outside the Old City in east Jerusalem before being shot and injured at the scene.

May 22, 2022: *Al-Jazeera* reported that an Israeli court sentenced six Palestinian prison escapees to another five years in prison for tunneling out of their cell in 2021 and escaping from a high-security facility. The escapees, who were members of Palestinian armed groups, were recaptured days later. Five were members of the Islamic Jihad; four were serving life sentences. Zakaria Zubeidi is a member of the secular Fatah group of Palestinian Authority President Mahmoud Abbas. Five other inmates charged with assisting the escapees were sentenced to an additional four years in jail.

May 28, 2022: The *Jerusalem Post* reported that the Defense Ministry's Crossing Points Authority at the Meitar crossing arrested two residents of Hura attempting to smuggle hundreds of bullets from Israeli to Palestinian territory in the South Hebron Hills. Authorities became suspicious and a search of their car yielded sacks loaded with bullets.

May 29, 2022: Police arrested a Palestinian, 21, a resident of Nablus, who was planning on conducting a stabbing attack at the entrance to the Old City in Jerusalem on the Temple Mount on Jerusalem Day. Police said he was acting suspiciously and was carrying a knife.

June 6, 2022: The *Jerusalem Post* reported that Border Police special forces (YAMAM) and Shin Bet officers arrested two Palestinians from Nablus in south Tel Aviv under suspicion of planning a terror attack.

June 15, 2022: *Reuters, AFP,* and *BBC* reported that the Beersheba District Court found Palestinian aid worker Mohammad el-Halabi, head of Gaza operations for World Vision, an international Christian aid group, guilty of 13 charges of supporting a terror organization but acquitted him of treason. Israel had held him since arresting him at the Erez crossing in June 2016 on charges he funneled $50 million (£41.5 million) in relief funds to pay Hamas fighters, buy arms including rockets, and fund Hamas's activities, including digging tunnels used to attack Israel. He was indicted in August 2016. A sentencing hearing was scheduled for July. He had refused several plea deal offers. He was represented by Maher Hanna, who denied media reports that his client had confessed. He vowed to appeal. Israel's Corporation Authority (ICA), which oversees NGO activities, petitioned a Jerusalem court to dissolve World Vision in Israel.

On August 30, 2022, the *Washington Post* reported that the Beersheba District Court sentenced Mohammed al-Halabi to 12 years in prison after convicting him of siphoning $40 million and tons of steel to Hamas's military wing. He ran the group's Gaza operation from 2014 until he was arrested.

June 28, 2022: The *Jerusalem Post* reported that a Palestinian man tried to stab a police officer at an entrance gate to al-Aqsa Mosque in Jerusalem's Old City during the night. No one was injured. Police detained him later that evening elsewhere on the mosque compound.

July 2, 2022: *Naharnet* reported that the IDF shot down three unarmed reconnaissance drones launched by Hizballah aimed at an Israeli gas platform in the Karish field, which Israel claims is within its internationally recognized economic waters in the Mediterranean Sea. Lebanon disputes that claim.

July 28, 2022: The *Jerusalem Post* reported the IDF's Battalion 636 returned fire after a night-time shooting attack by a squad of armed Palestinians in a vehicle on a military post at the entrance to Nablus. One of the gunmen got out of the car and fired. The IDF soldiers returned fire and hit several of the gunmen, arresting one of them. There were no IDF casualties.

August 14, 2022: The *Washington Post, CBC News,* the *Times of Israel, al-Jazeera,* and *NPR* reported that Palestinians were suspected in a gun attack on a bus waiting in a parking lot near Jerusalem's Western Wall in the Old City at 1:30

a.m. Eight people, including five Americans, were injured. A pregnant woman, 35, was shot in her abdomen and underwent an emergency caesarean procedure; both mother and baby were in serious condition. Another person was also critically injured. Two Americans were treated at the Hadassah Medical Center; three others were treated at the Shaare Zedek Medical Center. Israeli media earlier reported that four American victims were tourists and members of the same New York family. The shooter ran into the adjacent Palestinian neighborhood of Silwan. He turned himself and his weapon in to police after an hours-long manhunt. *CNN* reported that he is a Palestinian with Israeli citizenship, born in 1996, from East Jerusalem. He had a criminal record and spent time in prison. No group claimed credit, although Hamas cheered the "heroic operation". 22081401

August 17, 2022: The *Jerusalem Post* reported that during the night, Islamic Jihad terrorists shot at an IDF vehicle near Joseph's Tomb in Nablus, damaging the vehicle but causing no injuries. PIJ claimed credit. Palestinian media reported that the IDF killed a shooter, Waseem Nasr Khalifa, 18 (*Al-Jazeera* and *Wafa* said he was 20, from the Balata refugee camp). Four other Palestinians were injured.

August 21, 2022: *News 360* reported that the Israeli Army announced it would formally charge Baseem Saadi, 61, Islamic Jihad's West Bank leader, with membership in a terrorist group, conducting operations for such a terrorist group, incitement, and supporting terrorism. He was arrested in early July. The *Times of Israel* reported on August 21 that an Israeli court extended Saadi's pre-trial detention until August 25, 2022. Israeli authorities had jailed and released Saadi seven times. On August 25, 2022 *Hamodia* and *Reuters* reported that Israel indicted Sheikh Bassam al-Saadi.

September 19, 2022: The *Jerusalem Post* reported that earlier in the month, Shin Bet had arrested seven Hamas-affiliated Palestinians from Hebron and Nablus who were planning bombing attacks against Israeli forces and civilians. The detainees told Shin Bet that they were recruited and trained in explosives by Hamas operative Yahya Amer Muhammad Abu Sayfan, 26, a resident of the Nuseirat refugee camp in the Gaza Strip. Israeli security forces confiscated weaponry, explosives, and other equipment and substances. Authorities identified the suspects as Massab Himouni, Ahmad Abu Dawid, Aziz a-Din Al-Zin, Amad Abu Khalaf, Abdullah Quwasma, and Maamoun and Khamel Hanani.

September 20, 2022: *AFP,* the *Jerusalem Post,* and *News 360* reported that Palestinian Mousa Sarsour, 28, of Qalqilya in the West Bank, was suspected of beating an Israeli woman, 84, to death with a metal pole in Holon, outside Tel Aviv. He had entered Israel with a valid work permit. The next day, a passerby found his body hanged at the corner of Bar Kochba and Dizengoff Streets in the heart of Tel Aviv, an apparent suicide. The Israeli army arrested 11 suspects in raids across the West Bank, including "five individuals suspected of assisting in the terror attack".

September 22, 2022: *News 360,* the *Times of Israel, DPA,* and *ZUMA Wire* reported that authorities arrested a Palestinian who rammed a stolen vehicle into a security barrier at the entrance to Ben Gurion Airport. He fled after security forces shot at him. No casualties were reported. Authorities found the vehicle at a gas station in the airport complex and soon arrested the individual, believed to be residing in the West Bank.

September 26, 2022: The *Jerusalem Post* reported that an obstacle was found during the night on a railroad track between Akko and Carmiel. No one was injured and no damage was reported. Authorities arrested but later released an Israeli Arab in his 20s on suspicion of involvement. Shin Bet was searching for additional suspects in the planning of the attempted derailment.

October 8, 2022: *News 360, UPI,* and *al-Jazeera* reported that the Israel Defense Forces announced that Corporal Noa Lazar, 18, of Bat Hefer, died from her gunshot wounds during a 9 p.m. attack at a Border Police checkpoint in the Palestinian Shuafat refugee camp in East Jerusalem. The attacker fled into the camp. Three soldiers were injured. The *Times of Israel* added that a seriously wounded security guard un-

derwent neurosurgery overnight at Hadassah Medical Center in Jerusalem and was put on a respirator. Lazar was posthumously promoted to sergeant with the Erez Battalion of the Israeli Military Police. Three suspects from Shuafat, Beit Hanina, and Anata were arrested, as were three members of the alleged attacker's family. Israeli police claimed the gunman was driven to the checkpoint by an accomplice, got out of the car, opened fire, and ran into the camp. The driver sped away but turned himself in to authorities. The *Jerusalem Post* reported that the driver claimed he was taking a hitchhiker to Modi'in when the car stopped at the checkpoint and the hitchhiker fired seven rounds until his weapon jammed.

The *Jerusalem Post* reported on October 18, 2022 that security forces were still looking for the shooter, Udai Tamimi, 22, of East Jerusalem. Police said seven detained suspects, who resided in the Shuafat refugee camp and the nearby West Bank town of Anata, were relatives and acquaintances of Tamimi. A security guard, 30, remained in serious condition with bullet wounds to the head; he underwent surgery following the attack. He was sedated and ventilated in severe condition in the neurosurgery intensive care unit at Hadassah Ein Kerem in Jerusalem.

Numerous residents of Shuafat shaved their heads in an attempt to confuse Israeli troops searching for Tamimi. The *Jerusalem Post* reported that 15 people were arrested in connection to the attack, including family members and those suspected of assisting him.

AFP and *Reuters* reported on October 20, 2022 that Udai Tamimi shot at Israelis at the entrance to Maale Adumim, one of the largest Jewish settlements in the West Bank, injuring a security guard in the hand. A second security guard shot Tamimi to death. Palestinians went on strike in protest, shuttering shops, offices, and schools in the West Bank cities of Bethlehem and Nablus, as well as Jerusalem's Old City.

November 3, 2022: *Reuters, al-Jazeera,* and *AFP* reported that Israeli police said a Palestinian who was ordered to stop for inspection instead stabbed an officer in his upper body in Jerusalem's Old City before being shot dead by two other officers. Two other officers were injured in the friendly fire.

November 23, 2022: *UPI* and *CNN* reported that two bombs were remotely detonated at bus stops in Jerusalem in the morning, killing Aryeh Shechopek, 16, an Israeli-Canadian yeshiva student who lived in the Har Nof neighborhood, and injuring 18. One bomb went off at the entrance of a Givat Shaul Junction bus station in west Jerusalem at 7:06 a.m., injuring at least 12 people, four seriously, including a 45-year-old; Shechopek later died. The *Jerusalem Post* added that the first bomb contained black metal screws to increase collateral damage. At 7:30 a.m., a smaller bomb exploded near a Ramot Junction bus stop in northern Jerusalem, lightly injuring three people. One bomber was suspected. Police said he rode an electric bike to the sites. *AFP* reported on November 26 that Tadesa Teshuma died of his wounds at Jerusalem's Shaare Zedek hospital. No one claimed credit, but Hamas celebrated the attack.

The *Jerusalem Post* reported on November 28 that the FBI contacted the family of American-Israeli Naomi Pilichowski, 18, who was injured at the bus stop, en route to Bet Shemesh to do her national service. She had moved to Israel eight years ago. The FBI's Victim Services Division said she was a potential victim of a federal crime. The FBI offered to provide the family with the assistance they might need. Mom Aliza is the mayor of Mitzpe Yeriho and dad Rabbi Uri Pilichowski is an American-Israeli educator who works at Nefesh B'Nefesh.

Reuters reported on December 27, 2022 that Israel's police and domestic security service announced the November 29 arrest of a Palestinian male suspect, Islam Farouh, 26. 22112301

November 24, 2022: The *Jerusalem Post* reported that anti-Arab nationalists torched three vehicles in Abu Gosh and two in Ein Naqquba in Jerusalem during the night. No casualties were reported. Graffiti nearby read "the nation of Israel lives", and "enough [terrorist] attacks, evict the Arabs".

December 18, 2022: Israel deported to France Palestinian-French lawyer and activist Salah Hammouri, claiming he had ties to the PFLP. He had worked as a lawyer for Adameer, a rights group that assists Palestinian prisoners but Israel had banned for alleged PFLP ties. Hammour, born in Jerusalem but with French citizenship, had been jailed for seven years for a plot to kill a prominent rabbi. He was released in a 2011 prisoner exchange with Hamas. Israel said he was guilty of "breach of allegiance".

JORDAN

May 24, 2022: *UPI* reported that the U.S. Departments of State and Treasury imposed economic and financial sanctions against a Jordanian Hamas finance official and an expansive network of facilitators and companies across the Middle East and North Africa that generate funds for Hamas. The Departments named four people and six companies with sanctions targeting Hamas's Investment Office, which holds assets estimated to be worth more than $500 million including companies in Sudan, Türkiye, Saudi Arabia, Algeria, and the United Arab Emirates. Those sanctioned included

- Ahmed Sharif Abdallah Odeh of Jordan, believed in charge of the international investment portfolio until 2017

- Usama Ali, who was involved in the business activities of the companies maintained in the investment portfolio as head of the Investment Office

- Türkiye-based Jordanian Hisham Younis Yahia Qafisheh, believed to have transferred funds for companies linked to the investment portfolio

- Kuwait-based Jordanian Abdallah Yusuf Faisal Sabri, who has worked for the Hamas Finance Ministry for several years

The Hamas-affiliated companies were listed as Agrogate Holding, Al Rowad Real Estate Development, Anda Company, Itqan Real Estate JSC, Sidar Company, and Trend Gyo.

LEBANON

February 22, 2022: *AFP* reported that the Interior Ministry claimed that Internal Security Forces (ISF) had thwarted an ISIS plan to conduct three suicide bombings targeting Shi'ite religious compounds in Beirut's Hizballah-controlled southern suburbs. Interior Minister Bassam Mawlawi announced that "A terrorist group had recruited young Palestinian men in Lebanon to carry out major bombing attacks using explosive belts." ISF said instructions came from an ISIS operative based in the Ain al-Hilweh Palestinian refugee camp; he was also communicating with Sunni extremists in Syria. An undercover agent working for ISF as a penetration of ISIS warned ISF that on February 7, he was instructed to prepare attacks on a Shi'ite religious compound in the al-Laylaki neighborhood, the Imam al-Kazem compound in Haret Hreik, and the al-Nasser religious center in Beirut's Ouzai suburb. He was to use three explosive vests and other weapons to conduct the attacks on February 16. Security forces identified four suspects residing in the Ain al-Hilweh camp who are believed to have been involved in the plot. Authorities arrested two suspects. ISIS asked bombers to record a confessor video, saying the attacks were conducted in honor of the late ISIS imam Amir Mohammed Said Abd al-Rahman al-Mawla, alias Abu Ibrahim al-Hashimi al-Qurayshi, alias Haji Abdullah, who was killed in a U.S. raid on February 2.

April 3, 2022: The *Jerusalem Post* and *al-Ahed* news reported that in a nighttime attack, a member of the Palestinian Authority's National Security Forces (NSF) was shot and killed in a market in the Ain al-Hilweh refugee camp.

April 24, 2022: *Al-Jazeera* and *UPI* reported that IDF tanks fired dozens of artillery shells into southern Lebanon at an infrastructural target after a rocket was launched from Lebanon into an open area near Mazuva, a kibbutz in northern Israel.

May 17, 2022: The *Washington Post* reported that final vote tallies showed that Hizballah and its allies lost their parliamentary majority.

August 24, 2022: The *Jerusalem Post* reported that Lebanese Interior Minister Bassam Mawlawi asked security forces to investigate death threats against the Saudi embassy in Lebanon after the Saudi Ambassador Walid bin Abdullah

al-Bukhari shared a recording containing threats on his *Twitter* account. The Interior Ministry believed that voice was of a Saudi living in Beirut's southern suburbs, a stronghold of Iran-backed Hizballah. The Interior Ministry added that Saudi authorities wanted the individual for "terrorist crimes". He said if his family was harmed, "no employee at the Saudi embassy will remain alive... I will annihilate everyone in the Saudi embassy, everyone who is related to the Saudi embassy."

September 7, 2022: A bomb exploded outside of the home of Hizballah-backed caretaker Public Works Minister Ali Hamieh in the eastern Bekaa valley. The bomb was wrapped in electrical wires and detonated in his garden.

September 16, 2022: *The Independent* reported that Judge Steven L. Tiscione of federal court in Brooklyn, New York, ordered Lebanese Hizballah to pay $111 million in damages under the U.S. Anti-Terrorism Act to a group of Americans who sued saying they were wounded by the group's rockets during a war with Israel in 2006.

December 1, 2022: *Reuters, UPI,* and the *Jerusalem Post* reported that the U.S. Department of the Treasury's Office of Foreign Assets Control (OFAC) sanctioned two individuals and two companies, all Lebanon-based, for providing financial services to and facilitating weapons procurement for Hizballah. Another individual was involved in facilitating weapons procurement. Those sanctioned included

- Adel Mohamad Mansour, 56, who led al-Qard al-Hassan, a Hizballah-run quasi-financial institution designated by the U.S. in 2007

- Hassan Khalil, 43, obtained weapons

- Naser Hassan Neser, variant Naser Hasan Neser, 59, who worked with Auditors for Accounting and Auditing, an entity that provided financial services

- al-Khobara for Accounting, Auditing and Studies (Mansour is its CEO)

- Auditors for Accounting and Auditing, controlled by Ibrahim Daher, sanctioned in

May of 2021 for serving as the chief of Hizballah's Central Financial Unit

December 14, 2022: The *Washington Post* and *BBC* reported that a 121st Infantry Battalion United Nations Interim Force in Lebanon (UNIFIL) armored vehicle was surrounded by a mob and came under small arms fire in al-Aaqibiyeh outside Sidon. Irish Pte Seán Rooney, 23, was killed in the attack on the two-vehicle convoy carrying eight UNIFIL peacekeepers to Beirut's airport. Four people were hospitalized; Pte Shane Kearney, 22, from Killeagh in County Cork, underwent surgery and was in serious condition. Two other soldiers sustained minor injuries. Rooney, from Newtowncunningham, County Donegal, joined the Irish Defence Forces in March 2019. Senior Hizballah official Wafiq Safa denied involvement. 22121401

Libya

February 10, 2022: *CNN, Reuters,* and regional *al-Jazeera TV* reported that in the morning, gunmen fired on the car of western-based Libyan Prime Minister Abdulhamid al-Dbeibah, who escaped unharmed as he was returning home. The attackers fled. Bullets hit the windshield, headlight, and chassis. *AFP* reported that parliamentary spokesman Abdullah Bliheg announced that the eastern-based House of Representatives in Tobruk unanimously voted to replace Dbeibah with Fathi Bashagha to head the government.

July 21-22, 2022: *Al-Jazeera, Anadolu, al-Ahrar TV, News360,* and *Reuters* reported that clashes between militia factions in Tripoli's central district near the Radisson Blu Hotel killed five people, including a man and a child. Fighting began in the Ain Zara region between units of the Presidential Council's security force and the Special Deterrence Force (RADA). Fighting was also reported in Zauiya al-Dahmani and al-Furnaj. The *Libya Observer* reported that nine were killed.

August 26-27, 2022: *Reuters* and *Economic Times of India* reported that fighting broke out in Tripoli's city center during the night and into the next morning between supporters of rival governments. *AP, CNN,* and *AFP* reported that 32 people died, with 159 wounded.

October 6, 2022: *News 360* and the *Libya Observer* portal reported that in the morning, gunmen attacked the headquarters of the Security Directorate of the parallel government of eastern Libya in Rebiana, killing two policemen and wounding seven other people, who were transferred to the Educational Hospital in Kufra. Authorities arrested several gunmen.

Morocco

September 29, 2022: *News 360* and *MAP* reported that the Central Bureau of Judicial Investigations (OCIJ) announced that a brigade of the special force of the Directorate General of Territorial Surveillance (DGST) in Casablanca arrested a suspected ISIS member, 29, who was preparing an attack against security force targets and planned to join the group in Morocco, Syria, or Iraq. Authorities seized computer equipment.

October 26, 2022: *News 360* reported that Moroccan security forces in Casablanca, Kenitra, Sidi Yahya Zaer, Inezgane-Ait Melloul, and Chichaua Provinces arrested five suspected ISIS sympathizers, aged between 20 and 45, who were planning attacks against basic services and security force targets. Authorities seized weapons and ammunition. Several of the detainees were being trained in the manufacture of explosives.

Qatar

November 19, 2022: *USNWR* and *Reuters* reported that AQAP called upon the world's Muslims to shun the soccer World Cup in Qatar, but made no threats. AQAP complained that Qatar was "bringing immoral people, homosexuals, sowers of corruption and atheism into the Arabian Peninsula", thereby diverting attention from the "occupation of Muslim countries and their oppression".

RED SEA

January 3, 2022: Houthi rebels announced on their *al-Masirah* satellite news channel that they had hijacked the Emirati ship *Rwabee* in the Red Sea off the coast of Hodeida. The Houthis claimed the ship was carrying military-style inflatable rafts, trucks, and other vehicles, a landing craft that lowers a ramp to allow equipment to roll on and off, and rifles. The vessel is owned by the Abu Dhabi-based Liwa Marine Services. Coalition forces said the ship carried medical equipment from a dismantled Saudi field hospital. Saudi state television said the Houthis moved the weapons onto the ship. *Al-Jazeera* added on January 17 that the Houthis rejected a UN Security Council call to release the ship and its 11-member crew, claiming on *al-Masirah* television that the ship was carrying "military assets". The UAE countered that the "civilian cargo vessel" *Rwabee* was leased by a Saudi company and had been in international waters. 22010303

March 24, 2022: *AP* reported that the anti-Houthi Saudi-led coalition said it destroyed two booby-trapped boats that approached oil tankers in the Red Sea. It claimed the boats were launched from the Houthi-controlled port of Hodeidah, Yemen.

SAUDI ARABIA

January 24, 2022: The government announced that the military had shot down ballistic missiles heading toward Dhahran. Another missile fell in Jazan region, injuring two foreign nationals and damaging vehicles and industrial workshops. Yemeni Houthis were suspected. 22012402

February 10, 2022: *Reuters, al-Arabiya TV,* and *Iran International* reported that Saudi air defenses shot down an explosives-laden drone over Abha Airport. A dozen people, including two Saudis and citizens of Bangladesh, Nepal, India, the Philippines, and Sri Lanka, were hit by shrapnel. Yemen-based Houthis said they hit a military target with a Qasef 2 drone. 22021001

February 21, 2022: *Al-Jazeera, Ekhbariya,* and the Saudi state news agency *SPA* said that Yemeni Houthis fired a drone from Sana'a International Airport toward King Abdullah Airport in the southwestern Jizan Province. Authorities intercepted the drone, but 16 people, including foreign nationals, were injured by shrapnel. Three travelers were critically injured. 22022101

March 10, 2022: *SPA,* the *Jerusalem Post,* and *Reuters* reported Yemen's Iran-aligned Houthi movement targeted a Saudi Aramco refinery in Riyadh using three drones. 22031001

March 11, 2022: The *Jerusalem Post* and *Reuters* reported that Yemeni Houthi rebel spokesman Yahya Sarea said it targeted Aramco facilities at the Saudi Arabian cities of Jizan and Abha. 22031101

March 12, 2022: *SPA, AP,* and *Reuters* reported that Riyadh executed 81 men, including 73 Saudis, seven Yemenis, and one Syrian, for terrorism and other offences including holding "deviant beliefs", murder, and membership in militant groups. Riyadh announced that some of the death row convicts were members of al-Qaeda, ISIS, and backers of Yemeni Houthi rebels. It was believed to be the largest mass execution in recent Saudi history.

March 20, 2022: *Reuters* and *Devdiscourse*.com reported that Yemeni Houthis fired missiles and drones at a petroleum products distribution terminal in the Jizan region, a natural gas plant, and the Yasref refinery in the Red Sea port of Yanbu, causing no casualties. 22032001

March 25, 2022: *AP, Livemint.com, al-Ekhbariya,* and *Reuters* reported that for six hours, Houthi rebels in Yemen fired drones at 16 oil facilities and other state institutions. Some drones hit Aramco facilities in Jeddah, others landed in two oil refineries and an electricity plant in the south, still others hit Riyadh. Other drones hit civilian housing and water tanks belonging to the national water company. Houthi military spokesman Yahya Sarea said the group attacked the Ras Tanura and Rabigh refineries. No casualties were reported. Houthi leader Abdel-Malek al-Houthi blamed Yemen's seven-year civil war on the United States, saying that Saudi Arabia is a mere "executor". The second-ever Saudi Arabian Grand Prix F1 race was scheduled for Jeddah for March 27. 22032501

Syria

January 2, 2022: *Al-Jazeera* and *SANA* reported that at 7 p.m., ISIS fired rockets in the Badia area, hitting a military transport bus, killing five soldiers and injuring 20.

January 12, 2022: *AFP* reported on January 17 that the Kurdish Red Crescent Aid announced that two ISIS members shot to death a health worker, 26, "while carrying out his humanitarian duties" in the al-Hol camp for displaced people. The terrorists entered the medical center with faked IDs.

January 13, 2022: The *Jerusalem Post* reported that a car bomb planted near a local transport office in Azaz near the Turkish border killed one civilian and wounded several bystanders.

January 20, 2022: The *Washington Post* reported that ISIS attacked Ghwaryan prison in the Kurdish-controlled area of Hasakah Province in the night, sparking a firefight leading to dozens of casualties by the next day. The incident began with an inmate revolt, followed by ISIS setting off two car bombs. Syrian Democratic Forces spokesman Mervan Qamishlo said, "Our forces killed around 20 terrorists that tried to attack the prison… Now there are clashes taking place in the neighborhoods near the prison, and Daesh is hiding behind civilians and using them as human shields." He said at least three civilians, seven inmates, and a member of the internal security forces were killed and seven wounded. The SDF said 89 prisoners were recaptured.

The *Washington Post* and *AP* reported on January 24 that Farhad Shami, a spokesman for SDF, said at least 160 suspected militants and 27 members of the U.S.-backed force had been killed in the battle to retake control of the prison. The SDF announced it had retaken the prison on January 26, but later admitted that some ISIS gunmen were still holed up in the facility. The

New York Times reported on January 30 that as of the previous day, 60 ISIS fighters remained.

February 2, 2022: *ABC News, Reuters,* the *Washington Post, CNN, UPI, BBC, AP, al-Jazeera, USA Today,* and the *Wall Street Journal* reported that an overnight raid in northwest Syria near the Turkish border by U.S. Special Forces had killed the leader of ISIS, Amir Mohammed Said Abd al-Rahman al-Mawla, alias Abu Ibrahim al-Hashimi al-Qurayshi, alias Haji Abdullah, who had succeeded Abu Bakr al-Baghdadi upon the latter's death on October 27, 2019. Pentagon press secretary John Kirby said that "U.S. Special Operations forces under the control of U.S. Central Command conducted a counterterrorism mission this evening in northwest Syria… The mission was successful. There were no U.S. casualties." The mission included Apache gunships, airstrikes, and Reaper drones. *NPR* reported that one helicopter experienced mechanical difficulties and had to be destroyed on the ground. *USA Today* reported that the clash against a two-storey house in a rebel-held area surrounded by olive groves in Idlib Province lasted for two hours.

The area is infested with Hayat Tahrir al-Sham (HTS) terrorists formerly affiliated with al-Qaeda, which battles defectors who joined the al-Qaeda-linked Hurras al-Din. The Syrian Observatory for Human Rights said an HTS member was inadvertently killed.

President Biden said that "Knowing that this terrorist had chosen to surround himself with families, including children, we made a choice to pursue a Special Forces raid at a much greater risk to our own people rather than targeting him with an airstrike. We made this choice to minimize civilian casualties… We do know that as our troops approached to capture the terrorist—In a final act of desperate cowardice he, with no regard to the lives of his own family or others in the building, he chose to blow himself up—not just in the vest but the blow-up that third floor, rather than face justice for the crimes he has committed, taking several members of his family with him. Just as his predecessor did." The opposition-run Syrian Civil Defense first responders claimed that 13 people, including six children and four women, were killed and two people were injured. The UK-based Syrian Observatory for Human Rights said that nine people, including two children and a woman, were killed. A U.S. official told *ABC News* that the civilian casualties occurred when al-Qurayshi set off an explosive device at the beginning of the operation near Atmeh and Dar Ballout. U.S. forces speaking Arabic used loud speakers to warn women and children to leave the area. Witnesses said the helicopters arrived at 1 a.m. and left around 3:20 a.m.

AP reported on February 6 that some 50 U.S. commandos attacked the three-storey house. Al-Qurayshi lived on the top floor; a lower-ranking ISIS leader and his family were on the second floor; an unwitting family was on the first floor. A raider speaking an Iraqi dialect said through the megaphone "If you don't leave, we have orders. We will fire missiles toward the house. There are drones overhead." Ten people left, including a man and woman from the first floor and eight children from the first and second. The ISIS lieutenant and possibly his wife fired on the commandos in a long gun battle and were ultimately killed. Several al-Qaeda adherents "began maneuvering with weapons toward U.S. forces," according to Central Command General Frank McKenzie. A U.S. helicopter killed two of them.

March 4, 2022: *AFP* reported that ISIS attacked an army bus east of Palmyra desert, killing three soldiers.

March 6, 2022: *AFP* and *SANA* reported that ISIS attacked an army bus in the Palmyra desert, killing 15 soldiers and wounding 18, many seriously.

March 8, 2022: *UPI* reported that the Biden administration named Katibat al-Tawhid wal Jihad, a Syria-based al-Qaeda-affiliated group, as a Specially Designated Global Terrorist Organization, accusing it of operating in Syria's Idlib Province with other terrorist designated groups, including Katibat al-Imam al-Bukhari and Islamic Jihad Group. The U.S. Department of State said the group was behind the April 2017 St. Petersburg subway bombing that killed 14 passengers and injured 50 others and the 2016 bombing of the Chinese Embassy in Bishkek, Kyrgyzstan, that injured three.

March 28, 2022: *Al-Jazeera* reported that an ISIS cell attacked the Kurdish Syrian Democratic Forces-run al-Hol camp in al-Hasakah Province. Three civilians, including a child, and an ISIS terrorist died and ten people were wounded. The Kurdish *Hawar* news agency said the three-hour gun battle pitted ISIS, armed with Kalashnikovs, pistols, and rocket-propelled grenades, against the SDF's Asayish Forces.

April 7, 2022: *Reuters* reported that a rocket attack on the Green Village base in the east slightly injured two U.S. personnel. One was treated and released; the other was checked for traumatic brain injury. *Military Times* reported the next day that four American troops were treated for minor injuries and evaluated for TBI after two rockets hit two support buildings. *AP* reported on April 18 that Combined Joint Task Force—Inherent Resolve changed its assessment and now believed that the explosive charges were deliberately placed by one or more individuals at an ammunition holding area and shower facility on the base.

CNN, AP, Military Times, and *CBS News* reported on June 6, 2022 that the U.S. Army's Criminal Investigation Division and the Air Force Office of Special Investigations were looking into whether an American service member set off explosives in an insider attack on the Green Village U.S. base in northern Syria that wounded four service members with traumatic brain injuries on April 7, 2022. The suspect is back in the United States.

CBS News, AP, NBC News, Air Force Times, and *CNN* reported on June 21 that military law enforcement authorities arrested an American airman who worked in explosive ordnance disposal and placed him in pretrial confinement. Charges were pending.

Task and Purpose reported on August 4, 2022 that Air Force spokesperson Ann Stefanek announced that the Air Force charged Tech. Sgt. David W. Dezwaan, Jr., of the 75th Air Base Wing at Hill Air Force Base, Utah, with dereliction of duty; destroying military property; reckless endangerment; access of a government computer with an unauthorized purpose; obtaining classified information; and aggravated assault for his alleged involvement in an explosion at a U.S.

military outpost in northern Syria that injured four American troops in April 2022. His preliminary hearing was scheduled for August 23 at Hill Air Force Base in Utah. *CNN* had reported that the blast was caused by explosive charges deliberately placed at an ammunition holding area and shower facility in the Green Village within the base. The Air Force Personnel Center said the airman worked in the explosive ordnance disposal career field. He was assigned to the 775th Civil Engineer Squadron at Hill Air Force Base, where he served as the non-commissioned officer in charge of the EOD base support equipment. He joined the Air Force in October 2007 and received the Joint Service Achievement Medal, the Navy Achievement Medal, and the Air Force Commendation Medal. He had been confined by the Air Force since June 2022. 22040701

April 17, 2022: *Al-Jazeera* reported that in an audio message entitled Vengeance for the Two Sheikhs, ISIS spokesman Abu Omar al-Muhajir called on ISIS fighters to avenge the deaths of then-leader Abu Ibrahim al-Qurayshi and his official spokesperson.

April 28, 2022: *Al-Jazeera* reported that ISIS was suspected when gunmen on motorcycles killed seven people and wounded four others at a Ramadan iftar gathering in Deir Az Zor Province. Nouri Hamish, former spokesperson of the Syrian Democratic Forces, had hosted the dinner at his home in Khashab. The *Euphrates Post* reported he was killed. The gunmen fled after villagers confronted them.

May 13, 2022: *Reuters* and *SANA* reported that a rocket attack on a military bus in Aleppo killed 10 soldiers and wounded nine.

May 30, 2022: The *Jerusalem Post* and *Anadolu* reported that there was a rocket attack on the U.S.-controlled Omar oil field in eastern Syria. The rockets fell nearby, causing no damage or casualties. 22053003

June 16, 2022: *Al-Jazeera, ABC News, AFP,* and *Reuters* reported that the U.S.-led Operation Inherent Resolve coalition announced that in an early-morning Chinook and Black Hawk helicopter raid in the village of al-Humaira (variants Hmeirah, al-Humayrah), 2.5 miles south of the Turkish border, it had detained Hani Ahmed al-Kurdi, a senior ISIS leader in Raqqa who was an experienced bomb maker, planner, and facilitator. *AFP* reported that the four men and six women who lived in the safe house did not socialize with the rest of the village. The raid lasted seven minutes. No civilians were injured.

June 20, 2022: *Al-Jazeera* reported that at 6:30 a.m., the Ministry of Defense announced that gunmen attacked a civilian bus on the Raqqa-Homs highway in the al-Jira area, killing 11 soldiers and two civilians and wounding three army personnel.

June 27, 2022: *ABC News* and *al-Jazeera* reported that U.S. Central Command announced that an airstrike killed Abu Hamzah al-Yemeni, a senior leader of al-Qaeda-affiliated Hurras al-Din, as he was riding alone on a motorcycle in Idlib Province.

July 12, 2022: The *Washington Post, AP, CNN, UPI,* and *Military Times* reported that U.S. Central Command announced that it killed Maher al-Agal, leader of ISIS in Syria, and seriously injured an ISIS senior official in drone strike on a motorcycle outside Jindaris in Khaltan village, near the Turkish border. A humanitarian group said the individual eventually died from his wounds. Al-Agal, one of the top five leaders of ISIS, had also worked to build ISIS networks outside of Iraq and Syria.

July 24, 2022: *News360* reported that Türkiye's intelligence services announced it had "neutralized" Sahin Tekintangaç, alias Kendal Ermeni, leader of Kurdish militias in Kobane, in the Aleppo region. *Hurriyet* reported that Türkiye accused him of involvement in "terrorist activities" in Agri, Kars, Bingöl, and Bitlis Provinces and of being part of the People's Protection Units (YPG), linked to the Kurdistan Workers' Party (PKK).

Türkiye announced the arrest of Savas Çelik a member of the Union of Kurdistan Communities, also linked to the PKK, who was accused of organizing an attack against Commander Arslan Kulaksiz in 2015, shot dead while in his vehicle.

August 15, 2022: *AP* and *Military Times* reported that in the morning, a drone attacked the al-Tanf garrison run by U.S. troops and U.S.-backed Syrian Maghaweir al-Thowra opposition fighters near the junction of the borders of Syria, Jordan, and Iraq, causing no casualties or damage. No one claimed credit.

August 24, 2022: *UPI* and *Military Times* reported that groups linked to Iran's Islamic Revolutionary Guard Corps fired rockets at 7:20 p.m. that landed inside the perimeter of Mission Support Site Conoco and near the vicinity of Mission Support Site Green Village, two coalition bases in Deir ez-Zor, injuring three U.S. service members. U.S. helicopters returned fire and destroyed three vehicles as well as equipment to launch the rockets and killed two of three terrorists involved. The next day, AH-64 Apache helicopters, AC-130 gunships, and M777 artillery killed four terrorists and destroyed seven rocket launchers. 22082401

September 11, 2022: ISIS killed six U.S.-backed Kurdish-led Syrian Democratic Forces fighters near the eastern village of Ruwaished in Deir el-Zour Province. The group said in a video on *Amaq* that it was retaliating for an ongoing operation inside a sprawling camp housing tens of thousands of family members of ISIS. The six were captured alive and shot dead that evening.

The previous week, SDF fighters arrested dozens of ISIS terrorists and rescued four women who were chained inside tents at the al-Hol camp that houses ISIS families in Hassakeh Province.

September 16, 2022: *News 360* and *Anatolia* reported that a Turkish Armed Forces drone strike killed Mehmet Gurbuz, alias Rojhat Karakocan, a commander for the Euphrates region of the Kurdish-Syrian militia People's Protection Units (YPG), along with his bodyguard, in Ain Issa in Raqqa Province. Türkiye charges that YPG is an offshoot of the PKK.

A second drone strike killed three other YPG members and destroyed two Grad missiles and ammunition.

September 18, 2022: *Al-Jazeera* reported U.S. Central Command said that at 7:05 p.m., three 107-mm (4.2-inch) rockets were fired at the U.S. military's Green Village base, but failed to hit the U.S. or coalition forces and equipment. Authorities found a fourth rocket and rocket tubes at the launch point three miles away.

October 5, 2022: *CNN* reported that U.S. Central Command announced it had conducted a nighttime special operations raid targeting a senior ISIS official in the northeast. *The Drive*, *CNN*, and *Reuters* added that the helicopter assault, supported by a few U.S. troops on the ground for less than an hour, occurred in Muluk Saray in Qamishli, which is controlled by the government of Syrian President Bashar al-Assad. *Al-Jazeera*, *CNN*, and Syrian media said Rakkan Wahid al-Shamman, an ISIS smuggler of weapons, money, and fighters, died, another was wounded, and two others were captured. The *Washington Post* reported that al-Shamman had beheaded two members of the Syrian Defense Forces.

October 6, 2022: *Military Times*, the *Washington Post*, and *AP* reported that a 6:23 p.m. U.S. airstrike in northern Syria killed Abu-Hashum al-Umawi, alias Abu 'Ala, the No. 2 ISIS leader in Syria and one of the group's top five leaders, and Abu Mu'ad al-Qahtani, an ISIS leader responsible for prisoner affairs.

Earlier in 2022, U.S. forces killed senior ISIS bombmaker Hani Ahmed al-Kurdi, alias the Wali of Raqqa.

October 8, 2022: *Reuters* reported that a rocket fired at a compound hosting U.S. troops and partnered local forces caused no injuries or damage. 22100801

October 28, 2022: *News 360* and *Sham FM* reported that an ISIS suicide bomber set off his explosive belt at a house in Daraa Province during a meeting in which former Free Syrian Army (FSA) leader Ghassan Akram Abazid was participating, killing four people and injuring two.

November 15, 2022: *Al-Jazeera*, *AP*, and *AFP* reported that the beheaded bodies of two Egyptian girls, aged 11 and 13, were discovered in sewage waters at the al-Hol detention camp hosting people linked to ISIS.

November 25, 2022: *Al-Jazeera* reported that U.S. CENTCOM noted that two rocket attacks against its patrol base in al-Shaddadi caused no injuries. Syrian Democratic Forces (SDF) found a third unfired rocket. 22112501

November 25, 2022: Mazloum Abdi, commander of the Syrian Democratic Forces, announced that the Kurdish-led force had halted operations against ISIS following a week of Turkish airstrikes on the SDF.

December 2, 2022: *Al-Jazeera* and *Reuters* reported that the Syrian Democratic Forces (SDF) announced that "all coordination and joint counterterrorism operations" with the U.S.-led coalition battling remnants of ISIS in Syria as well as "all the joint special operations we were carrying out regularly" had been halted because of Turkish attacks on its forces. Türkiye blamed SDF for the November 13 Istanbul bombing, which killed six people, and claiming that the suspected bomber had confessed to having been trained by the PKK in Syria.

December 11, 2022: *Task and Purpose* and *UPI* reported that at 3 a.m., U.S. Central Command helicopter-borne forces killed two ISIS leaders, including ISIS Syria Province official Anas, in al-Zer in eastern Deir el-Zour.

December 16, 2022: The Syrian Democratic Forces said it detained a wanted ISIS terrorist in a raid in Deir el-Zour and seized two cellphones, a dozen SIM cards, an Internet router, a Syrian-issued identity document, and a pistol with three magazines.

December 20, 2022: U.S. Central Command conducted three raids in eastern Syria in 48 hours and arrested six ISIS terrorists, including al-Zubaydi, a Syria Province senior official involved in planning and facilitating attacks in Syria. Two three raids took place in the Deir el-Zour and Hassakeh regions. Syrian Democratic Forces were also involved. Four detainees were Turkmen weapons dealers affiliated with ISIS. Two SDF fighters were wounded.

December 26, 2022: *Reuters* reported that an ISIS suicide attack on a security forces center in Raqqa killed two members of the SDF and two members of the region's Asayish internal security forces. One suicide bomber was killed and another would-be bomber detained.

December 29, 2022: *Task and Purpose* reported that CENTCOM announced that in 2022, U.S. troops in Iraq and Syria conducted 313 missions against ISIS, killing at least 686 suspected ISIS fighters, including the terrorist group's former top leader.

December 30, 2022: Rockets were fired at a bus carrying oil industry employees at the al-Taym gas field in Deir el-Zour Province, killing ten. No one claimed credit, but ISIS was suspected.

Kurdish-led forces arrested 52 members of ISIS sleeper cells.

TUNISIA

March 26, 2022: *Reuters* reported that a National Guard spokesman announced that police had dismantled about 150 militant cells in the past six months.

UNITED ARAB EMIRATES

January 17, 2022: The *Jerusalem Post, CNN, AP, AFP,* and state news agency *WAM* reported that Houthis claimed credit for a morning drone attack on three fuel tankers in Abu Dhabi's Musaffah industrial area near storage facilities of the ADNOC oil firm that killed three people—a Pakistani and two Indians—and injured six when a fire broke out at a storage facility at Abu Dhabi International Airport. The *Washington Post* added that Nasraddin Amer, the deputy minister of information in Houthi-controlled Sana'a, Yemen, said that the rebels had launched the attack in response to the "UAE's escalation" in Shabwa and Marib. *Defense News* reported that this was the first use in a military operation of the multibillion-dollar Terminal High Altitude Area Defense System (THAAD), made by Lockheed Martin and developed by the U.S. military. The THAAD intercepted a midrange ballistic missile aimed at an Emirati oil facility near al-Dhafra Air Base, which hosts U.S. and French forces. 22011701

The *Washington Post* reported on January 18 that Houthi officials claimed that nearly a dozen people were killed and others injured in overnight retaliatory airstrikes on Sana'a. Local residents said 14 died.

January 24, 2022: The UAE shot down two more ballistic missiles launched by Yemen's Houthi rebels. No casualties were reported. 22012401

January 31, 2022: *NPR* and *CNN* reported that UAE officials said the government had shot down a ballistic missile that Yemeni Houthi rebels had fired. No damage was reported. Israeli President Isaac Herzog was visiting the UAE. 22013101

February 2, 2022: *Reuters* and *CNN* reported that the UAE Defense Ministry tweeted it had intercepted three drones that entered its airspace over unpopulated areas at dawn. The little-known True Promise Brigades claimed credit. Its only other claim was in January 2021, when it said it launched a drone at Saudi Arabia.

West Bank

January 11, 2022: The *Jerusalem Post* reported that an IDF soldier, 19, was lightly injured in a car-ramming attack on Road 465 near the settlement of Neveh Tzuf in the West Bank. The attacker and a passenger in his car were detained.

February 8, 2022: *AFP* and *Reuters* reported that Israeli border police killed three Palestinians in a car in Nablus in what Israel described as an operation against a "terrorist cell". The border police reported that the trio were responsible for recent shooting attacks on Israeli troops and civilians. Fatah identified two of the dead as Adham Mabrouk and Muhammad al-Dakhil, who were affiliated with the al-Aqsa Martyrs Brigades.

February 22, 2022: The *Jerusalem Post* reported that the IDF fatally shot a Palestinian, 14, who was throwing Molotov cocktails at civilian vehicles near the village of al-Khader in the Gush

Etzion region. The Palestine news agency *Wafa* identified the teen as Mohammad Shehadeh.

March 1, 2022: *Al-Jazeera* and *AFP* reported that Israeli forces shot to death Palestinian Ammar Shafiq Abu Afifa, a resident of the al-Aroub refugee camp north of Hebron, near Beit Fajar.

Israeli border police and Palestinian health authorities announced that before dawn, authorities shot to death two other Palestinians after coming under fire in the Jenin refugee camp during an arrest raid against a suspect "wanted for terrorist activity". *Wafa* identified them as Abdullah al-Hosari, 22, and Shadi Khaled Najm, 18. Troops arrested Imad Jamal Abu al-Heija, a freed prisoner.

March 6, 2022: A Palestinian was killed after he attacked Israeli troops with Molotov cocktails.

March 31, 2022: *Reuters* and *AFP* reported that Palestinian Nidal Jumaa Jafara, 30, stabbed with a screwdriver and moderately wounded a male passenger, about 30, in the torso, on an Israeli bus south of Bethlehem near the Gush Etzion Jewish settlement in the West Bank. Another passenger shot Jafara to death.

During Israeli military raids in the morning in a refugee camp in Jenin to "apprehend terrorist suspects" linked to the Bnei Brak attack, residents fired on Israeli forces. Troops fired back, killing two gunmen. An Israeli soldier was slightly wounded. The Palestinian health ministry said two Palestinians, aged 17 and 23, were killed and another 15 were wounded. The Secretary General of Islamic Jihad, Ziad al-Nakhala, announced that IJ's armed wing would step up activities "in light of the storming of Jenin camp by the Zionist enemy army".

April 1, 2022: *UPI* and the *Times of Israel* reported that Israeli Defense Forces in Hebron shot and killed a Palestinian man after he threw a Molotov cocktail at them during weekly protests against Israeli settlements. Palestinian news outlet *Wafa* said he was Ahmad Younes al-Atrash, 29.

April 2, 2022: *UPI*, the *Times of Israel*, and the *New York Times* reported that Israeli Defense Forces and ISA security forces killed three Palestinian militants in a shootout in Shuweika after the men fired on border police who had stopped them on a tip they were about to carry out an attack in Israel. The Islamic Jihad confirmed their deaths. Four Israeli soldiers were injured, one seriously. Authorities arrested another armed suspect.

April 10, 2022: *Reuters, al-Jazeera,* and *Today Only* reported that Israeli troops in Bethlehem near Husan shot to death Ghada Ibrahim Sabatien, a Palestinian woman in her 40s running at them and ignoring their warning fire and calls to stop. She sustained a torn artery and massive blood loss. No weapon was found. *Wafa* reported that she was a widowed mother of six.

Israeli troops shot to death a Palestinian woman who stabbed and slightly wounded a paramilitary border policeman in Hebron, outside the Tomb of the Patriarchs, which Muslims call the al-Ibrahimi mosque.

April 13, 2022: *U.S. News and World Report* and *Reuters* reported that the Palestinian Health Ministry said Israeli soldiers shot dead two Palestinians, one a 14-year-old near Bethlehem who had thrown a petrol bomb at the soldiers, and the other a lawyer in Nablus, on a main street near Joseph's Tomb. Attorney Muhammad Hassan Muhammad Assaf, 34, worked for a department of the Palestine Liberation Organization that documents and lobbies against Israeli settlement activity on land Palestinians seek for a state. The PLO said he was driving his nephews to a school and had stopped on the side of the road to watch clashes at the tomb. *Al-Jazeera* added that a third Palestinian was killed in clashes that erupted after Israeli forces conducted an arrest raid. Shin Bet said it had arrested three Palestinians planning to carry out an imminent attack against Israelis. The military and police said about 20 "terror" suspects were detained.

May 8, 2022: *AFP* reported that Palestinian armed with a knife infiltrated the Tekoa settlement before being shot by a resident. The Palestinian health ministry identified him as Motasem Attalah, 17.

June 1, 2022: *USNWR, ABC News,* and *Reuters* reported that authorities shot to death a knife-wielding Palestinian woman who the IDF said threatened an Israeli soldier conducting routine security near al-Aroub village. The Palestinian Foreign Ministry called it a "field execution", observing, "She was en route to her work and there were no incidents there or danger to the criminals." The Palestinian Prisoners Society said she had been jailed by Israel for three months before being released in early April 2022. *Al-Jazeera* added that the Palestinian Health Ministry said Ghufran Hamed Warasneh, 31, had been shot in the chest at 8 a.m. at the entrance to the camp, located between Bethlehem and Hebron. Warasneh had started a new job at *Dream Radio*, a location station in Hebron, three days earlier. She died at al-Ahli hospital in Hebron of a bullet that pierced her heart. She lived in the nearby village of al-Shuyukh.

June 2, 2022: *AFP* and *al-Jazeera* reported that Israeli troops shot to death Ayman Mahmoud Mheisen, variant Ayman Muhaisen, 29, a Palestinian, in a pre-dawn raid at the Dheisheh refugee camp near Bethlehem. The father of three had spent three years in Israeli jails.

June 17, 2022: *USNWR* and *Reuters* reported that Israeli troops killed three Palestinian gunmen in Jenin. Hamas said one gunman was a Hamas member. Islamic Jihad said the trio were PIJ members.

June 21, 2022: *Wafa* reported that the Palestinian Health Ministry announced that Ali Hassan Harb, 27, was stabbed in the chest by an Israeli settler and died near the Ariel settlement in the north.

August 9, 2022: *UPI* and *Haaretz* reported that Israeli Police and the IDF killed Ibrahim al-Nablusi, 26, a member of the al-Aqsa Martyrs Brigade, and at least one other person, Islam Sabouh, in a morning gun battle in the streets of the Old City of Nablus as troops were attempting to arrest him at his residence. Troops found "a large quantity of explosives and additional weapons" at his home. Al-Nabulsi was wanted on accusations of being behind a series of shootings targeting IDF personnel and civilians. No troops were injured, but a 9-year-old elite unit K-9 named Zili died. The Palestinian Health Ministry said Hussein Jamal Taha, 16, was also killed in the raid. The *Jerusalem Post* reported that 30 Palestinians were wounded.

August 18, 2022: *Al-Jazeera, Times of Israel, Haaretz,* and *News 360* reported that the Israeli Army raided seven Palestinian civil society organizations in the West Bank. Six had been outlawed by Israel as "terrorist" organizations in October 2021, and accused of ties to the Popular Front for the Liberation of Palestine (PFLP). They included Addameer Prisoner Support and Human Rights Association, al-Haq rights group, the Union of Palestinian Women Committees (UPWC), the Union of Agricultural Work Committees (UAWC), the Bisan Center for Research and Development, and the Palestine chapter of the Geneva-based Defence for Children International. The seventh organisation was the Union of Health Work Committees (UHWC).

August 28, 2022: The *Jerusalem Post* reported that terrorists fired at a military pillbox post north of the Israeli settlement Ofra in northern West Bank during the night, causing no casualties. An hour later, shots were fired at a military position in Silwad, a Palestinian town northeast of Ramallah. The IDF added that it returned fire after shots were fired at a military position near Nablus. The IDF reported no casualties.

August 30, 2022: *AFP* reported that Palestinians shot at Israeli Jews who snuck into Nablus to visit the Joseph's Tomb shrine, wounding two, and torched their vehicle.

September 2022: The *Jerusalem Post* reported on September 19 that earlier in the month, Palestinians fired on a bus carrying troops from the Kfir Brigade in the Jordan Valley, injuring five soldiers and a civilian. One soldier sustained serious neck wounds; two others were moderately injured. The driver of the bus was shot in the face. The IDF arrested two Palestinians; a third remained at large.

Several days later, nine bullets hit two Israeli vehicles near Huwara. One Israeli was hospitalized with light injuries. A week later, the IDF and Shin Bet arrested the gunmen and seized weapons used in the attack.

September 2, 2022: *Reuters* reported that a Palestinian stabbed an Israeli soldier and was shot by another at a military outpost near Hebron. The assailant died; the soldier was moderately wounded.

September 4, 2022: *USNWR, AFP,* and *Reuters* reported that Palestinians in a pickup truck overtook and then fired on an Israeli bus on a desert highway within driving distance of Jenin and Nablus, wounding six soldiers and the driver. The terrorists tried to torch the bus when it stopped, but a firebomb went off inside their car. Authorities detained two suspected gunmen trying to escape. A Hamas spokesman called the "heroic" attack "proof that all attempts by the Occupation (Israel) to stop the escalating resistance operations in the West Bank have failed".

September 7, 2022: *News 360, AP, Times of Israel,* and *Kan* reported a Palestinian teen injured an Israeli soldier by hitting him in the face with a hammer near Beitin, east of Ramallah. The IDF shot to death the attacker, who carried a knife. The soldier had gone to an abandoned military post to relieve himself. The Palestinian Health Ministry identified the attacker as Haitham Mubarak, 17. No group claimed credit.

September 12, 2022: The *Jerusalem Post* reported that in a drive-by shooting, gunmen fired at Israeli soldiers on patrol near the Jalame crossing near Jenin. No injuries were reported.

September 14, 2022: *Al-Jazeera* and *AP* reported that two Palestinian men identified as Ahmad Ayman Abed, 23, and Abdul Rahman Hani Abed, 22, both from Kufr Dan village, and Israeli Major Bar Falah, 30, died in an exchange of fire at the Jalama (Gilboa) military checkpoint north of Jenin in the morning. Fatah said the duo belonged to its al-Aqsa Martyrs Brigades. One was a Palestinian Authority (PA) intelligence officer. The Jenin Brigades said the duo died after "intense armed clashes with occupation forces". Hamas called the duo "heroic martyrs".

The *Jerusalem Post* reported that two Palestinians shot to death Major Bar Falach as authorities were approaching the pair, who had acted suspiciously near a security barrier near Jenin.

Troops fired back, killing the two, one of whom had been an intelligence officer in the Palestinian Authority Security Forces.

September 15, 2022: The *Jerusalem Post* reported that a man, 18, was hit by gunfire in Carmel in the Mount Hebron area, sustaining moderate injuries. Another car was fired on outside the settlement, possibly by the same gunman, who fled the scene.

September 19, 2022: The *Jerusalem Post* reported that three shots hit an Israeli civilian car driving through Huwara south of Nablus before dawn. No injuries were reported. The IDF believed it was a drive-by from a passing vehicle.

September 24, 2022: *AFP* reported that Israeli troops killed a Palestinian driver who tried to ram them during a patrol outside Nablus. Palestinians deemed it a traffic accident. The Palestinian foreign ministry said the driver was Muhammad Ali Hussein Awad, 36, from Beit Ijza, near Jerusalem.

September 28, 2022: *Reuters* reported that Israeli forces killed three Palestinian gunmen in Jenin. Israeli police said they were targeting two Palestinians suspected of carrying out attacks. The Palestinians opened fire and set off a bomb as commandos closed in, and were shot. Palestinian medics said 40 people were wounded. The Dens of Lions Palestinian militant umbrella group said one of the slain gunmen also worked for the security services of the Palestinian Authority (PA). DL said a second Palestinian man killed was the brother of a Palestinian who shot dead three people in Tel Aviv in April.

October 23, 2022: *Reuters, AFP, News 360, Times of Israel, al-Jazeera*, and the *Jerusalem Post* reported that a limpet bomb on a motorcycle in the Old City of Nablus went off at 1:30 a.m. as Lions' Den fighter Tamer al-Kilani walked by, killing him. An Israeli military official said was connected to a shooting the previous week that killed an Israeli soldier, plus several other attacks in the northern West Bank. The PFLP and its military wing, the Abu Ali Mustafa Brigades, said al-Kilani had been a member of its military wing when he was younger. He spent eight years in Israeli prisons for membership in the Brigades. He left behind a wife, 11-year-old son, and five-month-old daughter. Palestinian groups blamed Israel.

October 25, 2022: *BBC* and *Bloomberg* reported that during an Israeli Defense Forces raid on a safehouse of the recently formed Lions' Den Resistance Brigades in the Old City in Nablus, five Palestinians, including three LD gunmen, were killed. Palestinian medical sources claimed that Israeli troops shot to death Qusai Tamimi, 19, a sixth Palestinian in Nabi Saleh, and wounded more than 20 Palestinians. The IDF said the site apparently was used as a bomb-making factory and headquarters of the group. Among the dead was LD senior commander and founder Wadi al-Houh, variant Wadee al-Houh, 31. The official Palestinian news agency *Wafa* and the *Jerusalem Post* said the others were Hamdi Sharaf, 35; Ali Antar, 26; Hamdi Qayyim, 30; and Mishaal Zahi Baghdadi, 27. Reports conflicted as to whether all five were LD members, or whether two were civilians uninvolved with the group.

Israeli Army Radio said Houh was involved in several terrorist attacks in the Nablus area, including the shooting that killed IDF St.-Sgt. Ido Baruch. Houh was a close friend of Mosab Shtayyeh, the senior Hamas operative who was arrested by the Palestinian security forces in Nablus a few weeks ago. Shtayyeh was also considered one of the top commanders of the Lion's Den group. Houh had been a senior member of al-Aqsa Martyrs Brigades, the armed wing of Fatah. He served in Israeli prison for security-related offenses. In 2020, Palestinian Authority officers in Nablus briefly detained him. He since posted on *Facebook* criticism of the PA for cracking down on Palestinian activists in the West Bank.

Mahmoud al-Banna, was with Houh during the military raid, was seriously injured.

October 26, 2022: *News 360* reported that in overnight raids, the IDF arrested 18 Palestinians allegedly involved in terror offenses, including three members of the Lions' Den militia.

October 28, 2022: *Reuters* reported that Israeli forces killed two Palestinian militants after a drive-by shooting at soldiers by individuals in "two suspicious vehicles" near Nablus. The Palestinian Health Ministry said the dead were Emad Abu Rasheed, 47, and Ramzi Zabara, 35, both from Askar refugee camp near Nablus. A third man was wounded. The al-Aqsa Brigades said the two men were members. The Palestinian Civil Guard, the Palestinian Authority's emergency and rescue service, said the two men worked for them.

October 29, 2022: *News 360* reported that a Palestinian fired an assault rifle, killing an Israeli citizen between the entrance to the Kiryat Arba settlement and Hebron. Three other Israelis and a Palestinian were wounded. A security guard rammed attacker Muhamad al-Jabari, 35, with his truck and pinned him to the ground. An off-duty military officer shot the attacker to death. The next day, *AP* reported that the IDF arrested one of the attacker's brothers and prepared the al-Jabari family home for demolition. No group claimed al-Jabari as a member, although Palestinians in Hebron celebrated.

October 30, 2022: *News 360* reported that a Palestinian driver hit and injured five Israeli servicemen at two locations south of Jericho. He rammed a group of servicemen near the Nabi Musa Junction before crashing his white car into a bus stop in Almog. The *Times of Israel* reported that two servicemen were moderately injured; the other three were lightly injured. *Yedioth Aharonoth* and *AFP* reported that security forces and a civilian shot dead the driver.

November 2, 2022: *Al-Jazeera* reported Israeli forces killed Palestinian Habis Abdel Hafeez Rayan, 54, who the Israeli army accused of carrying out a vehicle ramming and stabbing attack on an Israeli soldier at a military checkpoint near a Jewish settlement of Modiin. The Army reported that "The assailant got out of his vehicle with an axe to attack the officer, who fired at the attacker and neutralised him." Israeli army radio said the soldier was seriously injured and taken to Shaare Zedek Medical Center in Jerusalem. Rayan was from the village of Beit Duqqu northwest of Jerusalem. He left behind a son, Asem, imprisoned in an Israeli jail. *Reuters* reported that the next day the IDF raided Rayan's home.

November 15, 2022: *UPI, BBC, Washington Post, AFP, Reuters, Times of Israel, News 360,* and *CNN* reported that in the morning, a knife-wielding Palestinian attacker, 18 or 19, killed three people and critically injured three others at the Ariel Industrial Park. He stabbed a security guard at the entrance of the Park, then went to a nearby gas station to continue the attack. He fled in a stolen vehicle, caused a major traffic accident, and ran over another person on the nearby Route 5 highway, killing him. He hopped out of the car to stab other people. An IDF soldier shot him to death north of Salfit. *Wafa* identified the terrorist as Mohammed Murad Souf, variant Muhammad Murad Sami Souf, from the village of Hares, variant Haris. He had a permit to enter Israel. The dead included fathers Tamir Avihai, Michael Ledigin, and Moti Ashkenazi. The trio left behind 11 children. The IDF was searching for an accomplice. Souf had no criminal record, unlike his father, a Fatah member who had been imprisoned in Israel. Some reports said Souf stole two cars in his spree.

The *Jerusalem Post* reported that several Palestinian factions, including Hamas, Palestinian Islamic Jihad, PFLP, and the Democratic Front for the Liberation of Palestine, praised the attack as an "heroic operation".

November 21, 2022: The *Jerusalem Post* reported that a car exploded near an IDF post near the Mevo Dotan settlement. The vehicle had three gas cylinders, explosives, and a wire that may have allowed for a remote detonation of the devices. Authorities found a PFLP flag near the car.

November 29, 2022: *AFP* reported Israeli troops shot dead a suspected car-ramming attacker who had moderately wounded a female Israeli soldier, 20, north of Jerusalem near the Migron settlement.

November 30, 2022: The *Jerusalem Post* reported on December 3 that authorities in the Nablus Casbah confiscated a vehicle suspected of being used in an attempted shooting attack on a military post near the Jit junction on November 30.

December 1, 2022: The Palestinian Islamic Jihad threatened to retaliate after Israeli troops killed two of its leaders in Jenin.

December 2, 2022: The *Jerusalem Post* reported that the IDF, Shin Bet and Border Police arrested Ahmad Bassam Haraz, 22, a Palestinian suspected of carrying out shooting attacks in Nablus. He was earlier imprisoned for producing explosives and selling weapons. Israeli forces seized a handgun and military equipment. During the raid, Palestinian terrorists shot at Israeli forces and threw explosives at them. The soldiers returned fire and seriously injured an assailant.

The *Jerusalem Post* and *Channel 12* reported that Palestinian Ammar Hadi Mefleh, variant Mifleh, variant Mufleh, 22, attempted to use a stone to break into a locked vehicle with an Israeli couple inside, then stabbed a responding Israel Border Police officer in the face, lightly injuring him. Mefleh attempted to grab the officer's rifle. An IDF officer shot the attacker to death on Route 60 in Huwara. UN Special Coordinator for the Middle East Peace Process Tor Wennesland tweeted that he was "horrified by today's killing of a Palestinian man, Ammar Mifleh, during a scuffle with an Israeli soldier near Huwara in the ["occupied"] West Bank. The *Jerusalem Post, Yediot Aharonot,* and *KAN* added that UN Special Rapporteur for the Occupied Palestinian Territories Francesca Albanese and Tor Wennesland could face Israeli sanctions following their statements.

December 3, 2022: The *Jerusalem Post* reported that during the night, the IDF, Shin Bet, and Border Police arrested seven wanted men in the Judea and Samaria region in Ein Kiniyye, Dayr 'Amr, and Beit Furik, plus two people in the Binyamin region, two in the Yehuda region, and a third pair in the area where the Etzion Brigade operates. A suspicious vehicle drove full speed at the security forces, who shot at the vehicle, injuring and arresting the driver. A similar incident occurred soon after.

December 7, 2022: *Reuters* reported that Israeli forces killed a Palestinian driver who had fired on a military post. Soldiers conducting routine activity responded with live fire and pursued the driver who shot at one of its posts near the Ofra settlement. The al-Aqsa Martyrs Brigades said the man was a member of the group. The Palestinian Prisoners Club said the man, 32, had pre-

viously been imprisoned by Israel and was from the town of Silwad.

YEMEN

January 17, 2022: The *Jerusalem Post* reported that the Saudi-led coalition claimed that it had shot down three drones launched in the direction of Saudi Arabia. 22011702

January 26, 2022: *Reuters* and *SABA* reported that a nighttime Houthi missile attack on Marib killed five and injured 34.

February 11, 2022: *U.S. News and World Report* and *Reuters* reported that gunmen kidnapped five United Nations staff in the Governorate of Abyan who were returning to Aden after a field mission. *AFP* reported on September 6, 2022 that on September 3, AQAP released a video of a United Nations worker whom it abducted with four other UN staffers in Abyan Province in February. The video apparently was recorded on August 9. Hostage Akam Sofyol Anam urged "the UN, the international community, the humanitarian organizations, to please come forward... and meet the demands of my captors". 22021101

February 14, 2022: *Al-Jazeera* and the official Saudi news agency *SPA* reported that a Saudi-led military coalition airstrike destroyed a telecommunication system used to control drones in Sana'a. A spokesman told *SPA* that "The Houthis are using the Ministry of Telecommunications and Information Technology in Sanaa for hostile operations." The Houthi-run *al-Masirah* television station reported a coalition attack targeting the telecommunication ministry, destroying the TeleYemen telecoms company building and damaging another building. The coalition said it was responding to the February 10 drone attack on Abha Airport that injured 12.

Al-Jazeera reported that the coalition had conducted more than 24,000 air strikes in Yemen since 2015. *Jane's* noted that the Houthis had used four attack drones: the Qasef-1, Qasef-2K, and Sammad 2 and 3, and four reconnaissance drones: the Hudhed 1, Sammad 1, Raqib and Rased.

February 23, 2022: *Al-Jazeera* reported that Treasury Under-Secretary Brian E. Nelson said that the U.S. Department of the Treasury imposed sanctions on alleged members of an illicit network organized by lead financier Sa'id al Jamal that funds Yemen's Houthi rebels. The sanctions were aimed at front companies and ships that worked with a branch of Iran's Islamic Revolutionary Guard Corps to smuggle petroleum and other commodities around the Middle East, Asia, and Africa to help fund the Houthis. The sanctions also targeted traders and money exchange houses based in Yemen, the UAE, Türkiye, and other countries. The UAE blacklisted businessman Abdo Abdulla Dael Ahmed and five entities that had been sanctioned by the U.S.

February 28, 2022: *UPI* reported that the United Nations Security Council imposed an arms embargo on Yemen's Iran-backed Houthis, labelling them a terrorist group. The UAE-sponsored resolution passed 11-0-4 (Brazil, Ireland, Mexico, and Norway abstaining).

March 2, 2022: *AFP* reported that in the morning, Houthis fired a missile at a military camp in Midi in Hajjah Province near the Saudi border, killing nine Sudanese soldiers and wounding 30. 22030201

March 6, 2022: *Reuters* reported that gunmen kidnapped two Medecins Sans Frontieres (Doctors Without Borders) foreign employees—a German and a Mexican—from their car in Hadramout Governorate. AQAP was suspected. 22030601

March 20, 2022: *U.S. News and World Report*, Saudi state media, and *Reuters* reported that the Saudi-led coalition intercepted and destroyed a "hostile air target" aimed towards Jeddah.

March 23, 2022: *AFP* reported that Major General Thabet Jawas and four soldiers died in a car bomb explosion in al-Madina al-Khadra village, six miles north of Aden. No one claimed credit. He was a main commander fighting Houthi rebels.

April 1, 2022: The *New York Times* reported that the Yemeni government and Houthi rebels agreed to a U.N.-brokered two-month ceasefire to begin on April 2.

June 15, 2022: *Reuters* reported that Yemeni journalist Saber al-Haidari, 40, was killed in Aden in the night when a bomb hidden in his car exploded.

June 29, 2022: *Al-Jazeera* reported that a bomb planted in a car exploded within the convoy of a Yemeni military official in Aden, killing five civilians and one military officer and seriously wounding six others. Saleh al-Sayed, head of the security forces of the separatist Southern Transitional Council (STC) in Lahaj Province, survived the assassination attempt. AQAP was suspected.

August 28, 2022: *AFP* reported that rebels conducted a nighttime attack near Taez, killing ten soldiers and wounding several others.

September 6, 2022: *AFP* reported that AQAP attacked positions held by the UAE-trained Security Belt group in Abyan Province. The three-hour clash killed 21 separatists, including an officer, and six AQAP members.

September 12, 2022: *News 360* and the Saudi *Arab News* daily reported AQAP killed three Yemeni soldiers and wounded six other soldiers in a nighttime attack with several homemade bombs in Mudia in Abyan Province.

November 11, 2022: *News 360* and *Arab News* reported that Houthis fired a guided missile at a military vehicle carrying troops and residents in Qadash in Lajh Province, killing four soldiers and two civilians and wounding several other people.

November 12, 2022: *News 360* reported that Houthis killed a Yemeni soldier in Tur al-Bahah in Lajh Province.

November 17, 2022: *News 360* reported that a bomb exploded in Wadi Oemran in Abyan Province, causing no injuries. It was targeted at two senior members of the security forces. AQAP had announced a bombing campaign against the military.

November 19, 2022: *News 360* and the Yemeni portal *South24* reported that a bomb exploded in Wadi Oemran in Abyan Province, killing three military personnel and injuring two.

NORTH AMERICA

CANADA

February 14, 2022: *Newsweek* reported that the Alberta Royal Canadian Mounted Police (RCMP) arrested 11 people at one of the Freedom Convoy trucker protests in Coutts against COVID-19 restrictions after finding a cache of weapons and ammunition. Three trailers associated with the group contained 13 long guns and hand guns, body armor, a machete, ammunition, and high-capacity magazines.

March 19, 2022: *CNN* reported that at 7 a.m., during the dawn prayer of Fajr, worshipers at the Dar al-Tawheed Islamic Centre in Mississauga subdued Mississauga resident Mohammad Moiz Omar, 24, who had discharged bear spray and was swinging a hatchet. Omar said nothing, gasping for breath after inhaling bear spray. The mosque posted on *Facebook* that he was armed with "numerous other sharp edged weapons". *CNN* reported on March 21 that Peel Regional Police said Omar faced multiple charges for "a hate-motivated incident".

Charges included assault with a weapon; administering a noxious substance with intent to endanger life or cause bodily harm; possession of a weapon for a dangerous purpose; uttering a threat to cause death or bodily harm; carrying a concealed weapon; and mischief to religious property.

May 26, 2022: *Reuters, CTV,* and *CNN* reported that during the afternoon, two Toronto police shot and killed a man carrying a gun while walking down a street in the Scarborough area, near three schools. Five nearby schools, including the William G. Davis Junior Public School, Joseph Howe Senior Public School, Charlottetown Ju-

nior Public School, and Sir Oliver Mowat Collegiate Institute, were placed under precautionary lockdowns.

September 4, 2022: *CNN* reported that authorities were searching for Damien Sanderson and Myles Sanderson, possibly brothers, after a mass stabbing spree in which ten people were killed and 19 injured across 13 crime scenes in an Indigenous community and the surrounding area in Saskatchewan in western Canada. Victims ranged in age from 23 to 73 years old. Police believed the attackers were riding in a black Nissan Rogue with Saskatchewan license plate 119 MPI. Their vehicle was reportedly spotted at 11:45 a.m. in the Regina area, 186 miles south of the Cree site.

Police received the first stabbing report came at 5:40 a.m. at the James Smith Cree First Nation community. The *Washington Post* reported that Rhonda Blackmore, assistant commissioner of the Saskatchewan Royal Canadian Mounted Police, said that some of the victims appeared to have been targeted and some were random. One attack occurred in the neighboring community of Weldon.

Police increased security at Mosaic Stadium, site of the Saskatchewan Roughriders vs. Winnipeg Blue Bombers Canadian Football League game.

Authorities said Damien Sanderson, 31, was 5-feet-7-inches tall and 155 pounds with black hair and brown eyes. Myles Sanderson, 30, was 6-feet-1-inch tall and 240 pounds with brown hair and brown eyes. In May 2022, Saskatchewan CrimeStoppers listed Myles Sanderson as "unlawfully at large". Saskatoon police told *CBC* that in May he had stopped meeting with his parole officer. He was give statutory release from a five-year federal sentence for assault, robbery, mischief, and uttering threats.

The RCMP announced that police charged the duo with first degree murder, attempted murder, and breaking and entering into a residence. Myles Sanderson faced three counts of first-degree murder; Damien Sanderson was charged with one count of first-degree murder.

WOKV reported on September 5 that Rhonda Blackmore, commanding officer of the

Saskatchewan RCMP, said in the evening that Damien Sanderson was found dead in a grassy area on the James Smith Cree Nation, with wounds that did not appear to be self-inflicted.

CBC reported that one of the victims was Lana Head, 49, who worked as a security guard at the Northern Lights Casino and was a commissionaire officer. She was survived by two daughters, Sable, 31, and Sage, 30, according to her former partner, Michael Brett Burns.

The *Globe and Mail* reported on September 6 that crisis response worker Gloria Lydia Burns, 62, was killed on James Smith Cree Nation. The assailants burst into her home while she was attending to a call, killing her and two unidentified victims she was assisting.

Assistant Commissioner Rhonda Blackmore said the youngest victim was believed to have been born in 1999.

Weldon residents identified one of the victims as Wes Petterson, 77, a widower who ran coffee events on Sundays and drove around the community in the evenings to ensure everyone's safety. His adult grandson in his late 20s lived with him.

The *Washington Post* named Earl Burns, who served in Princess Patricia's Canadian Light Infantry regiment of the Canadian Army, as another victim. *BBC* added that Bonnie Goodvoice-Burns, 48, and her son Gregory Burns, 28, were killed. She died protecting her three young sons, one of whom survived his stab wounds. Also killed were Gloria Burns and Carol Burns.

BBC reported on September 7 that parole documents of Myles Sanderson showed that since he was 18, he had 59 convictions, including assault, threats, and robbery. His traumatic childhood included acts of violence and substance abuse.

CNN reported on September 7 that police received a call at 2:07 p.m. regarding a breaking and entering by Sanderson, who was standing outside of a home northeast of Wakaw with a knife. He stole a white Chevrolet Avalanche truck and fled the property. The RCMP received more than 20 calls about potential sightings of the truck. An RCMP officer saw the truck going 90 mph on a nearby highway. The *Washington*

Post reported that Sanderson was taken into custody around 3:30 p.m. near Rosthern, 80 miles southwest of the Nation. Police found a knife in his vehicle. Sanderson died after going into "medical distress" while in police custody.

The Saskatchewan Coroner's Service and RCMP identified the victims, nine of whom were from the James Smith Cree Nation, as:

- Thomas Burns, 23

- Carol Burns, 46

- Gregory Burns, 28, son of Bonnie Burns. He worked in the community, building homes.

- Lydia Gloria Burns, 61, a first responder and sister of Darryl and Ivor Burns

- Bonnie "Goodvoice" Burns, 48, sister of Saskatoon Tribal Chief Mark Arcand. She died trying to save her son Gregory, who had been stabbed several times at his home, but was herself stabbed twice. She worked at a local school and was fostering two other children. She was of the Wahpeton Dakota Nation and married into the James Smith Cree Nation.

- Earl Burns, 66

- Lana Head, 49

- Christian Head, 54

- Robert Sanderson, 49

- Wesley Petterson, 78, the only victim from Weldon, Saskatchewan

Authorities announced that all but one of the injured were adults; one was a teen. The Saskatchewan Health Authority announced that three patients were in critical condition; seven were in stable condition.

October 22, 2022: *CNN* reported that at 4 p.m., a "potential explosive" device was found on a bicycle parked near the island-side ferry terminal of Billy Bishop Toronto City Airport. Police moved the bike while passengers were evacuated and two Air Canada flights were diverted to Hamilton. Police disarmed the device and took two people into custody.

UNITED STATES

January 11, 2022: *AFP* reported that a court in Washington State convicted and sentenced Kaleb Cole, 25, a leader of the neo-Nazi Atomwaffen Division, to seven years in prison for threatening journalists and activists campaigning against anti-Semitism by mailing threatening communications, cyberstalking, and other activities. *NBC News* reported that he and three other neo-Nazis were arrested in early 2020 for a "Swatting" scheme. Prosecutors said the four planned to intimidate Jewish journalists and journalists of color by mailing threatening posters to their homes; one designed by Cole read "You have been visited by your local Nazis." Another poster showed a hooded figure preparing to throw a Molotov cocktail at a house. U.S. Attorney Nick Brown noted that Cole "repeatedly promoted violence, stockpiled weapons, and organized 'hate camps'". The *Jerusalem Post* added that Cole was convicted of one count of interfering in a federally-protected activity due to religion, three counts of mailing threats, and one count of conspiring to commit said crimes in addition to cyberstalking.

The three other Atomwaffen members pleaded guilty and were sentenced earlier. Cameron Shea, 25, was sentenced to three years in August 2021.

January 11, 2022: The U.S. Supreme Court refused to hear the appeal of Hoda Muthana, a woman who left home in Alabama to join ISIS in 2014, apparently after becoming radicalized online, but then decided she wanted to return to the United States. She was represented by attorney Hassan Shibly. Muthana was born in New Jersey in October 1994 to a diplomat from Yemen and grew up near Birmingham, Alabama. While she was overseas, Washington determined that she was not a U.S. citizen and revoked her passport, citing her father's status as a diplomat at the time of her birth. A federal judge ruled in 2019 that the U.S. government correctly determined Muthana was not a U.S. citizen because children of diplomats are not entitled to birthright citizenship. Muthana surrendered to U.S.-backed Syrian Democratic Forces. She had a son of a man she met while living with ISIS; he later died.

January 15, 2022: The *Fort Worth Star-Telegram* reported that a gunman took four people, including Rabbi Charlie Cytron-Walker, hostage during Sabbath services at Congregation Beth Israel on the 6100 block of Pleasant Run Road in Colleyville, Texas, northeast of Fort Worth. The livestream on *Facebook*, being watched by 8,000 people, began at 11 a.m. and was taken down around 2 p.m. *AP* reported that the individual told the rabbi that he had spent the winter night outside; the rabbi brought him inside and gave him tea. *Newsweek* reported that the man appeared to have a British accent. The individual claimed to have bombs at several locations. He claimed that Jews in America were powerful enough that they could get him what he was demanding. After the individual freed a male hostage at 5 p.m., the terrorist became more agitated. Drawing upon the Congregation's hostage survival training, at 9 p.m., Rabbi Cytron-Walker threw a chair at the terrorist, then led the other two hostages in fleeing through the door. The hostage-taker died in a firefight with the FBI SWAT Hostage Rescue Team. The FBI confiscated one firearm. The *Washington Post* quoted Stacey Silverman, a member of the Congregation, saying that the suspect could be heard saying that he had flown to the area from 5,000 miles away. No other injuries were reported. *NPR* said the FBI identified the attacker as British citizen Malik Faisal Akram, 44. President Joe Biden condemned the "act of terror".

ABC reported that the suspect claimed his "sister" is Aafia Siddiqui, 49, alias Lady al-Qaeda, a Pakistani terrorist incarcerated at Federal Medical Center Carswell women's prison in Fort Worth. He demanded her release. She was held since 2010 on charges related to the attempted murder and assault of United States officers and employees in Afghanistan in 2008. Siddiqui earned a bachelor's degree in biology from the Massachusetts Institute of Technology (MIT) and a PhD in neuroscience from Brandeis University. She was captured in Afghanistan in July 2008, with a flash drive containing documents on chemical and biological weapons and handwritten notes detailing a "mass casualty attack" on several New York City spots. When FBI agents and U.S. military personnel were interviewing her in Afghanistan, she grabbed a rifle and opened fire on the Americans before she was shot. She was convicted in federal court in New York of attempted murder and sentenced to 86 years in prison. She was married briefly to Amjad Khan then to Ammar al-Baluchi, nephew of Khalid Sheikh Mohammed. She told her attorney she was assaulted by another inmate in her cell on July 30, 2021. Another woman reportedly smashed a coffee mug with scalding hot liquid into Siddiqui's face. In several instances, al-Qaeda, AQAP, and ISIS demanded her release. She was represented by attorney Marwa Elbially, who said the suspect was not a member of Siddiqui's family.

Newsweek, Insider, and *The Guardian* reported that Counter Terror Policing North West of the Greater Manchester Police arrested two teens in South Manchester linked to Akram on January 16. *ABC News* reported on January 17 that the duo were Akram's children.

NPR and *The Guardian* reported on January 17 that British authorities said Akram came from Blackburn, Lancashire.

CNN and *NBC News* reported that Akram arrived at New York's JFK Airport on December 29, 2021. Akram was not on British or U.S. government watch lists. *CNN* reported that UK security services briefly investigated him in 2020, but determined that he was no longer a threat. Union Gospel Mission Dallas CEO Bruce Butler said that between January 6 and 13, Akram spent three nights at the group's homeless shelter.

Akram demanded that Siddiqui be brought to the synagogue so they could both die together, according to a law enforcement source.

NBC News and *Sky News* reported on January 17 that Akram's family members apologized, but added that they said there was nothing they could have done to get him to surrender during the incident. Gulbar Akram said his brother was "suffering from mental health issues". 22011501

CNN reported on January 18 that ten days before the attack, Akram argued with officials at the Islamic Center of Irving and was escorted from the property. He became belligerent after mosque employees refused to let him sleep inside the building, citing city ordinances prohibiting overnight guests.

ABC News and the *Insider* reported on January 20 that counterterrorism officers detained a man in Birmingham and another in Manchester.

CNN and *BBC* reported on January 26 that police arrested two men. *The Hill* reported on February 1 that Greater Manchester Police announced the duo's release. One was freed on January 26, the other on January 31.

AP reported that on April 9, 2022, the synagogue reopened.

On October 25, 2022, *UPI* reported that Chief U.S. District Judge David Godbey of the Northern District of Texas sentenced Henry "Michael" Dwight Williams, 33, to 95 months for selling Malik Faisal Akram a semiautomatic pistol at a South Dallas intersection two days before the attack. Police had arrested Williams on January 24, 2022 on an outstanding state warrant. He pleaded guilty in June 2022. Williams was earlier convicted for aggravated assault with a deadly weapon and attempted possession of a controlled substance.

January 18, 2022: *UPI* reported that Under Secretary of the Treasury for Terrorism and Financial Intelligence Brian E. Nelson announced that the U.S. Department of the Treasury had blacklisted three Lebanese men—Adel Diab, Ali Mohamad Daoun, and Jihad Salem Alame—accused of being financiers for Hizballah and the Dar Al Salam for Travel and Tourism company they own and operate. The sanctions included freezing all property and interests in property under their names and barring U.S. citizens from doing business with them under the risk of also being sanctioned.

The U.S. accused Diab of using his business to raise funds for Hizballah and of sharing assets with Ali al-Sha'ir, an assistant to Hizballah fundraiser Hasib Muhammad Hadwan, a member of the terrorist organization's general secretariat who works with its secretary general, Hasan Nasrallah. Al-Shair and Hadwan were blacklisted earlier.

Treasury accused Daoun of being a Hizballah official and Alame for materially assisting the organization.

January 28, 2022: *CNN* and *UPI* reported that Allison Elizabeth Fluke-Ekren, nee Allison Elizabeth Brooks, alias Umm Mohammed al-Amriki, 42, a former Kansas teacher, was detained in Syria, then sent to the U.S. to face federal charges of providing and conspiring to provide material support to a foreign terrorist organization by joining ISIS and leading an all-woman battalion in Syria. The Department of Justice said she allegedly wanted to recruit operatives to attack a U.S. college campus in the Midwest and was accused of discussing a terrorist attack on a shopping mall, adding, "To conduct the attack, Fluke-Ekren allegedly explained that she could go to a shopping mall in the United States, park a vehicle full of explosives in the basement or parking garage level of the structure, and detonate the explosives in the vehicle with a cell phone triggering device." The complaint was filed under seal in 2019. DOJ said that beginning in 2016, while in Syria, she led and trained 100 women and children to use AK-47 assault rifles, grenades, and suicide belts for ISIS. She also allegedly provided ISIS members with "lodging, translating speeches made by ISIS leaders... and teaching extremist ISIS doctrine", and organized and led the all-female Khatiba Nusaybah Battalion of ISIS. She faced 20 years in prison. Her next hearing was scheduled for January 31, 2022 in the U.S. District Court in Alexandria, Virginia.

Prosecutors said she moved to Egypt with her second husband, an Ansar al-Sharia member, in 2008, then moved in 2011 to Libya. She spent time in Mosul, Iraq, when it was ISIS-controlled. She also lived in Benghazi, Libya in 2012. Her husband's group was responsible for the September 11, 2012 attack on the U.S. special mission in Benghazi, Libya. He brought home a box of documents from the U.S. government buildings, which the couple read through. He delivered the American papers to officials in Ansar. The couple left Libya after determining that Ansar was not conducting sufficiently high-mortality attacks. They moved to Türkiye before settling in Syria in late 2012 or early 2013, where her husband trained ISIS snipers. A witness told the FBI that she and her late husband brought $15,000 to Syria to purchase the AK-47s, as well as grenades, handguns, and other weapons. A witness saw her young children, who were about five years old, holding a machine gun in her home in Syria. Her first husband died in February 2016 during an airstrike on Tell Abyad while attempting to conduct a terrorist attack on behalf of ISIS in Syria. She later married a Bangladeshi ISIS member who specialized in drones. He died in late 2016. She remarried a prominent ISIS leader, who has been responsible for ISIS's defense of Raqqa. Court documents indicated she was married five times; she was separated from her fifth husband.

She was behind the creation of an ISIS Women's Center in 2017 that offered medical services, and child care, and advanced weapons training.

She was smuggled out of ISIS-controlled territory in 2019. She turned herself in to local Syrian police in Qabasin in the summer of 2021 and was held in a Syrian prison for seven months. She was brought to U.S. custody on January 28, 2022 and flown to Virginia to face charges filed in 2019, according to *UPI*.

She told the court she had a U.S. master's degree in teaching. *CBS News* reported that she studied biology at the University of Kansas and attended a college in Indiana.

Amy Amer, an American writer based in Türkiye, met Fluke-Ekren in Kansas City in the 2000s and kept in touch with her until 2016. She noted that the teen mom was a Bible-beating Christian before her conversion.

U.S. District Judge Leonie M. Brinkema set sentencing for October 25, 2022. Her plea deal allowed for a maximum of 20 years in jail. She was represented by attorney Joseph King, who noted that his client was not charged with violent offenses.

On June 7, 2022, *AP* and *CBS News* reported that Allison Fluke-Ekren pleaded guilty in federal court in Alexandria, Virginia to conspiring to provide material support to a foreign terrorist organization, which carries a maximum 20-year prison sentence. First Assistant U.S. Attorney Raj Parekh said it was the first prosecution in the U.S. of a female ISIS battalion leader. The *Washington Post* reported she was the first U.S. woman to be prosecuted for a leadership role in ISIS.

AFP reported on October 30, 2022 that sentencing was scheduled for November 1 for Fluke-Ekren. *BBC* reported that Judge Leonie Brinkema sentenced her to 20 years in prison.

January 28, 2022: The *Florida Times-Union* reported that a Miami federal court sentenced Jonathan Guerra Blanco, a Cuban-born naturalized U.S. citizen, to 16 years in federal prison for distributing ISIS propaganda videos online. He had pleaded guilty in December 2020 to attempting to provide material support or resources to a designated foreign terrorist organization. He translated ISIS materials into Spanish for his target audience. Many of the videos called for attacks on Spanish authorities.

February 1, 2022: *CNN, WTOP, WGCL, WJLA,* the *Florida Times-Union, al-Jazeera,* and *AP* reported that more than a dozen Historically Black Colleges and Universities (HBCU) locked down and/or postponed classes after receiving bomb threats on the first day of Black History Month. Howard University, Southern University and A&M College in Baton Rouge, Louisiana, Bowie State University, Delaware State University, Bethune-Cookman University, and Albany State University had also received bomb threats on January 31. The later targets included Coppin State University, Alcorn State University, Tougaloo College, Morgan State University, Jackson State University, Kentucky State University, Fort Valley State University, Spelman College, Edward Waters University, the University of the District of Columbia, and Xavier University in New Orleans. Daytona Beach Police Chief Jakari Young said the Atomwaffen was behind the Bethune-Cookman threat.

    CNN reported on February 3 that the FBI had identified suspects, although no arrests were made. The threats are being investigated as hate crimes. The investigation involved more than 20 FBI field offices. No bombs were found.

February 8, 2022: *CNN* reported that a bomb threat was called in to Dunbar High School in Northwest Washington, D.C., during a visit with students and faculty by Second Gentleman Doug Emhoff, husband of Vice President Kamala Harris. The Secret Service evacuated the school and the children were sent home for the day. No bomb was found.

February 22, 2022: *Navy Times* reported that a three-judge panel of the 4th U.S. Circuit Court of Appeals upheld a prison sentence of 13 years and four months for former Coast Guard officer Christopher Hasson, who pleaded guilty to possessing unregistered and unserialized silencers, being a drug addict in possession of firearms, and illegal possession of tramadol, an opioid painkiller. He was accused of stockpiling weapons and plotting politically motivated killings inspired by Norwegian far-right mass murderer Anders Behring Breivik. The terrorism enhancement ruling in Hasson's case raised his guidelines range from 41 to 51 months to 151 to 188 months. The 4th Circuit panel said original sentencing judge Hazel "reasoned that Hasson's rhetoric and weaponry viewed separately would not justify applying the terrorism adjustment, but in combination they revealed 'that he was actually in the process of formulating a plan that makes this a case where the terrorism enhancement (applies).'"

March 21, 2022: Congressional confirmation hearings began for Judge Ketanji Brown Jackson, who was nominated by President Joe Biden to replace retiring Justice Stephen Breyer on the U.S. Supreme Court. Early in her career, while serving in a public defender's role, she worked on the cases of an al-Qaeda bomb expert, a Taliban intelligence officer, a man trained to fight U.S. forces in Afghanistan, and a Taliban-associated farmer.

March 24, 2022: *CNN* reported that in the morning, an individual broke into the Husseini Islamic Center in Sanford, Seminole County, Florida. The facilities manager, 59, confronted the attacker, dying after being bludgeoned and beaten with a shovel, but saving children at the center's school and daycare. The attacker broke a window with a propane tank and entered the mosque. No one at the center knew the suspect, who posted on social media that he was a descendant of Julius Caesar and he needed to defend Caesar's property. Sheriff Eric Flowers said the attacker escaped in the victim's vehicle, which was seen on a license plate reader in Indian River County. They found the vehicle in a Sam's Club parking lot. He exited the vehicle, but refused to put his hands up, instead reaching into his pocket, then pointing his hands like guns before diving back into the vehicle. Deputies fired, hitting him three times. He was hospitalized and likely to face murder charges.

March 29, 2022: *AFP* reported that jury selection began in the trial El Shafee Elsheikh, alias George (*CNN* said his alias was Ringo), 33, an alleged member of the ISIS kidnap-and-murder cell known as the "Beatles" because of their British accents. He was accused of involvement in the murders of American journalists James Foley and Steven Sotloff and relief workers Peter Kassig and Kayla Mueller. U.S. District Judge T.S. Ellis presided in the federal court in Alexandria, Virginia. Opening arguments began on March 30. The ISIS Beatles were believed involved in the kidnappings in Syria from 2012 to 2015 of 27 people from at least 15 countries, including the United States, Denmark, France, Japan, Norway and Spain. Elsheikh was represented by attorney Edward MacMahon.

The *Guardian* reported on April 2 that the case could establish a precedent that international terrorism cases could and should be tried in U.S. civilian courts.

On April 14, 2022, *CNN* reported that a jury in Virginia convicted ISIS Beatle El Shafee Elsheikh of eight counts, including four conspiracy charges relating to his work with ISIS and four charges of hostage taking resulting in death of Americans James Foley, Steven Sotloff, Kayla Mueller, and Peter Kassig between 2012 and 2015. On August 19, 2022, *Deutsche Welle* reported that U.S. District Court Judge T.S. Ellis sentenced ISIS "Beatle" El Shafee Elsheikh to eight concurrent life terms after being found guilty in April 2022 of hostage-taking and conspiracy to commit murder and support a terrorist organization.

April 2022: The *New York Times Magazine* reported in a long article on May 29, 2022 that in 2018, Cuban authorities at Jose Marti International Airport in Havana arrested Joseph Mahmoud Dibee, 50, a U.S. citizen and civil engi-

neer who was traveling from a business trip in Ecuador to his home in Russia, where he lived with his wife and stepson. On August 9, 2018, following several days of questioning by police and Cuban intelligence, Cuban officials handed him over to the FBI to face a 2006 indictment of participation in a series of arsons by the Earth Liberation Front. Dibee had spent years in Syria, Russia, and Mexico. In April 2022, he pleaded guilty to arson and conspiracy to commit arson. In the summer of 2022, he was scheduled to be sentenced in Oregon by Judge Ann Aiken.

The asthmatic Dibee was born in Syria after his parents moved from the United States. Until age 8 he spoke only Arabic. His father was an avid outdoorsman.

In December 2005, following mass arrests of ELF radicals, the FBI called in Dibee for questioning on a grand jury subpoena. He declined to cooperate and fled to Mexico, Beirut, and Syria. In Syria, he taught environmental engineering at the university level and helped plan a national project on renewable energy. He fled the civil war and landed in Russia, where he married and began a business recycling used fuels into biodiesel. Following a 2009 *New York Times* story that noted that Dibee was accused of being a domestic terrorist and that the FBI offered a $50,000 reward for his capture, the FAA revoked his U.S. pilot's license. After he contracted COVID-19 while in federal custody, he was conditionally released to house arrest.

April 6, 2022: *Newsweek* reported that U.S. citizen Bernard Augustine of California was sentenced to 20 years for attempting to provide material support to ISIS in Libya. He said he intended to encourage more English speakers to join the group and would "do it again" if acquitted. He had planned to give English voiceovers to ISIS propaganda videos, and watched such violent videos as "The Flames of War". He called videos showing executions of Syrian captives and beheadings as "good" and "really cool". He tried to join ISIS in 2016, using the search terms "how to safely join ISIS" and "how does a Westerner join ISIS", attempting to determine whether there was a recruitment process or application to be filled out. He posted that "the Islamic State is the true Islam" and the caliphate "can't be established and maintained except through the blood of the mujahideen who practice the true belief", according to the U.S. Department of Justice. In 2016, he traveled to Tunisia, hoping to join ISIS. He headed toward the ISIS-controlled region of Libya but was detained by local authorities before crossing the border. He was sent back to the U.S. in 2018 to face charges. His trial began in August 2021, lasting one week before the jury found him guilty. He represented himself during the trial.

April 12, 2022: *WABC* and *CNN* reported that at 8:24 a.m., a 175-180-pound, 5' 5" Black man entered the Kings Highway Subway station, put on a gas mask, set off a gas canister, and fired a handgun 33 times into a crowd of commuters on a Manhattan-bound N subway train waiting to enter the 36th Street and Fourth Avenue subway stop in Sunset Park in Brooklyn. At least ten people were hit by bullets, according to acting FDNY Commission Laura Kavanagh. Some reports indicated that 29 people were hospitalized for gunshots, smoke inhalation, shrapnel, and trampling during the panic. Five were in stable but critical condition. The train continued to the 25th Street station in Greenwood Heights. The gunman, wearing a green construction-type vest with a hooded gray sweatshirt, fled in the panic.

The individual left behind a bag containing a Glock 9 mm handgun, three extended magazines, two detonated smoke grenades, two non-detonated smoke grenades, bank cards in the suspect's name, a hatchet, and keys to a U-Haul van.

Police offered a $50,000 reward for information leading to his arrest.

CNN reported that the New York Police Department said it was searching for person of interest Frank James, 62, a Black man who rented a U-Haul van found near the scene of the shooting. James has addresses in Wisconsin and Philadelphia, the latter where he rented the vehicle. Authorities found the van's key at the subway crime scene; the van was recovered on a street in Brooklyn. NYPD Commissioner Keechant Sewell said social media postings connected to James mentioned homelessness, New York, and Mayor Eric Adams.

Patrol officers from the 9th Precinct downtown arrested Frank James in the East Village in New York City at 1:40 p.m. on April 13. They had received a tip on the Crime Stoppers hotline. *CNN* reported that James had called the tip line to say he was awaiting them in a McDonald's; subsequent reporting said he was picked up wandering the streets. Breon Peace, U.S. Attorney for the Eastern District of New York, said James was charged in Brooklyn federal court with violating a law that prohibits terrorist and other violent attacks against a mass transportation system. He was to be arraigned in federal court in Brooklyn. He faced life in prison.

NYPD Chief of Detectives James Essig explained that James got off at the 36th Street station, boarded an R train across the platform and rode to the 25th Street station stop. Less than an hour later, he boarded the subway at 7th Avenue and 9th Street station. Essig added that James, a New York City-area native, purchased the Glock at a pawn shop in Columbus, Ohio in 2011, and used a credit card to rent the U-Haul. Police believed the gun jammed during the shooting. Police said James bought the gas mask on eBay. James may have slept in the vehicle. Police said a license plate reader detected the van driving over the Verrazzano Bridge from Staten Island into Brooklyn around 4 a.m.

Among the injured was photojournalist Derek French, who told *CNN* he applied his Red Cross first aid training to help victims. While helping, French noticed that he was bleeding from a gunshot in his ankle.

Hourari Benkada, 27, a housekeeping manager at the New Yorker Hotel, was shot in the back of the knee, while sitting next to a man with a duffel bag who appeared to be wearing an MTA vest. He said the man let off a "smoke bomb". He recalled that gunfire began 20 seconds after the train left the 59th Street station and felt like it lasted for nearly two minutes.

Claire Tunkel, 46, was hospitalized for smoke inhalation.

James apparently had posted several videos on a *YouTube* channel, a screenshot from which was featured on a Crime Stoppers flyer. He talked about violence, mass shootings, and that he had thought about killing people who have presumably hurt him. "I've been through a lot of s**t, where I can say I wanted to kill people. I wanted to watch people die right in front of my f**king face immediately. But I thought about the fact that, hey man, I don't want to go to no f**king prison." He also complained about abuse in churches and racism in the workplace, employing misogynistic and racist terms. He claimed he had PTSD and had left his Milwaukee home on March 20, heading to the "danger zone... You know, it's triggering a lot of negative thoughts of course... I do have a severe case of post-traumatic stress." In a February video, he slammed Mayor Adams's plan to address safety and homelessness in the subway via increasing the presence of mental health professionals.

CNN reported on April 14 that Judge Roanne Mann denied bail. James did not enter a plea at his initial federal court appearance. Assistant U.S. Attorney Sara Winik called the attack as "premeditated and carefully planned". Defense attorney Mia Eisner-Grynberg requested a psychiatric evaluation.

The neon construction jacket, which James left on the subway platform, had a receipt for a storage unit in Philadelphia registered to James. The unit held more weapons and ammunition, including a threaded 9 mm pistol barrel that allows for a silencer or suppressor to be attached. Law enforcement searched an apartment James apparently rented for 15 days beginning on March 28, finding an empty magazine for a Glock handgun, a taser, a high-capacity rifle magazine, and a blue smoke canister.

James had a robust criminal record, racking up nine arrests in New York from 1992 to 1998, including possession of burglary tools, criminal sex act, and theft of service. He added three arrests in New Jersey in 1991, 1992, and 2007 for trespassing, larceny, and disorderly conduct. That said, he had no felony convictions, which allowed him to purchase a gun.

CNN, AP, and the *Florida Times-Union* reported on May 7, 2022 that Frank James, 62, was indicted on two federal counts: one of terrorist attack and violence against a mass transportation system and one count of discharging a firearm during a crime of violence. Both counts carry a

life sentence; the firearms count has a 10-year mandatory minimum sentence. Prosecutors said his DNA was obtained through a search warrant. The victims ranged in age from 16 to 60. He was jailed without bail. *CNN* reported on May 13, 2022 that James pleaded not guilty at his arraignment in front of U.S. District Judge William Kuntz. NYPD Chief of Detectives James Essig said James had nine prior arrests in NYC dating from 1992 to 1998 for offenses including possession of burglary tools, a criminal sex act, and theft of service. James was represented by Mia Eisner-Grynberg.

The *New York Times* reported on May 15, 2022 that the individuals who spotted James were attempting to obtain U.S. visas reserved for victims, witnesses, and informants who help law enforcement, or obtain humanitarian parole or political asylum. They included

- A Mexican woman, Ms. Flores, 37, who gave police her cellphone images of James

- Zach Tahhan, 22, an American-born Syrian who fled the civil war, who was represented by attorney Rifat A. Harb. Tahhan's parents are refugees in Türkiye.

- Mohamad Cheikh, a Lebanese student, who was represented by Mr. Harb. Cheikh earned his computer engineering Master's degree at City College in the fall of 2021.

- Francisco Puebla, manager of Saifee Hardware and Garden in the East Village in Manhattan, where Tahhan and Cheikh worked. He was directing security camera installers when James walked by. His attorney, Luis Gomez Alfaro, said Puebla's actions could make him eligible for an S visa for informants.

CNN and *NPR* reported on January 3, 2023 that Frank James, who faced ten counts of randomly shooting passengers, pleaded guilty to terrorism charges in federal court. He was indicted in December of committing a terrorist attack or other violence against a mass transportation system, and one count of discharging a firearm during a crime of violence.

April 20, 2022: *AP* and *ABC News* reported D.C. Metropolitan Police Chief Robert Contee announced that uniformed U.S. Secret Service officers shot and killed an intruder in the rear yard of the Peruvian Embassy in the Forest Hills neighborhood of Washington, D.C. The individual was smashing windows of the Peruvian ambassador's residence. The ambassador's relatives called the police around 8 a.m. The suspect waved a metal stake at police, who reported that tasers had no effort on him. Two officers were being evaluated for injuries. Some observers believed it was a burglary attempt.

April 29, 2022: *CNN* reported that U.S. District Judge T.S. Ellis in federal court in Alexandria, Virginia, sentenced ISIS "Beatle" Alexanda Kotey to life in prison. Kotey in September 2021 had pleaded guilty to taking part in hostage-taking that led to the deaths of American, Japanese, and British citizens in Syria. After serving 15 years in the U.S., Kotey will be transferred to the UK, where members of his family live, to serve the rest of his term.

May 1, 2022: *CNN* reported that Weather Underground member Kathy Boudin, 78, a 1960s radical imprisoned for a fatal robbery with life partner David Gilbert of an armored Brinks truck in Nyack, New York, died of cancer. Her son, Chesa Boudin, was San Francisco's District Attorney. She had founded Columbia University's Center for Justice. She had pleaded guilty to a single felony charge and was sentenced to 20 years to life. She was released in 2003 after serving 22 years. She had graduated in 1965 from Bryn Mawr College. She became the first woman to earn a master's degree while incarcerated in a New York state prison, later earned a doctorate from Columbia University Teachers College in 2007, and taught at the Columbia School of Social Work. Her brother, Michael Boudin, is a retired federal appellate judge. When she was jailed, Chesa, then 14 months old, was adopted by fellow radicals Bernadine Dohrn and Bill Ayers.

May 6, 2022: The *Oregonian* reported that police arrested freelance journalist Michael Edgar Bivins, 34, of Portland on suspicion of intentionally setting a fire at a Muslim community center, breaking windows at two Jewish congregations, and leaving graffiti on one of them. He was booked into the Multnomah County Detention Center at 4 a.m. on May 7 on five charges of arson and criminal mischief. Four charges are felonies. He had posted multiple hateful tweets in recent weeks. Authorities suspected him of spraying an antisemitic death threat in yellow paint on the outside of Congregation Beth Israel, the city's reform synagogue in Northwest Portland. He was suspected of breaking a window at Congregation Shir Tikvah on Northeast Sandy Boulevard on April 30. During the night of May 3, a surveillance camera recorded a man dressed in a blue hooded sweatshirt pouring something on the back of the Muslim Community Center of Portland's building on North Vancouver Avenue and then lighting it on fire at 6:48 p.m.

May 8, 2022: *CNN* affiliate *WISC* and the *Wisconsin State Journal* reported that in the morning on Mothers' Day, vandals damaged and torched the Madison, Wisconsin office of Wisconsin Family Action, a conservative political organization that lobbies against abortion rights and same-sex marriage. A passerby saw fire coming from an office building and called emergency dispatchers around 6 a.m. No injuries were reported. Police said a Molotov cocktail was thrown inside the building but did not ignite. A separate fire was started. Police also found graffiti at the scene, saying, "If abortions aren't safe, then you aren't either."

May 9, 2022: *UPI* and *AP* reported that Under Secretary of the Treasury for Terrorism and Financial Intelligence Brian Nelson announced that the U.S. Department of the Treasury's Office of Foreign Assets Control imposed financial sanctions on a network of five ISIS financial facilitators accused of smuggling children from Syrian refugee camps to fight in their terrorist cause. The network also transfers funds collected in Indonesia and Türkiye into Syrian displaced-persons camps to support ISIS efforts there, including for the recruitment of child fighters. Those sanctioned included:

- Dwi Dahlia Susanti, accused of being an ISIS financial facilitator since at least 2017.

Treasury claimed she had facilitated money transfers from Indonesia to displaced-persons camps in Syria with some of the funds used to smuggle teens out to the desert where they are picked up as recruits by ISIS foreign fighters.

- Muhammad Dandi Adhiguna and Dini Ramadhani were sanctioned on accusations of providing her assistance on multiple occasions and aiding her with financial and personal matters.

- Rudi Heryadi and Ari Kardian were also sanctioned.

A 2019 United Nations report indicated that of the 40,000 foreign ISIS members identified in Iraq and Syria, 12 percent were children under the age of 18.

May 11, 2022: *BBC, AP, CNN,* and the *Dallas Morning News* reported on May 18 that Jeremy Theron Smith, 36, was arrested for firing 13 shots from a .22 rifle that injured three women of Korean descent—the owner, a stylist, and a customer—inside the Hair World Salon in the Koreatown neighborhood of Dallas, Texas. The FBI opened a hate crime investigation. Authorities believe Smith, a Black man, may have been behind two other attacks on Asian businesses on May 10 and April 2. Dallas Police Chief Eddie Garcia told reporters that following a car accident involving an Asian male two years ago, Smith "has had panic attacks and delusions when he is around anyone of Asian descent". Smith was charged with three counts of aggravated assault with a deadly weapon.

May 13, 2022: The U.S. Department of State notified Congress that it planned to remove five defunct groups from its list of foreign terrorist organizations, including:

- the Basque separatist group Basque Fatherland and Liberty (ETA)

- the Japanese cult Aum Shinrikyo (Supreme Truth)

- the radical Orthodox Jewish group Kahane Kach (or Kahane Chai)

- the Mujahidin Shura Council in the Environs of Jerusalem, an umbrella group of several jihadist organizations based in Gaza

- Gama'a al-Islamiyya (Islamic Group–IG), an Egyptian Sunni Islamist movement that fought to topple Egypt's government during the 1990s

May 14, 2022: *CNN* reported that at 2:30 p.m. a gunman from another New York County nearly 200 miles away shot to death ten people and injured three others at the Tops Friendly Markets supermarket on Jefferson Avenue in Buffalo. Buffalo City Court Chief Judge Craig Hannah said that Payton S. Gendron, 18, a white man, was charged with first-degree murder and that the district attorney's office was planning on bringing additional charges in the racially-motivated attack. The supermarket is located near the predominantly Black neighborhoods of Masten Park and Kingsley. Gendron pleaded not guilty. *Yahoo!* reported on May 19 that a grand jury indicted Gendron for first-degree murder. Buffalo Police Commissioner Joseph Gramaglia said Gendron began by firing in the parking lot, killing three and injuring one, then moved inside, firing before he surrendered to police. Eleven victims were African American; two were White. Stephen Belongia, FBI Special Agent in Charge of the Buffalo field office said the Bureau was investigating the shooting as both a hate crime and a case of racially motivated violent extremism. The shooter livestreamed the incident on *Twitch*. He was wearing tactical gear with a tactical helmet and fired an assault weapon. Security guard Aaron Salter, Jr. (a retired Buffalo police lieutenant) shot the suspect, but the bullets were stopped by his heavy armor. The shooter killed Salter. Gendron put the gun to his neck, but two police officers talked him into dropping the gun, taking off some of his gear, and surrendering. He faced life in prison without parole.

Erie County Sheriff John C. Garcia said the shooting was a "straight up racially motivated hate crime from somebody outside of our community…This was pure evil."

Investigators said a purported 180-page manifesto was posted online in which the author said he was a fascist, a White supremacist, and an anti-Semite. The writer said he was radicalized by reading online message boards. He cited the "great replacement" theory of the far right. He noted that the Buffalo supermarket was in the 14208 Zip code, which "has the highest black percentage that is close enough to where I live". He said he bought a Bushmaster XM-15 from a gun store before "illegally modifying it".

Gendron was from Conklin, 3½ hours from Buffalo.

Four of the people shot were store employees.

Buffalo City Court Chief Judge Craig Hannah said Gendron pleaded not guilty to first degree murder.

CNN reported that on May 15, the Buffalo police identified the victims as:

- Roberta A. Drury, 32, of Buffalo, was buying food for dinner. She often shopped for her adoptive brother, Christopher Moyer—who was recovering from leukemia—and his family. *Syracuse.com* reported that she had lived in Syracuse but was in Buffalo to help her brother. She had attended school in the North Syracuse Central School District.

- Margus D. Morrison, 52, of Buffalo, was the father of three children.

- Andre Mackneil, 53, of Auburn, New York, was engaged to Tracey Lynn Maciulewicz. He died on their son's third birthday. He had gone to Tops to pick up a surprise birthday cake.

- Aaron Salter, 55, of Lockport, New York, had worked at the supermarket for several years after retiring as a police lieutenant.

- Geraldine Talley, 62, of Buffalo, was doing her regular grocery shopping with her fiancé, who escaped unharmed. She was a mother of two.

- Celestine Chaney, 65, of Buffalo, a grandmother to six—who ranged in age from four to 28—and a great-grandmother, was a cancer survivor who was buying shrimp and strawberry shortcake. She enjoyed bingo and shopping, and regularly attended church.

- Heyward Patterson, 67, of Buffalo, worked as a driver who gave rides to residents to and from the grocery store and helped with their groceries. He attended the State Tabernacle Church of God, serving as the pastor's armor-bearer and working in the soup kitchen. He left behind a wife, Tirzah.

- Katherine "Kat" Massey, 72, of Buffalo, a member of the community group We Are Women Warriors, which hosted a forum in February to discuss preventing youth violence following an incident in a local high school. In 2021, the group organized a giveaway of masks and PPE for people in Buffalo. She wrote for the *Buffalo Challenger* and *The Buffalo Criterion* newspapers, which serve the city's Black residents, and wrote frequent letters to the editor of the *Buffalo News*, in May 2021 expressing worry about "the escalating gun violence in Buffalo and many major U.S. cities... There needs to be extensive federal action/legislation to address all aspects of the issue… Current pursued remedies mainly inspired by mass killings – namely, universal background checks and banning assault weapons – essentially exclude the sources of our city's gun problems. Illegal handguns, via out of state gun trafficking, are the primary culprits."

- Pearl (or Pearly) Young, 77, of Buffalo, a substitute teacher for Buffalo Public Schools who also worked at Emerson School of Hospitality. She was preceded in death by her husband Ollie. She ran a weekly food pantry for 25 years, feeding people in Central Park every Saturday.

- Ruth Whitfield, 86, of Buffalo, mother of retired Buffalo Fire Commissioner Garnell Whitfield. She had visited Garnell's father in the nursing home, as she does every day, then stopped to buy groceries.

- Zaire Goodman, 20, of Buffalo, was treated and released from hospital

- Jennifer Warrington, 50, of Tonawanda, New York, was treated and released from hospital

- Christopher Braden, 55, of Lackawanna, New York, had non-life threatening injuries

New York Governor Kathy Hochul announced $2.8 million in funding for the victims and their families.

Buffalo Police Commissioner Joseph Gramaglia said "There was evidence that was uncovered that he had plans, had he gotten out of here, to continue his rampage and continue shooting people... He'd even spoken about possibly going to another store... He was going to get in his car and continue to drive down Jefferson Avenue and continue doing the same thing."

Investigators suggested that Gendron was in Buffalo the day before the shooting and did some reconnaissance at the store.

Investigators were treating the attack as a hate crime and terrorism.

Police noticed Gendron in June 2021, when, as a student at Susquehanna Valley Central High School, he made a "generalized threat" that was not racially motivated. Gendron was given a mental health evaluation and released after a day and a half.

Al-Jazeera added that the *Twitch* broadcast showed a racial epithet scrawled on the rifle used in the attack, as well as the number 14, possibly a reference to a white supremacist slogan.

A grand jury indicted Gendron of first-degree murder on May 18; he pleaded not guilty. He was held in jail without bail. *CNN* reported on June 1 that a grand jury returned a 25-count indictment, including 10 counts of first-degree murder, 10 counts of second-degree murder as a hate crime, three counts of attempted murder as a hate crime, domestic terror, and a weapons charge. He was on suicide watch. Federal prosecutors were also developing charges regarding a hate crime and a case of racially motivated violent extremism.

Yahoo! and the *Buffalo News* reported on May 19 that assistant office manager Latisha Rogers said a 911 dispatcher hung up on her for whispering when she called emergency services during the attack. The dispatcher was placed on administrative leave and her termination was to be sought at a May 30 disciplinary hearing. "She was yelling at me, saying, 'Why are you whispering? You don't have to whisper' And I was telling her, 'Ma'am, he's still in the store. He's shooting. I'm scared for my life. I don't want him to hear me. Can you please send help?' She got mad at me, hung up in my face." Rogers then called her boyfriend, who called 911 to report the shooting.

BBC reported on June 15, 2022 that that U.S. Department of Justice filed 26 federal hate crime and firearms charges—including 10 counts of hate crime resulting in death, three counts involving bodily injury, three counts of use and discharge of a firearm during a violent crime, and 10 counts of use of a firearm to commit murder and in relation to a violent crime—against Payton Gendron, 18. He faced the death penalty. He had pleaded not guilty to separate New York state charges of domestic terrorism and murder.

CNN reported on November 28, 2022 that Payton Gendron, 19, pleaded guilty to state charges including one count of domestic act of terrorism motivated by hate, 10 counts of first-degree murder, three counts of attempted murder, and a weapons possession charge. He faced a mandatory sentence of life in prison without the chance of parole. He was represented by attorney Brian Parker. Sentencing was scheduled for February 15, 2023.

May 15, 2022: *AFP* and *AP* reported that a gunman opened fire with two handguns at the Taiwanese-American congregation in Geneva Presbyterian Church (also known as the Irvine Taiwanese Presbyterian Church) in Laguna Woods, California, killing one person and injuring five others, four critically. The wounded were four Asian men aged 66, 75, 82, and 92, and an Asian woman, 86. Authorities said he was motivated by hatred of Taiwan and its people. U.S. citizen David Chou, 68, superglued door locks and chained the doors, hoping to trap the parishioners partaking in a post-service 1:30 p.m. banquet. His bags contained Molotov cocktails and spare ammunition. Police said he had emigrated from China; he was born on Taiwan in 1953. He worked as a security guard in Las Vegas. He planned to attack other victims. Parishioner John Cheng, a doctor, tackled Chou, dying in the gunfire but giving the rest of the congregation enough time to subdue and hogtie Chou.

May 18, 2022: *CNN* reported that the U.S. House of Representatives voted 222-203 to pass the Domestic Terrorism Prevention Act of

2022, aimed at preventing domestic terrorism and combating the threat of violent extremism by White supremacists. The bill will require 60 affirmative votes in the Senate. The Act would establish offices specifically focused on domestic terrorism at the Department of Homeland Security, the Department of Justice, and the FBI. The bill was sponsored by Democratic Rep. Brad Schneider (D-Illinois) and cosponsored by Reps. Brian Fitzpatrick (R-Pennsylvania), Don Bacon (R-Nebraska), and Fred Upton (R-Michigan). On May 26, 2022, the Senate did not pass the Act.

May 19, 2022: *UPI* and *al-Jazeera* reported that Under Secretary of the Treasury for Terrorism and Financial Intelligence Brian Nelson announced that the U.S. Department of the Treasury imposed economic sanctions against Lebanese businessman Ahmad Jalal Reda Abdallah and his network of five associates and eight companies in Lebanon and Iraq for funding Hizballah.

May 24, 2022: *CNN* reported that Salvador Ramos, 18, shot and critically injured his grandmother, crashed his vehicle in a ditch near Robb Elementary School in Uvalde, Texas, fired at two people at a neighboring funeral home, conducted a gun battle with a security guard and two police officers, barricaded himself in a classroom, and killed 19 students and two teachers before a Border Patrol officer killed him. The attack came two days before the students were to begin summer break.

The school has 2nd through 4th grades for 535 students.

Ramos had stopped regularly attending Uvalde High School, where he was often bullied. He had legally purchased two weapons for his 18th birthday on May 17 and 20, and used them in the shooting. He left one rifle in his crashed truck, and fired a rifle and a handgun. He posted photos of three AR-15s. He had worked at a local Wendy's.

NBC News, Yahoo! and *Occupy Democrats* reported that the victims included

- Eva Mireles, 44, a 4th-grade teacher for 17 years whose husband Ruben Ruiz was a police officer with the Uvalde school district

- Irma Garcia, 48, a teacher who shielded students with her body. She was in her 23rd year of teaching at Robb. She left behind a husband, two sons, and two daughters. Two days later, husband Joe Garcia had a fatal heart attack. They were high school sweethearts and married for 24 years.

- Nevaeh Alyssa Bravo ("Heaven" spelled backwards)

- Jacklyn Cazares, 9

- Makenna Elrod, 10

- Jose Flores, Jr., 10

- Eliana "Ellie" Garcia, 10

- Uziyah Garcia, 10, a 4th grader who was survived by two sisters

- Amerie Jo Garza, 10, who was shot while trying to call 911

- Xavier Lopez, 10, an honor roll student whose relatives raised more than $70,000 within 24 hours via a GoFundMe page

- Jayce Carmelo Luevanos, 10

- Tess Marie Mata, 10

- Miranda Mathis, 11

- Alithia Ramirez, 10

- Annabelle Guadalupe Rodriguez, 10, a 3rd-grader. Her cousin was killed in the same classroom.

- Maite Yuleana Rodriguez, 10

- Alexandria "Lexi" Aniyah Rubio, 10, an honor roll 4th-grade student with all-As and a good citizen award. Her father, Felix Rubio, a deputy with the Uvalde County Sheriff's Office, was one of many authorities who responded to the scene of the shooting.

- Layla Salazar, 10

- Jailah Nicole Silguero, 11

- Eliahana "Elijah" Cruz Torres, 10

- Rogelio Torres, 10

Another 15 people were wounded, including 11 children; a woman, 66, in serious condition; two police officers; and a Border Patrol agent.

Authorities found a backpack with seven 30-round magazines. They noted that the unemployed, friendless shooter lived with his grandparents in Uvalde, had no criminal history or gang affiliation, and no girlfriend. He was wearing a tactical vest.

Many observers noted that it was easier to get a gun in the U.S. than a pet or baby formula.

Many pundits questioned why the killer was in the school between 40 minutes and an hour before police were able to enter. Police authorities said that the 19 police were awaiting additional equipment to breach the classroom and the on-scene commander thought that no children remained inside. However, students inside the classroom called 911 numerous times, pleading for police intervention. Federal agents ultimately ignored the police commander and breached the classroom door, killing the attacker. The U.S. Department of Justice opened an investigation of the police response, including why a school district police officer—Uvalde Consolidated Independent School District Police Chief Pete Arredondo—had the authority to hold back the city's officers.

Ramos had no known criminal record or mental health history.

May 24, 2022: *NBC News, CNN,* and *Forbes* reported that the FBI alleged that Iraqi citizen Shihab Ahmed Shihab, of Columbus, Ohio, who entered the U.S. in September 2020, plotted to kill former President George W. Bush, traveling to Dallas to surveil the former president's home on February 8, 2022. The Bureau said he wanted to provide material support to ISIS, telling an FBI informant that he wanted to smuggle people into the country "to murder former President George W. Bush", whom he said was responsible for killing numerous Iraqis in the 2003 invasion of the country. Shihab was represented by public defender Soumyajit Dutta, who said that his client worked odd jobs and as a food vendor and has no close relatives in the U.S. Prosecutors charged Shihab with aiding and abetting the attempted murder of a former federal official in retaliation for the performance of official duties, and attempting to bring a foreigner to the U.S. for financial gain. The Bureau said he entered the U.S. legally in September 2020 and applied for political asylum. He tried to marry a U.S. woman to improve his immigration status. He told an FBI informant that he drove a transport vehicle with bombs in Iraq and was linked with the late ISIS leader Abu Bakr al-Baghdadi. In June 2021, he allegedly said that he would pay $5,000 to smuggle four former Ba'ath party members in Iraq, Türkiye, Egypt, and Denmark into the U.S. by crossing the Mexico border. They were to obtain firearms and a large van with a sliding door to carry out the assassination. He said two of the plotters were ex-Iraqi intelligence agents. One of the Iraqis was the secretary of an ISIS financial minister. He planned to use a car dealership in Columbus, Ohio, as a "hawala" to launder money from the U.S. to the ISIS financial minister's secretary. Shihab called himself a "soldier waiting for directions from the leadership in Qatar".

May 26, 2022: *UPI* reported that a federal jury in Brooklyn found senior ISIS member Mirsad Kandic, 40, guilty of one count of conspiracy to provide material support to ISIS and five substantive counts of providing the terrorist organization with support in the form of personnel, services, weapons, property, equipment, and false documentation and identification. Prosecutors said Kandic, from Brooklyn recruited thousands of people from Western countries to fight for ISIS in Syria and disseminated propaganda. The Department of Justice said one of his recruits was a New Yorker who became an ISIS sniper and trainer and Australian teenager Jake Bilardi who committed a suicide attack on March 11, 2015, in Ramadi, Iraq, killing himself and 30 Iraqi soldiers and an Iraqi police officer. Kandic gave ISIS battlefield fighters and commanders, including Bajro Ikanovic, who U.S. officials said commanded an ISIS training camp in Syria, intelligence and maps as well as conspired to dig tunnels under the Türkiye-Syria border to move more than 1,000 fighters into ISIS's ranks at a time.

Kandic arrived in Syria in late 2013 after several tries to leave the U.S. He initially tried to leave to join ISIS in the summer of 2012 but he was denied boarding a plane at a U.S. point of departure as he was on a no-fly list. In January 2013, he was turned away for the same reason for a flight from Toronto, Canada, to Istanbul. In

November 2013, he took a two-day bus trip from New York City to Mexico, then flew through Panama, Brazil, Portugal, Germany, Kosovo, and Türkiye before making it to Syria. He was arrested in June 2017 in Sarajevo, Bosnia and Herzegovina. He faced life in prison.

June 1, 2022: *CNN* reported that a man carrying a rifle and pistol from a parking lot walked up to the second floor orthopedic center of the Natalie Medical Building on the campus of St. Francis Hospital at 65th Street and Yale Avenue in Tulsa, Oklahoma, killing four people, including two doctors, and wounding ten. Some may have been injured in the chaos to escape. The shooter was reported dead at the scene, probably of a self-inflicted gunshot. Gun Violence Archive said it was the 233rd mass shooting (at least four people, not including the shooter, injured or killed) in 2022, on the 152nd day of the year.

    CNN reported the next day that the gunman bought an AR-15-style rifle the day of the shooting. *NPR* and *CNN* said he bought the 4.0-caliber semiautomatic handgun on May 29. He blamed surgeon Dr. Preston Phillips for post-surgery pain, and carried a letter saying he intended to kill Dr. Phillips and anyone who got in his way. He also killed Amanda Glenn, a receptionist at the hospital's Warren Clinic, and mother of two boys. Also killed was Dr. Stephanie Husen, a doctor of osteopathic medicine. William Love, a patient who was killed, had held a door to let others escape. Gunman Michael Louis, 45, of Muskogee, Oklahoma, underwent back surgery on May 19 and was released on May 24. Dr. Phillips saw him again on May 31. Louis parked his car in a nearby garage, and went through unlocked doors to get to the second floor office.

June 3, 2022: *NPR* and *CNN* reported that at 5 a.m., U.S. Capitol Police charged retired New York police officer Jerome Felipe of Flint, Michigan with unlawful possession of high-capacity magazines and unregistered ammunition. He had parked his 2017 Dodge Charger near the Capitol and allowed police to search it. USCP reported that they found a "BB gun, two ballistic vests, several high capacity magazines, and other ammunition". He showed USCP officers a fake

badge with the words Department of the INTERPOL printed on it, and claimed that he was a criminal investigator with the agency.

June 7, 2022: Amherst Police suggested that a 3 a.m. fire at a CompassCare anti-abortion center in a Buffalo suburb was likely arson. The center's director blamed women's rights extremists, saying the vandals who set the fire wrote "Jane was here" on the building.

June 8, 2022: *CNN* and the *Washington Post* reported that at 1:50 a.m., Montgomery County police arrested an armed Simi Valley, California man near the Maryland home of Supreme Court Justice Brett Kavanaugh, against whom he had made threats. *ABC News* and the *VC Star* reported that the man had a Glock 17 with two magazines, a tactical knife, ammunition, pepper spray, zip ties, a hammer, a crow bar, duct tape, and burglary tools in a suitcase and backpack. *NBC News* reported that he took a taxi to Kavanaugh's house, but spotted two U.S. deputy marshals nearby. He walked a block away, called the Montgomery County Emergency Communications Center to say that he intended to kill Kavanaugh and himself, and was arrested. The *VC Star* reported that Nicholas John Roske, 26, appeared in U.S. District Court in Maryland before U.S. Magistrate Judge Timothy J. Sullivan on charges of attempted murder of a federal official. Roske was upset about the draft Supreme Court decision that would overturn *Roe v. Wade*, and about the recent Uvalde school shooting. He said killing Kavanaugh would give his life purpose. He faced 20 years in prison. At his initial hearing, he told U.S. Magistrate Judge Timothy J. Sullivan, "I think I have a reasonable understanding [of court proceedings], but I wouldn't say I'm thinking clearly." He claimed to be a college graduate, and was taking medication. He was represented by federal public defender Andrew Szekely. A follow-up court date was set for June 22. Roske committed a minor traffic infraction in 2015. Jake Finch, a spokeswoman for Simi Valley Unified School District said that Roske graduated from Simi Valley High School in 2014 and ran cross country for two years. He left his job at Valley Guard Pest Control in Simi Valley in 2021.

CNN reported on July 27, 2022 that in the previous weeks, Roske researched how to assassinate individuals. Search terms included "most effective place to stab someone", "assassin skills", "how to be stealthy", and "quietest semi auto rifle". He also examined the Court's website's list of current members. He told an individual on *Discord* in May that he was "gonna stop roe v wade from being overturned" and "remove some people from the supreme court". His interlocutor replied "Two dead judges ain't gonna do nothing... You would die before you killed them all." Roske observed, "yeah but I could get at least one, which would change the votes for decades to come, and I am shooting for 3."

Roske pleaded not guilty to the charge of attempting to assassinate a U.S. Justice.

June 10, 2022: The *Daily Beast* and *Rolling Stone* reported on July 26, 2022 that former Marine Matthew Belanger, a member of the neo-Nazi Rapekrieg, was arrested on June 10, 2022 on federal firearms charges related to a straw purchase of an assault rifle and a handgun. He allegedly was planning a mass murder and rape spree to "decrease the number of minority residents" and "increase the production of white children" in America. Prosecutors filed a detention memo in Honolulu federal court indicated that he wanted to oust the "Zionist Order of Governments". He served in the Marine Corps from 2019 through May 2021, when he was given an Other Than Honorable Discharge. Investigators found in Belanger's barracks "1,950 images, videos and documents related to white power groups, Nazi literature, brutality towards the Jewish community, brutality towards women, rape, [and] mass murderers", including convicted domestic terrorist Dylan Roof.

June 11, 2022: The *Wall Street Journal* and *AP* reported that police in Coeur d'Alene, Idaho arrested 31 suspected white nationalist members of the Patriot Front on suspicion of conspiracy to riot near the annual LGBT Pride in the Park event and in other areas downtown. Police searched a U-Haul rental van after a citizen called to report people with masks and military gear loading the vehicle in a parking lot of a downtown hotel. Ten minutes later police

stopped the van. The individuals were wearing shin guards and carrying shields and other riot gear. Police confiscated a smoke grenade. They were expected to appear in court on June 13. The individuals came from 11 states, including Washington, Oregon, Texas, Utah, Colorado, South Dakota, Illinois, Wyoming, Virginia, and Arkansas. One was from Idaho.

June 25, 2022: *CNN* reported that a pickup truck hit several abortion rights demonstrators in Cedar Rapids, Iowa, who were protesting the Supreme Court reversal of *Roe v. Wade*.

June 30, 2022: *CNN* reported that Floyd County Sheriff John Hunt said that Lance Storz, 49, a suspect who used multiple firearms in a six-hours-long eastern Kentucky shootout that killed three officers and injured several others was "a terrorist on a mission". On July 1, Storz was charged in Floyd County court with several counts of murder, including murder of a police officer, and assault on a service animal. The judge set his bond at $10 million cash. Storz appeared via video with multiple bruises and lacerations on his face. The judge said he would appoint a public defender.

Deputies were serving a domestic violence warrant in Allen when Storz opened fire before they could even contact him. The dead included Floyd County Deputy William Petry and Prestonsburg Police Capt. Ralph Frasure, a 39-year police veteran. The Prestonsburg Police Department said officer and canine handler Jacob R. Chaffins was killed. He had also served as an EMT and fire fighter. A police canine officer also died. Four peace officers and one civilian were wounded. A deputy who took cover under a running patrol vehicle sustained carbon monoxide poisoning.

Storz was jailed in Pike County. A preliminary hearing was set for July 11 at 1:30 p.m.

July 1, 2022: *WOKV* and *WTOP* reported that the Richmond, Virginia Police Department on July 6 announced that, acting on a tip from a "hero citizen" caller that someone was "threatening to do a mass shooting on or about July 4", they had arrested an individual and seized several guns, preventing a mass shooting at a July

4 event at Dogwood Dell. *WWBT* reported that on July 4, police arrested Julio Alvarado, 52, at his home and booked him on a recommended charge of being a non-U.S. citizen in possession of a firearm. Police arrested Rolman Balacarcel, 38, on July 5 on the same charges. Police seized two assault rifles, a handgun, and more than 200 rounds of ammunition.

July 4, 2022: *NPR* and *CNN* reported that around 10 a.m., a gunman fired 90 rounds from a high-powered AR-15-style rifle from the roof of a commercial building into a crowd at a July 4 parade on Central Avenue in Highland Park, Illinois, killing seven and hospitalizing 38, ranging in age from eight to 88, before escaping. The shooter left behind the rifle, which he had legally obtained. Police tracked him down using the rifle's serial number. Police said the white male was between 18 and 20 years old. Highland Park Police Chief Lou Jogmen named as a person of interest Robert "Bobby" E. Crimo, III, 21, believed to be driving a silver 2010 Honda Fit, Illinois license plate DM80653. Police said the shooter used a ladder in an alley to get to the roof of a business. He was arrested later that evening after a North Chicago police officer saw him driving his mother's car and requested backup. Police believed Crimo had planned the attack for several weeks.

Police said Crimo wore women's clothing to cover up his multicolored neck and face tattoos, and to more easily blend in with the fleeing crowd. He then went to his mother's house. He lived in Highwood.

Highland Park Mayor Nancy Rotering told *NBC* she knew Crimo as a child. "I know him as somebody who was a Cub Scout when I was the Cub Scout leader."

Christopher Covelli, deputy chief of the Lake County Sheriff's Office, told a press conference that Crimo had considered a second attack in Madison, Wisconsin, where he had driven after the Highland Park shooting, using a second weapon in his car.

CNN reported on July 5 that police identified the victims:

- Irina McCarthy, 35, and Kevin McCarthy, 37, married in Chicago. Their son, Aiden, 2, was found alive. Relatives set up a Go-FundMe account for Aiden. By July 5, it had raised $820,000.

- Katherine Goldstein, 64, of Highland Park

- Jacquelyn Sundheim, 63, of Highland Park, a lifelong member of the North Shore Congregation Israel in Glencoe and member of the staff. She had been a preschool teacher and events coordinator.

- Stephen Straus, 88, of Highland Park, biked into his 80s.

- Nicolas Toledo-Zaragoza, 78, of Morelos, Mexico, father of eight and grandfather of many, was visiting his family. He enjoyed fishing, painting, and walking in the park with his family. His family set up a GoFundMe account to repatriate him to Mexico. Six of his eight children lived in the United States. One was injured in the shooting, as were two other Toledo family members. *AP* reported that granddaughter Xochil Toledo's father tried to shield Nicolas and was hit in the arm. Her boyfriend was hit in the back.

- A seventh victim died at a hospital outside of Lake County.

Barbara Medina, 46, was injured in the stampede as people fled. She was marching in the parade, representing Community Partners for Affordable Housing (CPAH). Her arm was broken as she fell while trying to get her daughter Carolina, 7, to safety. They were separated from her son, 12, and her father in the melee.

CNN reported on July 7 that Cooper Roberts, 8, who was attending the parade with his parents and twin brother, was shot in the chest, suffered a severed spinal cord, and was paralyzed from the waist down.

The Mexican Director for North American Affairs tweeted that two Mexicans were injured.

Lake County State's Attorney Eric Rinehart announced that prosecutors charged Crimo with seven counts of first-degree murder. Crimo faced life without the possibility of parole. Police said he confessed, providing details of how he got on the roof.

Crimo was represented by attorney Thomas Durkin.

Crimo had many warning signs. He tried to commit suicide with a machete in 2019, and in September 2019, threatened to kill people, according to a family member. Police fielded 22 disturbance calls to the family home.

Crimo did not appear to be employed, although he worked at Panera before the COVID-19 pandemic.

Crimo's father, Robert, Jr., had run for mayor of Highland Park in 2019, calling himself "a person for the people". He owned the house in front of his son's apartment.

Rabbi Yosef Schanowitz told *CNN* that Crimo attended a Passover service in April 2022 at Central Avenue Synagogue.

Crimo had attended High Park High School. Classmates described him as odd and withdrawn. His few friends tended toward rebelliousness.

Police were searching for a female witness who saw Crimo drop a rifle inside of a red blanket behind a Ross's store at 625 Central Avenue immediately following the shooting.

CNN reported on July 27, 2022 that the Lake County State's Attorney's Office announced that a grand jury in Lake County, Illinois, returned 117 felony counts against Crimo, including 21 counts of first-degree murder, three counts for each deceased victim, 48 counts of attempted murder, and 48 counts of aggravated battery with a firearm for each victim who was struck by a bullet, bullet fragment, or shrapnel. Arraignment was scheduled for August 3, 2022. He faced life in prison.

July 7, 2022: The *St. Augustine Record, Florida Times-Union,* and *USA Today* reported that a judge sentenced former St. Augustine resident Romeo Xavier Langhorne, 32, to 20 years in prison for attempting to provide material support to a designated foreign terrorist organization—ISIS. He also received 15 years of supervised release.

July 21, 2022: *CNN* reported that in the evening, a man climbed on stage during a Republican campaign event in Fairport, New York and attempted to stab U.S. Representative Lee

Zeldin, the Republican nominee for New York governor. The Zeldin campaign announced that Zeldin "grabbed the attacker's wrist to stop him until several others assisted in taking the attacker down to the ground". Zeldin, a 2020 election denier, finished his speech. The Monroe County Sheriff's Office charged David G. Jakubonis, 43, of Fairport, with attempted assault in the second degree. He was released on his own recognizance. *CNN* added on July 23 that the U.S. Attorney's Office in the Western District of New York announced that Jakubonis was arrested on a federal charge of assaulting a member of Congress with a dangerous weapon. Jakubonis appeared before US Magistrate Judge Marian W. Payson in Rochester. Court records indicated the weapon was a self-defense keychain. Steve Slawinski, assistant federal defender for the Western District of New York, represented Army veteran Jakubonis. A bail hearing was scheduled for July 27. The criminal complaint indicated that Jakubonis told authorities he had consumed whiskey on the day of the campaign event and "must have checked out" as he walked on the stage to ask if Zeldin was disrespecting veterans.

July 27-28, 2022: *AFP* reported on August 2, 2022 that the NYPD on July 28, 2022 arrested Khalid Mehdiyev, a man found with a loaded assault rifle outside the Brooklyn New York City home of Iranian-American journalist Masih Alinejad, 45, who has criticized Iran's regime. U.S. federal prosecutors said four Iranian intelligence agents plotted to kidnap her in July 2021. Police found a loaded AK-47 and 66 rounds of ammunition in his Subaru. Authorities charged him with one count of possessing a firearm with an obliterated serial number. A judge ordered him detained without bond.

Alinejad founded the My Stealthy Freedom movement, which encourages women to remove their hijabs.

July 29, 2022: The *Washington Post, UPI, AFP, Reuters,* and *Deutsche Welle* reported that U.S. District Judge T.S. Ellis, III of the Eastern District of Virginia sentenced to life in prison Saudi-born Canadian jihadi Mohammed Khalifa, 39, who was radicalized online, joined ISIS in Syria, and narrated in English 15 ISIS propaganda videos. Khalifa pleaded guilty in December 2021 to conspiring to provide material support to terrorism resulting in death. Prosecutors requested life; the defense, including attorneys Edward Ungvarsky and Cary Citronberg, said he merited only 20 years, saying he killed only two Syrian soldiers and no Americans and had a wife and three children.

Khalifa admitted to being in the final scenes of two documentary-length ISIS videos: "Flames of War: Fighting Has Just Begun" and "Flames of War II: Until the Final Hour", executing Syrian soldiers who had been forced to dig their own graves.

Khalifa earned a college degree in computer systems technology in Toronto, and was wooed by online videos by al-Qaeda organizer Anwar al-Aulaqi. He wrote to the judge that he abandoned a "comfortable home," "promising career", and marriage prospects to fight against Bashar al-Assad's attacks against Muslims in Syria. He joined ISIS in 2013, twice swearing a fighting oath to ISIS emir Abu Bakr al-Baghdadi. He joined the Muhajireen Wal-Ansar battalion. The Syrian Democratic Forces captured him in January 2019 and transferred him to U.S. custody in late September 2019.

He called journalists and humanitarian workers "disbelievers" with whom ISIS "had no covenant". He lauded Omar Mateen, the 2019 Pulse nightclub shooter, as "our brother" who killed "filthy crusaders" and "sodomites".

Prosecutors observed, "When he had the opportunity to surrender to the Syrian Democratic Forces in Syria in 2019, the defendant threw multiple grenades and fired his AK-47 at Syrian soldiers to continue his murderous campaign on behalf of ISIS." In Abu Badran, Khalifa, "alone and armed with three grenades and an AK-47, threw a grenade on the roof of a house where SDF soldiers were standing... The grenade detonated and the defendant ran into the house and attempted to go to the roof, but an SDF soldier was firing from the stairs... The defendant began firing at the SDF soldier and attempted to use all three of his grenades during the attack. The defendant fired most of his ammunition during the assault before his AK-47 jammed. The defendant was unable to clear his weapon. The defendant

received shrapnel injuries to his left leg, right leg, left arm and other parts of his body during the firefight." He then surrendered.

August 5, 2022: *CNN* reported that authorities in Albuquerque, New Mexico, announced that a fourth Muslim man was killed overnight and observed that there is "reason to believe" his death is related to three other recent killings of Muslim men. Just before midnight, a shooting in the area of Truman Street and Grand Avenue killed a South Asian Muslim man in his 20s. *NBC News* identified him as Naeem Hussain, 25. The previous day, police found a connection between the killings in southeast Albuquerque of Pakistani Muslims Muhammed Afzaal Hussain, 27, on August 1 and Aftab Hussain, 41, on July 26. Detectives sought to link the murders to the November 7, 2021 death of Mohammad Zaher Ahmadi, 62, a Muslim from Afghanistan who was killed outside of a business he ran with his brother. Police offered $15,000 for information leading to an arrest.

Ehsan Shahalami said his brother-in-law, Naeem Hussain, fled persecution as a Shi'ite in Pakistan and became a U.S. citizen in July 2022. Had had opened a trucking business in 2022. The day he was killed, he had attended a funeral for the two other victims.

Española Mayor John Ramon Vigil said Muhammad Afzaal Hussain worked on the planning team for the city. Hussain had studied law and human resource management at the University of Punjab in Pakistan. He earned BA and MA degrees in community and regional planning from the University of New Mexico.

CNN reported on August 9, 2022 that Albuquerque Police Chief Harold Medina tweeted that the police detained the "primary suspect", a father who was traveling to Texas after authorities found a vehicle believed involved in the attacks. *NBC News* identified the individual as Albuquerque resident Muhammed Syed, 51, who was held for the July 26 and August 1 murders which stemmed from a personal conflict. Following a tip, police stopped him on a road near Santa Rosa, New Mexico, more than 100 miles east of Albuquerque. *CNN* reported that Syed appeared before Bernalillo County Metropolitan Court Judge Renée Torres via video from a detention center on August 10. His case was to be transferred to a district court. He was held without bond. The Sunni Muslim spoke Pashto and was assisted by an interpreter. He was represented by attorney Megan Mitsunaga. Authorities found firearms in his residence. On gun was linked to bullet casings found at the scenes of two of the killings; casings for a handgun found in his car were linked to one of the scenes. Police considered him the primary suspect in the other two murders but did not initially press charges.

Syed, a father of six, moved to the U.S. with his family from Afghanistan six years earlier. His daughter said in February 2018 she married a man who was friends with victims Aftab Hussein and Naeem Hussain. Syed initially did not approve of her marrying a Shi'ite, but eventually accepted it. Police said Syed had "a few minor misdemeanor arrests (from the Albuquerque Police Department) from domestic violence" and some other incidents. His three previous domestic violence charges were dismissed.

Al-Jazeera reported on August 23 that Syed was charged on August 22 with murdering trucking business owner Naeem Hussain after evidence from mobile phones linked him to the attack. Syed's son Shaheen remained in federal custody on charges of providing false information to investigators about the guns and vehicle used in the attacks.

August 10, 2022: *The Hill, UPI, Military Times,* and *AP* reported that prosecutors charged Shahram Poursafi, alias Mehdi Rezayi, 45, a member of Iran's Revolutionary Guard, in an October 2021 murder-for-hire plot to kill Trump administration officials, including National Security Advisor John Bolton, in retaliation for an airstrike that killed IRGC Quds Force leader General Qassim Soleimani at Baghdad International Airport in January 2020. Department of Justice prosecutors said he offered $300,000 in cryptocurrency to people in Maryland and D.C. to "eliminate" Bolton. He said the individual behind the plot wanted video confirmation of Bolton's death. Poursafi faced ten years in prison and a fine of up to $250,000 if convicted of using interstate commerce facilities to commission a murder-for-hire scheme, and up to 15 years in prison and a fine of up to $250,000 if convicted

of attempting to provide material support for a transnational murder plot. Poursafi remained at large, having fled in January 2022. Poursafi told a U.S. informant that a second $1 million hit had had surveillance completed by someone "working on behalf of the IRGC-QF".

August 11, 2022: *AP* and *CNN* reported that at 9:15 a.m., Trump supporter Ricky Shiffer, 42, clad in body armor and carrying an AR-15-style rifle, fired a nail gun while attempting to breach the Visitor Screening Facility of the FBI field office in Cincinnati. He then led a car chase down Interstate 71 and State Road 73, followed by an hours-long standoff in rural Wilmington, Ohio before he was shot to death at 3:45 p.m. by a police officer on Smith Road after he had fired at police. He was believed to be protesting the seizure by the FBI earlier in the week of classified documents at Trump's Mar-a-Lago estate. Shiffer was believed to have been present at the January 6, 2021 riot at the U.S. Capitol, although he was not charged with any crimes.

AP and *Military Times* reported on August 15 that Shiffer apparently went on social media and called for federal agents to be killed "on sight". One message on Trump's *Truth Social* media platform, apparently posted after Shiffer's attack, read, "If you don't hear from me, it is true I tried attacking the F.B.I." Another *Truth Social* posting from @rickywshifferjr included a "call to arms" and urged people to "be ready for combat". The *New York Times* reported on August 14 that he had posted on *Truth Social* "Violence is not (all) terrorism… Kill the F.B.I. on sight."

Shiffer posted that he worked as an electrician. Public records indicated that he was a registered Republican who voted in the 2020 primary from Columbus, Ohio, and in the 2020 general election from Tulsa, Oklahoma. The Ohio Department of Taxation filed suit against him in June 2022, seeking a $553 tax lien judgment. Court records listed him at an address in St. Petersburg, Florida. He also previously lived at several addresses in Columbus and Omaha, Nebraska. After graduating from West Perry High School in Elliottsburg in central Pennsylvania, he enlisted in the Navy and served on the *U.S.S. Columbia* submarine until 2003. He was also an infantry soldier in the Florida Army National

Guard from 2008 to 2011, when he was honorably discharged.

August 12, 2022: *AP* and *CNN* reported that at 10:45 a.m., a man ran onto the stage of the Chautauqua Institution in western New York and began punching and stabbing twice in the neck Salman Rushdie, 75, the author whose *The Satanic Verses* led to a death threat fatwa from Iran's Ayatollah Ruhollah Khomeini in 1989. Moderator Henry Reese, 73, co-founder of the Pittsburgh nonprofit City of Asylum, suffered a minor head injury. After surgery, Rushdie was put on a ventilator and could not speak. A state trooper arrested the attacker, who was restrained by members of the audience. An Iranian religious foundation in 2012 offered $3.3 million to anyone who kills Mumbai-born Rushdie.

Rushdie's agent said, "Salman will likely lose one eye; the nerves in his arm were severed; and his liver was stabbed and damaged."

NBC News identified the suspect as Hadi Matar, 24, from Fairview, New Jersey. *CNN* reported on August 13, 2022 that Matar was arraigned on charges of attempted murder in the second degree and assault in the second degree. He was assigned a public defender and remanded without bail to the Chautauqua County Jail. The *Los Angeles Times* reported that his attorney, Nathaniel Barone, entered a not guilty plea in a New York court.

Matar was born in the United States to Lebanese parents who emigrated from Yaroun, Lebanon, a Hizballah stronghold.

NPR reported on August 14 that Rushdie was off the ventilator and able to talk about the attack.

Newsweek and *The Guardian* reported on August 14 that after she expressed sympathy for Rushdie, British author J.K. Rowling received a threat from a *Twitter* account under the name Meer Asif Asiz that praised the attack and added "Don't worry you are next."

BBC reported on August 17 that Matar said that he had read only two pages of *The Satanic Verses*. Matar told the *New York Post* that Sir Salman was "someone who attacked Islam".

Iran blamed Rushdie and his supporters for the attack.

CNN reported on August 18 that a grand jury indicted Matar, who pleaded not guilty to attempted murder.

Chautauqua County District Attorney Jason Schmidt said the Booker Prize-winner suffered three stab wounds to his neck, four stab wounds to his stomach, puncture wounds to his right eye and chest, and a laceration on his right thigh.

The Independent and *El Pais* reported on October 22, 2022 that Salman Rushdie's literary agent Andrew Wylie said Rushdie lost sight in one eye and the use of a hand because of cut nerves in one arm. Rushdie, 75, sustained three serious wounds to his neck and 15 more wounds to his chest and torso. Hadi Matar, 24, of Fairview, New Jersey, was jailed after pleading not guilty to attempted murder and assault.

August 13, 2022: *CNN, Fox 10 Phoenix,* and *Business Insider* reported that in the morning, Trump supporters brandishing handguns and "assault-style weapons" gathered outside the Phoenix FBI office to protest what they call the "unlawful" search of Mar-a-Lago. They carried "honor your oath" and "Abolish FBI" signs. The FBI announced that 25 demonstrators were exercising their First Amendment rights. One person waved a Confederate flag.

August 13, 2022: *CNN* reported that police arrested a man who drove his car into a crowd of people at 6:15 p.m. outside the Intoxicology Department bar in Berwick in Columbia County, Pennsylvania, killing one person and injuring 17 others, four critically, before killing a woman in a neighboring county later that night. The victims were participating in an all-day community event to raise money for victims of a deadly house fire that killed ten people, including three children. Pennsylvania State Police responded to a call about a male suspect who was physically assaulting a woman, Rosa D. Reyes, 56, in the Nescopeck Borough of Luzerne County. State troopers found her dead of multiple traumatic injuries after being struck by a vehicle and a hammer. Authorities identified the suspect as her son, Adrian Oswaldo Sura Reyes, 24, of Nescopeck. He was arraigned on two counts of criminal homicide. He was denied bail and was held in the Columbia County Correctional Facility.

August 14, 2022: *NPR* and *CNN* reported that at 4 a.m., a man crashed his car into a barricade at East Capitol Street and Second Street near the U.S. Capitol Building, setting the care on fire. He exited the car, fired several shots in the air, then turned the gun on himself. Congress was in recess until September. U.S. Capitol Police Chief Tom Manger said that the man had a criminal history from "over the past 10 years or so".

August 19, 2022: *News 360* reported that a Texas court sentenced former Colombian ELN guerrilla Henry Trigos Celón, alias Moncho Picada, to 46 months in prison for international distribution of cocaine. It was the first U.S. conviction of an ELN member. He and another ELN member were extradited to the U.S. in August 2021.

August 20, 2022: *NewsNation* reported that the FBI arrested the leaders of Black Hammer, an extremist group with alleged ties to the Russian FSB intelligence service. The Bureau acted on an unsealed federal indictment accusing the group's leader, Augustus Romain, Jr., alias Gazi Kodzo, of taking money from Russian national Aleksandr Ionov. The group was accused of conducting protests in March 2022 outside the headquarters of Meta, *Facebook*'s parent company, after *Facebook* placed restrictions on content supporting Russia's invasion of Ukraine. Romain and his aide, Xavier Rushin, alias Keno, were charged with kidnapping, aggravated assault, false imprisonment, conspiracy to commit a felony, and taking part in street gang activity. *NewsNation* reported that the duo also allegedly tried to harm homeless people and turn them into a de facto security force. The *Atlanta Journal Constitution* reported allegations that Romain forced some group members into sexual acts in order to advance within the group.

August 23, 2022: *CNN* and *WUSA9* reported on August 28 that Howard University received telephoned bomb threats on August 23 and 26. The Cook Hall freshman male residence hall was evacuated on August 23; the East and West Towers residence halls were evacuated on August 26. It was the eighth bomb threat of the year. The FBI reported that since January, 57 HBCUs across the U.S. had received bomb threats via phone calls, e-mails, instant messages, and anonymous online posts since January. No arrests had been made.

August 26, 2022: The *Florida Times-Union* reported that the U.S. Attorney's Office in New Mexico announced the arrest of Herman Leyvoune Wilson, 45, of Albuquerque, on charges of trying to provide support to ISIS and establishing an Islamic State Center in New Mexico.

August 27, 2022: *CNN* reported that at 6:42 p.m., shots were fired at the Sikh temple in Stockton, California, hospitalizing three Sikhs. Police arrested the suspected gunman, also a Sikh.

September 3, 2022: The *BBC, CNN, WTVA, AP,* and *The Guardian* reported that at 5 a.m., a pilot who was circling the area called E911 and threatened to crash a stolen small plane, possibly a King Air type, into a Walmart West on West Main in Tupelo, Mississippi. The plane landed in a field near Ashland, Mississippi at 10:07 a.m. The pilot was taken into custody.

September 13, 2022: *CNN* reported that a Northeastern University staff member, 45, sustained minor hand injuries when a package he was opening in the virtual reality center exploded at 7:16 p.m. The package was delivered to Holmes Hall, center of the Boston school's Writing Center. Several federal law enforcement sources said that the package contained a note that criticized *Facebook* founder Mark Zuckerberg and the relationship between academic institutions and the developers of virtual reality. The note was in a hard plastic container and detonated when the victim opened the latches and lifted the lid.

October 7, 2022: The *Florida Times-Union* and *USA Today Network* reported that at 2:40 p.m., a police officer shot and critically injured an ax-wielding man trying to get inside Ruth N. Upson Elementary School in Jacksonville/Duval County, Florida. The man was unable to get through the locked doors—the school at 1090 Dancy Street in the Murray Hill community was in lockdown. School district police officers found the individual outside a nearby church. He approached officers, who warned him to drop the ax, then shot him.

October 8, 2022: The White House announced that Presidential approval will be required before a suspected terrorist is added to the target list for potential lethal action outside war zones, including drone strikes and special operations raids. The policy was used in the Obama administration, but loosened during the Trump administration.

October 17, 2022: *Deutsche Welle* reported that a court in the U.S. sentenced Canadian man Abdullahi Ahmed Abdullahi to 20 years in prison for aiding ISIS in Syria by assisting half a dozen North American nationals to travel to Syria, where they joined ISIS in 2013 and 2014. One was the first known American to die fighting for ISIS. The six included Abdullahi's three cousins from Edmonton, Canada, his cousin, 18, from Minneapolis, and San Diego resident Douglas McAuthur McCain. All six were subsequently killed in combat. Abdullahi is from Edmonton. Canada extradited him to San Diego in 2019. In December 2021, he pleaded guilty in a federal court in San Diego to providing material support to terrorists. He also admitted to committing an armed robbery at a jewelry store in Edmonton in 2014 to raise money to finance the foreign fighters.

October 19, 2022: *Reuters* and *USA Today* reported that police at the U.S. Capitol arrested Tony H. Payne, 80, of Tunnel Hill, Georgia, around 4 p.m. on charges of possessing an unregistered firearm, possessing unregistered ammunition, and carrying a pistol without a license. He had two handguns and a shotgun in his illegally parked van and claimed to be in Washington to deliver documents to the Supreme Court.

October 28, 2022: *CBS News* reported that Tamirat Yehualawork, 36, an Ethiopian man living in Falls Church, Virginia, allegedly drove his Ford Expedition through a security checkpoint at the South Secure Parking lot of the Pentagon and ran over a second security barrier, driving over a sidewalk and through grass towards the Pentagon Mall Entrance. Pentagon Force Protection Agency police pulled their guns and used their vehicles to pin and stop his car near the complex. He yelled "F*** America" and told officers "I hate America and I was trying to kill people." He was accused of attempting to attack federal police officers. He had no prior criminal record. He was remanded to the custody of U.S. Marshals.

October 28, 2022: *CNN* reported that at 2:27 a.m., a man armed with a hammer and yelling "Where is Nancy?" broke into the back of the San Francisco home of House Speaker Nancy Pelosi and attacked her husband, Paul Pelosi, 82, hospitalizing him. Paul Pelosi underwent surgery and was expected to make a full recovery. *NPR* reported that he suffered a skull fracture and injuries to his right hand and arm. Authorities arrested suspect David DePape, 42, who had posted memes and conspiracy theories about alleged deadliness of COVID-19 vaccines, My Pillow CEO Mike Lindell's false allegations about the 2020 election, the Great Reset, the January 6, 2021 riot, claims that George Floyd died of a drug overdose, and transphobic images on *Facebook*. Two relatives said he is estranged from his family. He grew up in Powell River, British Columbia, Canada, leaving 20 years ago for a relationship in California. He was booked at San Francisco county jail on charges of attempted homicide, assault with a deadly weapon, elder abuse, and several other additional felonies. Police said the attacker tried to tie up Paul Pelosi "until Nancy got home". *NPR* reported that police said they found another hammer, tape, rope, and zip ties, and that DePape planned to "kneecap" Speaker Pelosi.

CNN reported on October 31 that the US attorney's office and San Francisco district attorney announced that DePape was federally charged with one count of "attempted kidnapping of a US official", which carries a maximum of 20 years in prison; and one count of assault of an immediate family member of a U.S. official with the intent to retaliate against the official, which carries a maximum sentence of 30 years in prison. State charges include attempted murder, residential burglary, assault with a deadly weapon, elder abuse, false imprisonment of an elder, and threats to a public official and their family; he faced 13 years to life on those charges.

CNN reported that the FBI debunked a conspiracy theory tweeted (and later deleted) by Elon Musk and supported by former *Breitbart* writer Raheem Kassam, Louisiana Rep. Clay Higgins, Sebastian Gorka, Donald Trump, Jr., and Dinesh D'Souza that the attacker and Paul Pelosi were gay lovers in a spat.

On October 31, the *Washington Examiner* suggested DePape was an illegal immigrant.

The *Florida Times-Union* reported on November 11, 2022 that a federal grand jury indicted David DePape on charges of assault and attempted kidnapping in the break-in of Speaker Nancy Pelosi's home and the bludgeoning of her husband. The charges superseded those of a federal complaint filed on October 31. DePape was represented by public defender Adam Lipson, who had entered a not guilty plea to state charges of attempted murder, burglary, and elder abuse. *CNN* reported on November 15, 2022 that DePape pleaded not guilty in a San Francisco federal court. He faced 20 years in federal prison, three years of supervised release, a $250,000 fine, and possible restitution on the kidnapping charge. He faced another 30 years in federal prison, five years of supervised release, a $250,000 fine, and possible restitution on an assault charge. He was represented by public defender Angela Chuang. His next federal court appearance was scheduled for November 30.

November 4, 2022: Federal officials announced that they had identified a man who had posted threats against New Jersey synagogues. They did not believe he was going to conduct a specific attack. He said he had been bullied and was angry with Jews.

November 9, 2022: *UPI* reported that the U.S. Departments of State and Treasury announced sanctions against two men connected to jailed Australian-based businessman Ahmed Luqman Talib, whom the United States sanctioned in 2020 on accusations of being an al-Qaeda facilitator. Australian authorities arrested him in March 2021 on charges of plotting incursions into foreign states for the purpose of engaging in hostile activities. Those sanctioned were his brother-in-law Musad Turkmen, who lives in Türkiye, and Sri Lankan-based businessman Mohamad Irshad Mohamad Haris Nizar. Treasury said the duo were business partners in Sri Lanka since at least 2018. Together, their dealings generated nearly $200,000 a year in profits.

November 19, 2022: *CNN* reported that New York Police Commissioner Keechant Sewell announced that the Metropolitan Transportation Authority (MTA) arrested two men as they were entering Penn Station in Manhattan for making online threats to attack a New York City synagogue. Christopher Brown, 21, from Aquebogue, New York, was charged with making a terroristic threat, aggravated harassment, and criminal possession of a weapon. Matthew Mahrer, 22, of Manhattan, was charged with criminal possession of a weapon. Police seized a large hunting knife, an illegal Glock 17 firearm, a 30-round magazine, and several other items. Threats began appearing on a *Twitter* account on November 12; they were traced to a computer at a veterinary clinic where one of the suspects worked. One post said, "Gonna ask a priest if I should become a husband or shoot up a synagogue and die." One suspect had a Nazi armband.

November 19, 2022: *CNN, AP,* and *WOKV* reported that an 11:57 p.m. shooting at Club Q, an LGBTQ nightclub in Colorado Springs, Colorado, killed five people and wounded 25, seven critically. Two customers subdued Anderson Lee Aldrich, 22, who was wearing a flak jacket and firing an AR-15-style semiautomatic weapon. Aldrich was placed in custody and given medical treatment. *CNN* reported on November 21 that he faced five counts of first degree murder and five counts of a bias-motivated crime causing bodily injury.

The Colorado Springs Police Department tweeted that the dead were

- Raymond Green Vance (he/him), 22, was visiting Club Q for the first time with his longtime girlfriend Kassy Fierro, her parents, and some of her parents' friends. They were celebrating a birthday. *AP* reported that one of those who subdued the gunman was Army veteran Rich Fierro, Kassy's father.

- Kelly Loving (she/her)

- Daniel Aston (he/him), 28, Club Q bar supervisor and performer and trans person, according to *WFMZ*

- Derrick Rump (he/him), bartender at Club Q and a native of Berks County, Pennsylvania, who graduated from Kutztown Area High School in 2002

- Ashley Paugh (she/ her) left behind a daughter, Ryleigh. Paugh worked at Kids Crossing, a nonprofit that works with the LGBTQ community to find homes for foster children. She enjoyed hunting, fishing, and riding four-wheelers.

Barrett Hudson was shot seven times in the back with an AR-15 but survived.

Colorado Springs Police Chief Adrian Vasquez said that one of the patrons who stopped the attack was injured during the incident.

CNN reported that in June 2021, Aldrich was arrested after his mother told police that he threatened her with a homemade bomb. Following a standoff at her El Paso County, Colorado apartment, the charges were dropped and records sealed. Police said he and his mother were not cooperating with police. The *New York Times* reported on December 9, 2022 that District Attorney Michael J. Allen said Aldrich's mother and grandparents had refused to cooperate and the June 18, 2021 case could not move forward without victim testimony. A judge dismissed the case in July 2022. Authorities did not return a rifle and "ghost" pistol (lacking a serial number, make, or model) seized from Aldrich. Judge Robin L. Chittum of El Paso County ordered the case unsealed in December 2022.

CNN noted that he legally purchased the AR-style rifle and the handgun he brought to Club Q.

NPR reported on November 21 that authorities decreased the number of injured to 19, of which 17 were hit by gunfire.

AP reported that Army veteran Rich Fierro grabbed the gunman's body armor and called for patron Thomas James to move the rifle out of reach. James is a U.S. Navy information systems technician stationed at the Defense Intelligence Agency base in Colorado Springs. He was injured. A transgender woman kicked her high heel in the shooter's face. Fierro grabbed the shooter's handgun and hit him in the head with it. Fierro spent three tours in Iraq and one in Afghanistan as a field artillery officer, retiring as a Major in 2013. Fierro sustained injuries to his hands, knees, and ankle.

Aldrich, who identifies as nonbinary and uses "they" and "them", was represented as of December 2022 by public defender Joseph Archambault.

November 21, 2022: *CNN* reported that at 10:45 a.m., a dark-colored SUV crashed through the front window of an Apple store in Hingham, Massachusetts, killing one person and injuring 16.

November 26, 2022: *Vice News* and *Raw Story* reported on December 13, 2022 that Luke Kenna, 43, an armed man with ties to white supremacist and neo-Nazi extremist groups was arrested during a taillight traffic stop in New York. Police found a loaded "ghost" gun—an untraceable firearm usually built at home—tucked into his pants. He was charged with being in possession of a loaded firearm, the unlawful wearing of body armor, and driving without a license. He pleaded not guilty. *Vice* noted that he had posted on *Instagram* the sonnenrad (a runic symbol popular with modern neo-Nazis), a German Imperial flag, and other images such as a person with a Totenkopf (the death's head symbol popular in Nazi Germany). He allegedly had connected to the Wolves of Vinland, a group that has been described by the Southern Poverty Law Center as a Neo-Volkisch hate group whose adherents base their spirituality on the survival of the European race and tend to lean into certain forms of paganism.

November 28, 2022: *NPR* reported that an individual in Ethiopia could be responsible for hundreds of "swatting" calls—false reports of active shooters across the U.S., principally at schools. *NPR* reported an example on October 24, 2022 when 3 p.m. on a September day, police in Chillicothe, Ohio, received a message from dispatch that an active shooter injured 24 students at Chillicothe High School and was at the scene. *NPR* noted that 182 schools in 28 states, including Virginia, Minnesota, Ohio, and Florida, received hoax calls about threats between September 13 and October 21. In March and April, authorities in Minnesota and Louisiana received fake calls from an individual with a similar North African accent regarding bombs at schools. A Sheriff's investigation established that the call came from a VOIP number tied to IP addresses in Ethiopia owned by the AFRINIC network, and specifically to the Ethiopian state-owned phone and Ethio Telecom Internet service based in Addis Ababa. On a single day in September, 80 places in Louisiana, Arizona and New Mexico received such calls from this number. *NPR* established that call logs between March 12 through April 21 showed that the VOIP number received or made 437 calls on 10 of those days; 80 percent of that activity was outgoing calls to schools, law enforcement agencies, fire departments, and emergency dispatchers. *NPR* suggested that the caller was using the TextNow service and a Gmail account. Between September 19 and 23, the caller used at least eight different phone numbers; six numbers were offered through TextNow. On November 25, TextNow banned Ethiopia from use of its service. *NPR* reported that on November 30, police in Georgia responded to ten swatting calls.

December 2, 2022: *CNN* reported that the Ukrainian Foreign Ministry announced that the Ukrainian Embassy in the United States received a letter with a photocopy of a critical article about Ukraine.

December 3, 2022: *Al-Jazeera* and *AP* reported that around 7 p.m., facility gates were breached and gunfire damaged two electrical grid substations in Moore County in North Carolina, causing millions of dollars of damage to equipment. *CNN* reported that all county public schools and many businesses were closed and a 9 p.m. to 5 a.m. curfew was imposed. *Poweroutage.us* reported that 34,000 utility customers were without power as of late December 5; initially, 45,000 customers were affected. Authorities called the attacks "intentional" and "targeted". Moore County Sheriff Ronnie Fields observed that the shooters "knew exactly what they were doing".

CNN reported on December 7 that police recovered nearly two dozen shell casings from a high-powered rifle from the sites where gunfire disabled the two substations.

Duke Energy reported on December 7 that it had completed repairs.

December 14, 2022: *UPI* reported that prosecutors with the Eastern District of New York unsealed an indictment against the three men and one woman—including three Americans and a Canadian—charging them with attempting to provide support to both ISIS and the Islamic State of Iraq, raising and donating more than $35,000 to those groups. They were identified as Mohammad Hashimi, 35, of Potomac Falls, Virginia, Abdullah At Taqi, 23, of Queens, New York, and Seema Rahman, 25, of Edison, New Jersey, who were arrested in those municipalities. Canadian authorities, acting on a request from U.S. prosecutors, arrested Khalilullah Yousuf, 34, of Ontario, Canada. The four defendants were denied bail pending trial on charges of conspiring to provide material support to a foreign terrorist organization, which carries a maximum statutory penalty of up to 20 years in prison.

Prosecutors said Hashimi and Yousuf were members of a group chat on an encrypted social media and mobile messaging electronic communication service. The group reportedly began working in early April 2021, formulating plans to post donation links disguised as humanitarian causes. The Justice Department claimed that Yousuf provided a link to a specific Bitcoin address and another member of the group posted a link to a PayPal campaign. U.S. Attorney for the Eastern District of New York Breon Peace said, "As alleged, this crowdfunding network used cryptocurrency, Bitcoin wallets, GoFundMe and PayPal to collect and raise blood money to support ISIS, not for needy families as they falsely claimed in their attempt to deceive law enforcement."

December 25, 2022: *CBS News* reported that vandals attacked four power substations in the Tacoma, Washington, area, knocking out power to more than 14,000 customers on Christmas Day. At 5:30 a.m., vandals damaged equipment at a Tacoma Public Utilities substation in Spanaway, Washington and a nearby TPU substation. Power went out around 2:30 a.m. after vandals hit a Puget Sound Energy substation. Around 7:30 p.m., a fire was reported at a Puget Sound Energy substation in Pierce County, cutting power to the Kapowsin and Graham neighborhoods; the latter has a population of 32,000.

December 31, 2022: *CNN* reported that a man, 19, injured three New York City police officers during a machete attack at 10:11 p.m. on West 52nd Street and 8th Avenue, outside a Times Square New Year's Eve security screening zone. The *New York Post* identified him as suspected jihadi Trevor Bickford of Wells, Maine. The attacker hit a police officer on the head with an 18" Gurkha machete, then struck two other officers before rookie officer Michael Hanna shot him in the shoulder. Paul Cozzolino, who graduated from the police academy on December 30, sustained a skull fracture and a large laceration to his head. Louis Iorio, an 8-year veteran Staten Island officer, suffered a laceration. The two were treated at Bellevue Hospital. Hanna, who joined the force in April, was taken to Mt. Sinai West. *NBC News* reported that police found personal writings, terrorist propaganda, $200, and a knife in his backpack. Bickford likely arrived in New York City via Amtrak on December 29 and checked into a hotel on Manhattan's Lower East Side. Federal authorities had interviewed him in mid-December after a tip-off from a relative. *NBC* added that he wrote in his diary that he was prepared to die in the attack, wanted to send his belongings to others, and described where he wanted to be buried. *Forbes* and *CNN* added on January 2, 2023 that Bickford wrote of his hope to join the Taliban in Afghanistan.

The NYPD on December 30, 2022 had warned law enforcement agencies of lone offender attacks following a video release from an ISIS-Aligned Media Unit.

The *New York Post* reported that on January 2, 2023, the three police were released from the hospital.

Bickford's father died of an overdose in 2018.

UPDATES OF PRE-2022 INCIDENTS

AFRICA

BURKINA FASO

October 15, 1987: *Al-Jazeera* reported on March 22, 2022 that the trial for the October 1987 assassination of former Burkina Faso President Thomas Sankara and his colleagues continued. Military prosecutors requested 30 years in jail for former President Blaise Compaore for Sankara's murder. Sankara changed the country's name from Upper Volta to Burkina Faso, which means "land of the honest men".

Al-Jazeera reported on April 6, 2022 that after a six-month trial, a court in Ouagadougou sentenced former president Blaise Campaore to life in prison for the murder of Thomas Sankara and 12 others on October 15, 1987. Campaore was tried with 13 others.

CENTRAL AFRICAN REPUBLIC

May 2019: *News 360* reported on October 31, 2022 that the Special Criminal Court (SPC) of the Central African Republic sentenced three members of the Return, Reclamation and Rehabilitation militias (3R movement), identified as Issa Sallet Adoum, Ousman Yaouba, and Tahir Mahamat, to sentences ranging from 20 years to life imprisonment for "crimes against humanity" for perpetrating a massacre in mid-May 2019 in the northwest of the country in which 46 civilians were killed. They were also found guilty of engaging in "murder, inhumane acts and humiliating and degrading treatment". *Radio France Internationale* reported that Sallet Adoum was sentenced to life imprisonment, while Yaouba and Mahamat were sentenced to 20 years.

CONGO

March 12, 2017: *BBC, Reuters,* and *AFP* reported on January 29, 2022 that following a four-year trial, a military court in Kananga issued death sentences to 51 militia members, many in absentia, for their involvement in the kidnap/murder of UN experts Swedish-Chilean Zaida Catalan and American Michael Sharp and their interpreter, Betu Tshintela, in the Kasai region in 2017. They were investigating alleged mass graves. Their bodies were found 16 days after their abduction; she had been beheaded. The country had declared a moratorium on executions in 2003; the defendants were likely to experience life in prison on several charges, including terrorism, murder, and act of a war crime through mutilation. Army Colonel Jean de Dieu Mambweni, who met with Catalan and Sharp before their mission, received a 10-year sentence for violating orders. A journalist and a police officer were acquitted. *Reuters* added that Thomas Nkashama, local immigration official who met with Catalan and Sharp the day before the attack, was among those sentenced to death. Tresor Kabangu represented several defendants in the trial. Congolese officials blamed the Kamuina Nsapu militia.

IVORY COAST

March 13, 2016: *Reuters* reported that the trial began in Abidjan on November 30, 2022 of 18 foreign AQIM jihadis accused of responsibility for the March 13, 2016 attack on a beach resort in Grand Bassam that killed 19 people and wounded 33. Public prosecutor Richard Adou said that the defendants were charged with terrorism, assassination, attempted assassination, harboring of criminals, and illegal possession of firearms and ammunition. Only four of the 18 defendants were present; the others remained at large.

VOA reported on December 28, 2022 that Judge Charles Bini in a court in Abidjan issued life sentences to four Malian men convicted of abetting the AQIM jihadi attack. Among the dead were nine Ivorians, four French citizens, a Lebanese, a German, a Macedonian, a Malian, a Nigerian, and an unidentified person. Several dozen people were later arrested. Defendants Hantao Ag Mohamed Cisse, Sidi Mohamed Kounta, Mohamed Cisse, and Hassan Barry were present in court. Seven of the 14 at-large defendants were handed life sentences in absentia. The other seven were acquitted.

KENYA

January 5, 2020: *AP* reported on March 10, 2022 that two military reviews by U.S. Africa Command and an independent investigation led by Gen. Paul Funk, commander of Army Training and Doctrine Command, attributed poor leadership, inadequate training, and a "culture of complacency" among U.S. forces across the board to the poor response against an al-Shabaab attack on Manda Bay Airfield in Kenya on January 5, 2020 that led to three American deaths, three wounded, and six destroyed aircraft. Eight Air Force personnel received some form of administrative punishment, including written reprimands and loss of certification. They included junior enlisted airmen and officers below the general ranks.

Task and Purpose and Georgia news station *13WMAZ* reported on September 14, 2022 that Air Force Master Sgt. Mathue Snow was award-ed a Bronze Star on September 9, 2022 for his efforts defending Camp Simba, a U.S. facility within the larger U.S. and Kenyan base called Cooperative Security Location Manda Bay. Thirty al-Shabaab terrorists attacked the base and its airfield with rocket-propelled grenades, mortars, and small arms. Snow was a 22-year veteran.

MALI

April 8, 2021: The *Washington Post, AFP, AP, Reuters,* and *al-Jazeera* reported on May 5, 2021 that Christophe Deloire, the chief of Reporters Without Borders, announced that Group to Support Islam and Muslims (Jamaa Nusrat al-Islam wal-Muslimin, JNIM) jihadis kidnapped French journalist Olivier Dubois, 46, on April 8, 2021 while he was working in Gao. He was going to interview JNIM leader Abdallah Ag Albakaye who then kidnapped him. Dubois did not return to his hotel after lunch. He works for *Liberation* and *Le Point Afrique.* JNIM released a 21-second video on May 5 in which Dubois said, "I'm Olivier Dubois. I'm French. I'm a journalist. I was kidnapped in Gao on April 8 by the JNIM (an al-Qaeda-linked group). I'm speaking to my family, my friends, and the French authorities for them to do everything in their power to free me." *Reuters* and *RTL* radio reported on May 23 that French Foreign Affairs Minister Jean-Yves Le Drian confirmed that Dubois had probably been taken hostage by jihadis. *Insider* reported on January 7, 2022 that Dubois remained missing. He had lived in Mali since 2015. *21040801*

AFP reported on March 14, 2022 that the previous day, a video appeared on social media apparently showing French journalist Olivier Dubois addressing the French government, his parents, and his partner, from whom he says he receives messages. The previous month, Reporters Without Borders projected a photo of Dubois on to the side of the Pantheon in Paris. Dubois, 47, started working as a freelance journalist in Mali in 2015. In a May 5, 2021, video, he claimed he was kidnapped in Gao by the al-Qaeda-linked Support Group for Islam and Muslims (GSIM).

NIGER

October 4, 2017: *Army Times* reported on May 18, 2022 that the Army decided to award the Silver Star to Sgt. 1st Class Jeremiah Johnson, one of four U.S. troops killed by Islamic State in the Greater Sahara terrorists near Tongo Tongo in Niger on October 4, 2017. Helmet camera footage recovered in 2021 showed his heroism. He had earlier posthumously received a Bronze Star with Valor.

NIGERIA

April 14, 2014: *BBC* reported on April 16, 2022 that rescued hostage Hassana Adamu, one of the 276 Chibok schoolgirls who had been kidnapped by Boko Haram on April 14, 2014, had received different treatment from her former classmates. A Boko Haram terrorist declared her married to him two years after her kidnapping; they had two children. He later surrendered to the government. She and classmates Ruth Ngaladar and Halima Ali Maiyanga were reunited with their families in January 2022. Bring Back Our Girls/ Enough Is Enough reported that 103 were freed following negotiations, 57 escaped, seven were found, and 109 remained missing. Many attended the American University of Nigeria (AUN) in Yola on full government scholarships.

Al-Jazeera reported that on June 14, 2022 troops of 26 Task Force Brigade found another kidnapped Chibok schoolgirl, Mary Ngoshe, later identified as Mary Dauda, carrying her baby son near Ngoshe village in Borno State, near the border with Cameroon. Dauda was 18 when she was kidnapped, and married at different times to Boko Haram fighters in the Sambisa forest. She added, "They would starve and beat you if you refused to pray." She told her husband she was visiting another Chibok girl in Dutse village near Ngoshe, then fled. "All the remaining Chibok girls have been married with children. I left more than 20 of them in Sambisa... I'm so happy I'm back."

Al-Jazeera reported on June 22, 2022 that Nigerian troops found another former schoolgirl, carrying a baby, on June 12. Hauwa Joseph was found along with other civilians around Bama after troops dislodged a Boko Haram camp. She explained, "I was nine when we were kidnapped from our school in Chibok and I was married off not long ago and had this child," Her husband and father-in-law were killed in a military raid when her son was 14 months old. "We were abandoned, no one cared to look after us. We were not being fed."

AFP, BBC, and *Reuters* reported on July 27, 2022 that the Nigerian army announced the discovery of two more female students abducted by Boko Haram in Chibok eight years earlier. The two hostages gave birth while in captivity. One was found with a child; the other had two.

SOUTH AFRICA

April 10, 1993: On November 21, 2022, Constitutional Court Chief Justice Raymond Zondo announced that South Africa's Constitutional Court unanimously ordered the release of Polish citizen Janusz Walus, 69, who was jailed for killing anti-apartheid leader Chris Hani, born Martin Thembisile Hani, SSA, SBS, CLS, DMG, MMS, leader of the South African Communist Party and chief of staff of Umkhonto we Sizwe, the armed wing of the African National Congress, on April 10, 1993. Hani died outside his home in Boksburg, east of Johannesburg. Walus was serving a life sentence. Several justice ministers had rejected his parole applications. He was convicted with Clive Derby-Lewis, who was released on medical parole in 2015 and died of cancer in 2016 at age 80.

Al-Jazeera reported on November 29, 2022 that Hani's gravesite in Ekurhuleni was vandalized over the weekend. *AFP* reported that a pillar was badly damaged, one side fell off, and the electric lighting system was stolen.

Deutsche Welle and *AFP* reported on November 29, 2022 that Janusz Walus was stabbed in prison, allegedly by a fellow inmate, ahead of his release on parole. Correctional services department spokesman Singabakho Nxumalo said his condition was stable and that he was receiving medical attention.

The South African Communist Party petitioned the Constitutional Court and the High Court to reverse the parole order. Walus was held in the Kgosi Mampuru II Correctional Centre in Pretoria. *AP* reported on December 8, 2022 that Walus was released from prison and placed on parole effective December 7, 2022.

ASIA

BANGLADESH

February 27, 2004: *Al-Jazeera, Bdnews24,* and *AFP* reported on April 13, 2022 that a court sentenced four members of Jama'atul Mujahideen Bangladesh (JMB) to hang for the murder of prominent writer and academic Humayun Azad, 56, on February 27, 2004. He was hacked by cleavers en route home from a book fair in Dhaka. He died in August 2004 while being treated in Germany. JMB was banned in 2005. Additional Metropolitan Sessions Judge Al-Mamun identified the killers as Mohammad Mizanur Rahman Minhaz, Anwarul Alam, Nur Mohammad Shamim, and Salehin Sani; the latter two remained at large. A fifth suspect, Hafez Mahmud, was killed while attempting to flee a prison van in 2014.

Azad was professor of Bangla literature at Dhaka University. His 60+ publications included seven poetry books, 20 novels, and dozens of non-fiction books. He received the 1986 Bangla Academy Award, the nation's most prestigious literary award. In 1995, the government banned his *Nari*, a book published in 1992 on modern feminism, for offending "Muslim religious sentiment". The ban was lifted after a five-year legal battle. Muslim right-wing groups in Bangladesh threatened him after the 2004 publication of his novel *Pak Sar Jamin Sad Bad* (*Blessed Be the Sacred Land*), which criticised religious fundamentalism. A week before the attack, Muslim preacher and then-member of parliament Delwar Hossain Sayeedi told the house Azad's work should be banned and a case of blasphemy be filed against him. Charges of inciting the killing against the hardline politician were dropped. In 2014, the government commuted Sayeedi's death sentence for crimes against humanity during the 1971 war for Bangladesh's liberation from Pakistan to a life sentence.

February 26, 2015: The *Daily Beast, al-Jazeera,* and *Reuters* reported on November 21, 2022 that suspected extremists on motorbikes sprayed chemicals in a police constable's eyes, punched another in the face, and rode off with Mainul Islam Shamim and Abu Siddique Sohel, Ansar Ullah Bangla Team terrorists who were being taken to court in Dhaka and facing the death penalty for the February 26, 2015 machete murder of American-Bangladeshi writer and anti-extremist blogger Avijit Roy. His wife Rafida Bonya Ahmed lost a thumb in the attack. Authorities offered a two million taka (about $19,350) reward for information about the escapees' whereabouts. A dozen men were facing charges at Dhaka Anti-Terrorism special tribunal. The U.S. government offered a $5 million reward for information about the killers.

Shamim, Sohel, and six others were convicted and sentenced to death for killing publisher Faisal Arefin Dipan, who published much of Roy's controversial writings.

May 12, 2015: *Al-Jazeera* reported on March 30, 2022 that a court sentenced four people to death for killing blogger and science writer Ananta Bijoy Das, who criticized hardline religious thought. He was attacked by masked men with machetes near his home in Sylhet on May 12, 2015. Judge Nurul Amin Biplob of the Sylhet Anti-Terrorism Tribunal lamented that "if these accused are not given exemplary punishment, people of other terrorist, extremist ideologies will be encouraged to commit such killings… The main purpose (of the killing) was to spread fear and apprehension among writers who wrote or spoke about liberalism, progressivism, science and prejudice prevalent in the society through the brutality and horror of the killing." Those sentenced to death were Abul Hossain, 25; Abul Khayer Rashid Ahmed, 24; Faysal Ahmed, 27; and Mamunur Rashid, 25. Safiur Rahman Farabi was acquitted for lack of evidence but was already serving a life sentence for U.S.-based Bangladeshi blogger Avijit Roy's murder three months earlier in Dhaka. Farabi and Rashid Ahmed were present in court; the others remained at large. Prosecution attorney Misbah Uddin Siraj said he was "not entirely satisfied" with the acquittal of Farabi and would appeal to the high court. Among the defense attorneys was Abdul Ahad, who also planned to appeal.

September 29, 2021: *Al-Jazeera* reported on June 13, 2022 that Bangladesh police charged 29 Rohingya over the murder of popular community leader and head of a Rohingya rights group Mohib Ullah, 48, on September 29, 2021. *AFP* reported that prosecutor Faridul Alam said that police had arrested 15 suspects; the rest remained at large. Four confessed. Ullah's family blamed the Arakan Rohingya Salvation Army (ARSA), which denied involvement. His family was relocated to Canada in April 2022.

INDIA

May 21, 1991: *BBC* reported on May 18, 2022 that a three-judge bench of the Supreme Court ordered the release of A.G. Perarivalan, who had been sentenced to death in 1998 for the May 21, 1991 murder of former Prime Minister Rajiv Gandhi. The sentence was commuted. He had been arrested at 19 for procuring batteries that were used in the bomb used by a female suicide bomber as he addressed an election rally in Tamil Nadu State. Perarivalan was a member of the Liberation Tigers of Tamil Eelam (LTTE) and one of seven convicts in the case. In 2000, the Tamil Nadu State governor commuted the death sentence of Nalini, a female convict in the case. In 2014, the Supreme Court had commuted the death sentences of all the others.

Al-Jazeera, NDTV, and *AFP* reported on November 12, 2022 that the last six co-conspirators jailed for the assassination of Rajiv Gandhi were released from prison, a day after India's Supreme Court ordered their release. Nalini Sriharan, her husband Murugan, and Santhan left two prisons in Vellore. Robert Pais, Jaikumar, and Ravichandran left prisons in Chennai and Madurai in the same state. Three were initially condemned to death. Earlier in 2022, the court freed AG Perarivalan, another convict involved in the assassination.

July 26, 2008: On February 18, 2022, *Reuters, AP, al-Jazeera, BBC,* and *UPI* reported that Special Judge A.R. Patel sentenced 38 Muslim men to death by hanging and ordered life in prison for 11 others for twenty Harkat-ul-Jihad-al-Islami (Indian Mujahideen) bombings on July 26, 2008 in Ahmedabad in Gujarat State that killed 57 people and injured 200. All of them were convicted of murder and criminal conspiracy. Special Judge AR Patel ordered compensation of 100,000 rupees (£982; $1,337) each to families of the victims. Defence lawyer Khalid Shaikh vowed to appeal the verdict. Another 28 defendants were acquitted. One of the bombings hit a hospital where victims of an earlier blast were being treated. Others, hidden in lunch boxes and bicycles, hit residential areas, buses, market places, public transport, and hospitals. Several unexploded bombs were found. The government banned the terrorist group in 2010 after it was accused of an attack on a German bakery in Pune in which 17 people were killed and scores injured. The *Indian Express* reported that prosecutors examined 1,163 witnesses during the trial.

The Indian Mujahideen had claimed it was avenging 2002 religious riots in the state in which at least 1,000 people—mostly Muslims—were hacked, shot, and burned to death. Those riots in turn were sparked by the death of 59 Hindus in a train fire, for which 31 Muslims were convicted of criminal conspiracy and murder.

Authorities foiled a 2013 escape attempt by more than a dozen defendants to tunnel out using food plates as digging tools. One suspect was bailed after a schizophrenia diagnosis.

May 1, 2019: The *Free Press Journal* reported on April 15, 2022 that alleged Maoist leader Nirmala Uppuganti, 59, who was accused in the May 2019 Gadchiroli bombing that killed 15 security personnel from the Gadchiroli Quick Response Team and one civilian, died of cancer at the Shanti Avedna Sadan hospice care center on April 9. Her husband Satyanarayan Rani, co-accused in the case, was held in the Arthur Road Central Prison.

INDONESIA

October 12, 2002: *BBC* and *AFP* reported on January 19, 2022 that the presiding judge at East Jakarta District Court sentenced Aris Sumarsono, alias Zulkarnaen, to 15 years in jail. The Jemaah Islamiah jihadi had been convicted of masterminding the October 12, 2002 Bali bombings that killed 202 people from 21 nations and other deadly attacks in Indonesia. He had been on Indonesia's most-wanted list until his arrest in December 2020. Prosecutors said other attacks carried out by a special unit under his command included Christmas and New Year church bombings in Indonesia in 2000 and 2001, a bombing of the Philippines embassy in Jakarta in 2000, the 2003 Jakarta Marriot hotel bombing, and the Australian embassy bombing in Jakarta in 2004. The U.S. had offered a $5 million bounty for his capture. He was a trainer at militant camps in Afghanistan and the Philippines.

On August 19, 2022, the *Daily Beast, AFP,* and *al-Jazeera* reported that the government on August 17, 2022 reduced the prison sentence of Bali bomb maker Umar Patek, 52. The Bali bombings on October 12, 2002 by Jemaah Islamiyah killed 202 people, including seven Americans, 88 Australians, 38 Indonesians, and 23 Britons, and injured 209. The sentence reduction from its original 20 years made Patek eligible for release in August 2022. He was convicted in 2012 of helping to mix the bombs. Patek's sentence was reduced by five months, coinciding with Indonesian Independence Day, and making Patek eligible for parole from Porong Prison in East Java Province. His sentence had been reduced several times. He had been arrested in Abbotabad, Pakistan in 2011. *AFP* reported on December 7, 2022 that Patek was released on parole at 8 a.m. after serving half of his sentence. He was to follow a training program until 2030.

Among those injured was Thiolina Ferawati Marpaung, 47, who sustained permanent eye damage from shards of glass. Chusnul Chotimah suffered 70 percent burns across her face and body.

The *Washington Post* reported on November 19, 2022 that Ali Imron, 43, a Jemaah Islamiyah terrorist who was imprisoned in the Greater Jakarta Metropolitan Regional Police Headquarters (Polda Metro Jaya) for the bombing, said that "Two hours was all it took me to convince someone to become a suicide bomber… So I know the power of terrorists. I know how compelling they can be." He claimed he had dedicated himself to preventing others from making the same decisions he made and that he could do more if he were freed. Indonesian authorities have allowed him to visit schools and conduct television interviews from prison. In 2007, he published a book warning others about the dangers of terrorist ideologies.

PAKISTAN

July 14, 2021: *Al-Jazeera* reported on November 15, 2022 that the previous week, an anti-terrorism court sentenced Muhammad Hasnain and Muhammed Ayaz to death for involvement in the killing of 13 people, including four Pakistanis and nine Chinese engineers working on the Dasu Hydropower Project in Upper Kohistan, in a suicide bombing of a bus on July 14, 2021 in Kohistan district of Khyber Pakhtunkhwa Province. Another 20 people were injured. Pakistan's then-foreign minister Shah Mahmood Qureshi blamed Tehreek-e-Taliban Pakistan (TTP) members who planned the attack in Afghanistan. Four men were acquitted. Four other suspects were believed hiding in Afghanistan.

PHILIPPINES

September 2015: The *Los Angeles Times* reported on June 17, 2022 that Sulu military commander Maj. Gen. Ignatius Patrimonio and other security officials said that Abu Sayyaf commanders Almujer Yadah and Bensito Quitino, accused of beheading kidnapped Canadian tourists Robert Hall and John Ridsdel in 2015 and German hostage Jurgen Gustav Kantner in 2017 in the southern Philippines, surrendered to military officials in Jolo town in southern Sulu Province and turned in their assault rifles. Sulu provincial police chief Col. Jaime Mojica said they will face multiple murder and other criminal and terrorism charges.

SRI LANKA

April 21, 2019: *Al-Jazeera* reported on January 12, 2022 that the trial of 25 men accused of plotting the 2019 Easter Sunday bombings in Sri

Lanka that killed nearly 270 people, including 45 foreigners, and injured 500, was adjourned until March to allow time for the indictments, which included more than 23,000 charges including conspiracy to murder, collecting arms and ammunition, as well as aiding and abetting the attacks, to be translated into Tamil. Former National Police Chief Pujith Jayasundara was charged with failing to act on repeated intelligence warnings of a possible "terror" attack. Former Defence Secretary Hemasiri Fernando was charged with negligence of duty by failing to prevent the attacks despite receiving intelligence information in advance.

Australia/Oceania New Zealand

March 15, 2019: The *Florida Times-Union* reported on November 9, 2022 that Brenton Tarrant, who had been convicted of killing 51 Muslim worshippers and sentenced to life in prison, filed an appeal with the Court of Appeal.

Europe

Austria

November 2, 2020: *Deutsche Welle* and *Reuters* reported on October 18, 2022 that the trial began of six men accused of helping ISIS supporter Kujtim Fejzulai, 20, plan and procure weapons for his November 2, 2020 rampage in which he killed four and wounded 23 more before police shot him dead in Vienna. Fejzuali was an Austrian citizen with parents from North Macedonia. Four defendants are aged between 21 and 23. Four defendants are Austrian, one is Chechen, and one is Kosovar. *AFP* reported that the attorney for a Chechen defendant, 32, charged with weapons trafficking, said that her client claims he did not know what the gun would be used for. *Reuters* reported that prosecutors said one defendant accompanied the shooter on a failed attempt to buy ammunition in Slovakia while an-

other allegedly supplied the assault rifle he used.

Fezjulai was convicted in 2019 for traveling to Syria and trying to join ISIS. He was sentenced to 22 months in prison, but was paroled within eight months.

Domestic intelligence had been aware of the ISIS sympathies of five of the defendants. Defense attorneys said the men would plead not guilty.

Ismail Bayandir was accused of taking part in preparations for the attack in the gunman's apartment. Attorney Manfred Arbacher-Stoeger said, "He visited the attacker ... but he did not provide a psychological contribution... He found out through the media that there had been an attack in the city center and when he saw the images he immediately went to the police himself and said 'I think I know him. I think this was a close friend of mine.'"

Belgium

March 22, 2016: *Deutsche Welle, News 360, Le Soir,* and *AP* reported on September 12, 2022 that the trial began of ten defendants accused of involvement in the three coordinated suicide bombings in Brussels on March 22, 2016 that killed 32 and wounded 340. French jihadi Salah Abdeslam, 32, refused to take the stand; he joined defense attorneys in complaining that it was unfair that the accused had to participate in glass compartments. Most of the ten were charged with murder, attempted murder, and membership of, or participation in the activities of a terrorist group. They faced 30 years in prison. Suspected mastermind Osama Atar was believed to have died in U.S. counterterrorism operations in Syria. Michel Bouchat represented Abdeslam.

Reuters reported on September 16, 2022 that Presiding Judge Laurence Massart ordered that the nine defendants not be put in glass boxes and that an alternative be found by October 10. Jury selection was scheduled for October 13.

Reuters reported on November 30, 2022 that jury selection began for the trial, chaired by presiding judge Laurence Massart, of 10 men accused of involvement in the March 22, 2016 bombings in Brussels that killed 32 people and injured 340. Some 700 potential jurors went through airport-style security checks. Charges included murder and attempted murder in a terrorist context and leading or participating in the activities of a terrorist group over the twin bombings at Brussels Airport and third bomb on the metro. Eight defendants identified themselves to the court. Osama Krayem, a Swedish national accused of planning to be a second metro bomber, refused to answer questions. One defendant, believed killed in Syria, was tried in absentia. The trial was scheduled to run through June 2023.

AFP reported on December 1, 2022 that Zaventem airport computer technician Philippe Vandenberghe, 51, recalled that using techniques acquired while studying for his first aid certificate, "I intervened on 18 different people, I'm sure I saved one, probably two or three." He developed PTSD, and after treatment, left his airport job in 2019. He is now a Red Cross volunteer and hopes to become an ambulance driver.

Danielle Iwens, 58, who was working at a check-in desk near the site of the blast, sustained permanent hearing damage, including "60 percent less in the left ear". She also had memory loss and finds it difficult to concentrate. The experience worsened her Parkinson's symptoms. She lost a work colleague in the bombing and retired early as an airport logistics contractor in 2022 at the urging of her doctors.

Christian De Coninck, 62, a 40-year police veteran, served as police spokesman at the Brussels metro bombing. He was diagnosed with PTSD a year later, consulted with a psychiatrist, and left the force.

Al-Jazeera and *Reuters* reported on December 5, 2022 that the trial began in the Court of Assizes in Brussels of 10 men accused of involvement in the two March 22, 2016 ISIS suicide bombings. The dead included 15 men and 17 women—Belgians, Americans, Dutch, Swedish, British, Chinese, French, German, Indian, Peruvian, and Polish. Nine men were charged with multiple murders and attempted murders in a "terrorist" context, and faced life sentences. All ten were charged with participating in the activities of a "terrorist group". Among them were Mohamed Abrini, who prosecutors claimed went to the airport with two suicide bombers but fled without setting off his suitcase of explosives,

and Swedish national Osama Krayem, accused of planning to be a second bomber on the Brussels metro. Salah Abdeslam was accused of having hosted or helped certain attackers. The indictment ran 486 pages. Prosecutors planned to call 370 experts and witnesses during a trial expected to run seven months and cost 35 million euros ($36.9 million).

Among the survivors were

- Christelle Giovannetti, who wears hearing aids due to injuries in the metro bombing

- Sylvie Ingels, who was near the first airport bomb, who suffered repeated nightmares in the runup to the trial

FRANCE

January 7, 2015: On September 12, 2022, *Reuters* and *France Inter* radio reported that an appeals trial began in a Paris court for Ali Riza Polat and Amar Ramdani, who were found guilty in December 2020 as accomplices of brothers Said and Cherif Kouachi, who attacked the *Charlie Hebdo* satirical magazine and Amedy Coulibaly, who attacked a Jewish supermarket in Paris on January 7, 2015. Polat was sentenced to 30 years in prison for helping the Kouachi brothers secure weapons. Ramdani was given 20 years for supplying weapons and financing the attacks.

November 13, 2015: *BBC* and *Insider* reported on January 25, 2022 that senior French orthopaedic surgeon Emmanuel Masmejean faced legal action and possible misconduct charges after he tried to sell an X-ray of one of his patient's injuries as a digital artwork without her consent. He put the image of a woman's forearm with a Kalashnikov bullet lodged near the bone up for sale online as an NFT (non-fungible token). She was shot in the November 13, 2015 Bataclan attack, then was treated at Paris's European Hospital Georges Pompidou. He described the patient as a young woman who had lost her boyfriend during the 2015 massacre in Paris by ISIS gunmen. *Mediapart* reported that he listed the NFT on the OpenSea trading sites for £2,057 ($2,776; €2,446). *AFP* reported that her lawyer said, "This doctor, not content with breaking the duty of medical secrecy towards this patient, thought it would be a good idea to describe the private life of this young woman, making her perfectly identifiable." She wished to remain anonymous. Martin Hirsch, head of Paris's public hospitals, tweeted that a criminal and professional complaint had been lodged against the surgeon for his "heinous behavior".

Deutsche Welle and *Reuters* reported on February 9, 2022 that Salah Abdeslam, alleged to have rented a black VW Polo car that was seen outside the Bataclan concert hall during the 2015 ISIS attacks that killed 130, testified during his trial that he killed no one. *AFP* said that the verdict was expected in May.

AFP reported on February 14, 2022 that *One Year, One Night*, a Spanish film directed by Isaki Lacuesta, about the aftermath of the 2015 Bataclan attack premiered as one of 18 contenders for the Golden Bear top prize at the 72nd Berlin film festival. The movie stars Nahuel Perez Biscayart, 35, and Noemie Merlant, 33, as Ramon and Celine, portraying a young couple who survived the attack. Lacuesta had read *Peace, Love and Death Metal* by Spanish author Ramon Gonzalez, who was at the Bataclan with his girlfriend and other friends.

Reuters and radio *France Inter*'s website reported on April 15, 2022 that defendant Salah Abdeslam, 32, apologized to the victims of the November 13, 2015 ISIS attacks on six Paris restaurants and bars, the Bataclan concert hall, and the national soccer stadium that killed 130 people. He is the only one of 20 defendants accused of murder, attempted murder, and hostage taking. The French national of Moroccan origin said, "I ask you to hate me with moderation...I ask you to forgive me. It will not heal you, but I know that good words can help, and if this helps even only one of the victims, it will be a victory for me."

AFP reported on June 8, 2022 that the prosecution's closing arguments began in the Paris trial of Salah Abdeslam and 19 alleged accomplices over the November 13, 2015 attacks that killed 130 in Paris. The trial began in September 2021.

The *Washington Examiner* reported on June 12, 2022 that prosecutors requested life sentences for 12 of the 20 defendants.

CNN, UPI, and *The Guardian* reported on June 29, 2022 that Presiding judge Jean-Louis Peries announced that the court found Salah Abdeslam guilty on all five counts and sentenced him to life without the possibility of parole. Abdelslam was represented by attorney Olivia Ronen. The *Los Angeles Times* reported that the special court also convicted 18 on various terrorism-related charges, and Farid Kharkhach on a lesser fraud charge. They were given suspended sentences up to life in prison. Mohamed Abrini, a childhood friend of Abdeslam, was accused of transporting the attackers and weapons. He was sentenced to life with 22 years as a minimum term.

AP and *AFP* reported on July 12, 2022 that the Paris chief prosecutor Remy Heitz announced that Salah Abdeslam had not appealed his whole-life sentence for the Bataclan attack. The 19 others who were sentenced in the case also did not appeal. Abdeslam's attorneys Olivia Ronen and Martin Vettes said his silence "does not mean that he agrees with the verdict and the resulting life sentence without parole... He has simply resigned himself to it... Although such a punishment is unacceptable, we respect the decision of the one we have been assisting... There is no honour in condemning somebody who is defeated by despair."

The U.S. Supreme Court announced on October 3, 2022 that it would hear the case of the relatives of Nohemi Gonzalez, 23, a U.S. citizen studying in Paris. The Cal State Long Beach student was killed in the ISIS attack on several locations in Paris on November 13, 2015. Her relatives sued Google, owner of *YouTube*, saying it had allowed ISIS to post hundreds of videos that incited violence and recruited supporters. A lower court judge had dismissed the case and a federal appeals court upheld the ruling.

July 14, 2016: *AFP* reported on September 2, 2022 that the trial was to begin on September 5, 2022 of eight suspects, including one woman, in the July 14, 2016 attack on the Promenade des Anglais in Nice where ISIS sympathizer Mohamed Lahouaiej-Bouhlel, a 31-year-old Tunisian, killed 86 people and injuring 450 by driving a truck into thousands of locals and tourists celebrating France's Bastille Day national day. The defendants were accused of crimes from being aware of his intentions to providing logistical support and supplying weapons. Three were charged with association in a terrorist conspiracy and five others with association in a criminal conspiracy and violating arms laws. Ramzi Kevin Arefa faced a life sentence if convicted as a recurring offender. The others faced between five and 20 years in prison. Brahim Tritrou was to be tried in absentia, after fleeing judicial supervision to Tunisia where he was believed to be under arrest.

AP added on September 5, 2022 that Jean-Marie Fondacaro had created a L'Ange de la Baie statue along Nice's Promenade des Anglais commemorating the victims. Bruno Razafitrimo lost his wife, Mino, in the attack, and was raising their two young sons alone. Veronique Marchand lost her husband.

The *Washington Post, CBS News,* and *AFP* reported that on December 13, 2022 a Paris court found eight people guilty of aiding Mohamed Lahouaiej Bouhlel. Prison sentences ranged from two to 18 years. Presiding judge Laurent Raviot sentenced Franco-Tunisian Mohamed Ghraieb, 47, from Bouhlel's Tunisian home town, and Chokri Chafroud, 43, also a Tunisian, to 18 years in prison for "terrorist criminal association" and renting the delivery truck. Six other defendants, including a woman, were sentenced to two to 12 years for their roles in the attack, including for having supplied arms and the truck to Bouhlel. Ramzi Arefa, 28, who admitted to selling Bouhlel the semi-automatic pistol he fired at police, was sentenced to 12 years. A Tunisian and four Albanians were sentenced to prison terms of two to eight years for weapons trafficking or criminal conspiracy. Brahim Tritrou was tried in absentia after fleeing judicial supervision to Tunisia. Aurelie Amani-Joly, 52, continued to be treated for her injuries. Laurence Bray was also injured.

July 26, 2016: *AP, Deutsche Welle, AFP, Radio Franceinfo, DPA,* and *Reuters* reported on February 14, 2022 that the trial began in the Palais de Justice courthouse of four French-born men charged with conspiring to commit a terrorist act and "criminal terrorist association" in connection with the ISIS murder of Catholic priest Father Jacques Hamel, 85, by two 19-year-old attackers as he celebrated Mass inside a Saint-Etienne-du-Rouvray, Normandy church on July 26, 2016. Two nuns and an elderly couple were held hostage before the terrorists slashed Father Hamel's throat and seriously wounded the other man, Guy Coponet, now 92. Police fatally shot both attackers as they left the church.

Three of the accused were present at the opening of the trial; Rachid Kassim, a Frenchman and ISIS recruiter, was tried in absentia, believed to have been killed in a drone strike in February 2017 near Mosul, Iraq. Kassim had received a life sentence in absentia in 2019 for having ordered a failed attack in Paris, in which two women who pledged allegiance to ISIS blew up a car in 2016 near Notre Dame cathedral.

The trio faced 30 years in prison. They were identified as:

- Jean-Philippe Steven Jean-Louis, 25, who travelled to Istanbul with attacker Abdel-Malik Petitjean. Jean-Louis wanted to go to Syria. He allegedly knew that Petitjean intended to commit an attack in France. He was accused of having set up an online money collection site to help finance the project. He had spread ISIS group propaganda via *Telegram.*

- Farid Khelil, 36, Petitjean's cousin, was accused of having known about and supporting the attack.

- Yassine Sebaihia, 27, was in contact with one of the attackers.

The verdict was scheduled for March 11.

On March 9, 2022, *Reuters* reported that three acquaintances, aged between 25 and 36, of Adel Kermiche and Abdel-Malik Petitjean who cut the throat of Father Jacques Hamel, 85, were respectively sentenced to 8, 10, and 13 years in prison for criminal terrorist association. The killers said they belonged to ISIS.

GERMANY

September 5, 1972—West Germany—On June 2, 2022, Joachim Herrmann, senior security official in Bavaria, announced that the state was releasing all of its previously unpublished files on the attack at the 1972 Munich Olympics following criticism from relatives of the 11 Israeli athletes and coaches who died there. He added that federal authorities might still hold confidential files.

AP reported on July 27, 2022 that the German government indicated that it was willing to pay additional compensation to the families of the eleven Israeli athletes killed at the 1972 Summer Olympics in Munich by Black September Palestinian terrorists. Family members of the athletes called the proposed amount as "insulting". The Interior Ministry said that in 1972, Germany paid the relatives of the victims about 4.19 million marks (about €2 million or $2.09 million). *DPA* reported that in 2002, the government paid the surviving relatives another €3 million.

In Israel, Ilana Romano, the widow of Yossef Romano, a weightlifter who was killed, told public broadcaster *Kan*, "The offer is degrading, and we are standing by our stance that we are boycotting the {50ᵗʰ anniversary} ceremony… {the German government}threw us to the dogs. They mistreated us for 50 years… They decided to take responsibility — very nice after 50 years."

Ankie Spitzer, widow of Andre Spitzer, a fencing coach with the Israeli Olympic team, told *RedaktionsNetzwerk Deutschland*, "The sum we have been offered is insulting… We are angry and disappointed." *RND* reported that Germany had offered €10 million to the families, which would include the earlier payments.

Al-Jazeera and *DPA* reported on September 2, 2022 that the German government announced that the families of 11 Israeli athletes killed by Black September at the 1972 Munich Olympics would receive a total of €28 million ($28 million) in compensation, including payments already made.

September 18, 1991: *DW, AFP,* and *AP* reported on April 4, 2022 that prosecutors arrested right-wing extremist Peter S. 49, regarding a 1991 arson on a home for refugees in Saarlouis that killed Samuel Yeboah, 27, of Ghana, and injured two people. Yeboah suffered severe burns and smoke inhalation. Authorities believed S. was inspired by racist violence. Federal prosecutors charged him with murder, attempted murder, and arson leading to death. Prosecutors said that the night of the crime, S. and his racist cronies were discussing racist attacks in Hoyerswerda and suggested that same should be conducted in Saarlouis. Officials said he went to the residence, poured gasoline on the stairs, and torched it. Two residents broke bones jumping out of windows.

June 1, 2019: *Deutsche Welle* reported on August 25, 2022 that the Federal Court of Justice (BGH) in Karlsruhe upheld a life sentence handed in 2021 by a court in Frankfurt to Stephan Ernst, a neo-Nazi convicted of murdering Christian Democrat politician Walter Lübcke on June 1, 2019. The court also agreed that co-accused Markus H., 46, was not guilty of involvement in the murder. Markus H. was given a suspended sentence for arms offenses.

State prosecutors sought an additional conviction of Ernst for a knife attack on an Iraqi asylum-seeker in 2016. The court in Frankfurt had dismissed those charges.

November 6, 2021: *AP* reported on March 21, 2022 that German prosecutors believed that the Syrian suspected of knifing four people on an ICE high-speed train traveling from Passau, on the Austrian border, to Hamburg on November 6, 2021 was a jihadi ISIS supporter. They initially believed he was mentally ill, but a psychologist determined that he could be held criminally responsible. He was jailed in January 2022. The Syrian entered Germany in 2014 and was granted asylum in 2016.

Ireland

December 1972: *BBC* reported on October 19, 2022 that An Garda Síochána (Irish police) identified new lines of inquiry into a car bombing outside Farrelly's Bar and McGowan's Drapery in Main Street in Belturbet that killed Patrick Stanley, 16, from Clara in County Offaly, and Geraldine O'Reilly, 15, from Belturbet, and injured eight people. Loyalist paramilitaries were blamed. Patrick was in a telephone kiosk phoning his parents when the bomb went off; Geraldine was in a restaurant directly opposite the car bomb.

February 2016: *BBC* reported on September 28, 2022 that former Sinn Féin councilor Jonathan Dowdall, 44, of Navan Road in Dublin, pleaded guilty to facilitating the murder of David Byrne, 33, who was shot to death at the Regency Airport Hotel in Dublin during a boxing weigh-in in February 2016. He had provided a room at the hotel for a criminal organization or its members. His father, Patrick Dowdall, also pleaded guilty. Sentencing was scheduled for October 3, 2022. Jonathan Dowdall's trial had been scheduled for that date, when he was to be tried with Gerard Hutch, 58. Two other men were scheduled to be tried with facilitating the murder by providing vehicles to the organization which carried it out.

December 1, 2019: *AFP* reported on March 30, 2022 that defense lawyer Michael O'Higgins, representing Lisa Smith, 40, an Irish ex-soldier from Dundalk accused of being a member of ISIS, denied she was involved in terrorist activities, speaking on the final day of her 9-week trial in front of three judges at the Special Criminal Court. Smith earlier pleaded not guilty to membership of an unlawful terrorist group between October 28, 2015 and December 1, 2019, and denied funding terrorism by sending €800 ($900) to aid medical treatment for a Syrian man in Türkiye. Smith was a member of the Irish Defence Forces from 2001 to 2011 but left when she converted to Islam. Prosecutor said she moved to Raqqa in October 2015 and married a Briton involved with ISIS's armed patrols. She was arrested with her young daughter at Dublin airport on December 1, 2019.

MALTA

October 16, 2017: *Reuters* reported on July 5, 2022 that George Degiorgio, accused of detonating a car bomb that killed prominent Maltese journalist Daphne Caruana, confessed in an interview with *Reuters* and vowed to implicate others in plotting to assassinate her. He said that if he had known more about her "I would have gone for 10 million. Not 150,000... For me it was just business. Yeah. Business as usual! Of course I feel sorry." On June 22, 2022, the Appeal Court rejected legal challenges by Degiorgio to

the murder charges against him and his brother Alfred. The brother were represented by attorney William Cuschieri.

Al-Jazeera reported on October 14, 2022 that the trial began of Alfred and George Degiorgio, two brothers accused of the murder of Maltese journalist Daphne Caruana Galizia, 53, on October 16, 2017 in a car bomb explosion outside her home. The duo pleaded not guilty. They faced life in prison. The *Washington Post* reported on October 15, 2022 that George Degiorgio, 59, and Alfred Degiorgio, 57, pleaded guilty and were sentenced to 40 years in prison.

NORWAY

July 22, 2011: The *Washington Post, The Local, AP,* and *Reuters* reported on January 18, 2022 that Norwegian terrorist Fjotolf Hansen, nee Anders Behring Breivik, 42, who on July 22, 2011, killed 77 people by setting off a bomb outside the prime minister's office in Oslo and opening fire at a youth summer camp in Utøya, appeared in court at a high-security prison in Skien, south of Oslo, to demand parole from his 21-year prison sentence after being convicted on terrorism and murder charges. He gave a Nazi salute upon entering the court. He was represented by attorney Oystein Storrvik. His three-room cell contained video games, a DVD player, a typewriter, books, newspapers, and exercise equipment. *Newsweek* added that psychiatrist Randi Rosenqvist said Breivik cannot be trusted if he is released from prison and that he suffers from "asocial, histrionic and narcissistic" personality disorders. "He still has narcissistic traits. He still tends to construct scenarios. It is not psychotic, but he could in several contexts live out fables in reality."

U.S. News and World Report, AP, BBC, Newsweek, and *Reuters* reported on February 1, 2022 that a three-judge district court in Telemark unanimously rejected Breivik's parole application, ordering that he must stay in prison.

On March 15, 2016, *BBC*, citing the Oslo police, Norwegian government, and *NRK*, reported that the victims included:
In the Oslo bombing:

- **Hanna Endresen**, 61, Oslo, a receptionist in the security department of the Government Administration Services.

- **Tove Ashill Knutsen**, 56, Oslo, a secretary with the electricians and information technology workers union, who was en route to a subway station when bomb exploded.

- **Kai Hauge**, 32, Oslo, who owned a bar and restaurant in Oslo.

- **Jon Vegard Lervag**, 32, Oslo, an attorney who worked in the justice department.

- **Ida Marie Hill**, 34, Oslo, originally from Grue, Hedmark county, she worked as an adviser to the ministry of justice.

- **Hanne Ekroll Loevlie**, 30, Oslo, a senior government worker originally from Tyristrand, Buskerud county.

- **Anne Lise Holter**, 51, Valer i Oestfold, Oestfold county, a senior consultant to Norwegian Prime Minister Jens Stoltenberg's office.

- **Kjersti Berg Sand**, 26, Nord-Ordal, who worked on international issues in the Justice Department.

In the Utoeya island shooting:

- **Mona Abdinur,** 18, Oslo, a young politician

- **Maria Maageroe Johannesen,** 17, Noetteroey, Vestfold County, a student at Greve Forest High School who was interested in music, dance, and drama.

- **Ismail Haji Ahmed** 19 Hamar, Hedmark County, better known as Isma Brown after appearing on a talent show.

- **Ronja Soettar Johansen,** 17, Vefsn, Nordland County, an active blogger with a keen interest in music.

- **Thomas Margido Antonsen,** 16, Oslo, a student council representative.

- **Sondre Kjoeren,** 17, Orkdal, Soer-Troendelag County, who was heavily involved in efforts to get a new sports hall in his village.

- **Porntip Ardam,** 21, Oslo, also known as Pamela

- **Margrethe Boeyum Kloeven,** 16, Baerum, Akershus county, a student council leader

- **Modupe Ellen Awoyemi,** 15, Drammen, Buskerud county, the daughter of city council politician Lola Awoyemi, she was active in AUF discussions.

- **Syvert Knudsen,** 17, Lyngdal, Vest-Agder county, a student politician with a keen interest in music, he was believed to have been one of the first shot on the island.

- **Lene Maria Bergum,** 19, Namsos, Nord-Troendelag, had planned to start a summer job as a journalist.

- **Anders Kristiansen,** 18, Bardu, Troms County, an active young politician and leader of the AUF in his area.

- **Kevin Daae Berland,** 15, Akoey, Hordaland County, was active in Askoey AUF and local politics as well as being a member of the youth council.

- **Elisabeth Troennes Lie,** 16, Halden, Oestfold County, a board member of the Halden AUF.

- **Trond Berntsen,** 51, Oevre Eiker, Buskerud County, Crown Princess of Norway's step-brother. The off-duty police officer was killed while working as a security guard on the island.

- **Gunnar Linaker,** 23, Bardu, Troms County, regional secretary of Labour Party's youth wing.

- **Sverre Flate Bjoerkavag,** 28, Sula, Soer-Troendelag County, a union official concerned about justice, equality, and community thinking, who fought for pupils and students' rights and was training to become a nurse.

- **Tamta Lipartelliani,** 23, Georgia, secretary of the international committee of the Young Socialists of Georgia.

- **Torjus Jakobsen Blattmann,** 17, Kristiansand, Vest-Agder county, son of a former political adviser, he loved playing the guitar.

- **Eva Kathinka Lutken,** 17, Sarpsborg, Oestfold County, an active politician.

- **Monica Boesei,** 45, Hole, Buskerud County

- **Even Flugstad Malmedal,** 18, Gjoevik, Oppland County

- **Carina Borgund,** 18, Oslo

- **Tarald Kuven Mjelde,** 18, Osteroey, a big fan of the Chelsea football team

- **Johannes Buoe,** 14, Mandal, Vest-Agder county, interested in dogs, hunting, and snowmobiling, who took an active part in the youth community.

- **Ruth Benedicte Vatndal Nilsen,** 15, Toensberg, Vestfold County

- **Asta Sofie Helland Dahl,** 16, Sortland, Nordland County

- **Hakon Oedegaard,** 17, Trondheim, Soer-Troendelag County, a music student at Heimdal high school and member of the Byasen school marching band.

- **Sondre Furseth Dale,** 17, Haugesund, Rogaland County

- **Emil Okkenhaug,** 15, Levanger, Nord-Troendelag County

- **Monica Iselin Didriksen,** 18, Sund, Hordaland County, who was active in Sund AUF

- **Diderik Aamodt Olsen,** 19, Nesodden, Akershus County, Vice president of Nesodden AUF and the youngest member of editorial staff working on the organization's magazine.

- **Gizem Dogan,** 17, Trondheim, Soer-Troendelag County, who was elected as central member of the local AUF a month earlier.

- **Henrik Pedersen,** 27, Porsanger, Finnmark County, the leader of the Porsanger AUF.

- **Andreas Edvardsen,** 18, Sarpsborg, Oestfold County, director of the Sarpsborg AUF and active in in the Labour youth league regional committee in Oestfold.

- **Rolf Christopher Johansen Perreau,** 25, Trondheim, Soer-Troendelag County, a long-term member of the AUF who was elected to the board in October.

- **Tore Eikeland**, 21, Osteroy, Hordaland County

- **Karar Mustafa Qasim,** 19, Vestby, Akershus County, originally from Iraq.

- **Bendik Rosnaes Ellingsen,** 18, Rygge, Oestfold County, had a summer job at the justice ministry before attending camp. He was secretary of Moss Regional Labour Youth.

- **Bano Abobakar Rashid,** 18, Nesodden, Akershus County, leader of the Nesodden AUF.

- **Aleksander Aas Eriksen,** 16, Meråker, Nord-Troendelag County

- **Henrik Rasmussen,** 18, Hadsel, Nordland County, Treasurer of the Hadsel AUF.

- **Andrine Bakkene Espeland,** 16, Fredrikstad, Oestfold County

- **Synne Roeyneland,** 18, Oslo

- **Hanne Balch Fjalestad,** 43, Lunner, Oppland County, a Danish national who was killed while working on the island as a first aid assistant. She was with her 20-year-old daughter, who survived the shooting.

- **Ida Beathe Rogne,** 17, Oestre Toten, Oppland County

- **Silje Merete Fjellbu,** 17, Tinn, Telemark County

- **Simon Saebo,** 18, Salangen, Troms County

- **Hanne Kristine Fridtun,** 19 Stryn, Sogn og Fjordane County, a nursing student who was the local AUF county chairman.

- **Marianne Sandvik,** 16, Hundvag, Stavanger

- **Andreas Dalby Groennesby,** 17, Stange, Hedmark County

- **Fredrik Lund Schjetne,** 18, Eidsvoll, Akershus County

- **Snorre Haller,** 30, Trondheim, Soer-Troendelag County, a painter and union man who was a board member of the Joint Association's Central Youth Committee.

- **Lejla Selaci,** 17, Fredrikstad, Oestfold County, leader of the AUF in Fredrikstad.

- **Rune Havdal,** 43, Oevre Eiker, Buskerud County, who worked as a security guard on Utoeya island.

- **Birgitte Smetbak,** 15, Noetteroey, Vestfold County

- **Guro Vartdal Havoll,** 18, Oersta, Moere og Romsdal

- **Isabel Victoria Green Sogn,** 17, Oslo, AUF member

- **Ingrid Berg Heggelund,** 18, As, Akershus County

- **Silje Stamneshagen,** 18, Askoey, Hordaland County, active in the Askoey AUF and played in the school band.

- **Karin Elena Holst,** 15, Rana, Nordland County, a member of the Rana AUF who spoke to her mother during the shooting. Her mother had urged her daughter to hang up and hide.

- **Victoria Stenberg,** 17, Nes, Akershus County, the oldest of three siblings

- **Eivind Hovden,** 15, Tokke, Telemark County, who was involved in his local youth center and was attending his first summer camp

- **Tina Sukuvara,** 18, Vadsoe, Finnmark County

- **Jamil Rafal Mohamad Jamil,** 20, Eigersund, Rogaland County, originally from Iraq

- **Sharidyn Svebakk-Boehn,** 14, Drammen, Buskerud County, known as Sissi to friends and family

- **Steinar Jessen,** 16 Alta, Finnmark County

- **Havard Vederhus,** 21, Oslo, elected leader of Oslo Labour Youth in February 2011

- **Espen Joergensen,** 17, Bodoe, Nordland County, had recently become head of the Bodoe AUF

SWITZERLAND

November 24, 2020: *News 360, La Tribune de Geneve,* and *Le Temps* reported on September 19, 2022 that the Federal Criminal Court sentenced a woman, 29, to nine years in prison on terrorism charges, attempted murder, and maintaining ties to ISIS after she stabbed and wounded two people on November 24, 2020 in Lugano. One victim suffered serious neck injuries. The prosecution had requested 14 years in prison; the defense suggested eight years. Police said the attacker had psychiatric problems. The defense noted that she had not converted to Islam. Witnesses said she had shouted "Allahu Akbar" during the attack. The Swiss Federal Police Office (FEDPOL) said that she was investigated in 2017 and had a history of links to jihadist terrorism.

TÜRKIYE

January 1, 2017: The U.S. Supreme Court announced on October 3, 2022 that it would hear the case of the relatives of Jordanian citizen Nawras Alassaf, who died in the January 1, 2017 attack on Istanbul's Reina nightclub in which an ISIS gunman killed 39 people. The family sued Google, *Facebook*, and *Twitter*, saying the trio did not do enough to curb terrorist postings on their sites. A lower court permitted the case to proceed.

UNITED KINGDOM

November 21, 1974: *AFP* reported on February 25, 2022 that a man confessed to journalist Chris Mullin, 74, that he was involved in the 1974 British pub bombings that killed 21. West Midlands Police pressed him to disclose source material from an investigation he carried out between 1985 and 1986. Six men were initially convicted of the IRA attacks on two pubs in Birmingham. Mullin's investigation helped clear the "Birmingham Six"; a court quashed their convictions in 1991. Mullin had served as a junior foreign minister in Prime Minister Tony Blair's government. The dead included Michael William Beasley, Lynn Jane Bennett, Stanley James

Bodman, James Frederick Caddick, Thomas Frederick Chaytor, James Goodlety Craig, Paul Anthony Davies, Jane Elizabeth Davis, Charles Harper Grey, Maxine Hambleton, Anne Hayes, John Clifford Jones, Neil Robert Marsh, Marilyn Paula Nash, Pamela Joan Palmer, Desmond William Reilly, Eugene Thomas Reilly, Maureen Anne Roberts, John Rowlands, Trevor George Thrupp, and Stephen John Whalley.

AFP reported on March 22, 2022 that Judge Mark Lucraft ruled in favor of Mullin's legal challenge against the West Midlands Police attempt to force him to disclose the identity of the bomber. Mullin's lawyer, Louis Charalambous, hailed the "landmark" for freedom of expression.

June 15, 1996: *UPI* reported that during the night of September 8, 2022, Greater Manchester Police arrested a man at Birmingham Airport in connection with a 1996 Irish Republican Army bombing in Manchester City Center that injured more than 200 people. No one had been charged in 26 years.

December 21, 1988: *BBC, NBC News,* and *CNN* reported on December 11, 2022 that Libyan citizen and intelligence operative Abu Agila Mohammad Mas'ud Kheir al-Marimi, variant Masoud, 71, whom the U.S. charged on December 21, 2020 for making the bomb which destroyed Pan Am flight 103 over Lockerbie, Scotland, in 1988, killing 270 people, was in U.S. custody following extradition from Libya. The *Washington Post* added that prosecutors told Magistrate Judge Robin M. Meriweather in the U.S. District Court in Washington that they could not seek the death penalty, which the charges did not carry in 1988. Al-Marimi faced two charges, including destruction of an aircraft resulting in death, which since has carried the death penalty. The Tunisian-born al-Marimi faced life in prison. Al-Marimi told the judge he had the flu. Meriweather delayed the detention hearing until December 27. In an earlier interview with federal authorities, al-Marimi admitted making the bomb and assisting Megrahi and Fhimah in executing the plot.

February 23, 2015: *The World* and *BBC* reported on September 1, 2022 that Azadeh Moaveni,

author of *Guest House for Young Widows*, claimed that a Syrian asset of the Canadian Security Intelligence Services (CSIS) helped British citizen Shamima Begum, then 15, leave the UK for Syria on February 23, 2015, with her friends Kadiza Sultana and Amira Abase. Begum has been accused of joining ISIS. Then-British Home Secretary Sajid Javid withdrew her citizenship on February 19, 2019. Moaveni argued that she essentially was trafficked. *CNN* reported that Canadian Prime Minister Justin Trudeau promised to "follow up" on the allegations. The *Times of London* reported that she was in a refugee camp in Syria.

May 22, 2017: *UPI* reported on August 2, 2022 that authorities issued an arrest warrant for Ismail Abedi, 29, alias Ben Romdhan, older brother of Hashem Abedi, who aided the May 22, 2017 Manchester Arena bomber that killed 22 people.

Ismail failed to appear in Manchester Magistrates Court for an inquiry into what part he played in his brother's radicalization and whether his brother was trained in Libya. He was convicted in absentia in July 2022 for refusing to comply with the inquiry. He had been questioned for 14 days, but police lacked enough evidence to charge him. Police believed Ismail fled the UK in August 2021, using the alias Ben Romdhan, and went to Libya, where the rest of the family resides.

Hashem was found guilty in 2020 and sentenced to 55 years for helping the bomber, his brother Salman Ramadan Abedi, who blew himself up in the attack on an Ariana Grande concert.

Police had confiscated Ismail's laptop and cellphone in 2013, finding evidence that he was being radicalized by ISIS. Police found his DNA on evidence collected from a vehicle used by the two younger brothers to transport the explosives ahead of the attack.

Reuters reported on November 3, 2022 that chairman John Saunders of an inquiry examining emergency response announced that the group had determined that John Atkinson, 28, who was killed in a suicide bomb attack by Salman Abedi, 22, at a concert by U.S. singer Ariana Grande in Manchester on May 22, 2017, would probably have survived if the response by the emergency services had not been so flawed and if he had received more prompt medical treatment. Some 22 people died and more than 200 were injured. There was also a possibility that Saffie-Rose Roussos, 8, might have survived.

CNN reported on December 28, 2022 that pop singer Ariana Grande, 29, donated gifts to babies, children, and teenagers on pediatric wards at Royal Manchester Children's Hospital, Trafford Hospitals, Wythenshawe Hospital, and North Manchester General Hospital in Manchester as part of her long-standing relationship with Royal Manchester Children's Hospital Charity. *Manchester Evening News* reported that in 2021, she gave 1,000 presents to children in Manchester who were patients over Christmas, and in 2020, gave a £100 ($120.82) Amazon voucher to every young patient at Royal Manchester Children's Hospital and Manchester Royal Infirmary. She was named an honorary citizen following her One Love Manchester benefit concert, held to raise money for the victims of the May 22, 2017 Arena attack just weeks after the bombing that killed 22 people.

June 26, 2020: *UPI* and *BBC Scotland* reported on April 12, 2022 that a leaked report indicated that Sudanese asylum seeker Badreddin Abadlla Adam made 72 calls for help to the Home Office and its contractor Mears and Migrant Help before he stabbed six people at a hotel in downtown Glasgow on June 26, 2020 and was eventually shot by police. He stabbed six people in the Park Inn hotel, including three other asylum seekers, a police officer, and two hotel staffers.

November 14, 2021: At 11 a.m., a taxi exploded in front of Liverpool Women's Hospital, killing one passenger and injuring the driver, David Perry. *AP* and *Newsweek* reported on November 16 that the suspected bomber was Iraq-born Emad al-Swealmeen, alias Enzo Almeni, 32, an asylum-seeker claiming to be of Syrian and Iraqi background, who had converted from Islam to Christianity. He entered the UK in May 2014 with a Jordanian passport, falsely claiming to be a Syrian. He requested asylum in the UK in 2014, but was denied.

BBC reported on January 24, 2022 that al-Swealmeen reapplied for asylum under a new name.

October 15, 2021: *Reuters* and *AFP* reported on March 21, 2022 that prosecutor Tom Little told the Old Bailey court in central London that Ali Harbi Ali, 26, a British citizen and son of an ex-media adviser to a former prime minister of Somalia, had planned other attacks, including on cabinet minister Michael Gove. Ali was being tried for the October 15, 2021 stabbing murder of British lawmaker Sir David Amess, 69, at the Belfairs Methodist Church in Leigh-on-Sea, and preparing terrorist acts. Ali pleaded not guilty to murder and to preparing acts of terrorism. Prosecutors said Ali during earlier years had conducted reconnaissance on Gove and Conservative lawmaker Mike Freer. *AFP* reported that Little said Amess was "assassinated" in a "cold and calculated murder" by a "fanatical, radicalized Islamist terrorist". Little said Ali bought the knife in 2016.

AFP and *AP* reported on April 7, 2022 that Ali Harbi Ali, 26, accused of murdering UK lawmaker David Amess, 69, by stabbing him 21 times in a church in Leigh-on-Sea on October 15, 2021, told London's Old Bailey court that he was motivated by a grievance against parliamentarians who voted to bomb Syria. He "decided to do it because I felt that if I could kill someone who made decisions to kill Muslims, it could prevent further harm to those Muslims." He said that Amess had voted for airstrikes against ISIS in Syria in 2015, adding, "For one, he can't vote again...and perhaps send a message to his colleagues."

Reuters and *U.S. News and World Report* said on April 11, 2022 that Ali was found guilty of murder and preparation of terrorism after the jury took less than half an hour to reach a verdict. The jury deliberated for 18 minutes.

Reuters and *AP* reported on April 13, 2022 that London's Central Criminal Court sentenced Ali to whole life in prison, meaning Ali will never be eligible for parole, and will likely die in prison.

December 25, 2021: *AFP* reported on August 2, 2022 that police charged Jaswant Singh Chail,

20, from Southampton in southern England, with an offence under Britain's 1842 Treason Act after arresting him on Christmas Day 2021 armed with a crossbow at Windsor Castle where Queen Elizabeth II was enjoying the holiday. He was also charged with making threats to kill and possession of an offensive weapon. London's Metropolitan Police said he was scheduled to appear at Westminster Magistrates Court in London on August 17.

LATIN AMERICA

COLOMBIA

February 23, 2002: *AFP* reported on January 15, 2022 that on January 4, 2022, Judge Matthew Brann in U.S. federal court in Pennsylvania ruled that Lawrence Delloye, aka Lorenzo Delloye, the son of Ingrid Betancourt from her first marriage to Frenchman Fabrice Delloye, was entitled to $12 million in compensation and may "recover threefold the damages he… sustains and the cost of the suit, including attorney's fees", thereby ordering the former Revolutionary Armed Forces of Colombia (FARC) to pay $36 million in compensation for the kidnapping of presidential candidate Ingrid Betancourt, who was held hostage from 2002 to 2008. Delloye had sued 14 former FARC leaders in June 2018 for compensation under the Antiterrorism Act, which allows victims of terrorism to seek damages in U.S. federal courts. He was represented by law firm Scarinci Hollenbeck. Betancourt, now 60, a former Colombian senator with dual French citizenship, was kidnapped while campaigning in the Colombian presidential elections. Lorenzo was 13 at the time. The Colombian Army rescued her on July 2, 2008.

On January 18, 2022, Ingrid Betancourt announced that she would run for the presidency. She had founded the Green Oxygen Party while she was a congresswoman.

HAITI

July 7, 2021: *BBC,* the *Miami Herald, Newsweek, AP, UPI,* and *Reuters* reported on January 4, 2022 that the U.S. Department of Justice charged retired Colombian military officer Mario Antonio Palacios, 43, in federal court in Miami for having "participated in a plot to kidnap or kill the Haitian president", Jovenel Moïse, outside his Port-au-Prince home on July 7, 2021. Palacios had been arrested in Panama after being deported from Jamaica to Colombia. He faced a life sentence on charges of conspiracy to commit murder or kidnapping outside the United States, providing material support resulting in death, knowing or intending that such material support would be used to prepare for or carry out the conspiracy to kill or kidnap in connection with Moïse's assassination. He had been arrested in Jamaica in October 2021. Alfredo Izaguirre was appointed to represent Palacios. His next hearing was scheduled for January 31. Interpol had issued a red notice for Palacios for attempted murder, armed robbery, and conspiracy based on a request from the Haitian government. Palacios was with Colombia's military for 20 years. *Reuters* reported on April 4, 2022 that Palacios pleaded not guilty in the United States District Court for the Southern District of Florida to charges by U.S. prosecutors that he conspired to commit murder or kidnapping outside the United States in connection with the assassination of Moïse. He was represented by attorney Alfredo Izaguirre. The Haitian National Police said Palacios was part of a five-man "Delta Team" that entered Moïse's bedroom to kill him. The other four Deltas were in Haitian custody.

BBC, the *Miami Herald, AP,* and *NPR* reported that Jamaica Constabulary Force spokesman Dennis Brooks said Jamaican authorities on January 15, 2022 arrested former Haitian opposition senator John Joël Joseph as a prime suspect in the murder. Former National Police Chief Leon Charles said Joseph supplied weapons and planned meetings.

On January 19, 2022, *CNN* reported that a spokesperson for the Southern District of Florida said that the United States extradited a second suspect, Rodolphe Jaar, a Haitian who was presented with the charges on January 20 during his initial court appearance in Miami.

The *Washington Post* reported on April 8, 2022 that by that date, Haitian prosecutors had charged no one and a fourth judge, Judge Merlan Belabre, had been appointed to oversee the investigation but had yet to receive the case files after a month on the job.

UPI reported on May 9, 2022 that the United States charged former Haitian senator Joseph Joel John, variant Jean Joel Joseph, 51, with conspiring to kill Haitian President Jovenel Moïse, becoming the third person charged by U.S. authorities in the assassination plot. The specific charge was being present during a meeting where an unnamed co-conspirator identified as a dual Haitian-American citizen secured the signature of a former Haitian judge to arrest and imprison Moïse as well as providing them with immunity for their actions. He was also accused of obtaining vehicles and firearms to support the kidnapping operation. He faced life in prison. In mid-January 2022, Counter Terrorism and Organized Crime Unit authorities arrested John and three family members in Jamaica at a St. Elizabeth home on immigration-related charges. He was extradited to Miami on May 6, 2022.

The *Gal Times* reported on July 7, 2022 that the 37th High Criminal Court of Istanbul, Türkiye rejected the extradition request for Samir Nasri Salem Handal, a Jordanian businessman wanted for the assassination of Haitian President Jovenel Moïse and the subject of a red Interpol arrest warrant. The court freed Handal without charge. The Turkish press said some believed he had rented his house to Christian Emmanuel Sanon, who might have organized the murder. The *Daily Sabah* reported on November 21, 2021 that Turkish authorities had detained Handal at Istanbul Airport while traveling from the United States to Jordan in November 2021. Handal was also carrying Palestinian and Jordanian passports. He was held at Istanbul's Maltepe prison on the strength of Interpol's international arrest warrant for eight months.

Reuters reported on August 6, 2022 that a Turkish repatriation center freed a man wanted by Haiti over his alleged involvement in the assassination of President Jovenel Moïse and returned him to the United States.

October 16, 2021: *UPI* and *al-Jazeera* reported on July 7, 2022 that U.S. federal prosecutors in the U.S. District Court for the District of Columbia charged Haitian 400 Mawozo gang member Jean Pelice, alias Zo, 27, in connection with the armed kidnapping of one Canadian and 16 U.S. missionaries near Port-au Prince on October 16, 2021. The gang demanded $1 million for each Ohio-based Christian Aid Ministries hostage and the release of their leader, Joly "Yonyon" Germine. Pelice was transferred to U.S. custody on May 16, 2022. U.S. prosecutors had indicted Germine on May 10, 2022 for the kidnapping, claiming he directed the operation from his cell. Germine pleaded not guilty. Two hostages were released on November 18, three on December 5, and the others escaped on December 16, 2021.

Mexico

February 7, 1985: *Newsweek, Washington Examiner, El Universal,* and *AFP* reported that on July 15, 2022, Mexican Navy authorities arrested Rafael Caro Quintero, 69, alias El Narco de Narcos, in Sinaloa State. He was featured in the Netflix series *Narcos: Mexico*. He was wanted for the February 7, 1985 kidnap/murder of DEA agent Enrique "Kiki" Camarena. A court ordered his release on August 7, 2013 from Puente Grande State Prison in Zapotlanejo, Jalisco State. A female bloodhound search dog named Max found him hiding in the bushes in the mountains. Caro Quintero founded and led the Guadalajara cartel in the 1970s. U.S. Attorney General Merrick Garland said the U.S. will seek Caro Quintero's immediate extradition. Caro Quintero fled to Costa Rica after killing Camarena. He was soon arrested, returned to Mexico, convicted of murder, and sentenced to 40 years in prison. He was freed from prison after 28 years on August 9, 2013. Mexican courts reconsidered the ruling that he should have been tried in a state vice federal court and issued a warrant for his arrest. The FBI added him on the Ten Most Wanted Fugitives list, offering a $20 million reward for his capture. Charges against him included violent crimes in aid of racketeering; conspiracy to commit violent crimes in aid of racketeering; conspiracy to kidnap a federal agent; kidnapping of a federal agent; felony murder of a federal agent; aiding and abetting; and accessory after the fact. The *Washington Post* ran a long feature on July 23, 2022 regarding a dozen other failed operations to recapture Caro Quintero.

MIDDLE EAST

AFGHANISTAN

August 9, 2016: The *Washington Post* reported on August 13, 2022 that Australian teacher Timothy Weeks, 53, who was kidnapped in Kabul by the Taliban in 2016, then released in an exchange deal with U.S. officials in 2019, returned to Kabul on August 12, 2022 to "celebrate" the upcoming one-year anniversary of Taliban rule. He announced that he "stood behind" the Taliban regime. He deplaned wearing a black tribal turban and white Afghan tunic. He had converted to Islam during his captivity, taking the name Baar Muad Jibra'il after returning home. He told the media he was now "an Afghan and a Pashtun" and wants to help the Afghan people through a new charity in Australia.

January 31, 2020: Navy veteran and contractor Mark Frerichs, of Lombard, Illinois, was kidnapped in Kabul, possibly by the Haqqani network, a Taliban affiliate. On April 1, 2022, the *New Yorker* reported that a video was released showing him saying that it was recorded on November 28, 2021, adding "I'd like to ask the leadership of the Islamic Emirate of Afghanistan: Please release me. Release me so that I may be reunited with my family. Thank you." The *New Yorker* said it was given the video by "an unidentified individual in Afghanistan". It was the first time he had been seen since his disappearance. *CNN* reported on April 1, 2022 that his family called on the Biden administration to take "bold and decisive action" to bring him home.

The *Washington Post, AFP, al-Jazeera,* and *CNN* reported on September 19, 2022 that U.S. hostage Mark Frerichs, a civil engineering contractor and Navy veteran from Illinois, was released in exchange for granting clemency to an Afghan detainee held in U.S. federal prison. Bashir Noorzai, alias Haji Bashir Noorzai, a warlord and drug trafficker with ties to the Taliban, was convicted of drug trafficking and sentenced to life in federal prison in 2005 after being enticed to enter the United States. Acting Foreign Minister Amir Khan Muttaqi told a news conference that the duo were swapped at Kabul's international airport.

July 16, 2021: The *Washington Post* and *al-Jazeera* reported on March 22, 2022 that attorney Avi Singh, representing the family of Danish Siddiqui, 38, a 2018 Pulitzer Prize-winning Indian photojournalist for *Reuters* killed in Afghanistan on July 16, 2021, petitioned the International Criminal Court to investigate his killing and try top Taliban leaders for war crimes and crimes against humanity. Siddiqui died while accompanying an Afghan special forces unit to Spin Boldak in Kandahar Province. The *New York Times* had reported that his body was mutilated in the Taliban's custody. *Al-Jazeera* noted that Afghan commando Sediq Karzai died alongside Siddiqui.

GAZA STRIP

2015: *AP* reported on June 28, 2022 that Hamas released a video of Hisham al-Sayid, 34, an Israeli citizen and Bedouin Arab who had wandered from southern Israel into Gaza, and whom Hamas had held incommunicado since 2015. He was shown lying in a hospital bed and wearing an oxygen mask. There was no audio. The day before, Hamas said his condition was deteriorating. It was the first proof-of-life Hamas had released. The video was titled, "Footage of the soldier in the army of occupation, Hisham al-Sayid, detained by the Qassam Brigades". A TV in the background showed images of the Qatar Economic Forum, which was held in Doha the previous week. Rights groups said al-Sayid was mentally ill.

IRAN

September 22, 2018: *Reuters, ISNA, Mian Online,* and *Radio Free Europe* reported on January 18, 2022 that Branch 26 of a Revolutionary

Court in Tehran began the trial of Iranian-Swedish ethnic Arab separatist leader Habib Chaab, alias Habib Asyud, for the September 22, 2018 attack on a military parade that killed 25 people and several bombings. The judiciary's *Mizon Online* reported that he was accused of "managing and leading a terrorist group" and "planning and carrying out numerous bombings and terrorist operations" in Khuzestan Province.

Chaab was a founder and former leader of the Arab Struggle Movement for the Liberation of Ahwaz (ASMLA) separatist group who lived in Sweden for 14 years until he was apparently "lured" to Türkiye by Iranian intelligence agents. He vanished during a visit to Türkiye in October 2020. The next month, he appeared on Iranian state television. In December 2021, Türkiye arrested 11 people suspected of spying and involvement in the alleged kidnapping of Chaab on behalf of Iran.

IRAQ

June 10, 2014: On December 1, 2022, the *Los Angeles Times* reported that Christian Ritscher, head of a United Nations Investigative Team to Promote Accountability for Crimes team investigating atrocities in Iraq, told the U.N. Security Council that ISIS committed crimes against humanity and war crimes at Badush Central Prison in Mosul, Iraq, on June 10, 2014, where at least 1,000 predominantly Shi'ite prisoners were systematically killed. He said his group determined that ISIS was responsible for "crimes against humanity of murder, extermination, torture, enforced disappearances, persecution and other inhumane acts… war crimes of willful killing, torture, inhumane treatment, and outrage upon personal dignity".

January 8, 2020: *Military.com* reported on June 8, 2022 that the Pentagon in April 2022 awarded Purple Heart awards to nine members of the Ohio and New Hampshire National Guard, including aviation operations Staff Sgt. Aaron Futrell, for serious injuries they suffered in Iran's bombardment of the U.S. al-Asad Air Base northwest of Baghdad on January 8, 2020 in revenge for the killing of IRGC Quds Force General Qassem Suleimani.

ISRAEL

August 9, 2001: *Al-Jazeera* reported on July 11, 2022 that the U.S. continued to seek the extradition from Jordan of Ahlam al-Tamimi, a Palestinian woman convicted of aiding an August 9, 2001 bombing at a Sbarro pizzeria in Jerusalem in 2001 that killed 15 people, including Malki Roth, 15, an Israeli-American girl, and another U.S. citizen. Israel detained al-Tamimi weeks later, accused her of choosing the target and sending the bomber there, and sentenced her to 16 life terms. *AP* noted that she never expressed remorse and said she was pleased with the high body count. Israel released her from prison in 2011 in a prisoner exchange with Hamas, sending her to Jordan. In 2013, the U.S. Department of Justice charged her with conspiring to use a weapon of mass destruction against Americans, unsealing the charge in 2017. She faced the death penalty. Her name was also added to the FBI's Most Wanted Terrorists list. Jordanian courts denied extradition in 2017. *AP* reported that Roth's family sought a meeting with President Joe Biden during his visit to Jerusalem in July 2022.

July 31, 2002: The *Jerusalem Post* reported on August 1, 2022 that the Palestinian Authority had given a 14.29% raise in the monthly salaries given to four Palestinian terrorists who had bombed Hebrew University's Frank Sinatra Cafeteria on July 31, 2002. The bombers killed American student Janis Ruth Coulter, 36, Dina Carter, 38, David Gritz, 24, Daphna Spruch, 61, Levina Shapira, 53, American student Benjamin Thomas Blustein, 25, David Ladowski, 29, Revital Barashi, 30, and Marla Bennet, 24, and injured 80 others. The *Post* reported that during the previous two decades, the PA paid Wael Qassem, Wassim Abbasi, Alla Aldin Abbasi, and Muhammed Odeh more than NIS 8 million ($2.5 million). Their monthly payments were to increase from NIS 7,000 ($2,251) per month to NIS 8,000 ($2,572). They received an additional NIS 300 shekels ($96) per month because they were residents of Jerusalem. Per a Knesset law passed in 2018 calling for the withholding of funds given to terrorists, Israel's Security Cabinet deducted NIS 600 million from the taxes and tariffs Israel collects for the PA. PA refers to the payments as a "martyrs' fund"; Israelis call it "Pay for Slay".

August 8, 2019: The *Jerusalem Post* reported that on May 31, 2022, the Judea Military Court sentenced Hamas terrorist cell commander Ahmad al-Atzafra to life in prison plus 25 years, in connection with the stabbing murder of IDF Cpl. Dvir Sorek on August 8, 2019 near Migdal Oz, Israel. The court ordered al-Atzafra to pay NIS 1.5 million to Sorek's family. The IDF in October 2019 indicted al-Atzafra and four other Palestinians affiliated with Hamas—Qasem al-Atzafra, Nazir al-Atzafra, Yusef Zahur and Mahmoud Atuna—for the murder.

May 13, 2021: The *Jerusalem Post* reported on November 27, 2022 that the Tel Aviv District convicted Israeli-Arabs Muhammad Iyash and Ali Mutzri of causing aggravated bodily injury and of incitement to terror and violence against an IDF soldier on Sderot Jerusalem Street in Jaffa on May 13, 2021. The verdict was part of a plea bargain in a case running parallel to the case against Nur Yusef for attempted murder against the same soldier, known as L.S. The prosecution planned to request a jail sentence of five years on Mutzri and 22 months on Iyash.

November 2021: *AFP* reported on February 1, 2022 that an Israeli judge agreed to the early release of Spanish aid worker Juana Rashmawi, who was sentenced by a military court to 13 months in November 2021 for illegally funding the Popular Front for the Liberation of Palestine terrorist group, according to her lawyer, Avigdor Feldman.

LEBANON

February 14, 2005: *Reuters* reported on March 10, 2022 that presiding judge Ivana Hrdlickova announced that appeals judges at the Lebanon Tribunal overturned an acquittal and convicted in absentia Hassan Habib Merhi and Hussein Hassan Oneissi of several counts of terrorism and murder for their role in the February 14,

2005 bombing that killed 22 people, including former Lebanese prime minister Rafik al-Hariri.

AFP reported on June 15, 2022 that the Netherlands-based Special Tribunal for Lebanon (STL) was scheduled to sentence in absentia Hizballah members Hassan Habib Merhi and Hussein Hassan Oneissi on June 16, 2022 for the February 14, 2005 assassination in Beirut of former premier Rafik Hariri in a truck bombing that killed Hariri and 21 others and injured 226. The STL cost between $600 million and $1 billion since it opened in 2009. In March 2022, a court reversed the acquittal of Merhi and Oneissi.

Reuters and the *Jerusalem Post* reported on June 16, 2022 that presiding judge Ivana Hrdlickova handed down the maximum sentence of life in prison to Hassan Habib Merhi and Hussein Hassan Oneissi.

June 12, 2014: *News 360, Naharnet,* and *IMN TV* reported on June 13, 2022 that Lebanese authorities in Jbeil arrested Abdullah Yasser Sabawi al-Hasan, grandson of Sabawi Ibrahim al-Hasan, half-brother of Saddam Hussein, pursuant to an Interpol arrest warrant for his possible involvement in the massacre on June 12, 2014 at the Iraqi military academy of Camp Speicher in Tikrit Province, in which ISIS executed between 1,095 and 1,700 Iraqi cadets and Shi'ite militiamen. The Lebanese National Security Agency announced the arrest on August 19, 2022. Al-Hasan had fled to Yemen when Saddam's regime fell, then moved to Lebanon in 2018 with his family.

August 4, 2020: *AFP, NNA,* and *Reuters* reported on April 21, 2022 that Spanish authorities arrested Jorge Manuel Mirra Neto Moreira, 43, a Portuguese man wanted by Interpol for the August 4, 2020 Beirut port blast that killed over 200 people. Police arrested him at Madrid Airport on April 20, 2022 after he arrived on a flight from Santiago, Chile, where he had arrived on a flight but was immediately sent back to Madrid. Moreira was wanted in Lebanon for allegedly having brought explosives into the country. The next day, Spain's National Court ordered his conditional release and banned him from leaving the country. His passport was confiscated and he must appear before authorities on a weekly basis. Lebanon requested extradition for crimes of "terrorism" and "causing death through the use of explosives". The Portuguese daily *Jornal de Noticias* reported that Moreira ordered the ammonium nitrate as an employee of Mozambican firm Fabrica de Explosivos de Mocambique (FEM), a company he worked for until 2016. The ammonium nitrate arrived in Beirut in 2013 onboard the *Rhosus*, a Moldovan-flagged ship sailing from Georgia to Mozambique. In 2021 a Portuguese court rejected Lebanon's extradition request because it had not received all the necessary documents on time. In 2021, he was an executive at a frozen foods company in Braganca.

Saudi Arabia

December 30, 2021: *Reuters* and *BBC* reported on January 4, 2022 that French prosecutors opened a terrorism investigation into an explosion that went off under a French Sodicars Racing team support vehicle involved in the two-week Dakar rally in Saudi Arabia on December 30 in Jeddah. Driver Philippe Boutron sustained serious leg injuries. The bomb hit the vehicle soon after it left the Donatello Hotel for the race route. Five team members were in the vehicle. French newspaper *L'Equipe* reported that the explosion tore through the floor of the vehicle, which caught fire. *Reuters* reported on February 11, 2022 that investigators had determined that the explosion was caused by a bomb. 21123002

Syria

August 2014: *NBC News* and *AFP* reported on June 23, 2022 that Diane Foley, mother of American journalist James Foley who was beheaded by an ISIS cell dubbed the "Beatles", had met three times with Alexanda Kotey, 38, one of the imprisoned terrorists. Mohammed Emwazi, alias Jihadi John, killed Jim Foley in an execution ISIS filmed and broadcast. A U.S. drone strike killed Emwazi in 2015. She first met with Kotey twice in October 2021 inside a federal courthouse in Virginia.

Yemen

October 12, 2000: *UPI* reported on February 1, 2022 that the Biden administration told the D.C. Circuit Court of Appeals in a brief filed in the evening that it will not use statements obtained through enhanced interrogation techniques during any stage of the legal proceedings concerning Guantánamo Bay detainee and Saudi citizen Abd al-Rahim Hussein al-Nashiri, who was accused of being the mastermind behind the bombing of the U.S. Navy destroyer *USS Cole* that killed 17 U.S. sailors on October 12, 2000 and the attempted bombing of the *USS The Sullivans*. Colonel George Kraehe, interim chief prosecutor of the Military Commissions, signed the brief.

North America

Canada

June 23, 1985: *BBC, Deutsche Welle,* and the *Los Angeles Times* reported on July 15, 2022 that in the morning, a gunman shot to death Ripudaman Singh Malik in his car outside his clothing business in Surrey, British Columbia. Police called it a targeted killing. Police found a burnt-out vehicle nearby. Malik had been acquitted in March 2005 over the bombing of the June 23, 1985 Air India 182 flight that exploded over the Irish coast, killing 329 people. Malik denied involvement in the terrorist attack but police were accused of bungling the investigation. The bombings were attributed to Canadian-based Sikhs retaliating for India's deadly 1984 storming of the Golden Temple. Malik, a Sikh businessman, and Ajaib Singh Bagri were acquitted of mass murder and conspiracy charges for the Air India bombing and a second bomb that exploded prematurely on an Air India plane at Tokyo's Narita Airport in Japan, killing two baggage handlers. Inderjit Singh Reyat was the only man convicted in the bombings. He testified for the prosecution at Malik and Bagri's trial but was later convicted of perjury. Reyat was paroled in 2016.

February 21, 2017: *Reuters* and *USNWR* reported on May 27, 2022 that the Supreme Court upheld a 2020 decision by a Quebec court to lower Alexandre Bissonnette's parole eligibility to 25 years from the original 2019 sentence of 40 years of ineligibility. He was convicted of shooting to death six people in a Quebec City mosque in 2017. The Court deemed a 2011 law that allowed lengthy parole sentencing as unconstitutional. Bissonnette, 32, earlier pleaded guilty to six counts of first-degree murder and six counts of attempted murder.

April 23, 2018: *Reuters* reported on June 14, 2022 that Justice Anne Molloy announced that the Supreme Court sentenced Alek Minassian, 29, to life in prison. The incel was found guilty in 2021 of murdering ten and attempting to murder 16 when he drove a rented van into dozens of people on a busy Toronto street. Serving multiple life sentences concurrently, he would be eligible for parole in 25 years. Among the dead were Geraldine Brady and Amaresh Tesfamariam, a long-term care nurse from Eritrea, who was left a quadriplegic with severe health problems that hospitalized her for three and a half years before she died of her injuries.

March 31, 2020: *NBC Bay Area, The Guardian, CBC News, E! News,* and *Giant Freakin Robot* reported on June 15, 2022, that former *Riverdale* actor Ryan Grantham, 24, was given a mandatory life sentence. In March 2022, he had pleaded guilty before the British Columbia Supreme Court to second-degree murder for killing his mother, Barbara Waite, 64, in their townhouse while she played piano on March 31, 2020. Prosecutors in British Columbia argued that he planned to kill Canadian Prime Minister Justin Trudeau. *CBC* reported that the day after killing Waite, he packed in his car three guns, Molotov cocktails, ammunition, supplies for camping, and a map with directions to Rideau Cottage in Ottawa, where the Trudeau family lives. He allegedly moved to a plan to commit mass violence at his school, Simon Fraser University, or Vancouver's Lions Gate Bridge. Instead, he surrendered to the Vancouver police. He was represented by attorney Chris Johnson, who blamed mental illness.

TVLine reported that in 2019, Grantham guest-starred on *The CW's Riverdale,* playing Jeffery Augustine, who killed Fred Andrews (played by Luke Perry) in a hit-and-run. Grantham earlier played Redwood in *Becoming Redwood* in 2012 and Rodney James in *Diary of a Wimpy Kid* in 2010 and appeared in the 2009 Terry Gilliam movie *The Imaginarium of Doctor Parnassus.*

UNITED STATES

February 21, 1965: *Al-Jazeera* reported on July 14, 2022 that Muhammad Aziz, 84, who was exonerated after spending 20 years in prison for the 1965 assassination of Malcolm X, then 39, at the Audubon Ballroom in New York City announced that he had filed a lawsuit against New York City in federal court for $40 million in damages for its role in his wrongful conviction. He claimed the New York Police Department had withheld exculpatory evidence. Aziz and co-defendant Khalil Islam, who died in 2009, were exonerated in November 2021. Aziz was 26 when he was arrested. He had served multiple tours of duty with the U.S. Navy and was the father of six. Then-Manhattan District Attorney Cyrus Vance, Jr. apologized for what he called "serious, unacceptable violations of law and the public trust". Islam's estate also filed a similar lawsuit against New York City. Mujahid Abdul Halim, Islam, and Aziz were convicted in 1966. Halim was released from prison in 2010. The case was reopened in 2020 following the release of the Netflix docuseries *Who Killed Malcolm X.* The *New York Times* reported that New York State settled Aziz's wrongful conviction lawsuit for $5 million in April 2022.

June 5, 1968: *CNN* reported on January 13, 2022 that California Gov. Gavin Newsom denied parole for Sirhan Sirhan, 77, who was convicted of assassinating Senator Robert F. Kennedy in 1968. Sirhan had been recommended for parole in August 2021; two of Kennedy's sons—Robert F. Kennedy, Jr. and Douglas Kennedy—supported the release during their testimony at Sirhan's 16th appearance before the California Parole Board. Other family members disagreed. Robert F. Kennedy's widow, Ethel Kennedy, said in

September 2021 that Sirhan "should not have the opportunity to terrorize again… He should not be paroled."

March 30, 1981: *AFP* reported on June 1, 2022 that a Washington, D.C. judge granted unconditional release as of June 15 to John Hinckley, 67, who shot President Ronald Reagan on March 30, 1981. The ruling came six years after Hinckley was freed from a psychiatric hospital. *AFP* reported on June 15, 2022 that John Hinckley regained his freedom fully. He tweeted "After 41 years 2 months and 15 days, FREEDOM AT LAST!!!"

April 19, 1995: *CNN* reported on January 19, 2022 that Raymond Washburn, 75, who helped rescue five people from the rubble of the 1995 Oklahoma City bombing, had died at his home in Bristow, Oklahoma. Washburn was working at the fourth-floor snack stand he owned and operated when the bomb went off. He freed himself from the rubble, suffering cuts and bruises. Although blind, he then rescued four of his customers and an employee and led them to safety. Washburn was a member of the Yuchi Tribe of Native Americans and was the past president of the Randolph Sheppard Vendors of America, the Oklahoma Council of the Blind, and the Oklahoma League of the Blind Credit Union.

September 11, 2001: On February 11, 2022, U.S. President Joe Biden signed an executive order freeing $3.5 billion in Afghan assets held in the U.S. for families of American 9/11 victims.

CBS47-Jacksonville reported on June 2, 2022 that four retired FDNY firefighters died in late May 2022 from long-term illnesses related to the 9/11 attacks in New York.

Al-Jazeera reported on August 26, 2022 that U.S. Magistrate Judge Sarah Netburn in Manhattan recommended that 9/11 victims not be allowed to seize $10 billion of assets belonging to Afghanistan's central Da Afghanistan Bank (DAB) to satisfy court judgements they obtained against the Taliban. She held that seizing the funds would by extension give de facto recognition of the Taliban regime. The recommendation will be reviewed by U.S. District Judge George Daniels in Manhattan.

October 2002: *CNN* reported on August 28, 2022 that Maryland Court of Appeals Judge Robert McDonald ruled on August 26, 2022 that Lee Boyd Malvo, one of two serial snipers that conducted attacks in the Washington, D.C., area that killed ten people, must be resentenced because of U.S. Supreme Court guidance on juvenile offenders. The Supreme Court ruled that life without parole for youthful offenders is not permitted under the Eighth Amendment "if a sentencing court determines that the offender's crime was the result of transient immaturity, as opposed to permanent incorrigibility". Malvo, 17 at the time of the shootings, is serving life sentences in the Red Onion State Prison in Virginia.

April 15, 2013: *CNN* reported on March 4, 2022 that the U.S. Supreme Court in a 6-3 vote upheld the death sentence of 2013 Boston Marathon bomber Dzhokhar Tsarnaev. Justice Clarence Thomas, writing for the majority, held that "Dzhokhar Tsarnaev committed heinous crimes… The Sixth Amendment nonetheless guaranteed him a fair trial before an impartial jury. He received one." The court reversed a federal appeals court that had stopped the death sentence for Tsarnaev and ordered a new penalty-phase trial. He was represented by attorney Ginger D. Anders.

On April 7, 2022, the defense team for Boston Marathon bomber Dzhokhar Tsarnaev, 28, asked the 1st U.S. Circuit Court of Appeals to examine four constitutional claims not considered when his death sentence was appealed to the Supreme Court in March 2022. The Supreme Court upheld the sentence on March 4, 2022, overturning the 1st circuit court's vacating of the death sentence. His defense team argued that he was forced to stand trial in Boston; the trial court denied his challenges to two jurors accused of lying during voir dire; the court dismissed a potential juror because the person opposed the death penalty; and the court permitted the admission of Tsarnaev's "coerced confession".

NPR reported on April 19, 2022 that first-time runner Henry Richard, 20, finished the 2022 Marathon in honor of his late brother Martin, who at 8 years old, was the youngest victim of the 2013 Boston Marathon bombing.

August 15, 2017: *Al-Jazeera* and *Star-Tribune* reported on April 12, 2022 that two Illinois men who helped pipe-bomb the Bloomington, Minnesota Dar Al-Farooq Center mosque on August 15, 2017 were sentenced to far below the 35-year mandatory minimum that each man faced. Michael McWhorter, 33, was sentenced nearly16 years and Joe Morris, 26, was sentenced to nearly 14 years; they had pleaded guilty to multiple counts in 2019. Victims and prosecutors requested leniency after the men cooperated and testified in the 2020 trial of the mastermind of the attack Emily Claire Hari, who was known as Michael Hari at the time of the attack and leader of the small Illinois militia group "White Rabbits 3 Percent Illinois Patriot Freedom Fighters". Hari was convicted in December 2020 and sentenced in 2021 to 53 years in prison. McWhorter was represented by attorney Chris Madel; Morris by Robert Richman, who said his client has a "reduced mental capacity" and had suffered from undiagnosed mental illness, including schizophrenia and depression.

February 14, 2018: On October 13, 2022, *BBC* and *AP* reported that the jury recommended life in prison without the possibility of parole for Nikolas Cruz, 24, who had confessed to killing 17 people at Marjory Stoneman Douglas High School in Parkland, Florida on February 14, 2018. A sentencing hearing was scheduled for November 1, 2022. *BBC* reported on November 2, 2022 that Cruz was sentenced to life in prison without parole.

2019: The *Sarasota Herald-Tribune, USA Today*, and *Florida Times-Union* reported on July 9, 2022 that U.S. District Judge Kathryn Mizelle sentenced David G. Hannon, 67, of Sarasota County, Florida, to three years probation, a $7,000 fine, attend substance abuse and mental health treatment programs, refrain from drinking alcohol, and have no contact with U.S. Representative Ilhan Omar (D-Minnesota), for sending her a threatening e-mail in 2019. He had pleaded guilty in April 2022 to threatening a federal official. He had threatened to shoot Omar and the three other members of "The Squad" (U.S. Representative Alexandria Ocasio Cortez (D-New York), U.S. Representative Ayanna Pressley (D-Massachusetts), and U.S. Representative Rashida Tlaib (D-Michigan)) of progressive Members of Congress following a TV press conference on July 16, 2019 when they responded to President Trump's call for them to return to their "broken" countries, despite them being U.S. citizens (three were U.S.-born).

November 2019: *WOKV* and *AP* reported on May 18, 2022 that Milwaukee County Circuit Judge Jean Marie Kies sentenced Clifton Blackwell, 64, a White Wisconsin man, to a decade in prison for throwing acidic drain cleaner in the face of Latino man Mahud Vallalaz in November 2019 in a racist attack at a Milwaukee bus stop. She called Blackwell's actions "diabolical" and included five years of extended supervision. Villalaz testified that the vision in his left eye was permanently damaged by the attack. Villalaz suffered second-degree burns. Blackwell was represented by attorney Michael Plaisted, who said his client was diagnosed with multiple personality disorders. A jury convicted Blackwell in April 2022 of first-degree reckless injury with use of a dangerous weapon as a hate crime. Villalaz is a U.S. citizen who emigrated from Peru.

October 8, 2020: *WOKV* and *AP* reported on February 9, 2022 that Kaleb Franks pleaded guilty to conspiracy in the October 2020 plot to kidnap Michigan Governor Gretchen Whitmer, agreeing to testify before four other men—Adam Fox, Barry Croft Jr., Daniel Harris, and Brandon Caserta—faced trial scheduled for March 8.

Al-Jazeera reported on March 24, 2022 that during the trial of four individuals indicted for conspiracy to kidnap Michigan Governor Gretchen Whitmer, Ty Garbin, 26, who had pleaded guilty, told jurors that he and Adam Fox, Barry Croft, Jr, Daniel Harris, and Brandon Caserta wanted to attack before the 2020 election to prevent Joe Biden's victory.

The *BBC, CNN, NPR*, and *Washington Post* reported that on April 8, 2022, a federal jury in Grand Rapids, Michigan acquitted Daniel Harris, 24, and Brandon Caserta, 33, of conspiring to kidnap Michigan Gov. Gretchen Whitmer, 50, in October 2020, and deadlocked on the counts against Adam Fox, 38, and Barry Croft, Jr., 46, causing U.S. District Judge Robert Jonker to declare a mistrial for the latter duo. Federal authorities said they would pursue a second trial. Caserta was represented by Michael Hills; Fox was represented by Christopher Gibbons; Croft by Joshua Blanchard. Prosecutors had called as witnesses two admitted co-conspirators, Ty Garbin, 26, and Kaleb Franks, 27, who had pleaded guilty months earlier, and told the jury they had agreed to kidnap Whitmer from her lakeside home. The defense had claimed entrapment by the FBI and that Fox was high on marijuana when the plot was discussed.

On August 9, 2022, *AP* reported that jury selection began in a retrial of Adam Fox and Barry Croft, Jr., whose first trial ended with a hung jury regarding federal charges of conspiracy to kidnap Michigan Governor Gretchen Whitmer in 2020. Two other men who had pleaded guilty in the earlier trial were to testify.

CNN and *AP* reported on August 23, 2022 that after eight hours of deliberation, a jury convicted Adam Fox, 39, and Barry Croft, Jr., 46, of two counts of conspiracy related to the kidnapping scheme and attempts to use a weapon of mass destruction. Croft, a trucker from Bear, Delaware, was also convicted of another explosives charge. The conviction came on Whitmer's 51st birthday. They were represented by attorneys Christopher Gibbons and Joshua Blanchard, who argued entrapment by the FBI. Their clients faced life sentences. U.S. District Judge Robert Jonker did not set a sentencing date.

CNN and *BBC* reported on October 26, 2022 that a jury found Joseph Morrison, 28, his father-in-law Pete Musico, 44, and Paul Bellar, 23, guilty of providing material support for a terrorist act and two other state charges related to the 2020 plot to kidnap Michigan Governor Gretchen Whitmer, including gang membership and felony possession of a firearm. Sentencing was set for December 15, 2022.

On December 15, 2022, Judge Thomas Wilson sentenced Pete Musico, 45, to a minimum of 12 years; Musico's son-in-law Joe Morrison, 28, to 10 years; and Paul Bellar, 24, to seven years for plotting the kidnapping. The trio were convicted in October 2022 for providing material support for a terrorist act, which carried a 20-year maximum sentence, and for a gun crime and membership in a gang, the Wolverine Watchmen. They were not charged with having a direct role, but were members of a paramilitary militia that trained with Adam Fox, who faced a life sentence on federal charges on December 27, 2022. Defense lawyers planned to appeal.

CNN and *AP* reported on December 27, 2022 that Michigan federal Judge Robert Jonker sentenced ringleader Adam Fox to 16 years in prison on charges of kidnapping conspiracy and conspiracy to use weapons of mass destruction. Fox received credit for the more than two years in custody since his arrest. Judge Jonker added five years of supervised release. Fox was represented by defense attorney Christopher Gibbons.

CNN reported on December 28, 2022 that Judge Jonker sentenced Barry Croft, Jr., to 235 months in federal prison, the longest sentence of the people convicted.

January 6, 2021: On January 13, 2022, federal prosecutors charged Stewart Rhodes, founder and leader of the far-right Oath Keepers militia group, and 10 other members or associates, with seditious conspiracy in the violent attack on the U.S. Capitol on January 6, 2021. These were the first seditious conspiracy charges leveled regarding the attack. Rhodes, 56, of Granbury, Texas, and Edward Vallejo, 63, of Phoenix, Arizona, were arrested on January 13, 2022. The nine others were already facing criminal charges related to the Capitol attack. They faced 20 years in prison. Rhodes was a former U.S. Army paratrooper and Yale Law School graduate who founded the Oath Keepers in 2009.

On January 13, 2022, authorities arrested Alan Fischer, III, 28, of Tampa, Florida; Zachary Johnson, 33, of St. Petersburg, Florida; and Dion Rajewski, 61, of Largo, Florida with civil disorder. Fischer and Rajewski were also charged with assaulting, resisting or impeding certain officers with a dangerous weapon. Prosecutor was scheduled for a Washington, D.C. federal court.

Al-Jazeera reported on January 26 that U.S. District Judge John Bates in Washington sentenced Nicholas Languerand, 27, to 44 months in prison after he pleaded guilty in November 2021 to a single felony charge of assaulting law enforcement with a dangerous weapon by throwing objects at police and bragging about his actions on social media. He had been jailed since his arrest in April 2021 in South Carolina and received credit for time served. Prosecutors had recommended a 51-month sentence. Languerand's grandfather told the judge during the sentencing hearing that during Languerand's childhood, his father intentionally set fire to a trailer that he and his mother were living in, nearly killing them.

UPI reported on February 2, 2022 that Aaron Mostofsky, 35, pleaded guilty to the U.S. Attorney's Office in Washington, D.C., to one felony count of civil disorder, one count of theft of government property, and one count of entering and remaining in a restricted building, related to the insurrection at the U.S. Capitol on January 6, 2021 while dressed as a caveman in furs and wearing a stolen police vest and shield. Prosecutors agreed to drop a charge of obstruction of an official proceeding. *NBC News* reported that Mostofsky is the son of Judge Steven Mostofsky of the Kings County Supreme Court in New York. Aaron Mostofsky was to be sentenced on May 6, 2022. He faced up to five years in prison and a $250,000 fine on the felony charge and a year in prison and a fine of up to $100,000 for each misdemeanor.

Newsweek and the *Florida Times-Union* reported on February 23, 2022 that gluten-free TV chef Carol Kicinski was charged with four federal criminal counts for allegedly breaching the U.S. Capitol building. FBI Task Force Officer Shawn Walsh discovered GPS data from a mobile device that showed that she was near the first-floor northwest doors to the Capitol building at approximately 2:19 p.m. Video appeared to show that Kicinski and Jon Heneghan, who lives with her in a Dunedin, Florida home, left the Capitol by 2:51 p.m. Walsh said he had probable cause indicating that she did "knowingly enter or remain in any restricted building or grounds without lawful authority to do" and "knowingly, and with intent to impede or disrupt the orderly conduct of Government business or official functions, engage in disorderly or disruptive conduct in, or within such proximity to, any restricted building or grounds when, or so that, such conduct, in fact, impedes or disrupts the orderly conduct of Government business or official functions." He said she engaged in "loud, threatening, or abusive language, or engage in disorderly or disruptive conduct, at any place in the Grounds or in any of the Capitol Buildings with the intent to impede, disrupt, or disturb the orderly conduct of a session of Congress or either House of Congress." She had appeared on television broadcasts in the Tampa, Florida show *Daytime* on NBC affiliate *WFLA* since July 2009. She founded and served as editor-in-chief of *Simply Gluten Free* magazine.

The FBI announced that more than 725 people had been arrested in nearly all 50 states, in cases linked to the attack. More than 160 people had pleaded guilty to federal charges, including 22 felony offenses.

The *Florida Times-Union* reported on February 26, 2022 that U.S. District Judge Reggie Walton sentenced Adam Johnson, of Tampa, Florida, who posed for photographs with the podium of House Speaker Nancy Pelosi in the Capitol Rotunda, to 75 days in prison, a $5,000 fine, one year of supervised release, and 200 hours of community service. His plea agreement required him to relinquish compensation for any book, song, script, interview, or product bearing his name or likeness for five years. He had pleaded guilty in November 2021 to entering and remaining in a restricted building or ground. The stay-at-home father to five children had not worked for 11 years; his wife is an affluent doctor.

The *Florida Times-Union* reported on February 28, 2022, that U.S. District Judge Timothy J. Kelly sentenced northeast Florida warehouse worker Jeffrey Register, 39, to 75 days in prison for parading, demonstrating, or picketing inside the Capitol building and fined him $500. He had pleaded guilty in October 2021 to the single misdemeanor charge. The prosecution had called for five months in prison for having "arguably contributed to the circumstances" surrounding the shooting of rioter Ashli Babbitt. Assistant Public Defender Cara Halverson said Register was fired from his job for being charged in connection with the riot. He later found work at a distribution company.

CNN reported on March 7, 2022 that the Government Accountability Office reported that 114 police officers were injured during the January 6 Capitol riot.

CNN added on March 8, 2022 that a jury in a Washington, D.C. federal court found Guy Reffitt guilty of all five charges—wanting to obstruct the congressional certification of the 2020 presidential election, transporting guns into D.C., carrying a Smith and Wesson handgun onto the restricted grounds of the Capitol, interfering with Capitol Police protecting the Upper West Terrace, and obstructing justice by threatening his son and daughter when he returned to Texas. It was the first 1-6 federal trial. Judge Dabney Friedrich presided. Sentencing was scheduled for June 8. He faced 20 years in prison on the most serious charge. *CNN* reported on March 21 that Reffitt's attorney, Bill Welch, asked for a new trial before the D.C. Circuit Court of Appeals, saying Reffitt might have been guilty only of trespassing. *CNN* reported on August 1, 2022 that District Judge Dabney Friedrich sentenced Reffitt to 87 months in prison, the longest insurrection-related sentence to date. Reffitt, a recruiter for the right-wing Three Percenters militia, was the first rioter to go to trial rather than take a plea agreement. He said on a video posting, "I just want to see Pelosi's head hit every f**king stair on the way out. ... And (Republican leader) Mitch McConnell too." Reffitt's son Jackson testified against his father during the trial and said he "absolutely" deserved the sentence. Prosecutors wanted enhanced penalties to the sentence for terrorism. Prosecutor Jeffrey Nestler said, "We do believe he is a domestic terrorist."

CNN reported on March 18, 2022 that former West Virginia state lawmaker Derrick Evans, who resigned from the West Virginia House of Delegates after participating in the January 6, 2021, insurrection, pleaded guilty to a felony related to the riot. Prosecutors said that according to his plea agreement, he admitted that after he had won election as a state delegate, he livestreamed himself pushing inside the Capitol, screaming "We›re in, we're in! Derrick Evans is in the Capitol!" Prosecutors added that he also said, "If (Vice President Mike) Pence betrays us, you better get your mind right because we're storming that building." He faced five years in prison at a sentencing hearing in June 2022. He agreed to pay $2,000 in restitution for damage to the building. He was arrested on January 8, 2021.

On March 21, 2022, the trial in Washington, D.C., was to begin of conspiracy theorist Couy Griffin, 48, an Otero, New Mexico County Commissioner and founder of Cowboys for Trump, on charges of two misdemeanors for illegally entering Capitol grounds. *CNN* and *al-Jazeera* reported on March 22 that federal Judge Trevor McFadden found the former rodeo rider guilty of trespassing on U.S. Capitol grounds. Griffin was acquitted of a second misdemeanor charge of disorderly and disruptive conduct, claiming that he led others in prayer at the Capitol that day. Sentencing was scheduled for June 17; Griffin faced a potential fine, probation, or up to a year in jail for entering and remaining in a restricted area. *CNN* reported on June 16, 2022 that Otero, New Mexico County Commissioner Couy Griffin said that he planned to defy a State Supreme Court order and refused to vote to certify the results of a recent primary election because of concerns about Dominion voting machines. In June 2022, a D.C. federal judge sentenced Griffin to 14 days with time served and one year of supervised release after he was found guilty of trespassing during the riot. *CNN* reported that on September 6, 2022, New Mexico Judge Francis Mathew removed Griffin from his elected position as an Otero County commissioner because he violated a clause in 14th Amendment of the Constitution by participating in an "insurrection" against the U.S. government. Griffin was barred from holding any state or federal elected position in the future.

Newsweek and the *Daily Beast* reported on March 22 that Evan Neumann, 49, of California, who was indicted on 14 counts for the riot, received refugee status in Belarus. The six charges against him included engaging in physical violence in a restricted building with a deadly or dangerous weapon; civil disorder; assaulting, resisting, or impeding certain officers; and more. He fled the U.S. in February 2021, first landing in Ukraine, then in Belarus in August 2021. In November 2021, he asked for asylum on Belarusian state TV. A federal arrest warrant was issued for him in December 2021. The *BelTA* news agency reported, "U.S. citizen Evan Neumann has received refugee status in Belarus. The document was handed to him today in the Department of Citizenship and Migration of the Internal Affairs Directorate of the Brest Regional Executive Committee." He told Russian news site *Gazeta* that "I feel safe in Belarus. It's calm, I like it in this country. Today I am experiencing mixed feelings. I'm glad that Belarus has taken care of me. I'm upset that I wound up in this situation, that in my native country there were such problems."

CNN reported on March 25, 2022 that the FBI offered a $15,000 reward for information on the whereabouts of Jonathan Daniel Pollock, one of several Floridians accused of attacking multiple police at the Capitol. He was sought since June 2021. He was charged with assaulting several officers, theft of government property, and violent entry and disorderly conduct on Capitol grounds. Prosecutors said he punched two officers in the face, kneed a police officer, dragged an officer down stairs, charged at police with a flag pole, grabbed an officer's neck and pinned them to the ground, and rammed a police shield into an officer's neck. His sister, Olivia, was arrested earlier and pleaded not guilty to assaulting police. The FBI noted that he is a welder and ironworker.

The *Florida Times-Union* and *USA Today* reported that on March 29, 2022, Jonathan Daniel Carlton, 46, of Union County, Florida, a New River Correctional Institution in Raiford, Florida prison employee, pleaded guilty to a misdemeanor after admitting to parading, demonstrating, or picketing in a Capitol building. He faced six months in prison. He settled four misdemeanors filed by the FBI. He was represented by attorney Richard Landes of Jacksonville Beach, who told Senior U.S. District Judge Thomas F. Hogan that his client "did not battle with anyone and did not assault anyone". The prison "moved him to the mailroom" pending sentencing, which was scheduled for June 29. His companion, Baker County, Florida resident Bradley Weeks, still faced a felony charge of obstructing an official proceeding. The *Florida Times Union* and *USA Today* reported on June 16, 2022 that Jonathan Daniel Carlton, 46, was fired from his job as a guard after pleading guilty to a misdemeanor of parading, demonstrating, or picketing in a Cap-

itol building. Defense attorney Richard Landes noted that Carlton would also lose his subsidized housing as part of his employment. Sentencing was scheduled for June 29; Carlton faced up to six months in prison. The prosecution dropped three other misdemeanor counts as part of the plea deal. The *Florida Times Union* and *USA Today* reported on June 28, 2022 that Assistant U.S. Attorney Anne Veldhuis recommended in a June 22 sentencing memo to U.S. District Senior Judge Thomas F. Hogan that Carlton should serve three months in jail and be placed on three years of probation. Veldhuis argued that "As a corrections officer, Carlton would be well aware of the danger of a large mob against vastly outnumbered police officers. Moreover, he swore an oath to uphold the Constitution... As a law enforcement officer, Carlton held a special position of trust that he disregarded not only on January 6 but in the coming weeks when he lied to the FBI and hindered their investigation."

CNN reported on April 1, 2022 that a court sentenced Lonnie Coffman, 72, to 46 months in prison for parking his truck, containing 11 Mason jars filled with gasoline and Styrofoam, several unregistered firearms, hundreds of rounds of ammunition, a stun gun, machetes, and a crossbow with bolts, a few blocks from the Capitol on the day of the insurrection. Judge Colleen Kollar-Kotelly said "He had almost a small armory in his truck, ready to do battle... {He} spent two tours in Vietnam so he certainly knows what napalm can do." Coffman received credit for time served. He was also sentenced to three years probation and mandatory mental-health treatment. During his arrest that evening, police officers found that he was carrying two loaded, unlicensed handguns and had a contact card for a militia in Texas. He had taken a trip in 2014 with the American Patriots militia, bringing a shotgun and pistol to Camp Lonestar, where groups patrol the US-Mexico border. He had handwritten lists in his truck of homes of politicians, political operatives, and a federal judge with titles like "traitors" and "Obama's lap dog", or added to a "bad" category. He had faced seven federal charges and pleaded guilty in November 2021 to two: bringing destructive devices (the Molotov cocktails) and an unlicensed gun to Capitol Hill.

Police found 12 more Molotov cocktails in his home.

Business Insider reported that on April 4, 2022, a court sentenced Jason Riddle, of New Hampshire, who had pleaded guilty to two misdemeanor charges of illegally protesting inside the Capitol and theft of government property, to 90 days in jail and pay $750 restitution. He was also sentenced to three years of probation. Riddle had said in 2021 that he was running for the House seat of Rep. Ann Kuster (D-NH) in the 2022 midterms. (During the interview, he was told that Kuster was not a state representative but a representative from New Hampshire's 2nd Congressional District.) He had bragged to *NBC10 Boston* about drinking a lawmaker's wine during the riot. He also stole a red leather *Senate Procedure* book from an office, which he later sold for $40.

CNN reported on April 6, 2022 that Judge Trevor McFadden, an appointee of former President Donald Trump, found Matthew Martin not guilty of four federal misdemeanors related to trespassing. This was the first time a Capitol riot defendant was acquitted of all charges. Martin had worked for a government contractor. He claimed that a Capitol Police officer had waved him into the building. He was the first defendant to testify in his own defense, saying, "If the cops weren't letting people in, I would not have gone in. He called the activity outside the Capitol a "big block party... It was a magical day in many ways."

Meanwhile, the head of the West Virginia chapter of the Proud Boys pleaded guilty on April 6, 2022, saying he looked to Charles Donohoe, Proud Boys leader Enrique Tarrio, and others as leaders on January 6.

CNN reported on April 8, 2022 that Charles Donohoe, 34, a leader of the Proud Boys North Carolina chapter, pleaded guilty to two felony charges—conspiracy to obstruct an official proceeding and assaulting an officer—becoming the first member of the Proud Boys leadership to plead guilty. He faced more than seven years in prison and agreed to pay $2,000 in restitution for damage done to the Capitol. Prosecutors said he was a member of a small national leadership group of Proud Boys, self-entitled the Ministry

of Self Defense. Another Proud Boys member was slated to plead guilty later on April 8.

Five other alleged leaders of the Proud Boys, including Ethan Nordean, Joseph Biggs, Zachary Rehl, Enrique Tarrio, and Dominic Pezzola, earlier pleaded not guilty. *CNN* reported that Donohoe, Tarrio, Biggs, Nordean, Rehl, and others had an encrypted messaging channel entitled "MOSD Leaders Group", where they created the plan for January 6.

CNN reported on April 11, 2022 that a jury in Washington, D.C., found Thomas Robertson, a former sergeant of the Rocky Mount police in Virginia, guilty on all six charges, including impeding law enforcement officers, obstructing an official proceeding, entering and remaining in restricted grounds, and tampering with evidence in his actions around the U.S. Capitol attack. A D.C. Metropolitan Police officer testified that a man {Robertson} carrying a stick, hit him and another officer as they tried to pass through the mob of rioters during the attack. The Army veteran swung a large stick and wore a gas mask, confronting police officers. Robertson had posted online a month earlier calls for an "opened armed rebellion". Investigators found a rifle and bomb-making material in his home; he bought another 37 guns on line after his original arrest in January 2021. The *New York Times* reported on August 14, 2022 that Judge Christopher Cooper of U.S. District Court in Washington sentenced Robertson, 49, of Ferrum, Virginia to seven years and three months in prison, followed by three years of supervised release. His attorney, Mark Rollins, planned to appeal the conviction.

CNN reported on April 14, 2022 that Dustin Thompson, 38, told Judge Reggie Walton and a Washington, D.C. jury that "Besides being ordered by the President to go to the Capitol, I don't know what I was thinking... I was caught up in the moment." The government charged that he broke into the Senate parliamentarian's office twice, stole a bottle of bourbon and a coat rack, and then ran from a Capitol Police officer who tried to question him. The jury of seven men and five women deliberated for less than three hours before convicting the unemployed exterminator from Ohio of all six charges of obstructing an official proceeding, theft of government property, illegally entering the Capitol, illegally protesting in the Capitol, and two counts of disorderly conduct in the Capitol. It was a major precedent against the "President made me do it" defense that other defendants were expected to try. The obstruction of an official proceeding felony carries a sentence of up to 20 years in prison. Sentencing was scheduled for July.

CNN reported on April 28, 2022 that Josh Munn, 24, of Texas, pleaded guilty to U.S. District Judge Beryl Howell in federal court to illegally protesting inside the Capitol by climbing through a broken window and walking around the Capitol with his parents and two of his three sisters. Sentencing was scheduled for August 2022; he faced six months in prison. According to a plea agreement, he will pay $500 for damage done to the building. The parents Tom and Dawn, and sisters Kristi and Kayli, pleaded not guilty to separate charges. The family was the largest group of relatives to be charged. *CNN* reported on October 12, 2022 that five members of the Munn family from Borger, Texas, were sentenced together. The two parents received 14 days in jail. Three adult children—Kayli, Joshua, and Kristi—were given probation and some home confinement. D.C. Chief Judge Beryl Howell reprimanded parents Dawn, a nurse, and Thomas Munn for bringing four of their eight children—three adults and a minor child—to Washington with the intent to investigate the results of the 2020 election. Kristi Munn, the mother of three and oldest of the eight Munn children, received 90 days of home detention in addition to probation.

CNN reported on April 29, 2022 that Brian Ulrich, 44, of Georgia, one of the 11 Oath Keepers facing sedition-related charges, pleaded guilty in federal court to U.S. District Judge Amit Mehta to "obstruction of an official proceeding" and seditious conspiracy and admitted that he "intended to influence and affect conduct of the United States government and to retaliate against the United States government". He faced more than six years in prison, but Department of Justice prosecutors could suggest a lower sentence depending on his cooperation.

ABC News reported on May 2, 2022 that a jury found retired New York City police officer

Thomas Webster guilty on six charges, including assaulting D.C. Metro Police Officer Noah Rathbun, in the first federal assault case stemming from the Capitol attack. This was the fourth time a jury had heard his case; all four led to convictions on all charges. Webster called Rathbun a "rogue cop". On January 6, 2021, Webster wore bulletproof vest and waved a Marine Corps flag, yelling "commie mother------" at the officers, before yelling at Rathbun, "take your s--- off!" Webster was represented by defense attorney James Monroe. Webster was convicted on all charges, including assaulting, resisting, or impeding an officer using a dangerous weapon; civil disorder; entering and remaining in restricted grounds with a dangerous weapon; engaging in physical violence in restricted grounds with a dangerous weapon; and engaging in an act of physical violence on Capitol grounds. *CBS News* reported on September 2, 2022 that U.S. District Judge Amit P. Mehta sentenced Webster, 56, to 10 years—the longest sentence in the January 6, 2021 case—for several felonies, including assaulting a D.C. police officer with a flagpole, tackling the officer to the ground, and trying to pull off his gas mask.

USA Today and the *Florida Times-Union* reported on May 13, 2022 that U.S. District Judge Carl J. Nichols announced in Washington, D.C. on May 11 that Orange Park, Florida resident and bail bondsman Adam Avery Honeycutt, 41, may serve his current sentence that ends on May 23 but must then serve another 90 days behind bars for parading, demonstrating, or picketing during the Capitol riot. Honeycutt had pleaded guilty to one misdemeanor. Federal agents had arrested him in February 2021 when they found guns and marijuana paraphernalia in his home.

CNN reported on May 23, 2022 that Judge Beryl Howell, the chief judge of the Washington, D.C., federal court, had denied the request of Jason Douglas Owens, charged with assaulting a police officer at the U.S. Capitol riot, to go to the upcoming "2021 President's Club" five-day event in June in Cabo San Lucas, Mexico, as a reward from his employer, opioid maker Mallinckrodt Pharmaceuticals. His son, Grady Douglas Owens, is charged with assaulting an officer with a skateboard. Both pleaded not guilty.

CNN reported on May 27, 2022 that alleged Nazi sympathizer and white supremacist Timothy Hale-Cusanelli was convicted for his role in the riot after claiming he did not know Congress met there, believing that the "U.S. Capitol" was a suite of buildings. The Army reservist sports a Hitler-esque mustache. He told a jury that he was "from New Jersey" and was "idiotic" and ignorant. "I did not realize that Congress met in the Capitol." Hale-Cusanelli later said he knew about the Electoral College process and American politics generally, which he took classes on in college. Judge Trevor McFadden found the claim "highly dubious", suggesting that he was open to an enhancement against Hale-Cusanelli for obstructing justice. Sentencing was scheduled for September 16. He faced up to 20 years for the felony of obstructing an official proceeding. He was represented by defense attorney Jonathan Crisp.

CNN, al-Jazeera, and the *Washington Post* reported on June 6, 2022 that the U.S. Department of Justice issued a 10-count superseding indictment that charged the head of the Proud Boys, Henry "Enrique" Tarrio, 38, and four other leaders—Ethan Nordean, sergeant at arms of the Proud Boys and president of his local chapter in Washington State; Joseph Biggs, of Florida, organizer of Proud Boys events; Zachary Rehl, who runs the Philadelphia chapter of the Proud Boys; and Dominic Pezzola, alias Spaz, a Rochester, New York Proud Boy—with seditious conspiracy. They were earlier indicted on less serious conspiracy charges. Rehl was represented by defense attorney Carmen Hernandez. Tarrio was represented by Nayib Hassan. Seditious conspiracy is punishable by up to 20 years in prison.

The House of Representatives committee investigating the insurrection held prime-time hearings, beginning on June 9, 2022. Most networks carried the hearings live; *Fox News* did not.

AP reported on June 9, 2022 that FBI spokeswoman Mara Schneider announced the arrest in western Michigan of Ryan Kelley, 40, an Allendale Township real estate broker and Republican candidate for Michigan governor, on misdemeanor charges for his role in the riot, including disruptive conduct, injuring public property, and entering restricted space without permission. Michigan Democrats said Kelley has "no business seeking an elected position in the same government he tried to overthrow".

USA Today and the *Florida Times-Union* noted on June 10, 2022 that Florida had climbed into the lead of people arrested with 91, beating Texas's 72. Across the nation, 46 Proud Boys (16 from Florida) and 27 Oath Keepers (11 from Florida) had been charged. Polk County, Florida resident Jonathan Pollack remained a fugitive as of April, facing two charges of felony assault on a police officer by pulling one down stairs and punching another's face.

CNN reported on June 16, 2022 that District Judge Christopher Cooper sentenced Dr. Simone Gold, from Beverly Hills, who has spread debunked quackery about COVID-19, to 60 days in prison for illegally entering and remaining in the U.S. Capitol. The founder of America's Frontline Doctors was fined $9,500.

CNN reported on June 17, 2022 that rioter Mark Mazza, 57, pleaded guilty to carrying a loaded firearm—a revolver loaded with shotgun and hollow-point rounds—onto U.S. Capitol grounds and assaulting police officers with a stolen police baton. He told federal investigators he regretted not seeing House Speaker Nancy Pelosi during the riot and that they would "be here for another reason" if he had. He faced 20 years for assaulting officers with a dangerous weapon. *CNN* added on October 21, 2022 that Judge James Boasberg sentenced rioter Mark Mazza to 60 months in jail and fined him $2,000 for damages. Mazza said he lost on the west terrace a revolver called the "Judge" loaded with shotgun shells and hollow point bullets. Mazza took a baton from a police officer and hit him with it, yelling "This is our f***ing house! We own this house! We want our house! Get out of the citizens of the United States' way!"

The *Tallahassee Democrat, Florida Times-Union,* and *USA Today Network-Florida* reported on June 20, 2022 the arrest of three Saint Cloud, Florida residents accused of traveling to Washington with the Oath Keepers. Leslie Gray, 56, Tracy Isaacs, 52, and her husband, Luis Hallon, faced numerous charges. Gray and Isaacs faced a felony. Isaacs applied to join the Oath Keepers and offered to serve as a paramedic.

CNN reported on July 21, 2022 that District Judge Emmet Sullivan sentenced Capitol rioter Dawn Bancroft, 59, who had threatened to attack House Speaker Nancy Pelosi, to 60 days in prison, three years probation, and 100 hours of community service. Bancroft had said in a selfie video while leaving the Capitol, "We broke into the Capitol, we got inside, we did our part… We were looking for Nancy to shoot her in the frickin' brain, but we didn't find her." Bancroft pleaded guilty to unlawfully protesting in September 2021. Bancroft was represented by attorney Carina Laguzzi.

The same day, *CNN* reported that a jury in federal district court in Washington, D.C. convicted Memphis area moving company owner Matthew Bledsoe, 38, of five counts, including obstructing an official proceeding and four misdemeanors. He said he lived in Cordova, outside Memphis, when he was arrested. Bledsoe, also of Olive Brach, Mississippi, had asked "where those pieces of sh-t at?" during the Capitol breach. Sentencing was scheduled for October 21, 2022. He faced 20 years on the felony count and up to three years on the four misdemeanor counts. He was represented by attorney Jerry Smith. Bledsoe had scaled a wall on the West side of the Capitol, observing, "I chose the challenge of going up the wall." He did not take the stairs, because climbing "seemed funner for me at the time". Answering prosecutor Jamie Carter's question regarding whether climbing walls was a normal way to enter a building accessible to the public, Bledsoe quipped, "It wasn't a normal day." Chief Justice Beryl Howell rejected Smith's claim that Bledsoe was unaware he was on restricted grounds.

CNN reported on July 25, 2022 that far-right livestreamer Anthime Gionet, alias Baked Alaska, agreed to plead guilty to unlawfully protesting after abandoning a plea agreement in May during a hearing in which he proclaimed he was "innocent". He livestreamed a nearly 30-minute video in which he called on others in the mob to enter the building and saying, "We ain't leaving this b*tch." The plea agreement was filed on July 22. He had earlier claimed that he was acting as an independent journalist on January 6.

Insider reported on July 26, 2022 that Capitol rioter Alan Byerly, 55, of Pennsylvania, accused of attacking an *Associated Press* photographer and pulling a stun gun on police, pleaded guilty to two charges of assaulting, resisting, and impeding police, and striking, beating, and wounding a photographer on federal grounds that carried a 46-month prison sentence. He was arrested on June 2021. Sentencing was set for October 21, 2022. He faced a $150,000 fine.

AP and the *Florida Times-Union* reported on July 27, 2022 that U.S. District Judge Tanya Chutkan sentenced Washington, D.C. resident Mark Ponder, 56, to 63 months in prison for attacking police officers with poles during the riot. He claimed he "got caught up" in the chaos and "didn't mean for any of this to happen… I wasn't thinking that day." Prosecutors had requested 60 months. He was arrested in March 2021 and pleaded guilty in April 2022 to assault.

CNN reported on July 27, 2022 that George Tanios, who purchased two cans of bear spray and two cans of pepper spray prior to the riot, and was accused in the assault of Capitol Police officer Brian Sicknick, pleaded guilty to disorderly conduct and entering and remaining in a restricted area. He faced up to a year in prison. Sentencing was scheduled for December 2022. His co-defendant, Julian Khater, sprayed a line of officers, including Sicknick. The *Washington Post* reported that city's chief medical examiner, Francisco Diaz, indicated that Sicknick suffered several strokes and died of natural causes on January 7, 2021.

On August 10, 2022, Matthew Council, 50, of Riverview, Florida, pleaded guilty in the District of Columbia federal court to one felony count of assaulting, resisting, or impeding law enforcement officers, one felony count of interfering with a law enforcement officer during a civil disorder, and four misdemeanor offenses during the riot. Sentencing was scheduled for November 1, 2022. He faced up to 16 years in prison.

Military.com reported on August 23, 2022 that the Department of Justice announced the arrest of Marine Corps veteran and former combat videographer Kaleb Dillard, 26, in Columbiana, Alabama, on eight charges, including felony offenses of assaulting law enforcement officers and interfering with law enforcement during a civil disorder, plus six misdemeanor charges. He made his initial appearance in the Northern District of Alabama federal court. His military records said that in May 2019, he was a sergeant assigned to the Communication Strategy and Operations Office in Quantico, Virginia. Court filings noted that "Officer B.A. stated he was attempting to secure the Rotunda doors when he was approached from behind and thrown to the ground… Investigators have identified this individual as Dillard."

CNN reported on August 29, 2022 that Judge Timothy Kelly sentenced Proud Boy Joshua Pruitt, who nearly came face-to-face with then-Senate Minority Leader Chuck Schumer, to four years and seven months for obstructing the certification of the electoral college vote. Pruitt had pleaded guilty in early June 2022 to obstructing an official proceeding. Pruitt was sworn into the Proud Boys on President Joe Biden's Inauguration Day, two weeks later.

CNN reported that in August 2022, Robert Morss, Geoffrey Sills, and David Lee Judd were found guilty of obstruction of an official proceeding during a bench trial. Morss and Sills were also found guilty of assault.

The *Washington Post* reported that on September 9, 2022, Hawaii Proud Boys founder and "elder" Nicholas R. Ochs, 36, a former Marine and unsuccessful 2020 Republican-backed candidate for a state House seat in Honolulu, and associate Nicholas J. DeCarlo, 32, of Fort Worth, pleaded guilty to one felony count of attempting to impede or obstruct Congress and felonious defacing of the Capitol's Memorial door with the words "Murder the Media", their social media channel. They wrote in permanent marker on the door honoring two police officers fatally shot in 1988 while defending the Capitol from a gunman. They admitted to each throwing a smoke bomb at police, livestreaming the attack, stealing flexcuffs from a police duffel bag, and damaging federal property. They faced 20 years in prison. Under their plea deal, Chief U.S. District Judge Beryl H. Howell was likelier to sentence them to 41 to 51 months on December 9, 2022.

The *Washington Post* added that also on September 9, 2022, Oath Keepers general counsel Kellye SoRelle pleaded not guilty to a four-count indictment following her arrest in Texas. She was charged with conspiracy, obstruction of a federal proceeding, tampering with documents, and misdemeanor trespassing.

The *Washington Post* noted that also on September 9, 2022, Shane Jason Woods, 44, owner of Auburn Heating and Air in Auburn, Illinois, pleaded guilty to felony counts of assault on law enforcement and assault on a news photographer. His sentence was likely to range between 33 and 41 months. He was arrested in June 2021 and indicted in March 2022 on eight felony assault and disorderly conduct charges.

CNN reported on September 13, 2022 that District Judge Trevor McFadden announced guilty verdicts for three rioters following a bench trial. Patrick McCaughey was guilty of nine counts, including assault with a deadly weapon, for an attack against Washington, D.C., police officer Daniel Hodges. A video showed Hodges screaming in pain as he was crushed against a doorway and had his mask ripped off his face. Tristan Stevens was found guilty on nine charges. David Mehaffie was found guilty of four charges. Stevens and Mehaffie were acquitted on a single count of obstruction of an official proceeding. Prosecutors said that McCaughey and Stevens fought police, while Mehaffie directed members of the mob in and out of the Capitol's Lower West Terrace tunnel. Sentencing was scheduled for November 2022.

CNN reported on September 15, 2022 that District Judge Carl Nichols sentenced Robert Packer of Virginia, who was photographed wearing a "Camp Auschwitz" sweatshirt and an "SS" t-shirt inside the U.S. Capitol during the riot, to 75 days in jail. In January 2022, Packer pleaded guilty to misdemeanor trespassing. He had a lengthy rap sheet. He was represented by attorney Stephen Brennwald.

CNN reported on September 20, 2022 that the trial began of Douglas Jensen, who was seen on video at front of a mob that chased Capitol Police Officer Eugene Goodman near the Senate chamber. Jensen faced seven charges, including obstruction of an official proceeding, disorderly conduct, and assaulting, impeding, or resisting an officer. Jensen told investigators that his belief in QAnon conspiracy theories was the reason he breached the Capitol. Prosecutors told the jury that Jensen was one of the first 10 rioters who entered the building. Jensen was represented by attorney Christopher Davis.

CNN reported on September 27, 2022 that Judge Amy Berman Jackson sentenced Kyle Young, one of several rioters who attacked Washington, D.C., police officer Michael Fanone, to 86 months in prison. Young had pleaded guilty in May 2022 to assaulting Fanone by holding his wrist and pulling his arm while Fanone was dragged into the mob by other rioters, who beat and tased him in the neck. Fanone eventually lost consciousness. Fanone left the Metropolitan Police and is a *CNN* contributor. Daniel Rodriguez was charged with electrocuting Fanone several times in his neck and pleaded not guilty. Co-defendant Albuquerque Head pleaded guilty to the assault. *CNN* reported on October 27, 2022 that district Judge Amy Berman Jackson sentenced Head, 43, of Kingsport, Tennessee, who pulled former Washington, D.C., Metropolitan Police officer Michael Fanone into the crowd of violent rioters, yelling "I got one!" to 90 months behind bars. Head was detained in April 2021 and pleaded guilty in May 2022 to assaulting a police officer.

Fanone testified he felt Head "choke me and drag me out into the vicious crowd," while another rioter tased him. Fanone suffered a heart attack as rioters beat him and tased him in his neck repeatedly. Head was represented by attorney Nicholas Wallace.

AP and the *Florida Times-Union* reported that on September 27, 2022, jury selection began in the seditious conspiracy trial in a federal court in Washington, D.C. of Oath Keepers leader Stewart Rhodes and four of his followers—Kelly Meggs, Jessica Watkins, Kenneth Harrelson, and Thomas Caldwell—who allegedly collected weapons, organized paramilitary training, and created armed teams to stop Joe Biden from being named President.

CNN reported on October 3, 2022 that U.S. District Judge Randolph Moss sentenced Capitol rioter Lucas Denney, self-declared leader of

the Patriot Boys of North Texas, to 52 months in prison for assaulting a police officer. Denney had also formed his own militia, raised funds, and worked to recruit others to join him at the insurrection. Moss noted that Denney "came looking for a fight", citing messages from Denney talking about purchasing pepper spray and armor for his trip. Denney had pleaded guilty in March 2022 to the assault charge. He tried to pull barricades away from a line of police officers several times and later attempted to take a police officer's baton. He swung a pole made of PVC at a police officer but hit a photojournalist instead. Video showed him pushing on police officers with a riot shield. The judge said other video showed that "Mr. Denney was trying to take a swing at officer (Michael) Fanone." Denney was represented by attorney William Shipley.

CNN reported on October 6, 2022 that Jeremy Bertino, 43, a top lieutenant to Proud Boys leader Enrique Tarrio, agreed to plead guilty to seditious conspiracy and unlawful possession of a firearm by a prohibited person. He was the first member of the Proud Boys to plead guilty to seditious conspiracy. He was not alleged to have been in Washington, D.C. on January 6.

The *New York Times* reported on October 9, 2022 that Joseph Brody, 23, of Springfield in Fairfax County, Virginia, who was charged with assaulting a police officer with a metal barricade and breached several restricted areas, including the Senate floor and Speaker Nancy Pelosi's office, had worked for the Fairfax County Republican Committee for Glenn Youngkin, then a candidate for Governor. The FBI said Brody was associated with the white nationalist America First group, whose followers are called Groypers.

On October 13, 2022, the House of Representatives committee investigating the riot voted to subpoena former President Trump for records relating to the case and to appear before the committee to testify. *CNN* reported on October 21, 2022 that the select committee officially sent a subpoena to former President Donald Trump ordering him turn over documents by November 4 and "one or more days of deposition testimony beginning on or about November 14". He ignored the subpoena.

CNN reported on October 20, 2022 that the trial began of former U.S. Capitol police officer Michael Riley, who allegedly on January 7, 2021 told now convicted rioter Jacob Hiles in a private *Facebook* message "I'm a capitol police officer who agrees with your political stance… (t)ake down the part" about being in the Capitol building after Hiles made a *Facebook* post stating "I very simply made my way through the building." He also told the rioter he thought some of the "agitators" that day were Antifa. Riley pleaded not guilty to two counts of obstruction. Hiles pleaded guilty to unlawfully protesting in the Capitol in September 2021 and was sentenced to 24 months of probation. Riley was represented by attorney Christopher Macchiaroli. *CNN* added on October 28 that a jury found Riley guilty of obstruction for deleting his *Facebook* message telling another user to remove portions of a post that person made about entering the U.S. Capitol but did not reach a verdict (one juror would not convict) on a second obstruction count Riley faced for suggesting to the *Facebook* friend that he take down parts of his post, which federal prosecutors had alleged hampered their criminal investigation. The judge declared a mistrial on the second charge.

Riley was on the Capitol Police force for 25 years. He faced 20 years in jail.

AP reported that U.S. District Judge Carl Nichols on October 21, 2022 sentenced Trump ally Steve Bannon, 68, to four months in prison and fined him $6,500 for defying a subpoena from the House investigating committee. Bannon was convicted in July 2022 of one count of contempt of Congress for refusing to sit for a deposition and a second contempt count for refusing to provide documents. He was permitted to stay free pending an appeal by attorney David Schoen. Bannon faced separate New York charges of money laundering, fraud, and conspiracy.

USA Today and the *Florida Times-Union* reported that on October 21, 2022, John M. Pierce, attorney for Daniel Pearl Gray, 42, of Neptune Beach, Florida, argued that his client was entrapped. Gray was indicted in May 2021 on nine counts and faced 20 years in prison, accused of shoving police and causing a female police officer to fall down a flight of stairs in the Capitol rotunda. Pierce wrote "While Gray was lawfully standing and protesting outside the Capitol, Gray's cellphone device was unlawfully stolen… by an (apparent) law enforcement officer… Gray was forced to follow the apparent officer into the interior of the Capitol to seek recovery of his device… These facts establish a type of entrapment defense, because Gray was not intending to enter the Capitol prior to the unlawful actions of the alleged officer."

CNN reported on November 16, 2022 that a federal judge in Washington, D.C., found Larry Brock, 55, of Grapevine, Texas, guilty of five misdemeanors and the felony of obstructing an official proceeding during the Capitol riot. The retired Air Force lieutenant colonel entered the Senate chamber dressed in military gear, including a helmet and tactical vest and carrying plastic flexcuffs he found in the Rotunda that day. He faced 20 years behind bars. Brock chose a trial before a judge vice jury. Brock had rifled through Senators' desks. Sentencing was scheduled for February 2023.

The *New York Times* reported on November 20, 2022 that U.S. Judge Reggie Walton of the U.S. District Court for the District of Columbia sentenced Byron Thompson, 38, an unemployed exterminator from Columbus, Ohio, to three years in prison. Thompson said Donald Trump was responsible for his decision to storm the Capitol while wearing a bulletproof vest and steal a bottle of bourbon and a coat rack from the Senate parliamentarian's office. A jury convicted Thompson in April 2022 of a felony for obstructing an official proceeding and five misdemeanors, including theft of government property. Thompson was represented by attorney Andrew M. Stewart. Thompson and his wife, Sarah, met in 2004 while they attended Ohio State. Thompson's accomplice, Robert Anthony Lyon, 28, of Reynoldsburg, Ohio, pleaded guilty in March 2022 to misdemeanor theft of government property and disorderly and disruptive conduct in a restricted building or grounds. In September 2022, he was sentenced to 40 days in jail followed by supervised release.

CNN reported on November 29, 2022 that Oath Keepers founder and leader Stewart

Rhodes, 57, and fellow group member Kelly Meggs, 53, leader of the Florida chapter, were found guilty of seditious conspiracy in the criminal trial of five alleged leaders of the right-wing militia group. Rhodes, Meggs, transgender Jessica Watkins, 40, who had earlier led her own militia in Ohio, Florida Oath Keeper Kenneth Harrelson, 41, and Thomas Caldwell, 68, who claimed he was not an Oath Keeper member, were convicted of obstructing an official proceeding.

Specifics of the jury's verdict included:

Count 1: Seditious conspiracy

Stewart Rhodes: GUILTY

Kelly Meggs: GUILTY

Kenneth Harrelson: NOT GUILTY

Jessica Watkins: NOT GUILTY

Thomas Caldwell: NOT GUILTY

Count 2: Conspiracy to Obstruct an official proceeding

Stewart Rhodes: NOT GUILTY

Kelly Meggs: GUILTY

Kenneth Harrelson: NOT GUILTY

Jessica Watkins: GUILTY

Thomas Caldwell: NOT GUILTY

Count 3: Obstructing an Official Proceeding

Stewart Rhodes: GUILTY

Kelly Meggs: GUILTY

Kenneth Harrelson: GUILTY

Jessica Watkins: GUILTY

Thomas Caldwell: GUILTY

Count 4: Conspiracy to prevent an officer from discharging any duties

Stewart Rhodes: NOT GUILTY

Kelly Meggs: GUILTY

Kenneth Harrelson: GUILTY

Jessica Watkins: GUILTY

Thomas Caldwell: NOT GUILTY

Count 5: Destruction of Government Property and Aiding and Abetting

Kelly Meggs: NOT GUILTY

Kenneth Harrelson: NOT GUILTY

Jessica Watkins: NOT GUILTY

Count 6: Civil Disorder and Aiding and Abetting

Jessica Watkins: GUILTY

Count 7: Tampering with Documents

Stewart Rhodes: GUILTY

Count 8: Tampering with Documents

Kelly Meggs: GUILTY

Count 9: Tampering with Documents

Kenneth Harrelson: GUILTY

Count 13: Tampering with Documents

Thomas Caldwell: GUILTY

AP and *al-Jazeera* reported that on December 6, 2022, police who defended the U.S. Capitol received Congressional Gold Medals, the highest honor Congress can bestow, in the Capitol Rotunda. The medals were placed in the United States Capitol Police headquarters, the Metropolitan Police Department, the Capitol, and the Smithsonian Institution. Several honorees skipped shaking hands with Congressional Republicans who had downplayed the severity of the insurrection.

On December 14, 2022, *WCSC* reported that the Citadel suspended cadet Elias Irizarry, 21, of York County, after he pleaded guilty on October 26, 2022, for his role in the riot. He was arrested in March 2021. He was seen in various videos holding a metal pipe. The Citadel issued a statement saying that *"Following a Commandant's Board, he was found to have violated The Citadel's policies for "Conduct Unbecoming a Cadet." A sus-*

pension requires a cadet or student to leave the college for one semester; they may reapply for admission after that time." His sentencing was scheduled for March 15, 2023.

CNN reported on December 19, 2022 that the House committee investigating the insurrection announced that "That evidence has led to an overriding and straight-forward conclusion: the central cause of January 6th was one man, former President Donald Trump, who many others followed… None of the events of January 6th would have happened without him." The committee's report referred Trump to the Department of Justice on four criminal charges:

- Obstructing an official proceeding
- Defrauding the United States
- Making false statements
- Assisting or aiding an insurrection

The committee also made ethics referrals regarding House Minority Leader Kevin McCarthy, and Representatives Jim Jordan of Ohio, Scott Perry of Pennsylvania, and Andy Biggs of Arizona, for refusing to comply with committee subpoenas.

April 2021: *Military Times* reported on September 13, 2022 that James Bradley, 21, of the Bronx, and wife Arwa Muthana, 30, of Hoover, Alabama pleaded guilty on September 9 and 12, 2022 to attempting to travel to Yemen to join ISIS. Bradley told an undercover officer of his intentions to launch a terrorist attack on the U.S. Military Academy and ROTC cadets. The couple were indicted in the Southern District of New York in April 2021 for attempting to provide material support to a terrorist organization. The FBI was aware of Bradley's jihadi sympathies since July 2019. Bradley was married when he conducted a marriage ceremony with Muthana in January 2021. U.S. District Judge Paul Engelmayer scheduled sentencing in Manhattan federal court for February 2023. Each faced 20 years in prison.

In 2014, Muthana's younger sister, Hoda Muthana, used college tuition money to buy a plane ticket to the Middle East, where she became a wife to ISIS fighters. She later renounced ISIS and unsuccessfully tried to regain U.S. citizenship.

November 21, 2021: Darrell Brooks, Jr., 40, accused of driving his red SUV through a Christmas parade in Waukesha, Wisconsin, killing six, including a boy, 8, and several members of the Dancing Grannies group, and injuring dozens on November 21, 2021, withdrew his insanity plea on September 9, 2022. He faced nearly 80 charges, including six homicide counts, in Waukesha County Circuit Court. He had pleaded not guilty by reason of mental disease or defect in June 2022. The judge set a hearing for September 19, 2022.

CNN reported on October 26, 2022 that a jury found Brooks guilty of six counts of first-degree intentional homicide. He faced a mandatory sentence of life in prison. He was convicted of all other charges, including 61 counts of recklessly endangering safety with the use of a dangerous weapon, six counts of fatal hit and run, two counts of felony bail jumping, and one count of misdemeanor domestic battery.

Nicole White sustained injuries to her spine and tailbone and suffered ligament damage to her right knee.

CNN, WTMJ, and *BBC* reported on November 16, 2022 that Wisconsin Judge Jennifer Dorow sentenced Brooks to life in prison. Brooks represented himself in the four-week trial and declared himself a "sovereign citizen". Dorow said Brooks had chosen "a path of evil". The dead included Virginia Sorensen, 79; LeAnna Owen, 71; Tamara Durand, 52; Jane Kulich, 52; Wilhelm Hospel, 81; and Jackson Sparks, 8.

November 30, 2021: On October 24, 2022, Ethan Crumbley, 16, pleaded guilty to 24 charges, including terrorism and first degree murder, in the Oxford, Michigan High School shooting on November 30, 2021 that killed four students. His parents faced involuntary manslaughter charges for making the 9 mm Sig Sauer handgun accessible to him and ignoring his needs for mental health treatment. On November 29, 2022, the Michigan Supreme Court postponed the scheduled January 17, 2023 trial of his parents, ordering the state appeals court to hear an appeal from James and Jennifer Crumbley that the charge of involuntary manslaughter did not fit.

BIBLIOGRAPHY

GENERAL

"Art + Data; Describing (De)Radicalization) *RAND Review* March-April 2022, pp. 16-19.

Melissa Bauman "A Roster of Radicals" *RAND Review* March-April 2022, p. 21.

Daniel Byman *Spreading Hate: The Global Rise of White Power Terrorism* London: Oxford, 2022, 288 pp.

Ronald D. Crelinsten *Terrorism, Democracy, and Human Security: A Communication Model* Abingdon: Routledge, 2021.

Rita Katz *Saints and Soldiers: Inside Internet-Age Terrorism, from Syria to the Capitol Siege* Columbia University Press, 2022.

David McBride *Bioterrorism: The History of a Crisis in American Society: Epidemics, Bioweapons, and Policy History* Routledge, 2022.

David Miller and Tom Mills, eds. *The Politics of Terrorism Expertise: Knowledge, Power and the Media* Abingdon: Routledge, 2022.

The Origin and Evolution of the RAND Corporation's Terrorism Databases www.rand.org/t/ PEA1203-1

The Politics of Terrorism Expertise: Knowledge, Power and the Media Routledge, 2023.

Predicting Terror Activity Before It Happens www.sciencedaily.com/releases/2019/10/19100715345.htm

RAND Database of Worldwide Terrorism Incidents https://smapp.rand.org/rwtid/search_form.php

A Review of Public Data About Terrorism and Targeted Violence to Meet U.S. Department of Homeland Security Mission Needs www.rand. org/t/RRA1203-1

Alex P. Schmid, James J. F. Forest, and Timothy Lowe "Counter-Terrorism Studies: A Glimpse at the Current State of Research (2020/2021): Results from a Questionnaire Sent to Scholars and (Former) CT Practitioners" 15, 4 *Perspectives on Terrorism* August 2021, pp 155-183.

Judith Tinnes "Bibliography: Defining and Conceptualizing Terrorism" 14, 6 *Perspectives on Terrorism*, December 2020.

AFRICA

Bulama Bukarti *Inside Boko Haram: Unravelling the Myths of an African Catastrophe* Hurst, 2022.

Usman A. Tar *The Routledge Handbook of Counterterrorism and Counterinsurgency in Africa* Abingdon: Routledge, 2021.

EUROPE

W. Craig Reed *Terror in Frankfurt: The Untold Truth About the Worst Terrorist Attack in U.S. Air Force History* Permuted Press, 2022.

Thomas Renard *20 Years of Counter-Terrorism in Belgium: Explaining Change in CT Policy-Making Through the Evolution of the Belgian CT Doctrine and Practice Since 2001* Ghent University doctoral dissertation, 2021.

MIDDLE EAST

Mansoor Adayfi with Antonio Aiello *Don't Forget Us Here: Lost and Found at Guantanamo* Hachette, 2021, 384 pp.

Ethan Chorin *Benghazi: A New History of the Fiasco that Pushed America and Its World to the Brink* Hachette, 2022.

Cathy Scott-Clark and Adrian Levy *The Forever Prisoner: The Full and Searing Account of the CIA's Most Controversial Covert Program* Atlantic Monthly Press, 2022, 464 pp.

Michael Gordon *Degrade and Destroy: The Inside Story of the War Against the Islamic State* Farrar, Straus and Giroux, 2022.

Nelly Lahoud *The Bin Laden Papers: How the Abbottabad Raid Revealed the Truth about al-Qaeda, Its Leader and His Family* New Haven: Yale University Press, 2022, 362 pp.

Ido Levy *Soldiers of End-Times: Assessing the Military Effectiveness of the Islamic State* Washington Institute for Near East Policy, 2022, 258 pp.

Azadeh Moaveni *Guest House for Young Widows: Among the Women of ISIS* Random House, 2019

David Gartenstein-Ross and Thomas Joscelyn *Enemies Near and Far: How Jihadist Groups Strategize, Plot, and Learn* Columbia University Press, 2022.

Shahbaz Taseer *Lost to the World: A Memoir of Faith, Family and Five Years in Terrorist Captivity* Bantam, 2022.

NORTH AMERICA

Andy Campbell *We Are Proud Boys: How a Right-Wing Street Gang Ushered in a New Era of American Extremism* Hachette Books, 2022.

R. Scott Decker *Recounting the Anthrax Attacks: Terror, the Amerithrax Task Force, and the Evolution of Forensics in the FBI* Lanham, Maryland: Rowman and Littlefield, 2019, 300 pp.

James Gehring *Madman in the Woods: Life Next Door to the Unabomber* Diversion Books, 2022.

Sam Jackson *Oath Keepers: Patriotism and the Edge of Violence in a Right-Wing Antigovernment Group* New York: Columbia University Press, 2020, 240 pp.

Shahan Mufti *American Caliph: The True Story of a Muslim Mystic, a Hollywood Epic, and the 1977 Siege of Washington, D.C.* Farrar, Straus and Giroux, 2022.

Malcolm Nance *They Want to Kill Americans: The Militias, Terrorists, and Deranged Ideology of the Trump Insurgency* New York: St. Martin's, 2022, 320 pp.

Mark Oppenheimer *Squirrel Hill: The Tree of Life Synagogue Shooting and the Soul of a Neighborhood* Knopf, 2021, 320 pp.

John D. Woodward, Jr. "Terrorists and the Boston-Area Institutions of Higher Learning That Educated Them" 27, 1 *The Intelligencer: Journal of U.S. Intelligence Studies* Winter-Spring 2022, pp. 29-38.

RESPONSES

Mathieu Deflem "Responses to Terror: Policing and Countering Terrorism in the Modern Age" in C.A. Ireland, et al, eds. *The Handbook of Collective Violence: Current Developments and Understanding* Abingdon: Routledge, 2020.

Ofir Falk *Targeted Killings, Law, and Counter-Terrorism Effectiveness: Does Fair Play Pay Off?* Abingdon: Routledge, 2020.

K. Ford, A. Martini, and R. Jackson *Encountering Extremism: Theoretical Issues and Local Challenges* Manchester University Press, 2020

Andrew Glazzard and Alastair Reed "Beyond Prevention: The Role of Strategic Communications Across the Four Pillars of Counterterrorism Strategy" 165, 1 *RUSI Journal* 2020, pp. 74-88.

Christopher C. Harmon *A Citizen's Guide to Terrorism and Counterterrorism* Abingdon: Routledge, 2020.

Jason Hartley *Counter-Terrorism Community Engagement: Pitfalls and Opportunities* Abingdon: Routledge, 2021.

Lee Jarvis and Tim Legrand *The Proscription of Terrorist Organizations: Modern Blacklisting in Global Perspective* Abingdon: Routledge, 2020.

Patti Tamara Lenard *How Should Democracies Fight Terrorism?* Cambridge: Polity Press, 2020.

David Lowe and Robin Bennett *Prevent Strategy: Helping the Vulnerable Being Drawn Towards Terrorism or Another Layer of State Surveillance?* Abingdon: Routledge, 2020.

Alice Martini *The UN and Counter-Terrorism: Global Hegemonies, Power and Identities* Abingdon: Routledge, 2021.

Bill O'Reilly and Martin Dugard *Killing the Killers: The Secret War Against Terrorists* New York: St. Martin's, 2022, 288 pp.

Ted Schipper *Who the Hell Are You Simon Smith? A First Person Account of an Intricate UK Covert Operation to Infiltrate Muslim Terror Network* self-published, 2020, 361 pp.

Alex P. Schmid, ed. *The Handbook of Terrorism Prevention and Preparedness* The Hague: ICCT Press, 2021.

Alison Scott-Bauman and Simon Perfect *Freedom of Speech in Universities: Islam, Charities and Counter-Terrorism* Abingdon: Routledge, 2021.

Andrew Silke *Routledge Handbook of Terrorism and Counter-Terrorism* London: Routledge, 2020.

Ishaansh Singh "Anti- and Counter-Terrorism" in Alex P. Schmid, ed. *Handbook of Terrorism Prevention and Preparedness* The Hague: ICCT, 2021, pp. 1273-1288.

David Teiner "Bibliography: Civilian Casualties of Terrorism and Counter-Terrorism" 15, 1 *Perspectives on Terrorism* 2021, pp. 202-227.

Tewodros Workneh and Paul Haridakis, eds. *Counter-Terrorism Law and Freedom of Expression: Global Perspectives* Lexington Books, 2021.

Fiction

Jenifer S. Farmer *Blue Sky Gone* St. Augustine: Ancient City Press, 2021, 357 pp.

John Sandford *The Investigator* NY: Putnam, 2022, 392 pp.

Special Appendix: The Work of Richard Chasdi

Author's Note: Chasdi, of George Washington University has used the ITERATE dataset for several decades. Herewith is a catalog of his terrorism scholarship. I can include your terrorism vita in forthcoming editions if you send me a copy.

Books

Corporate Security Surveillance: An Assessment of Host Country Vulnerability to Terrorism Springer Nature Switzerland, AG, 2022.

Corporate Security Crossroads: Responding to Terrorism, Cyberthreats and Other Hazards in the Global Business Environment. Santa Barbara, CA: Praeger Publishers-ABC-CLIO, 2018.

Counterterror Offensives for the Ghost War World: The Rudiments of Counterterrorism Policy Lanham, MD: Lexington Books, 2010.

Tapestry of Terror: A Portrait of Middle East Terrorism 1994–1999 Lanham, MD: Lexington Books, 2002.

Serenade of Suffering: A Portrait of Middle East Terrorism 1968–1993 Lanham, MD: Lexington Books, 1999.

The Dynamics of Middle East Terrorism, 1968–1993: A Functional Typology of Terrorist Group-Types Ph.D. Dissertation: Political Science, Purdue University, August 1995.

Book Chapters

"Prevention of Major Economic Disruptions Following Acts of Terrorism – The Case of the Bali Bombings of 2002 and 2005." in Alex P. Schmid, ed. *Handbook of Terrorism Prevention and Preparedness* New York; ICCT, The Hague, 2021, pp. 1012-1058.

"Chapter 44A - Public Private Partnership Opportunities in the Realm of Virtual World Counterterrorism" in John R. Vacca, ed. *Online Terrorist Propaganda, Recruitment, and Radicalization* CRC Press, 2019, pp. 415-441.

Ronis, Sheila and Richard J. Chasdi. "Chapter 7 – Tools to Study Complexity in the Virtual World of Counterterrorism: Lessons Learned from the Stuxnet and Shamoon Viruses in John R. Vacca, ed. *Online Terrorist Propaganda, Recruitment, and Radicalization* CRC Press, 2019, pp. 113-122.

Ronis, Sheila and Richard J. Chasdi. "A Lone Wolf Visionario in the American Midwest" in Aaron Richman and Yair Sharan, eds. *Lone Actors – An Emerging Security Threat* Amsterdam, OIS Press, 2015, pp. 210-220.

"Center for Radicalization Prevention: A Model of Government Response to 'Lone Wolf' Terrorist Assaults" in Aaron Richman and Yair Sharan, eds. *Lone Actors – An Emerging Security Threat* Amsterdam, OIS Press, 2015, pp. 94-110.

"Terror in Rwanda in 1994 and the Failure of International Response" in Gillian Duncan, Orla Lynch, Gilbert Ramsay, Alison M.S. Watson, eds. *State Terror and Human Rights: International Responses Since the End of the Cold War.* New York: Routledge, 2013, pp. 114-141.

"An Analysis of Counterterror Practice Failure: The Case of the Fadlallah Assassination Attempt" in Richard Weitz, ed. *Project on National Security Reform – Vol 2: Case Studies Working Group Report.* Carlisle Barracks, PA: U.S. Army War College, Strategic Studies Institute, 2012, pp. 303-374.

Articles

"Implications of the New Taliban Government for the Biden Administration" *The International Journal of Intelligence, Security, and Public Affairs,* 2021 (https://doi.org/10.1080/23800992.2021.2011071).

"Research Note – The New Frontier of Enhanced Terrorism with the U.S. in Mind." 22, 2 *The International Journal of Intelligence, Security, and Public Affairs*, 2020, pp. 119-131.

"A Continuum of Nation-State Resiliency to Watershed Terrorist Events." 40, 3 *Armed Forces & Society* July 2014, pp. 476-503.

"Risks of Terrorism, Homicide, and Illness: a Methodological Consideration" 7, 6 *Perspectives on Terrorism* 2013 (http://www. terrorismanalysts.com/pt/index.php/pot/article/ view/316/html).

"Terrorist Group Dynamics Through the Lens of the Tigantourine Assault in Algeria" 2, 2 *Stability: International Journal of Security and Development*, pp. 1-10 (also translated into French and Arabic), 29 July 2013, (http://www. stabilityjournal.org/article/view/sta.bw/106).

"Forecasting the 'Arab Spring' of 2011: Terrorist Incident Data from 2000-2010 Offered No Early Warning" 7, 2 *Perspectives on Terrorism* 2013 (http://www.terrorismanalysts.com/pt/ index.php/pot/article/view/255/html).

"Research Note: Terrorism in Northwestern Africa: Mali, Mauretania, and Algeria: What START's Quantitative Data (1970-2011) Can and Cannot Tell Us" 6, 6 *Perspectives on Terrorism: a Journal of the Terrorism Research Initiative* 2012 (www.terrorismanalysts.com/pt/ index.php/pot/article/view/233/html).

"Terrorism in North America (Canada, United States & Mexico), 1970-2010: A Research Note" 6, 4-5 *Perspectives on Terrorism: a Journal of the Terrorism Research Initiative* 2012 (www. terrorismanalysts.com/pt/index.php/pot/article/ view/221/html).

"Trends and Developments in Terrorism: a Research Note" 6, 3 *Perspectives on Terrorism: A Journal of the Terrorism Research Initiative*, August 2012, pp. 67-76 (www.terrorismanalysts. com/pt/index.php/pot).

"What Is Known and Not Known About Palestinian Intifada Terrorism: The Criteria for Success" 27, 2 *Journal of Conflict Studies* Winter 2007, pp. 146-172.

"The Lair and Layers of Al-Aqsa Uprising Terror: Some Preliminary Empirical Findings" 14, 2 *Journal of Conflict Studies* Winter 2004.

"Middle East Terrorism 1968–1993: An Empirical Analysis of Terrorist Group-Type Behavior" 17, 2 *Journal of Conflict Studies* 1997, pp. 73-114.

"Terrorism: Stratagems for Remediation from an International Law Perspective" 12, 4 *Shofar: An Interdisciplinary Journal of Jewish Studies* 1994, pp. 59-86.

Non-Academic Publications

"Tackling Horizontal and Vertical Supply Chain Vulnerabilities: Risks from Interstate Conflict and Terrorism" 24, 4 *Journal of Counterterrorism & Homeland Security International*, May 16, 2019, pp. 10-14. (https:// issuu.com/fusteros/docs/iacsp_magazine_ v24n4_issuu/12).

"Terrorism." in Christopher G. Bates and James Ciment, eds. *Global Social Issues: An Encyclopedia*, Volume Three. Armonk, NY: Sharpe Reference, 2013, pp. 892-898.

"Mass Casualty Attacks and Strategic Targets" in Frank Shanty and Raymond Picquet, eds. *Encyclopedia of World Terrorism 1996–2002* Armonk, NY: M.E. Sharpe, Inc., 2003, pp. 533–536.

"Use of Conventional Weapons Technologies and Tactics." in Frank Shanty and Raymond Picquet, eds. *Encyclopedia of World Terrorism 1996–2002* Armonk, NY: M.E. Sharpe, Inc., 2003, pp. 566–570.

Academic Presentations

"Terrorist Attack Patterns of Business Targets in India, 2013-2018." Presented at the 2021 Biennial International Conference, Inter-University Seminar on Armed Forces and Society, Panel, "Terror, Intervention, and Trauma." Richard J. Chasdi, The George Washington University, Chair & Discussant; Drew Hogan, University of Minnesota, Kelsey L. Larsen, University of Central Florida, Richard J. Chasdi, The George Washington University.

"Part V of the Handbook of Terrorism Prevention & Preparedness." John D. Colautti, The University of Mass-Lowell; Richard J. Chasdi, George Washington University; Marie Robin, University of Southern Denmark; Tom Parker; Alex P. Schmid, Research Fellow, International Centre for Counter Terrorism – The Hague, Netherlands; International Centre for Counter Terrorism – The Hague, Netherlands, June 17, 2021.

"The Value of Complexity Systems Analysis for Counterterrorism." Presented at the 2017 Biennial International Conference, Inter-University Seminar on Armed Forces and Society, Roundtable, "Foresight Methods for a World of Complexity," Reston, Virginia, November 5, 2017.

"Strategic Counterterrorism." S. Rajaratnam School of International Studies (RSIS), Nanyang Technological University, August 18, 2017.

"A Comparison of Counterterror Practice Characteristics – Israel and the United States." Presented at the *Institute for National Security Studies (INSS)*, Forum of National Security Concept, Tel-Aviv, Israel. January 6, 2015.

"Center for Radicalization Prevention: A Model of Government Response to 'Lone Wolf' Terrorist Assaults." Presented at "Advanced Research Workshop – Lone Actors – an Emerging Security Threat" (sponsored by NATO Science for Peace and Security Programme), November 4-6, 2014, Jerusalem, Israel.

"Terrorism and the State." Richard J. Chasdi, Wayne State University, Chair and Discussant; Patricia Blacksome, Kansas State University; Michael A. Allen, Boise State University, Matthew DiGiuseppe, University of Binghamton, SUNY, Richard W. Frank, University of New Orleans; Stephen Charles Nemeth, Kansas State University, Jacob A. Mauslein, Kansas State University; Paul James Martin, Southern Illinois University, Carbondale. 2013 Midwest Political Science Association Conference, April 14, 2013, Chicago, Illinois.

"A 'Resiliency Continuum' of Terrorist Assaults at the Nation-State Level of Analysis." Presented at the 2011 Biennial International Conference, Inter-University Seminar on Armed Forces and Society, Panel, "National Resilience 2: Troubled Nations Demonstrating Various Resilience Patterns," Chicago, IL, October 21, 2011.

"American 'Hard-Line' Counterterror Practice Effectiveness in the Post 9/11 Era: The First Two Years." Presented at the World Summit on Counter-Terrorism: Terrorism's Global Impact, The International Institute for Counter-Terrorism (ICT) 11th Annual Conference, Workshop Panel, "The Role of Proactive Measures and 'Targeted Killings' in Modern Counter-Terrorism Strategies." Herzliya, Israel, September 14, 2011.

"Cyberterrorism Conceptualization and Dynamics – A Re-examination." Presented at Group Discussion Session at Center of Academic Excellence in National Security Intelligence Studies' 5th Annual National Security Colloquium, "Cyberterrorism: What? Where? Why?" Wayne State University, Detroit, Michigan, April 5, 2011.

"Case Study 1: 'The Fadlallah Affair'" Presented at The Project on National Security Reform (PNSR) Case Study Presentation on Interagency Reform, Minuteman Memorial Building, Reserve Officer's Association (ROA), 1 Constitution Avenue NE, Washington, D.C., October 19, 2010.

"Panel Session – Track 2: Enhancement of Data through Comparative Analysis and Statistical Modeling." Moderator, Richard J. Chasdi; Joshua B. Hill, Sam Houston State University; John M. Miller, Sam Houston University; Daniel J. Mabrey, University of New Haven; William M. Pottenger, Rutgers University; Victor Asal, University of Albany – State University of New York; R. Karl Rethemeyer, University of Albany – State University of New York, 2010 Annual Terrorist Incidents Conference, National Counterterrorism Center (NCTC), Herndon, Virginia, July 28, 2010.

"A 'Mini-Max' Counterterror Framework for Iraq and Afghanistan." Presented at Society for the Advancement of Socio-Economics (SASE) 22nd SASE Annual Meeting, Temple University, Philadelphia, Pennsylvania, June 26, 2010.

"Intelligence Compilation" Presented at Group Discussion Session at Center of Academic Excellence in National Security Intelligence Studies' 4th Annual National Security Colloquium, "Intelligence: Defending America in the New Age of Terrorism." Wayne State University, Detroit, Michigan, April 13, 2010.

"Terrorism: Definitions/Conceptualization" Presented at Group Discussion Session at Center of Academic Excellence in National Security Intelligence Studies' 3rd Annual National Security Colloquium, "Alternative Energy – A National Security Issue" Wayne State University, Detroit, Michigan, March 24, 2009.

"Panel 1: Global Security and Order" Presented at Uluslararasi Terörizm ve Sinirasan Suclar Arastirma Merkezi (International Terrorism and Transnational Crime Research Center). Presented at UTSAM panel program, "Countering Terrorism and Conflict Areas in the Middle East: Iraq and Palestine." Ankara, Turkey, March 17, 2009.

"Terrorist Groups in Social and Strategic Context" Richard J. Chasdi, Wayne State University, Chair and Co-Discussant with Joshua B. Spero, Fitchberg State College; Risa Brooks, Northwestern University; Mia M. Bloom, University of Georgia; Sherzod A. Abdukadirov, George Mason University; Jodi Vittori, University of Denver; Peter John Paul Krause, Massachusetts Institute of Technology. 104th American Political Science Association Annual Meeting, Boston, Massachusetts, August 28–31, 2008.

"Issues in National Security and the Root Causes of Terrorism" Detroit Council for World Affairs, and Center of Academic Excellence in National Security Intelligence Studies, Wayne State University, Detroit, Michigan, September 26, 2007.

"The Complex Set of Interconnections Between Empirical Research and the Rudiments of Counterterror Policy" Presented at the Symposium on Complexity and Business Analytics: Theory and Applications, Wayne State University, Detroit, Michigan, October 14, 2006.

"What is Known and Not Known About Palestinian Intifada Terrorism: Success Criteria" Presented at Centre for Conflict Studies and the Military and Strategic Studies Program, 25th Annual Conflict Studies Conference, "Terrorism in History: The Strategic Impact of Terrorism from Sarajevo 1914 to 9/11," University of New Brunswick, Fredericton, Canada, October 14-15, 2005.

"Empirical Trends in Middle East Terrorism: 1994–1999" Presented at The John F. Kennedy School of Government, Harvard University. Sponsored by the Belfer Center for Science and International Affairs, Middle East Initiative, Cambridge, Massachusetts, February 13, 2003.

"Tapestry of Terror: A Portrait of Middle East Terrorism" Presented at Muskingum College, Boyd Science Center, New Concord, Ohio, September 17, 2002.

"Understanding and Combating Terrorism" Richard J. Chasdi, College of Wooster, Chair and Discussant; Navin Bapat, Rice University; Stephen D. Collins, Johns Hopkins University; Leonard B. Weinberg, University of Nevada, Reno; Karl P. Mueller, Rand Corporation. 98th American Political Science Association Annual Meeting, Boston, Massachusetts, August 29–September 1, 2002.

"Causes and Consequences of September 11, 2001" Chair and Discussant: Richard Chasdi, Sharon Murphy, Lawrence Cline, Jon Dorschner, Michaela Hertkorn. New York State Political Science Association 56th Annual Conference, Niagara University, Lewiston, New York, April 19–20, 2002.

"Roundtable on the Middle East After September 11, 2001" Moderator: Abdul H. Raoof. Participants: Richard Chasdi, George Gregorian, Abdul Raoof, Abolghassem Sedehi. New York State Political Science Association 56th Annual Conference, Niagara University, Lewiston, New York, April 19–20, 2002.

"Perspectives on Terrorism" Jeffrey S. Lantis, Kent J. Kille, Richard J. Chasdi. Sponsored by International Relations; Political Science; Office of International Student Affairs, The College of Wooster, Wooster, Ohio, September 19, 2001.

"A Brown Bag Discussion on Understanding Terrorism" Richard Chasdi, Brad Roth. Program on Mediating Theory and Democratic Systems, Wayne State University, Detroit, Michigan, September 28, 1998.

"Some Behavioral Trends in Middle East Terrorism, 1968–1993: An Empirical Analysis of Middle East Terrorist Group-Types" Correlates of War Colloquium Series. University of Michigan, Ann Arbor, Michigan, April 4, 1997; and at International Studies Association/Midwest 1996 Annual Meeting, St. Louis, Missouri, October 1996; and at the 28th Annual Michigan Conference of Political Scientists, Wayne State University, Detroit, Michigan, October 1996.

"Middle East Terrorism." Presented at the Center for Peace and Conflict Studies Lunch Hour Seminars, Wayne State University, Detroit, Michigan, April 1996.

"Terrorism: Stratagems for Remediation from an International Law Point of View" Presented at International Studies Association/Midwest 1991 Annual Meeting, UrbanaChampaign, Illinois, October 1991.

BOOKS BY EDWARD MICKOLUS

TERRORISM

Terrorist Events Worldwide, 2021

Terrorist Events Worldwide 2019-2020

Terrorism Worldwide, 2018

Terrorism Worldwide, 2017

Terrorism Worldwide, 2016

Terrorism 2013-2015: A Worldwide Chronology

Terrorism 2008-2012: A Worldwide Chronology

Terrorism, 2005-2007

with Susan L. Simmons *Terrorism, 2002-2004: A Chronology* 3 volumes

with Susan L. Simmons *Terrorism, 1996-2001: A Chronology of Events and a Selectively Annotated Bibliography* 2 volumes

with Susan L. Simmons *Terrorism, 1992-1995: A Chronology of Events and a Selectively Annotated Bibliography*

Terrorism, 1988-1991: A Chronology of Events and a Selectively Annotated Bibliography

with Todd Sandler and Jean Murdock *International Terrorism in the 1980s: A Chronology, Volume 2: 1984-1987*

with Todd Sandler and Jean Murdock *International Terrorism in the 1980s: A Chronology, Volume 1: 1980-1983*

Transnational Terrorism: A Chronology of Events, 19681979

with Peter Flemming *Terrorism, 1980-1987: A Selectively Annotated Bibliography*

The Literature of Terrorism: A Selectively Annotated Bibliography

Annotated Bibliography on International and Transnational Terrorism available in Legal and Other Aspects of Terrorism

International Terrorism: Attributes of Terrorist Events, 1968-1977, ITERATE 2 Data Codebook

ITERATE: International Terrorism: Attributes of Terrorist Events, Data Codebook

Combatting International Terrorism: A Quantitative Analysis

with Susan L. Simmons *The 50 Worst Terrorist Attacks*

with Susan L. Simmons *The Terrorist List: North America*

with Susan L. Simmons *The Terrorist List: South America*

with Susan L. Simmons *The Terrorist List: Eastern Europe*

with Susan L. Simmons *The Terrorist List: Western Europe*

with Susan L. Simmons *The Terrorist List: Asia, Pacific, and Sub-Saharan Africa*

The Terrorist List: The Middle East, 2 volumes

INTELLIGENCE

Spycraft for Thriller Writers: How to Write Spy Novels and Movies Accurately and Not Be Laughed at by Real-Life Spies

More Stories from Langley: Another Glimpse Inside the CIA

Stories from Langley: A Glimpse Inside the CIA

The Counterintelligence Chronology: Spying by and Against the United States from the 1700s through 2014

with Cynthia Kwitchoff *The Secret Book of Intelligence Community Humor*

with Cynthia Kwitchoff *Two Spies Walk Into a Bar*

The Secret Book of CIA Humor

INSPIRATION

Harlan Rector and Ed Mickolus, eds. *I Still Matter: Finding Meaning in Life at All Ages*

Harlan Rector and Ed Mickolus, eds. *I Matter Too: Finding Meaning in Life at All Ages*

Harlan Rector and Ed Mickolus, eds. *I Matter: Finding Meaning in Life at All Ages*

with Cynthia Kwitchoff *His Words: Inspirational Quotations from Jesus Christ*

All the Presidents' Heroes: Inspirational Stories of the Honorees of State of the Nation Addresses (forthcoming)

EDUCATION

The Creativity Sourcebook

Briefing for the Boardroom and the Situation Room

with Joseph T. Brannan *Coaching Winning Model United Nations Teams*

HUMOR

More Funny COVID Memes

America's Funniest Memes: Coronavirus Edition

Food with Thought: The Wit and Wisdom of Chinese Fortune Cookies

FICTION

with Tracy Tripp *White Noise Whispers*

with Scott M. Baker, Clint Collins, Gene Coyle, Rodney Faraon, Susan Hasler, Tony Jordan, James Lawler, Clint Mesle, Susan Ouellette, Valerie Plame, Bill Rapp, Julie Savell-McCandless, Janice Sebring, J.R. Seeger, Paula T. Weiss, Terry Williams, and Scott Woodward *Naked Came the Spy* (forthcoming)

MISCELLANY

with Bill Wildey *Trivia Matters: A Trivia Host Sourcebook*

with Joe Rendon *Take My Weight, Please; Head-to-Toe Fitness for Seniors—The Cowboy Joe Way*

Made in the USA
Columbia, SC
01 March 2023

13048147R00120